James Ludington

Various Revelations

With an Account of the Garden of Eden, and the Settlement of the Eastern

Continent

James Ludington

Various Revelations

With an Account of the Garden of Eden, and the Settlement of the Eastern Continent

ISBN/EAN: 9783337090630

Printed in Europe, USA, Canada, Australia, Japan

Cover: Foto ©Lupo / pixelio.de

More available books at **www.hansebooks.com**

"BEHOLD, I STAND AT THE DOOR AND KNOCK!"
Rev. iii. 20.

Designed by Henry J. Saw. Copied from Harper's Weekly by permission.

VARIOUS REVELATIONS.

WITH

AN ACCOUNT OF THE GARDEN OF EDEN, AND THE SETTLEMENT OF THE EASTERN CONTINENT,

AS RELATED BY THE LEADERS OF THE WANDERING TRIBES.

FROM THE AGE OF ENOCH, SETH, AND NOAH, TO THE BIRTH OF JESUS OF NAZARETH,

AS RELATED BY MARY HIS MOTHER, AND JOSEPH THE FOSTER-FATHER;

WITH

A Confirmation of his Crucifixion and Resurrection,

AS RELATED BY PILATE AND THE DIFFERENT APOSTLES.

ALSO,

AN ACCOUNT OF THE SETTLEMENT OF THE NORTH AMERICAN CONTINENT, AND THE BIRTH OF THE INDIVIDUALIZED SPIRIT WHICH HAS FOLLOWED.

WITH

A REPORT OF THE IMPORTANT WORK OF ESTABLISHING ORDER IN THE DARK SPHERE OF THE SPIRIT:

WHERE THE TRIBES OF ISRAEL AND OF JUDAH, WITH THE GENTILE NATIONS, HAVE BEEN GATHERED TOGETHER AROUND A PLATFORM OF ETERNAL JUSTICE: WHERE JESUS, THE SAVIOUR, WITH THE APOSTLES, THE WITNESSES OF HIS EARTHLY MISSION, HAVE PRONOUNCED THE EXPECTED JUDGMENT.

ALSO,

MANY IMPORTANT REPORTS FROM STATESMEN, POETS, AND SCIENTISTS, FROM CLERGYMEN AND WARRIORS, WHO HAVE ATTAINED TO HONORABLE POSITION IN THE ANNALS OF AMERICAN HISTORY.

BOSTON,

1876.

BF 1291
.L85

Entered, according to Act of Congress, in the year 1876,
By JAMES LUDINGTON,
In the Office of the Librarian of Congress, at Washington.

PREFACE.

THE following revelations of the second advent of Jesus, the Saviour of man, give a statement of his labors among the spirits of the dark sphere, where order has been established, and the scattered tribes of Israel and of Judah, with the Gentile nations, have gathered around him on the great platform of eternal justice: where, with the twelve apostles, the witnesses of his earthly mission, the expected judgment has been pronounced; together with an account of many other important events, as given through the vocal organs of a trance media who has been guarded by one and the same controlling spirit, who gives the name of India at the opening and closing of the various sessions during the past twenty-three years.

The amanuensis, who is a witness that the following revelations were given and faithfully recorded, claims nothing for himself or the media but the rights of laborers.

They dedicate the work to the spirits who have indited it, and authorized its publication for the instruction and elevation of mortals through the coming cycle of time.

"The sceptre shall not depart from Judah, nor a lawgiver from between his feet, until Shiloh come: and unto him shall the gathering of the people be." — JACOB: Genesis xlix. 10.

"So they cast him out of the vineyard, and killed him; what, therefore, shall the Lord of the vineyard do unto them? He shall come and destroy these husbandmen, and shall give the vineyard to others." — JESUS: John xx. 15, 16.

"Therefore, if thou bring thy gift to the altar, and there rememberest that thy brother hath aught against thee, leave there thy gift before the altar, and go thy way; first be reconciled to thy brother, and then come and offer thy gift." — JESUS: Matthew v. 23, 24.

"For I say unto you, That except your righteousness shall exceed the righteousness of the scribes and Pharisees, ye shall in no case enter into the kingdom of heaven." — JESUS: Matthew v. 20.

"Therefore all things whatsoever ye would that men should do to you, do ye even so to them: for this is the law and the prophets." — JESUS: Matthew vii. 12.

"God is a spirit: and they that worship him, must worship him in spirit and in truth." — JESUS: John iv. 24.

"For I would not, brethren, that ye should be ignorant of this mystery, (lest ye should be wise in your own conceits,) that blindness in part is happened to Israel, until the fullness of the Gentiles be come in. And so all Israel shall be saved." — PAUL: Romans xi. 25, 26.

"For it pleased the Father that in him should all fullness dwell. And, having made peace through the blood of his cross, by him to reconcile all things unto himself; by him, I say, whether they be things in earth, or things in heaven." — PAUL: Colossians i. 19, 20.

"For if the casting away of them be the reconciling of the world, what shall the receiving of them be, but life from the dead?" — PAUL: Romans xi. 15.

"Beware therefore, lest that come upon you which is spoken of in the prophets; behold, ye despisers, and wonder, and perish: for I work a work in your days, a work which ye shall in no wise believe, though a man declare it unto you." — PAUL: Acts xiii. 40, 41.

"He walked and talked with spirits, and the highest spirit was God." — ENOCH.

"And all spirits are spirits of the Great Spirit." — INDIA.

REVELATIONS.

During the month of August, in the year eighteen hundred and sixty-seven, after years of investigation of the various reports of friends who had been called beyond the veil of the flesh, we entered into a covenant with the leaders of a band of spirits, who were working for the elevation of the inhabitants of the dark sphere.

Prominent among the workers were the names of Mrs. Townsend, a Quakeress, Margaret Fuller, and Mrs. Crow, and Miss Landon and others; while among the males, the names of Everett and King, of Pierpont and Paine, with Channing and many others whose names appear in the report of their labors, were the most noticeable. Among the representatives of the red man's race were Red Jacket and Metamora, and Tecumseh and the Forest Maidens. Our covenant was an arrangement for devoting two evenings a week, after the business affairs of the day had closed, in order to listen to the various statements which were then made, as each one was allowed to make his own report. The sessions were opened and closed by the leader with an invocation to the Great Spirit; and as time passed, from year to year, many hundreds of both sexes had told their own stories. The females, as a general thing, gave their names and places of residence, and appeared to have been selected from a class that had been favorably surrounded in their youth; but from disappointment in affairs of love, and other misfortunes, they had travelled the broad road to destruction, and, after a few years of dissipation and sorrow, found themselves deserted and friendless in the dark sphere in spirit, only to sigh and mourn over their unhappy condition. And the males who made their reports said they had been many of them the soldiers who were sent headlong from the battle-fields into the dark sphere of spirit during the late fratricidal war, where as yet they could hardly distinguish one from another. Pirates of the sea, and thieves and assassins who represented the land pirates, made their reports, and all made similar statements in regard to their spirit experience.

The soldiers gave their names and residence, the names of their officers and regiments, with many other things they seemed to be interested in. None appeared to comprehend the object of their call, while all were more than thankful for the attention they had received, saying it appeared to them like a resurrection from the dead. They said there was a commotion in their dark sphere in spirit, and when the different names were called, much anxiety was expressed in listening for the next name, although they did not know who called them, or where they were going. But as the weeks and the months passed away, we had listened to the voluntary reports of many hundreds with as much evident surprise as that manifested by themselves, as they told of their passage from the purgatories and hells of earth into the dark sphere in spirit; during which time, many others, who had occupied important positions among their countrymen, had been announced, from time to time, among those engaged in the work of apparent restitution. And on the 26th of September, 1869, after India's invocation to the Great Spirit, he announced the name of Webster, and then retired.

And Webster next spoke of the great pleasure it gave him to have an interest in a work that was but little understood. He spoke of its magnitude, and encouraged us to persevere, saying that in the end great good would be accomplished.

He then spoke of his own early home, surrounded by the gurgling streams on every side, and of the great pleasure it still afforded him to again survey the grand, majestic mountains that were familiar to him in the days of his youth. After saying he was interested in the work of investigation inaugurated by the higher powers, and should be often with us, he announced that his brother Red Jacket was waiting in order to speak, and retired.

When Red Jacket was the next heard in the council, where he too had come to the dedication of the white wigwam in the work of the Great Spirit, he spoke of the change that had taken place on the lower hunting-grounds of the red man's race, and said the red man was again on the war-path, and the watch-fires would not go out until the work of the Great Spirit was accomplished; the red man's tents were again everywhere seen on the hunting-grounds, and a guard was set around the wigwam; and as long as we were faithful in the work of the Great Spirit, nothing should harm the white brave or his squaw. After Red Jacket retired, others were presented, and made their several reports, when it was again arranged for the holding of a session twice a week — one for females, the other for males.

During the two following years, hundreds of both sexes had reported from every state and town, and, from the various conditions of life from which they had emerged, found a rough experience during their earthly pilgrimages; — girls who said they had been crushed at the fall of the Pemberton Mills at Lawrence; girls from the wreck of the Morning Star; and many girls from the brothels and hells of earth, gave their names, and circumstances connected with their misfortunes, and seemed to realize that some change had come to them in spirit. Soldiers from the battle-fields and from the prisons, from the wards and hospitals where they had left their perishable bodies, as they appeared and made their varied reports, from every state and from every town, — all expressed gratitude for the attention they had received, and seemed conscious of having been resurrected in spirit to a realization of their true condition.

At the session commencing the year 1870, after India's invocation to the Great Spirit, again giving thanks for all that had been accomplished, he said there would be a general review of the work which had been presented to the council in spirit, and guardians would be appointed for the ensuing year. After the names of our guardians were made known, he said Miss Landon was present, and would speak, upon which he retired. And Miss Landon was the next heard in the council, and said she had come with her school of little ones from what she called the paradise of God's love, in order to enliven and encourage the others in their work. She told the children to scatter their flowers, in token of the Great Father's endless love, among all that had been gathered together during the past year; and then, after expressing her own gratitude for the pleasure received, she withdrew.

White Fawn was the next in council, to which she had come from the upper hunting-grounds of her tribe, to ask that some of the children of the school might return with her and teach her and her tribes, who loved the Great Spirit, how to cultivate the beautiful flowers.

Shadow also reported as one of the leaders among the tribes, and said she was ever ready and willing to do the work of the Great Spirit. And the work of the year was blessed. Many spirits who had occupied every condition in life had made their reports. Franklin and Scott, Everett and King, with Parker, and Channing, and Booth, and many others, were reported among those engaged in the work during the year.

At the opening session commencing the year 1871, after India's invocation to the Great Spirit, giving thanks for continued blessings, and again asking for wisdom and for strength sufficient for their work, he said there would be a review of their labors during the past year, and that other guardians would be appointed. He expressed his gratitude for what had already been accomplished, gave encouragement concerning the final results, and then announced the name of Professor Hare, and that of Martha Washington, as those who were assigned to act as guardians for the ensuing year; and after saying that Everett was the next in order to speak, he again retired.

Whereupon Everett came before the council and expressed his approbation of what they had been engaged in during the past year, and said he desired to offer a few remarks in behalf of what had been denominated the literary class among mortals. He spoke of the necessity of cultivating the mind, and told them that order was the first law of nature, and that where that was obeyed the ordinary duties of life would soon become a pleasure. He spoke of the change which had already taken place around them, and encouraged all to persevere in their labors for the elevation of the race. After saying his brother King was present in order to make a few remarks, he expressed his gratitude for what had been accomplished, and retired.

King was the next in council, where he spoke of the accumulating evidence of the good results of their labors the past year, in the changed condition of those who were then gathered together around them. He then observed that it was his desire to offer a few remarks in behalf of the clergy, for he thought, as a general thing, their labors in order to elevate the people had been useful, and if some had advanced opinions which had proved to be injurious to the masses, he rejoiced to know the time had arrived for them to lay aside their former prejudice, and work together for the amelioration and elevation of all. He was thankful for what had been already achieved, and urged them to renewed perseverance, owing to the fact that their time must be limited; and after a few words of encouragement, he said his brother Booth was waiting for an opportunity to speak, and he retired.

And Booth was next in council, where he spoke in behalf of those of his own profession, and of the grand position they occupied as educators of the people. He was glad to know, as the race advanced, that the time had arrived when he could again make his appearance on the stage, surrounded by his countrymen, where each one had found the part they were called to perform in the grand drama of life. He encouraged them in their good work, told them to be ever ready to obey the promptings of the higher powers, and when the little bell tinkled for the green curtain to roll, all would be at hand to take their appointed places. He then spoke of the great pleasure he had found in having an opportunity of appearing before them, and retired. After which Margaret Fuller and Miss Townsend each spoke of the sorrowful conditions which had made an untimely sacrifice of so many of the fair young daughters of America, and then describing the fearful and the sad plight in which they had found them in the dark sphere in spirit; but still they felt that they could encourage all in their work, having the assurance that in the end they would be triumphant.

Scott then made a few appropriate remarks in connection with the soldiers who had been gathered together, and was then assigned to be their commander in spirit; and after speaking of his pleasure to be again surrounded with his former comrades, he announced the arrival of Miss Landon with her school-children, and retired.

Miss Landon was the next to make a few encouraging remarks in connection with what had been achieved during the past year, and she again directed the children to go to them all and scatter their celestial flowers, in evidence of the Great Father's approval of their labors.

India then spoke of the many millions of individualized spirits that were still in the dark sphere, and of their final triumph, if they persevered. He again closed the session by invocation to the Great Spirit, once more asking for wisdom and for strength sufficient for the accomplishment of their work.

During the following nine months many more had reported

who had represented all the varied conditions that were known to mortals, and each one was allowed to tell his own story without interruption. Plantation slaves, and sometimes their former owners, would make reports. One man, giving the name of Jackson, said he had owned a plantation near Memphis, and one near Helena, with four hundred bondmen, and that when the trouble commenced between the states, he had armed and drilled one hundred of his best men, and started with the intention of annihilating the troublesome Yankees; but he soon found himself shorn of his temporal power, and mixed up with others in the dark sphere of the spirits.

It is still sorrowful to remember the reports of the many tragedies related during these years of investigation. Young girls by the hundreds had told of their wrongs and of their terrible sufferings. The Irish girls told of the darkness of the purgatory they had left behind, and often prayed that they might never be made to return. An Irishman, known as the healer, often reported among others engaged in the work. He said he had been educated in a convent, where he devoted his time among the afflicted during his earthly life, for the love he had for the blessed Saviour, and that he was still working for the elevation of his countrymen in spirit. By the middle of the month of November, in the year eighteen hundred and seventy-one, representatives of every class and condition, and of various nationalities, had made their reports.

At the opening session, on the 19th of November, 1871, after India's invocation to the Great Spirit, he expressed his own gratitude at the results of their labors. He then spoke of the sorrowful and degrading condition of mortals that had filled the dark sphere with its unhappy spirits; but the time had arrived for a change. A platform of eternal justice was to be established, and that hereafter Justice and Charity, Judgment and Love, were the order marked out for their further labors. After his usual encouragement, he said that Columbus had been called, and would be present to answer and tell the condition of the inhabitants of this continent at the time he made its discovery.

Columbus was the next in council, and told of the friendly and harmless condition of the natives; said they were comparatively in a natural condition, had but few wants, and these were readily supplied from the abundance of natural productions by which they were surrounded; said there were "sages" and "seers" among their old men, who taught the tribes to venerate the Great Spirit, who was the author of their existence, and supplied them with their daily blessings.

Metamora was then announced, and spoke for his race at the time the Pilgrims landed at Plymouth. He said the red man's posterity was contented and happy on the lower hunting-grounds of the Great Spirit until his pale-faced brother came among them and taught them by their avarice how to lie and deceive one another; the red man and his tribes had been robbed of their hunting-grounds by their white brothers, and he had come to the council-fire by command of the Great Spirit to be a witness against them.

Washington was the next announced. He had been cited to appear and answer for the condition of the country of which he was called the Father. He spoke in high praise of the magnitude and grandeur of the country, and of its natural productions,— said it was an Eldorado full of lakes and rivers and valley lands that challenged the industry of the people, and that there was land enough for all, and it seemed to him as though they ought to have been contented and happy. It was evident the experiment had not proved successful, and the present corrupt condition of the people of his country was to him a source of great unhappiness.

Confucius was then announced. He reviewed their statements, and spoke of the error man had made in his struggles for earthly principalities. He then pointed up to the beautiful heavens, the living temple of the Great Father, and spoke of the perpetuity of His blessings. Then in sorrow he spoke of the sufferings man had entailed upon his race in his struggle for earthly power; and arraigned the apostles, and told them they had been an obstacle which had delayed the progress of others by their own apparent want of comprehension of the divinity and of the glorious and final triumph of their Master. And after congratulating the investigators for their perseverance, he retired, and India closed the session as usual by invocation to the Great Spirit.

NOVEMBER 22, 1871. — After India's invocation, he said Alexander was present, and would be permitted to speak; said there might be some doubt about the ancient people speaking the English language, but they had teachers and interpreters in spirit where information, conveyed by arbitrary signs, was soon overcome.

Alexander was then present, expressed his gratitude for the opportunity of speaking, and soon told of the terrible conditions which had so long surrounded him in spirit. He told of his wars, of the countries he had devastated, and of the starved and bleeding victims of his ambition; said that mothers with their children, in skeleton forms whose hands were like birds' claws, were with him and around him on every side; that no language was sufficient to portray his suffering; many had been his crimes in the wanton destruction of the homes of innocent thousands, and such had been his reward that he had prayed long and earnestly for relief, and leaped forth with renewed hope at the call of his name, trusting and anxiously hoping that some relief had come at last.

An ancient sage of the tribe of Benjamin was next present, — told of his knowledge of the communion of spirit during his pilgrimage below. The prophets and seers were men of age and experience through which the spirits of the spheres gave instruction to mortals in the same way and by the same laws he was then speaking. Then, as at the present time, the tribes disregarded the teachings of high spirits that would lead them to their promised land above their earthly Jordans, and followed after the ones that guided them into forbidden paths that led headlong to destruction.

One of the Forest Maidens was next present; said she came from the upper hunting-grounds of the red man. She told of the power and love of the Great Spirit; she had come to the council-fire of the white squaw, and listened to the talk of the pale-face braves, who had turned away from the councils of the Great Spirit, and lost the track that led to the upper hunting-grounds; they had wandered in their own darkness until poverty and crime had covered the lower hunting-grounds of the Great Spirit, where the red man's race had been contented and happy.

India closed the session by invocation to the Great Spirit.

NOVEMBER 26, 1871. — After India's invocation to the Great Spirit, in acknowledgment for his continued blessings, he said the Quaker woman and others of the band were present, and there would be a review of their labors. Mrs. Townsend was then present, and spoke, followed by Margaret Fuller. Both spoke in behalf of the class they had gathered from the dark sphere in spirit, and of the unhappy conditions which had caused their sufferings. Mrs. Crow and Miss Landon, with her band of juveniles, were also present, and both spoke in terms of approbation of the result of their labors.

Scott then spoke of his soldiers. He complimented them for their improved discipline and for the numbers added to their ranks; said he was beginning to feel as though his life had not been spent in vain, for he had got among men who had some respect for age and experience.

When Everett was next announced, with his band of vagrant boys who had been friendless and homeless, and who were found still hanging around the slums and purlieus of vice that infest the cities, he complimented his boys for their improved appearance and for their good behavior, assigned them a place for amusement, and told them, as long as they obeyed the rules that were established for their improvement, they would be supplied with everything necessary for their comfort. He then spoke of the sorrowful sights he had seen, and of the pleasure the improved condition of his boys had given him. Miss Landon's school-children — from the paradise of the Great Father's love — then mingled with those who had been unfortunate, and distributed their flowers to the gratification of all. And India closed the session by invocation to the Great Spirit.

NOVEMBER 29, 1871. — After India's invocation, he said Everett, with King and Shakspeare, would speak, and then Confucius.

Everett then addressed the statesmen and teachers, — spoke of the divided condition of the people, and of the fearful increase of pauperism and crime. He acknowledged that their system of legislation, their schools and colleges, had failed to secure the virtue and the industry and happiness of the people; the youth that were sent from the rural districts to a college for instruction, too often were known to return home in a debauched and corrupted condition, unworthy of the pure embrace of their mother, and unfit in every sense of the word for public teachers. He spoke feelingly of the terrible condition, acknowledging his own failings, and said he had been ignorant of the true condition of the people of his country. After which

King addressed the clergy, — told them all their efforts to redeem or reclaim the human race based on the atonement of the Saviour had proved a failure, and, now they knew their Master's work, they must turn away from their costly temples, where pride and extravagance had been engendered, and go into the streets among the beggars,— representing their false systems and modes of teaching.

Then Shakspeare spoke in glowing terms of the stage,— and of that portion of humanity that was not bound up by *priestcraft*,— said the design of the stage was to give man a higher estimate of his Creator, where he should learn to worship him everywhere in nature, by acts of fellowship and kindness to all; there were too many of the craft who quoted scraps of holy writ and seemed saintly when scheming some plan to rob their brother-man. After improvising an epilogue, he retired.

Confucius was then present, and spoke in earnest concerning the corruption of the age. He told them of their many errors, and of the necessity of their going to work and trying to make restitution in order to insure their own progression. He told them the present corrupt condition of society had resulted from the false teachings of a scheming and corrupt *priesthood;* the Great Father, whom they had misrepresented, was everywhere seen in nature, and was full of love for all. Every manifestation of his great power was a manifestation of his parental care for his children, whom he has raised up from the crawling worms of the dust that they might partake of his blessings. Man, in his avarice and in the evil of his thoughts, had turned away from the Great Father's love, and gone into forbidden paths and corrupted himself by his own abominations, and had taken delight in destroying each other in their struggle for power. After telling them again to turn back and forsake their evil ways, he retired, and India closed the session by invocation to the Great Spirit.

DECEMBER 3, 1871.— At this session, after India's invocation to the Great Spirit, acknowledging their dependence, and asking for more power in order to impress the minds of those in bondage, he said Lincoln, and Taylor, and Calhoun, had been cited to give in their testimony before the council.

And Lincoln was then present, and said, although he was still a living witness, he had been a bleeding martyr in the struggle for the black man's emancipation from bondage to his white brother. He told of his trials and sufferings when he was the "figure-head" for the nation, and of a dark cloud that followed him wherever he went as the time approached for his martyrdom. Said he was glad the time had arrived for a settlement, and that he felt more cheerful than he had at any time before since his advent into spirit-life; he was still ready and willing to do all in his power in order to forward the great and good work of emancipation.

When Taylor was the next to respond, he said that he too had been a martyr as well as a "figure-head" for his country, and, although he was but the agent to see that the commands of others were enforced, he knew of the corruption and deception of all that were ambitious for earthly power. He spoke of Davis as one who had been too ambitious, and of his own daughter who had been his wife, and of her anxiety in spirit for him when his head was a forfeit for treason to his country. He then said, although he had once been a martyr, he was ready and willing to do all he could in establishing the law of justice for his country's good.

Calhoun was then present, saying he was familiar with the conditions that followed man in his imperfection. He had devoted his life to the protection of the people of his State from the avarice of their Puritan brothers. Of the northern and eastern States he said, the bondage of the blacks had been fostered and encouraged by them as long as they had them to sell; and the public buildings in all their cities were erected with the money they got from their southern brothers for the negroes they sold into bondage; and he had long been tired of their hypocrisy, for he knew they would not be contented until they had saturated the earth with the blood of their brothers. If it were true the southern men had become corrupt, they were corrupted by association with their Puritan brothers; for Everett had acknowledged before them all, the other night, that their schools and their colleges had failed to increase the virtue and secure the industry and happiness of their countrymen. They had wrangled about the negro when the country was blessed with prosperity, and their colored servants of the south were contented and happy in their condition. They could now draw their own picture, and count up the white slaves in their own States, where pauperism and crime were increasing and the people starving, and then say if they were satisfied.

One of the Forest Maidens was next present; — said she had come to the wigwam of the white squaw, where the watch-fire was bright, and where the pale-face braves were in council. She had brought a band of fresh martyrs of her own race, which had just been butchered by their pale-face brothers on the western plains, and were still bleeding. The Great Spirit directed her to leave them with their pale-face brothers in council. She then told of the contentment and happiness of her race on the lower hunting-grounds of the red man, many moons before the pale-faces came to disturb them with their false gods and their weapons of destruction. She said the Great Spirit was good, and that the pale-faces would have much to answer owing to their errors and their covetousness, and their great injustice to the race of the red man.

After which, India again closed the session by invocation to the Great Spirit.

DECEMBER 6, 1871. — Again, after India's invocation to the Great Spirit, he said one of the Borgias would make a few remarks, and as he retired, the next one in council said he had been cited to answer for Alexander the Fourth, but he had got nothing to say in self-justification; his temporal struggle for transitory power had failed to secure happiness, and he was ready to do what he could in order to make restitution. He then withdrew.

A woman of ancient birth was next in council, where she told of her earthly pilgrimage, and of the suffering entailed upon the race from the errors inculcated by designing and crafty men for a wrong and selfish purpose. She spoke of the grandeur and harmony everywhere manifested in the works of nature as an evidence of the care and love of the Great Father for every object of his creation. The baneful effects resulting from the crafty promulgation of past errors stimulated the mind of men of the present age to search for a higher knowledge of the object and design of the Creator, and they were now looking for Him through the great power and wisdom manifested in all His works. And that the time had arrived for the resurrection and quickening of the spirit. Said it was a pleasure to them of a higher sphere to know there was a demand for more light among the inhabitants of earth; and that the good old father Confucius would be with them at the next session, and would review the history of the past.

One of the Forest Maidens was next in council, and spoke of the hardships and wrongs entailed upon her race from the avarice and injustice of their pale-face brothers. She spoke of the power and love of the Great Spirit, and of the endless variety of the manifestations of his wisdom; said they had found him, and had bowed in veneration and amazement at the evidence of the majesty and power seen throughout the vast universe. Whereupon, after a few instructions in regard to health, India closed the session by invocation to the Great Spirit.

DECEMBER 10, 1871. — At this session, after India's invocation, he said one of the Irish bishops desired to speak, after which Luther and Confucius would reply.

One of the Catholic bishops, without giving his name, was next in council, and spoke at length concerning the condition of the present inhabitants of the earth, acknowledged that great injustice had been fostered through errors inculcated by the Church, that the priesthood had corrupted themselves in their struggle for earthly power. They had disregarded the precepts and examples of the blessed Lord Jesus, and taken up too much with external signs and symbols. He was ready to join with the spirits and return to the scenes of his earthly life, and do all that lay in his power to undo the evils and remove the obstacles that prevented the progress of humanity; said he had been two hundred years in the spirit sphere, and had sorrowed much over the unhappy condition of mortals. He was thankful for an opportunity, and enjoyed the privilege of once more speaking for himself, and then gave way.

Luther was next in council. He was thankful he had been called and permitted to speak, for he knew now that many things he had inculcated had proved to be injurious, and retarded the progress of the human family. But he was honest in his opposition to Catholicism, for he knew that great wrongs were committed by the priesthood of the order, and upheld and sustained by the Church, and in his zeal to oppose them he had inculcated other errors. He thought the Bible contained many useful lessons calculated for the improvement of mortals, but they had been wrongly interpreted and used for building up and strengthening earthly principalities which had resulted in great injustice. He appealed to those of his own faith and to all others to accept of the light that was now offered to them, and go back and, if possible, undo all that proved to be wrong, and labor to impress mortals with a higher knowledge of their ultimate destiny. He then gave way.

The familiar voice of the good father Confucius was next heard. He addressed them in earnest and telling words, told them to go back with him to Adam's time with his fabled garden and vindictive God; then down to the time of Moses, and from Moses to the Judaites who crucified their Saviour with common malefactors, and showed them the records were marked with cruelty and stained with human blood. He told them that even now they kept the image of the One they professed to venerate hung up in their market-places with the appearance of blood streaming from the hands and sides, in order to gratify their cruel thirst for blood. He told them, now they had seen the evil of their errors, to lay aside their black robes and go back like men, and go to work in their Master's vineyard, and as far as possible make restitution, and the Great Father, who was ever loving and kind to his children, would forgive them. And after a few words of encouragement for all engaged in the work, he retired.

One of the handmaidens of Israel was next in council, where she addressed words of good cheer to all. She told them she had come with her sister spirits from over the waters, to join with them in their work for the elevation of spirits and mortals.

One of the Forest Maidens then spoke of the change on the lower hunting-grounds of the red man, and told of the time when her race was happy, and roamed at their leisure through the beautiful groves and around the fishing lakes the Great Spirit had given to the red man's race; but now she had come to the council-fire to listen to the talk of the pale-faces, and she would away back to tell of their injustice. And India again closed the session by invocation.

DECEMBER 13, 1871. — At this session, after India's invocation, he said the investigation would be continued.

And the next in council said he had tried to follow the examples of his blessed Master to the best of his knowledge. It was true he had been a Catholic priest, and known to his own as Father O'Brien; said he had never visited America during his earthly pilgrimage. He was thankful for an opportunity of being present, and spoke with much feeling to the friends of his order that were called before the council in spirit; told them great wrongs had been perpetuated among the inhabitants of earth by inculcating the errors and doctrines of the Church; told them, if they had been honest and faithful in their professions, they had nothing to fear. But now they knew their teachings had been erroneous, and they must accept of the present opportunity to assist in undoing their work. They had nothing to fear now, for their blessed Lord and Master would lead them in the right path.

The next speaker said he had been a mariner of the ocean, and was called to represent the noble men of his own profession, and ask that justice hereafter be extended to them; said, as a class, they had been treated as inferiors, although they perilled their lives in the distribution of the products of the nations for the benefit of the race; many improvements had been studied in spirit for the advantage of commerce, for which they received no compensation from their earthly friends. He wanted some provision made for the widows and orphans of the brave and noble mariners who often made a sacrifice of their lives through dangers and hardships in order to prolong the lives of others.

The next one said he was known as Paine. He had come before the council to ask that the assembled clergy would take it upon themselves now and see that justice was extended to him and his friends, for they had reviled his name and imprisoned his body, and burned up the books he had published for the advancement of the mind of man; and he would ask them who the infidels now were? Said it was well known the clergy had turned away from the covenants and commandments once held sacred, and preached to the people things they themselves never practised, and desecrated the temples they had falsely dedicated to God, and turned them into marts for traffic; they had warned the people to shun the truths given to the world through his organization, with all the venom of a nest of vipers. He invited them to take another investigation of their sacred book, and cited them to the history of Jonah and the whale, Samson and the foxes, and their saintly David and wise Solomon. " Well," said he, " what of them ? No wonder you hang your heads in shame. Throw off your black robes, and go back and undeceive the people, and learn justice." After speaking approvingly of the rapid progress freedom of thought and of speech was making among the people, he retired.

One of the Forest Maidens was present, and said she had come from the upper hunting-grounds of the red man by the command of the Great Spirit to listen to the talk of the paleface braves; told them they had much to answer to the Great Spirit for their injustice to her race on the lower hunting-grounds. She told them the Great Spirit was good, and when they learned to deal in justice with each other, He would receive and give them a home in his upper hunting-grounds. She then said the good old brave would not speak until the next council; but the watch-fire would be kept burning, for the red man's race was on the war-path by command of the Great Spirit, and they would guard the wigwam of the brave. Whereupon India closed the session by invocation.

DECEMBER, 19, 1871. — At this session, after India's invocation to the Great Spirit, in remembrance for his continued blessings, he said Franklin was before the council, and would speak in behalf of the laboring classes, whereupon he retired.

Franklin was present; said he felt a pride in responding to a call to speak in behalf of the toiling millions, for their interest had been neglected by their accepted guardians, and they were ground down by burdensome taxes until their lands were starving for necessary fertilizers, while the extravagance of those in control of the government and the laws had demoralized the people of the whole country; and the time had come that a change was necessary, and he was ready to suspend his investigation in the cause of science in spirit, and assist others in the work of establishing justice in behalf of the toiling and suffering inhabitants of the earth. Most cheerfully would his boys lay down their tools and shut up shop, and engage in the work.

The next one present said he was called in behalf of the pirates of the ocean. He had sailed under the name of Dexter, but belonged to the Montraville family of England; said if he had stayed ashore, he would have inherited the title of duke, but was led away by the false charms of a roving life, and became the leader of a band of pirates on the high seas. He said many of the wealthy families of the day were sporting with fortunes their forefathers stole when pirating on the ocean. He felt that great wrongs had been entailed upon the inhabitants of earth by the false teachings of what was called the Church. It had caused man's selfishness to increase until his hand was everywhere raised against his brother, and pirating had become fashionable all over the land. He was gratified to have an opportunity of speaking; and said he thought he could help some of his own profession who had long been tired of their condition.

Confucius was next in council, and spoke of the sorrowful effects everywhere seen flowing from the avarice of man. He then spoke to Franklin, complimenting him for the part he had been called to represent. He told of the hardships the toiling millions of the earth had endured from cycle to cycle; told him that Jesus, who was crucified as a malefactor, was a sacrifice in their behalf, and was now at the head of the masses in spirit who had been despised and cast out, leading them up to higher and better conditions; said the ancient of days, so long foretold, had come, and the covenants and commandments of the Great Father would be reinforced that all should partake of his blessings; and told them they were gathering up at the call of the angel of time, and must prepare themselves for the enforcement of the law of eternal justice.

An ancient Jewess was next present; said they had taken their harps down from the willows again, and were prepared to engage in the work; said they were standing by the river calling to their sisters, and asking permission to join with them in promulgating to the children of earth the news of their glorious resurrection.

A Forest Maiden then told of the power and wisdom of the Great Spirit, and spoke of his love for his earthly children; told of the progress the red race had made in their upper hunting-grounds; said the pale-faces would tremble at the power of the Great Spirit. Then she spoke to them about their injustice to each other, for their suffering victims were crying aloud for justice. After which India again closed the session by invocation to the Great Spirit.

DECEMBER 20, 1871. — After India's invocation to the Great Spirit, by whose power all things created were sustained, he said there was a gathering up of those who had appeared before the council, and so arranged for Confucius to address them. After speaking of the magnitude of their work and of the pleasure it was to those engaged in gathering up the forsaken and friendless, he retired, and the voice of the good Father Confucius was again heard. He commenced his remarks by referring to the power and wisdom and the perfection everywhere displayed in the works of the Great Father; and then addressed the popes and cardinals, the bishops and priests, and the pirates. He told them of the terrible sufferings which had been entailed upon the inhabitants of the earth through their injustice to their brothers. He asked them if their temporary gratification in their struggle for earthly power had paid them for all the human suffering they were still compelled to witness; said the time had now arrived, and they would be offered an opportunity to assist in undoing their work. He told them they had failed to do the work of Him they professed to follow; they had walked the streets in their pride, with their book under their arm, to their costly sanctuaries, and pandered to the demands of the rich and of those in power; while the poor, who had always been the suffering victims of the lovers of Mammon, and who were of the same mould of nature as themselves, were everywhere neglected. He told them they had all sold their Master, not for thirty pieces of silver, but they had sold him for the Mammon of unrighteousness and worldly position, and at last they had awakened to the knowledge that by so doing they had sold themselves. He then addressed himself to the others who had been gathered up, and who represented the various conditions of life, — to Everett, with his newsboys and vagrants and young thieves, whom he had been gathering up among the haunts of vice and suffering which they had found in every city. He complimented him for his perseverance in the work of his Master, and told him that all, whatever their condition, were the Great Father's children. Then to Scott with his soldiers. He told them they were looking much better than when they were sent to the spirit sphere crushed and mangled from the battle-fields, where brother warred against brother in their cruel struggles for the principalities of earth. He then spoke of the magnitude of the heavens above them; said the stars were the windows that opened into the heavens beyond, and that every star was an evidence of the Great Father's love for his children. Then he explained that at the next session they would all have their orders, and they must be prepared to return to the inhabitants of the earth, where they would have to labor as best they could until they had undeceived them.

One of the Forest Maidens then said she had come from the upper hunting-grounds of the red man by the command of the Great Spirit, to listen to the talk at the council-fire at the wigwam of the white squaw; the Great Spirit had heard the cry of suffering and sorrow that comes from the poor and friendless of the pale-faces who now inhabit the lower hunting-grounds of the red man. She would return to the Great Spirit, and tell him all that was said at the council.

After which, India again closed the session by invocation to the Great Spirit.

DECEMBER 24, 1871. — After India's invocation to the Great Spirit, asking for wisdom to guide their labors that all might be approved and mortals elevated from their darkness, he said the review would continue, and that Mrs. Townsend, the Quakeress, that Everett with King, and Metamora, would speak for those they had been appointed to represent; after which Confucius would address them. He then retired.

Mrs. Townsend was next in council. She spoke in behalf of the girls, and of the various conditions during their earthly lives, which had led them from the paths of virtue and happiness, and of the darkness and suffering in which they were found in spirit. She then spoke of the progress of their labors, and of the pleasure they received from the improved condition of those who left the dark sphere and were clothed in new garments, and prepared to engage in the work of amelioration.

Afterwards, Everett spoke in behalf of the boys and youth of the various cities, who had been friendless and without homes; said their condition was fearful to contemplate: many had found the end of their physical life in a loathsome prison, many had died in want of the most common necessaries of life, and still found themselves in the same condition in spirit. Said that he had felt an interest during his earthly life, and devoted much time in cultivating the young mind; but he had known nothing of the terrible destitution and suffering among the poor and unfortunate people who were cast off and neglected in every part of the country; said he felt ashamed when he was awakened in spirit to their true condition, and had gladly applied himself in the work of restitution; said he desired to introduce one of his New York boys before the council, and let him speak for himself. Upon which he withdrew.

The boy was then introduced, and told of his own sufferings, and of his efforts to obtain bread for his poor brokenhearted mother, with her five friendless children; how his father had died, and left them all destitute, from the effects of his own heavy burdens; how himself and his class were watched and hunted down by the officers of the law, and frequently unjustly imprisoned; spoke of their temptation to take from those living in luxury, and surrounded with wealth and ease, in order to keep their own from starving. He then spoke of their happiness in spirit since they had been furnished a good place to stay, where they were not called "vagrants" and then kicked out.

King next spoke of his class; said the difference between their Master's work and that of their own had shown itself on every hand, and he was thankful that even now he was permitted to take a part in spirit in the work of restitution; for he knew that millions had been hurried out of their physical bodies without any one to care for them, or to ask where they had gone, or what would be their fate. After finishing his remarks, he retired.

Metamora was then present, and spoke in behalf of his own race. He told of the freedom they enjoyed on their lower hunting-grounds before the pale-face race came among them with their avarice and their weapons of destruction. He spoke of their beautiful forests, where the deer was undisturbed by the sharp report of the deadly rifle; and of their lakes and rivers, full of fish from the bountiful supply of the Great Spirit. He told of his race, and how they were driven from their wigwams, and their forests cut down; and said the trail of the pale-faces was still marked with the blood of his race all over the red man's hunting-grounds.

The good father Confucius was next present, and spoke to the assembled host. He told of the rise and fall of empires, and of the untold suffering man had entailed upon his race in his terrible struggle for earthly power. He spoke of the perishable nature of earthly principalities that crumbled away before the natural action of the immutable laws of the Great Father; told them the time had now arrived for the law of justice to be enforced, and spoke of the suffering entailed upon the innocent from the errors that had been propagated by a designing priesthood. He told of the efforts of the inhabitants of the spheres to improve the condition of their earthly friends, and of how their labors had been received; asked them how the Master they had professed to follow could even trust his disciples in spirit, when they turned away and forsook him while in their physical forms. And told them all, the time had come for them to undo their work, and that all that were instrumental in producing the present unhappy condition among the inhabitants of the earth were held responsible by the law of Eternal Justice; and they must return and labor for the amelioration and elevation of their earthly brothers until the effects of their errors and falsehoods were destroyed. The Great Father had called for His children, and He knew them all by name; and they must hunt them up, and see that they were ready to answer. After saying he would soon address them again, he retired.

A woman of ancient days gave them encouraging words. She spoke of the wandering of her people among their earthly Palestines in search of their promised land. She told them the Great Father, who had watched over them all, and supplied them with blessings, was still good, and that when His children were in a proper condition, He was ready to receive them.

One of the Forest Maidens then spoke of her race when they were many and covered the lower hunting-grounds given to them by the Great Spirit; said they were happy and satisfied with the blessings the Great Spirit sent them, until the pale-faces came and disturbed them. Now the glory of the red man's race was departing from the lower hunting-grounds, and the pale-face race would have to answer for their injustice to their red brothers at the call of the Great Spirit; the red man's upper hunting-grounds were large, and the Great Spirit supplied and loved his red children.

The usual time having again expired, India, after commending their work to the care of the Great Spirit, closed by invocation.

DECEMBER 27, 1871. — After India's invocation to the Great Spirit in commemoration of continued blessings, he said Confucius would address the spirits concerning their new labors. After a few encouraging remarks, he retired. And Confucius' earnest voice was again heard. He told them of the necessity of taking Charity with them as they went out to engage in their labors with their earthly brothers; and he told them that Charity must be worn as a mantle, and used among the present generations, as they engaged in the work of removing the errors and their effects which had culminated from their own false teaching. He told them how short-sighted they had been when they set bounds to the love of the Great Father for his earthly children; told them to go back with him to the time when he was a pilgrim of the earthly sphere, and he would show them some of the inhabitants of this planet long before his time. He then said to them, as they looked through the opening of a sphere, "You see those bright spirits; they were all once inhabitants of the earthly sphere, where they long ago learned to deal in justice with their brothers, and who are now engaged in the higher pursuits of life." He then told them that the time had come for a work of purification, and that the toiling millions of earth must be restored to their rights, and the earth and man purified and prepared for a revisit of its ancient inhabitants. He told them not to be deceived: it was not the Saviour and his disciples they had been shown. It was a band of bright spirits that once inhabited the earthly kingdom, and learned the laws of Eternal Justice long before the days of Judaism. After a few general remarks connected with the council, he again retired.

Then one of the bishops made a few remarks; said his people had desired him to ask for one more sight of the bright spirits which had been shown to them. If it was true they were once inhabitants of this planet, they would cease their opposition, and do all in their power that was just and right in order to prepare to associate with those who had passed on beyond them. He then gave way.

A woman of ancient days next addressed the council. She encourged them as a band of reformers whose labors in the cause of justice would receive the approbation of the Great Father; said that she and her sisters had come to join with them in their work for the progress of humanity.

One of the Forest Maidens next spoke of the great power of the Great Spirit; said he was angry with his pale-faced children, who had not dealt in justice with their brothers on the lower hunting-grounds of the red man; said the winds and the floods would teach the pale-faces of the Great Spirit's power. She had listened to the talk in the council at the wigwam of the white squaw, and she was going to the mountains where the snows were deep, and where the red man and his squaw and pappoose had got nothing to eat.

And as the usual time had expired, India again closed the session by invocation to the Great Spirit.

DECEMBER 31, 1871. — After India's invocation, he said the woman would occupy the spare time, while Confucius made preparation to gratify the request of the monks that were anxious for another view of the progressed spirits.

Mrs. Jackson was then announced, and spoke of the work they were engaged in; said they still felt an interest in the welfare of their country, and were ashamed of the corrupt condition that was fast destroying the energies of the people and everything else that was American. She spoke of the habits of society of her time, — said the women then were satisfied with an eight-yard calico dress, and one of gingham for Sunday was all they required; and they were contented and satisfied with their homes as long as their country was blessed with prosperity. She regretted the extravagance and idleness of the age, and said her husband often remarked, by the Eternal! such things could not be sustained much longer in their country. She was pleased with an opportunity of speaking, but gave way for one of their companions.

Mrs. Adams was next announced. Said she was inclined to be charitable with her countrymen, for it was well known that foreigners had introduced the habits and customs of the older nations among the people, and they were disturbing elements that had a tendency to demoralize and corrupt society; and it was true the inhabitants of the day were more spiritual than at her time, and she thought that had a tendency to disturb and lead them into extravagance. It was true, many things were hard to endure, and were the cause of much suffering; but she thought it imparted its own lesson to the people, and might result in good. She, too, was thankful for the opportunity of speaking, and gave way for one who said that —

France was her native country; but she had crossed the water to join her sisters of the council, to engage with them in the work of restitution. She thought the time had come when all nationality should be set aside, and all that could work should work for the elevation of the toiling millions, who were crushed by craft and caste until their sufferings were past endurance. It was known that all inherited natural rights by their birth, and such rights must and would be respected when they enforced the law of Eternal Justice.

The familiar voice of Confucius was next heard. He addressed the assembled host in forcible language; told them to follow him back step by step to the time their sacred history commenced, and then told them the story of their Garden of Eden was a fable. He showed them a group of bright spirits who were inhabitants of this planet thousands of years in advance of the time when their records commenced, and told them the light of those they saw was reflected from others who had passed on before them. He then showed them a beautiful scene: it was the birth of a child into the physical world. He said, before mothers fell from their high and holy calling, the mother was surrounded by her friends, and her couch strewn with flowers, while anthems of praise were ascending to the Great Father in thanks that another child had been intrusted to their keeping. He told them then to lay aside their black robes and cowls, and return to the scenes of their earthly pilgrimage, and engage this time in the work of restitution, elevate the downcast millions, and teach them the Great Father is ever good, and that all are his children, and that all must stand on one and the same platform. After a few kind and encouraging words, he retired; and India closed by invocation.

JANUARY 1, 1872. — Unexpectedly our Irish friend, the "healer," was present this evening; said they were anxious to commemorate the advent of the new year, and had made their call for that purpose; and, after a few more appropriate remarks, said, if we had no objections, he would like to introduce a friend. No objections being made, his friend gave the name of Morgan.

Morgan said he was the man that was accused of divulging some of the mysteries of an Order that had been popular in our country. He was willing to converse on different subjects connected with the Order, but declined to tell how he was relieved of his body; said that was for the Order to answer. After saying what he desired, he thanked all for their attention, and retired.

One of the children from Miss Landon's school was next present, and delivered a beautiful epilogue. It related to the labors of the council, and was grand in its conception. And when asked how it was possible for her to commit such things to memory, her answer was it was inspiration; said she had only to open her mouth for it to flow out. She was delighted to be remembered, for we had divined who it was, as she had been before the council to speak before. After the girl retired, the "healer" made a few remarks; spoke of the pleasure the interview had given, and closed with an appeal to the blessed Saviour Jesus, who had labored and suffered for mortals.

JANUARY 3, 1872. — After India's invocation to the Great Spirit, he said remarks would be made by different individuals in regard to the labors they were about to engage in; when he retired.

A very intelligent advocate was present, and spoke in behalf of the African race; said he had investigated the history of the different nationalities back for many ages, and was unable to find any good cause why his race should be bound to serve his white brothers. He was satisfied that color was the effect of climate, and that all races should be protected in their natural rights in the pursuit of earthly happiness. He was glad the law of justice was to be enforced, and was satisfied the black man, with an equal opportunity, would soon make rapid progress. He was pleased with his opportunity to speak, and said he would be always ready to defend the rights of his race.

The next speaker thought it was best for them to commence their new labors with mortals by directing their energies among the different grades of society. They all knew that in spirit each one went to the sphere of his attraction; no one could stay where he was not in harmony from natural progress, as they all received their light from those who had passed on beyond them. He thought it could not be expected that the wealthy, who were the admitted guardians of the poor, were going down to associate with the poor and the depraved class by which they were surrounded; he thought it best for them to work with those nearest to them in condition, and so on to the bottom; said he was creed-bound during his earthly life, and left his body at Salem, Massachusetts, sixty years ago.

The next speaker said her name was Jones; she had been in the sphere over sixty years, and she did not agree with the former speaker; said the poor had been disciplined through their poverty, and were more virtuous and benevolent, and occupied a higher sphere in spirit than any of the so-called educated and wealthy classes. She said that millions of the toiling sons and daughters of earth, who were disciplined through poverty and suffering, and knew what truth and virtue were, would be an honor to the parlors of those who squandered their time in idleness and luxury, and the sooner their condition was ameliorated the better it would be for humanity.

Confucius then made a few cheering remarks; told them the Great Father had not forgotten them, and they must persevere, and all be faithful in their work of establishing the law of Eternal Justice. He then said at their next session the apostles would be called to an account.

One of the Forest Maidens was then present; said she had come to the council with her brave, who " was bold and true, and she no other brave had ever known." They had returned to the lower hunting-grounds of the red man by command of the Great Spirit, to keep the camp-fire burning until the pale-faces had learned to deal in justice; said the brave, who worshipped the Great Father, was then with a group of bright spirits, chanting an anthem in thankfulness for the harmony and good order of the council.

After which, India again closed the session by invocation to the Great Spirit.

JANUARY 7, 1872. — After India's invocation to the Great Spirit, again asking for wisdom to guide their councils, he said the apostles would have an opportunity to make their own statements; he then retired.

And Thomas was the next in council, and there made the following statement. Said he did doubt, for he could not believe in the bodily resurrection of his Master, for he had been told, time and again, through the organism of his Master, of the grandeur of the Spirit Sphere, and that flesh and blood, that belong to matter, had no inheritance there. He then said the story of their deprivations and sufferings had not half been told; they were hooted and stoned by the mob; often without food to appease their hunger, or clothing fit to be seen in public; said the mission of his Master was then but little understood, and those in power cared nothing for his beautiful teachings, and the opposition and hatred of the priesthood were past endurance; but when they retired to their frequent haunts in the forest, where they were undisturbed, they were encouraged by their Master, and by others who spoke through him, — the same, and by the same law, that he was then speaking, — and who encouraged their labors. And said their Master returned to them at four different times after his crucifixion, and spoke to them through the organism of one of their number; and told them of his triumph over death, and counselled them to persevere in their labors in elevating humanity; said they did try to follow the examples and precepts of their Master, whom they loved, but after all their labors and sufferings, they were misunderstood and misrepresented by mortals. He was glad an opening had been prepared, that he could speak again with his earthly brothers, and whenever he was called he would be ready to answer. After expressing his gratitude for the pleasure of speaking, he said one of his brothers was ready, and he would retire. And the next one said he was —

The terrible Judas Iscariot, and also was thankful for an opportunity to speak, and readily confirmed all his brother

Thomas had said, and was anxious to set himself right before the world in regard to his being so long called a traitor to his Master. All he desired was to state the facts, and let others judge for themselves. He then made the following statement. At one of their scanty meals in the forest, where they were secreted from the violence of the mob, his Master remarked that one of their number would betray them, or notify the priesthood of the place of their seclusion. When he went out, he thought nothing more of the remark, but was soon entranced by a Jew spirit, who informed the mob who was then in search of them, armed with authority for their Master's arrest. After he had led them back to their retreat, and had accomplished their design, the spirit left him, and he was conscious of what had been done. He did feel badly, and would have given a hundred lives in order to have restored his Master; but it was then too late, for the hatred of their traducers had no bounds. After the crucifixion, the body was entombed, and the armed guards stationed to watch it. They were overpowered with affright at the appearance of the angel band, who had come for their Master, who did afterwards appear, and confirmed the desired knowledge of a glorious resurrection. He then said the clairvoyant eye of his Master saw the Jew spirit that obsessed him, and knew what would be the result. He thought they were not responsible for the stories — promulgated by a designing priesthood — about the atonement and a bodily resurrection, and was thankful the time had arrived when he could speak with mortals in his own defence. He had long ago seen his Master in spirit, and received his forgiveness. But as his time now was limited, and his brother was then waiting, for the present he would retire.

And John was next in council. He had come to confirm the statements of his two brothers. All they had said was true. Although at the time they were the earthly companions of Jesus, their Master, they but poorly comprehended the beautiful teachings from the unseen world. His own vocal organs were also used for the purpose of instructing the people, and many a beautiful vision of the spirit spheres was shown to him for his own instruction, although at the time not fully comprehended. It was true, the guards stationed to watch the mangled form of their Master could give no account of his glorious resurrection; and when He stood in their midst, in the semblance of his physical form, it was materialized for the occasion, that they might have the evidence of his presence with them in spirit, and of his triumph over the powers of darkness. For his crucifiers had denied the evidence of his glorious mission, and scoffed at his humanity; and they themselves expected the literal fulfilment of many of their Master's sayings, which they have since learned were connected with the establishing of his kingdom in spirit; from which he did return, and hold communion with them after his ascension, and it was the knowledge of the communion of spirit upon which they based their association. They were not accountable for the corrupt condition of Christianity, nor for the corrupted records sustained and upheld by a designing and willing priesthood. After saying that the time had now arrived for the establishment of their Master's kingdom upon the platform of Eternal Justice, he retired.

One of the Jewish rabbi was next in council, where he said: "Here we are all the way along the river,—Jews on one side, and Nazarites on the other. How could they accept as truth the dogmas of a rabble grown up in their midst? They who were educated, and daily worshipped in their temples dedicated to the God of Abraham, and Isaac, and Jacob, as they had been taught by Moses, who was the prophet of God, that led the Israelites from their Egyptian bondage,— they knew nothing, and they cared nothing for the doctrines they claimed to promulgate, and they looked upon Jesus as a blasphemer when he proclaimed himself the Son of God, while all knew of his humble origin; and they put him to death as a troublesome leader of a ragged mob, who was constantly disturbing the public peace." They were still satisfied to worship the God of their fathers; although they had not seen him, still he had blessed them in basket and store, and they were looking for the time when their cities would be rebuilt; and their nation again united, as they had been before. But the time was long; they had waited, and his people must be patient; they wanted no other God to worship.

One of the Forest Maidens then addressed them, and told of the time when the race of the red man covered the lower hunting-grounds, and was blessed by the Great Spirit, many thousand moons before the Israelites or the Judaites had soiled the beautiful hunting-grounds with the trail of their many abominations. As she then retired, India closed by invocation to the Great Spirit.

JANUARY 10, 1872. — After India's invocation to the Great Spirit, asking for wisdom and strength to allay the opposing forces, that the result of their labors might in the end be approved, he said the new temple they were erecting in spirit, where Justice " would be enthroned." was fast taking shape and form, as each one called anxiously applied themselves in the new work, and that one familiar with the history of the Great Media and his disciples was present to speak of things in connection with the labors of the council. He then retired.

And one who spoke as one with authority said he was pleased to be a witness of the labors already performed by the council, for he knew what would be the result. He had been a familiar witness of the labors and sufferings of the humble and forgiving Nazarene, who willingly suffered martyrdom that he might accomplish the connection between "spirit" and "mortal;" and although his advent had been foretold by sages and seers, those who were looking for him rejected and cast him out; so again, when he returns in spirit, he has found but few laborers in his earthly vineyard, and those who were expecting his return, and have prepared for his reception, have turned away and rejected and crucified him again. But the angel of time has called, and the book of life was opened, and the nations of the earth must prepare for the Judgment. After speaking encouragingly of their labors, he said the time had now arrived — foretold by the ancient prophets — when the spirit kingdom would be established, when the poor and the toiling millions of earth, who were crushed and cast out through avarice, would be restored to their birthright. After his closing remarks, he retired, and India again closed with a beautiful invocation to the Great Spirit.

From the above session until the 27th of November, at the usual sessions, the time was occupied in gathering up promiscuous spirits from the dark sphere, and many heart-rending accounts were listened to from the different parties who were permitted to tell of their own sufferings before the council.

NOVEMBER 27, 1872. — At this session, after India's invocation to the Great Spirit, expressing thanks for the privilege of meeting together after the gathering in of another bountiful harvest, he said there were many anxious to join them in their labors, and the council had made the necessary preparation to listen to their various reports. After which the familiar voice of Madam Pitcher was again heard.

She was one of the workers, and had often encouraged all in their labors. She had brought up an old friend, by the name of Warren, she was desirous of introducing to the council; said she had known him many years past, when she was in her earthly form. Their labors in spirit were making rapid progress with the inhabitants of the dark sphere, and the time would soon arrive when justice would again find a place among the inhabitants of earth. After a few words of instruction, she gave way for her friend, who was glad to respond.

He said his name was Warren; that he belonged to a numerous family of that name, and had lived in Charlestown; said he was anxious for some change, for many of his own were looking to him for light; they were strongly tinctured with the old Puritan notions, which had failed to give them satisfaction in spirit. And he appealed to the old lady, whom they found to be a bright guide, who had kindly prepared the way and introduced him to the council; he remembered the old lady from an acquaintance of many years past in Boston, and right thankful he said he was for the opportunity to speak; said there was great disturbance among them, and he did not know what would be the result. He spoke of the terrible war the people had struggled through, and how much they were demoralized; he thought it had caused their disturbance in spirit.

The next one in council said his name was Tuckerman. He had lived in Boston, went from that place to New York, where he engaged in the business of a broker, and was a teacher part of his time during his earthly pilgrimage; said he found things in spirit altogether different from what he had anticipated. He was thankful for the opportunity to speak, and said he would gladly engage in a work that would forward the time when justice should have a hearing among the affairs of men.

The next one then said her name was Livermore. She was a native of Massachusetts, had lived in New York, was fifty-six years old at the time of her change, had been fifteen years in spirit, and was anxious to join with the band, and unite her labor with theirs in their great and good work for the elevation of the race.

Another one said her name was Bancroft. She was of

English birth, and was anxious about the condition of Mrs. Stuart, once a member of the so-called royal family, who desired a change; and she had sought the opportunity to speak in her behalf, hoping she might have a hearing at our next session; said she had been eighty years in the sphere, and was familiar with the labors of the council. She then remarked that the one known as Margaret Fuller had just entered with Mrs. Greeley, but she was then too feeble to give a communication. After speaking in high terms of the good that had already resulted from their labors, she retired.

And the companion of Mrs. Townsend, the Quakeress of Philadelphia, was then present. He spoke of the work they were all engaged in, told of its magnitude, and of the great results already accomplished by penetrating the dark sphere, where they were still gathering up the friendless and forsaken spirits, who were ignorant of any higher condition; said they were now well organized, and there would be no delay in their labors until all was finished, and justice once more found a resting-place among the inhabitants of earth. He told of the fearful conditions they found among the ignorant and degraded spirits who had not relaxed their claim on mortals, and of some of the results that must follow, and disturb our present relations in the affairs of life. After the usual encouragement, he retired.

One who claimed to be of Irish nationality spoke in warm terms in behalf of the people of his own country. He told them the time had now come for them to work their way up to the new Mecca, and they must be about it, and not be laggards in the good cause of human progress. They had all been sufferers in the past for the want of light that had been but dimly reflected; but now he knew the blessed Jesus, their Lord and Master, was at the head, and none should fear to follow. He thanked all who had been instrumental in assisting his people out of the purgatories in spirit, that were still connected with the purgatories of earth, where the good Lord only knew what had been their suffering. After speaking to his own people, and giving them instruction about what should be done, he said there was a warrior present, who gave the name of Tecumseh, who desired to speak at our next session. He then gave thanks, and asked the Master to remember them in his work.

One of the Forest Maidens then spoke of her own race, who were now in the upper hunting-grounds of the Great

Spirit, and of his power and love for his earthly children, who had turned away from his great law of justice, and built their storehouses so large that much suffering was caused, and the cry for bread had gone up to the Great Spirit from many of the pale-face race on the lower hunting-grounds. After which, India again closed the session by invocation to the Great Spirit.

DECEMBER 1, 1872. — After India's invocation to the Great Spirit, giving thanks for light and strength to sustain them, and after saying Confucius and Burns, Choate and Berry, were then before the council, he retired. And Confucius again spoke at length to the assembled spirits, gave them counsel in regard to their labors among mortals, told them of the sufferings that were entailed on the inhabitants of earth — the effects of their own errors which they had designedly propagated in order to strengthen their power; spoke of the love and forbearance of the Great Father, whose blessings were intended for all his children, and who never sanctioned any of their unholy abominations; told them to return and undo their work, and see that justice once more had a resting-place among their earthly brothers, and then — and not till then — could they expect to find rest. He then spoke favorably of what had been accomplished the past year, and gave renewed encouragement; told them their earthly witnesses must be protected in order to secure the benefit of their own labors, and labor they must to insure their own salvation. He again retired.

Burns once more spoke of the bonny lads and lasses of his own native country, repeated the story of Tam O'Shanter, and the devil who sat in the window of the old kirk, fiddling for the dance of the fairies. After relating some of his own experience in spirit, he improvised a beautiful poem connected with their labors. After repeating it, he said they had just brought a dead man into the council, and retired.

Choate was next present. Said the man referred to by Burns was Greeley, whose friends had just then arrived with him, and who was also anxious to speak, but said it was thought best he should delay until another session. He then spoke of the terrible condition of society in their own country — spoke of his Boston friends and of their recent affliction; said it was just, that nothing else would ever turn their attention from the worship of their worldly Mammon to the fulfilment of the law of Eternal Justice. He spoke to his spirit friends in regard to their labors as they returned from among mortals; said no one should shrink from his duty on account of a former friendship; told them they had much to undo, and none knew better than they did the evil effects of their own errors. After thanks for the opportunity of speaking, he retired.

Berry was next in council; said he was at one time connected with the "Banner," published in Boston. He had left that office, and went into the recent rebellion for the overthrow of chattel slavery; and he was delighted with his experience in spirit life, for the countless hosts of the spirit spheres were there working for the establishment of justice among the inhabitants of earth. He thought the baptism of fire that this country had been passing through would quicken the perceptions of all to the duties they owed each other.

The one known as Shadow was the next to speak. She complained of the hardship of her sister squaw, who was making a bath-tub of herself in order to clean up the filth that others had created; said they had got their work well organized, and the pale-faces would soon have evidence enough that the Great Spirit had not forgotten the red man's wrongs.

One of the Forest Maidens next told of the upper hunting-grounds of the red man, and of the wisdom and power of the Great Spirit manifested in all his works. She told of the degradation and suffering inflicted upon the remnants of her race from the covetousness and injustice of their pale-face brothers,— all of which she would go and tell to the Great Spirit. And then India said, Tecumseh, Mary Queen of Scotland, and Greeley, would speak for themselves at the next session, and again closed by invocation to the Great Spirit.

DECEMBER 4, 1872. — After India's invocation, again asking the Great Spirit for strength and wisdom to guide them in their investigations, so that in the end they might receive His approval, and after saying Mary, Scotland's queen, would be the next in council, he retired. Thereupon Mary was present, and told of her terrible suffering; said the scenes of her earthly life had been constantly before her, and she had found no rest for her troubled spirit. She was ready and willing to do all that was possible in order to obtain relief; the agonies she had endured in the dark sphere were beyond comprehension; she was thankful she had been called, and trusted it might open the way for her to improve her condition. After speaking again of her long and terrible suffering, she retired. And the old warrior—

Tecumseh announced himself; said he had come to the council with his braves, where the pale-faces had made the watch-fire burn at the wigwams of his white brother on the lower hunting-grounds of the red man, given to the red man and his posterity many moons since by the Great Spirit. They had come to the council of the pale-faces to listen to their talk about justice. The red man loved justice, and they had come to the council to ask about justice for the remnant of the red man's race that was still upon the lower hunting-grounds. It was not sanctioned by justice for them to be hunted down and robbed by their pale-face brothers. The Great Spirit had spoken to his red children in their upper hunting-grounds, and the red man's race was again on the war-path, and would ask for justice for all. They had come to rekindle the watch-fires on the mountains, and should come again to the council.

And then Greeley was the next present; said he was gratified to meet his friends in spirit, and pleased with the opportunity they had provided for him to again speak, for he felt keenly the ingratitude of his earthly friends, and was glad to get away from them, although everything seemed strange to him. It appeared like a dream, and he was not sure that he could trust his own vision, but seemed to be more natural at the end of the interview; spoke about his paper, and was anxious to get back to his office; finally concluded he wanted rest, and desired no one to tell where he was at present, for it was gratifying to believe he was among friends that would not desert him.

One of the Forest Maidens then said she had come from the upper hunting-grounds, as by the Great Spirit sent to listen to the talk of the pale-face braves at the wigwam of the white squaw, where all told of their many sorrows, and where they knew not of the love of the Great Spirit. She told them to go back and teach the pale-face race to learn justice, and they would see more of the love of the Great Spirit in the wonderful manifestation of his mighty power among his pale-face children, whose sorrows were the result of their own injustice.

Thereupon India told of the terrible condition of the millions sent friendless and homeless into the dark sphere in spirit, ignorant of all the duties of life; and closed the session by invocation to the Great Spirit, asking his acceptance of all that was acceptable in connection with their labors.

DECEMBER 8, 1872. — After India's invocation to the Great Spirit, he spoke encouragingly of what had already been accomplished, and said there were many that were anxious to unite with them in their investigation, and at the next session two or more would be introduced. Josephus, one of the historians of the Jews, would be the next in council. He then withdrew.

Josephus was then present, and told of his experience in connection with Jewish history. He said that many changes and alterations had found a place in the records of his own age through the ingenuity of modern writers. It was true they did fail to comprehend the mission of Jesus, their final Saviour, as many strong proofs of his being the true Messiah had been suppressed by those in power. His people were willing to join the Nazarites now, and follow the lead in spirit of him they crucified for telling them of the promised land above their earthly Palestines; they refused the light offered to them, and had wandered in darkness and doubts, looking and waiting for the rebuilding of their cities and temples, when they should have been pressing their way upward in search of "the temple not made with hands." He told of the terrible suffering they passed through after the rejection of their Messiah: they had wrangled and fought with each other, without any apparent cause, until their nationality was lost, and the remnant of their people become wanderers and living witnesses of the mistakes of their national *priesthood* throughout the civilized world. He was thankful for an opportunity to speak, and glad to be a witness that his people were anxious to bow before him they had crucified, and pray for his forgiveness, weary, and willing to find rest anywhere in his kingdom. After saying he would be ready to answer whenever he was wanted, he retired; and one of the ancients, who gave the name of Bebo, who had come to represent the inhabitants of South America nineteen hundred years ago, made his appearance.

He told of the progress of that age, of the customs and habits of the people, and said in many respects it was far in advance of the mass of the peoples of the present age; in agriculture and the mechanical arts they were well developed. But, like the nations before them, they lost the light that came from above, and became worshippers of the Mammon of unrighteousness, and were cut off by a terrible destruction from the face of the earth. He said they were a people of Jewish origin, but they had no knowledge of the flood spoken of at the time of Noah; he thought it did not reach their part of the country. But there were many ways in which the inhabitants of the earth were destroyed when they turned away from the covenants and commandments of the Creator, and disregarded the law of justice in their intercourse with each other. He was gratified to know he could speak again, and at some other time would give a more extended account of the tribes of his day After which he retired. And then—

Another of the ancients gave an interesting history of the changes of the planet as it progressed from the material up to the spiritual, where the inhabitants of its production would all eventually find a home. He then told of the working of the mighty hosts of the invisible world for the establishment of the law of justice among the affairs of men; said his name was Thomas, and he was familiar with the history of the Nazarene.

One of the Forest Maidens was then present. She had come from the upper hunting-grounds of the Great Spirit. She told of the numerous race of the red man who once covered the lower hunting-grounds of the Great Spirit, where they were taught the great law of eternal justice, long before the pale-face race with their avarice and their injustice had desecrated the lower hunting-grounds of the red man.

After which, India again closed the session by invocation to the Great Spirit.

DECEMBER 11, 1872. — After India's invocation, again asking the Great Spirit for light and strength that their labors in spirit might be approved, he said the parties referred to at a former session were waiting, and retired.

And Prout was the next in council. He had a desire to comprehend the wonderful mystery in order to be useful. He spoke of the magnitude of the eternal world of spirits, whose limits were incomprehensible; said he had but just entered upon its border. and was glad to be called into a sphere of labor where his former knowledge would be made useful. As far as he had been able to extend his geological investigations, he had found abundant evidence of the wisdom made manifest in the wonderful works of the Great Creator. After again expressing his thanks for an opportunity to speak, he introduced a friend by the name of Renfrew, who expressed his gratitude to find that he also had been remembered. He related things in connection with his earthly pilgrimage, and then spoke of his experience in spirit; said he had spent most of his time with a few of his former friends, who had preceded his own initiation. He was anxious for any position in which he could be useful and assist in the advancement of the human race. He had brought a friend to the council who was in trouble. He had been a clergyman of his acquaintance in a western State, and had been removed unexpectedly by an accident on one of the western roads. He was at the time engaged in the building of a church, and still felt an anxiety in their temporal welfare. After expressing thanks, he gave way to his friend, who introduced himself.

He said he had been known among his earthly friends by the name of Bullard, and was relieved of his physical form by the fall of the Gasconade Bridge at the opening celebration of the Pacific Railroad between St. Louis and Jefferson City, in Missouri. He spoke with much feeling, thought it was strange his congregation had paid no attention to his efforts to enlighten them since his release from his earthly body; said he had given many demonstrations of his presence in his church, where he had been so much interested; and if his followers believed in the manifestation of spirit so often and plainly reported in the scriptures of the past, he knew not why they had not been prepared to receive his testimony. He was very thankful for the opportunity to speak, and would do all in his power to hasten the advent of truth and justice among the inhabitants of his country.

One of the Forest Maidens next told of the wisdom and love of the Great Spirit, and of his mighty power everywhere manifest in his works. She had come to the council of the white braves, and had listened to their talk. She was pleased she could go and tell the Great Spirit his pale-faced children had been talking about his great law of eternal justice. She then withdrew.

India again closed by invocation to the Great Spirit in thanks for the good order in council.

DECEMBER 15, 1872. — After India's invocation to the Great Spirit, he said one of the ancients, known by the name of Maroni, would have the privilege of speaking, and while he was speaking, it would be decided who would be called to follow.

Maroni was then before the council, and made the following statement. Many ages past, he inhabited an earthly form, and after many trials and sufferings, he was disobedient to the known commands of the spirit, and for his disobedience had been assigned the duty of keeping a record of the things of time. And most terrible, he said, had been his suffering: he had wandered up and down the earth, but found no rest; he had time and again climbed to the mountain-top and cast himself down headlong, but could not be destroyed; in his agony of spirit he had time and again prayed for annihilation, but annihilation came not to relieve him. He had witnessed the rise and fall of nations, and kept a record of man's inhumanity to man, as he had watched over their mangled forms on the battle-field, where they had struggled for the powers of earth. But, thankful to the Great Father, his name at last had been called by the angel of time. O, how his spirit had leaped before the platform of Eternal Justice, where he could lay down his bundles and find rest!

After Maroni retired, one who gave the name of Brown, of Kentucky, was before the council, and said he was glad he had been called to represent his State, for they were willing that all they had accumulated in their traffic with the colored man should be destroyed; and they would also make every possible restitution in their power in order to satisfy the demands of the red man's race, who were again upon the warpath, with their watch-fires on every mountain. His people would present no obstacle to the law of eternal justice, for they were tired of the effusion of human blood, and would gladly throw down their weapons of destruction and enter into rest. After thanking all for the privilege of speaking, he retired, and a man of Irish nationality spoke in behalf of the people of his country.

He thanked the good Lord that the time long foreseen by the ancient prophets and seers had come at last, when the principalities and the powers of the earth must give way for the kingdom of their Lord and Master — a kingdom of righteousness and justice that would rule among men. How his spirit rejoiced in anticipation of the glory that would follow

the advent of his Master's kingdom of joy and peace in the
Holy Spirit, for the children of earth had suffered, O how
long! from the bigotry and injustice of their brothers. He
counselled his countrymen in spirit, who, from whatever
cause or condition, had been instrumental in propagating
error among mortals, to hasten back to earth, and, like good
soldiers of the cross, undo their work, and be ready to meet
their Master. He then expressed his gratitude for the attention his country people had received, and retired. And
another of the Forest Maidens was before the council.

She had come from the upper hunting-grounds as by the
command of the Great Spirit, to listen to the talk of the paleface braves. The Great Spirit heard many complaints of the
sorrows of his pale-face children from the avarice and injustice of their brothers. The Great Spirit's red warriors were
many, and he had sent them out to see that his law of eternal
justice was again established on the lower hunting-grounds
of the red man.

And then, after giving his usual directions, India closed the
session by invocation to the Great Spirit.

DECEMBER 18, 1872. — After India's invocation to the Great
Spirit, he said many of the friends of the media were present
and anxious to identify themselves, and the session would be
assigned to them for that purpose. And as he retired,

Eight others had the privilege of speaking through the
vocal organs of their earthly friends, and relating a variety
of circumstances by which they desired to be remembered.
Each one gave his name, and they told of their condition in
spirit, expressed much gratitude for the pleasure they enjoyed,
and were anxious to be remembered. One man, who gave
the name of Stone, said he had been well known in Boston,
where he was familiar with the covenant of the communion
of spirit, and had found his friends in spirit waiting for him
at the end of his earthly pilgrimage. He was rejoiced to
know the time foreseen by prophets and seers would soon be
ushered in, when the sorrows of doubting mortals would be
submerged by the ever healing tide that would flow from the
fountain of the Prince of Peace.

Another man, who gave the name of Hutchinson, had been
anxiously waiting for an opportunity to telegraph back to his
earthly friends, and he knew of no other way. He said he
was one of the travelling band of brothers that was known

in the States as the singing family, and he had gathered up all of his own who had laid aside the mortal, and they were still singing progressive anthems for the amelioration and the elevation of spirits who inhabited the dark sphere. He was gratified with an opportunity to speak, and also anxious to be remembered by his earthly friends; when he retired. India again closed the session by invocation to the Great Spirit.

DECEMBER 22, 1872. — After India's opening invocation to the Great Spirit, once more presenting the labor of the council for his approval, he said that many had presented themselves who were anxious to join the council, and be known by name to their earthly friends as coworkers in building up the platform of eternal justice, but time would only permit a few to enjoy that privilege. All that were then present of the different nationalities could pass, and as they passed he mentioned the names of many who had formerly occupied prominent positions in the affairs of life. He then gave the names of three bishops — Watson, Comer, and Waterhouse — who had been designated as the ones having the privilege of speaking, to be followed by Bruce. And as he then retired —

Watson was the next in council, where he addressed his people, and told them the time had now arrived for the ancient prophecies to have their fulfilment, and it was what they had long and earnestly prayed to see. For he had revised his hymns, and was ready to engage in the work of redemption; and wherever there was a spirit or a mortal in bondage caused by any errors of his teaching, he was ready to go and work until he had accomplished their release. They had long lamented the sad condition of mortals who had turned away and denied the spirit, and were blindly struggling to increase their earthly power, when all history repeated the story of decay and national destruction, the result of avarice, idleness, and pride. He counselled all to accept of the present opportunity, and assist in re-establishing the great law of eternal justice. After extending his thanks for the opportunity of speaking, he retired.

Then Comer addressed the council. He was thankful his name had been called, and that he was granted the privilege of speaking. He had heard the remarks of his brother, and was also anxious that mankind should be redeemed from their errors. It was of but little consequence, so far as he was concerned, by whom such errors had been inculcated; they had all found to their own sorrow they had been the dupes of the errors and falsehoods of others. Man had ever been struggling for the principalities and powers of earth, and had made to themselves gods who had sanctioned their inhumanity. He was willing the principalities of earth should all be destroyed, if by so doing justice could be established. But he thought the gods, who worked all things after the counsel of their own wills, wherever they were, must be responsible for the present condition of affairs. He would stand in his lot, and do what he could to assist in the progress of the race. After the usual expression of good will, he retired.

Waterhouse was then before the council, and told them that good men with angels and spirits had long prayed for the establishment of justice in the councils of men; said the terrible suffering entailed upon mortals through avarice and injustice had disturbed the harmony of the spheres. He had been to the council many times, and was pleased to add his testimony in favor of its important work. The ancient sages were gathering together and rejoicing at the birth of a new kingdom, where the scattered tribes would be gathered in, and unite in a new anthem of praise for their long-lost Messiah. He then spoke with encouragement to those who had been honest and sincere in what they had promulgated, and thought all should be anxious to engage in the great work of restitution. He felt grateful for the privilege he had been permitted to enjoy, and was thankful he could stand as a witness for his people; when he retired.

Bruce was next before the council, and said he willingly responded to the call, and would be a witness of the avarice and injustice of the nations in their struggle for power. Great had been his sufferings, and also the sufferings of his people unjustly inflicted upon them, from the tyranny of the trusted guardians of the English nation. His people were gathering up and had anxiously waited for the call of the angel of time, when the nations of the earth would have to appear and take their place around the platform of Eternal Justice. He then spoke of the terrible sufferings of the darkness and sorrow in spirit of those who through avarice and injustice had struggled for the perishable principalities of the earth, and who had travelled up and down fearfully waiting for the judgment. He said that his bonny lassy and himself had stood in their lot, and patiently waited for the unfolding of events, and felt grateful for the call.

An Indian girl gave the name of Signal Star. She had come to the council to learn, and the guards had let her pass; and she repeated a number of wise proverbs that were shown to her in spirit. After saying the things given in the council should not be given out until the Great Spirit gave directions, she retired.

One of the Forest Maidens then told them the Great Spirit had been bountiful with his blessings to his pale-faced children; He gave them seed-time and harvest, and his lower hunting-grounds produced enough for all. It was their own fault that the cry of sorrow had gone up to the Great Spirit; they had revelled and danced with their store-houses full, when the poor pale-face squaws and their pappooses were shivering in the cold, and crying to the Great Spirit for bread. When India closed again by invocation to the Great Spirit.

DECEMBER 25, 1872. — After India's invocation, thanking the Great Spirit for the privilege of gathering together to review their work at the end of another year, asking his approval of all that was just and right, and for wisdom to guide in council, he said it was the purpose of the present session to commemorate the birthday of the Great Media, who was a voluntary martyr in order to enlighten and save the tribes of the earth from their bondage to the perishable things of time, and again asking for protection and for wisdom to govern their councils the coming year. After a few more words of encouragement, he said Mrs. Townsend and Mrs. Fuller, and others of the council, would speak, and retired.

Mrs. Townsend was the next to speak, and said she felt grateful for the opportunity to meet with so many in council to commemorate the birthday of their blessed Saviour, he who had agonized in Gethsemane, and been cruelly nailed to the cross, in order to open the way for mortals, and lead them to their immortal home. She thanked the Great Father that they were now permitted to be coworkers with him in gathering up the lost and friendless spirits in their dark condition, in order to prepare them for their entrance with Jesus their Saviour into his Father's eternal kingdom. She then spoke to her coworkers in spirit, and congratulated them on the success of their labors; it was true they found many things incredible to believe from the sufferings of those who had been degraded and sent headlong into the invisible world, but they were encouraged by the thought that some time such things would have an end. She would gladly prolong her remarks, but their time was limited, and she would give way that others might have time to speak.

Margaret Fuller came next. She spoke of the beneficial results of their labors; they had gathered up from the dark sphere millions of unhappy spirits who were without friends, and knew of no other condition. They were now clothed and rejoicing in their salvation. And a mighty host had assembled from the higher sphere to witness the evening's exhibition, in acknowledgment of the glorious triumph of their Master's labors, whose birthday they had then assembled to commemorate. She spoke of Everett and his army of boys, who had been cast out from their friendless haunts about the various cities, and of their fearful condition; but now their eyes sparkled with delight as they responded to the call of their teachers. She then spoke of her friend Greeley, he also being delighted with his change; and after her usual encouragements, she gave way for another.

Everett was the next to respond. He was pleased that he could be a coworker with others in the accomplishment of such important results. It was true, during his earthly life he had no inclination to mingle with or look into the condition of the so-called lower orders of society; he had known but little of their many sorrows. He thanked the controlling powers that he had been aroused in spirit to a proper understanding of his duty, and he was beginning to realize something of the pleasure that flowed from a successful endeavor to ameliorate the sufferings of others; for he had been with some of his boys into every den of vice and demoralization and human suffering in the various cities, he had been into cold and slimy underground tenements where the light of the sun had never shone, and where human beings were compelled to live destitute of every human comfort, and that in cities where they had boasted of their Christian civilization. He encouraged all who had engaged in the work of restitution, told them the fruits of their labors were with them, and worthy of their leader whose birthday they had assembled to celebrate. He then addressed a few cheering words in behalf of their earthly witnesses, who had patiently sat in the council, when —

Webster was the next to speak. He told of the demoralized political condition of the country, told of the sufferings of the southern States resulting from the recent cruel conflict, and of the fearful increase of pauperism and crime in the northern and eastern States; and then told Washington it was the natural fruit resulting from his signing the national constitution with its provision for human bondage; told him, if he had refused to sign that declaration of human rights, until it made provision for the equal freedom of all mankind, the present fearful judgment of the Great Creator might have been averted. He still felt that his own counsel to his countrymen had been disregarded, and was pleased to realize the time had come when justice would soon have a hearing among the people. He never had owned a plantation, he had never enslaved the colored man, and he thanked the controlling powers for it, for he had been slave enough himself. After speaking of their present organization and its good results, he retired.

Then Shakspeare was before the council, and spoke of their various labors, and the gratifying results; told of the lost and forsaken females that had been gathered up, and of the noble sisters at their head; spoke of Scott and his army of soldiers who were ready to do battle again this time in the true cause of eternal justice. He spoke of Everett and his coworkers, and of the vast assembly of boys that were made thieves and ragged vagabonds, and crushed in their growth, in the lower world, from the avarice and injustice and inhumanity of man. He then encouraged them all in their work, and told them, although many of the scenes had been sorrowful, it was a noble play upon a large stage, and worthy of their great Leader. He then recited a beautiful epilogue, and retired.

The chieftain Metamora was next present. He had come to the council of the pale-faces, not to disturb their devotions in memory of the birth of an ancient brave, but he had come to the great council with the claims of the red man to the lands the Great Spirit had given to their forefathers. He told them his warriors were again out on the war-path, and the hatchet should not be buried until their rights were restored, and not until justice, which the pale-face race was talking about, was extended to the balance of the red man's race. He then spied out Forrest, and gave him the hand of fellowship, and told him to go with him and he would show him the upper hunting-grounds which the Great Spirit had assigned to the red man, and where his white brother would always be welcome. After a few words to his warriors, he withdrew.

One of the Forest Maidens next told of the time when the red man's race covered the lower hunting-grounds of the Great Spirit. She had come to the council by the command of the Great Spirit, who was not pleased with his pale-faced race, who had driven the red man from their hunting-grounds; and the Great Spirit's law of eternal justice would make much sorrow among his pale-faced children for their disregard of his high commandments given to their fathers. And as she withdrew, India closed the session by invocation to the Great Spirit.

DECEMBER 29, 1872. — After India's invocation, again thanking the Great Spirit for the success and harmony of their labors, he said Mrs. Washington, and Penn, and Booth, would speak before the council. After a few remarks to his coworkers, he retired.

And then Mrs. Washington was again before the council, and said it was a pleasure to answer the call in behalf of America, for she was gratified to know that her country — the America she had loved so well — would be permitted to retain its own in spirit, for the time had arrived when the nations were called to stand in their place, and must appear. She felt to rejoice that George and herself had been thought worthy to take a part in re-establishing the great cause of eternal justice. She encouraged all to persevere in their labors, and then gave way for her brother and coworker.

The next, Penn, was before the council. Said he was thankful the time was drawing near to its close when there must be a settlement, for the cry of the suffering and want from avarice and injustice had disturbed them all; and he had come with his parchments, and his red brothers that stood around him were witnesses that he had always dealt justly with them; and he had told King Charles, when he got the grants for his lands, they were not his to grant, — they belonged to the natives the Great Father in his wisdom had seen proper to place there. He had dealt with his red brothers the same as though he had had no king's grant. He then told the guardians of the people of the other States if they had any parchments, to get them ready to hand up to the council on the platform of Eternal Justice, for the time had arrived when there could be no more dodging. After a few pleasant remarks, he said his people claimed to be the descendants of Rachel, and that justice had been their coat of arms. He then gave way for his brother.

When Booth was again before the council, he spoke of the great stage on which they had been called to perform, for the time had now arrived in which each one had to take his part. He then discovered Greeley and Forrest in his audience. He told Greeley if he had taken the spirit of truth with him in his late contest, he would not have left his earthly home broken-hearted. He then said to Forrest that he had played well his part, and he could now make his appearance upon the great stage in the battle of the Almighty with his mammon-loving children of earth. He told Greeley he would instruct him in his part at the next session. He then addressed his coworkers in spirit, and told them to give heed to the prompter, as the scenes changed, that each one might take his place. He then withdrew.

The next one was a Miss Forrest. She said she was taken from her earthly home during her childhood, and had been schooled in the paradise of the Great Father's love. She had come to meet her brother, and assure him she still loved him, and to tell him that his own loved ones were waiting to give him a happy greeting. She then retired.

One of the Forest Maidens next told of the condition of her race, who still inhabited the lower hunting-grounds of the red man. Great wrongs had been inflicted upon them by their pale-face brothers. The Great Spirit had sent his red warriors back to claim their lands, and assist in re-establishing his great law of eternal justice on the lower hunting-grounds of her race. And India again closed by invocation to the Great Spirit, once more asking that their labors might be acceptable, and be approved.

JANUARY 1, 1873. — After India's invocation to the Great Spirit, he said the rational investigations would commence, and that Washington and others had been cited to answer before the council. After again asking for wisdom and for strength sufficient for the work, he retired.

And Washington was before the council, and questioned about the condition of America, of which he was called the father. He replied by saying he was aware that many wrongs existed at the time they adopted the national constitution, and that no one could regret the present disorganized and unhappy condition of the American people more than himself; but it was true, at the time they asked for and relied upon divine wisdom to govern them in their councils;

and it was shown that the enslavement of the African race was lawful and right among the Israelites, and that their divine laws were still in force with the American people, who had received it as sacred, and sanctioned its authority. He said it had been his desire that the principles advanced in the declaration, that all men were endowed by their Creator with just and equal rights in the various pursuits of life, should have been sanctioned and sustained by the constitution; but at the time it was thought the service of the colored man was necessary in order to develop the resources of the country, and their continued enslavement was sanctioned by the different States at the ratification of the national constitution. It was true great wrongs had been entailed upon the race of the red man, as well as the black, and he had suffered, and still sorrowed over the fearful results; but then what could one man do? He was willing and anxious to be judged by the One whose right it was to establish the law of Eternal Justice. The facts being before them, it was not necessary to extend his remarks, and he would give way for his brother.

And Paine was the next one in council. He had been charged with stirring up strife among the American people by scattering broadcast his infidel writings. But he claimed that priestcraft had proved a stumbling-block in the way of the intellectual progress of the human race, and that it was still, and always had been, an expensive and useless burden upon the people. At the time mentioned, he was compelled to write by an unseen power that was hastening the birth of American freedom. He said he had told Washington, when they were struggling to free themselves from the bondage of foreign despots, to see and have all mankind protected in their natural rights when they ratified the new constitution, for it was a divine right that all men should be free in the pursuits of daily happiness, and free to worship their Creator in accordance with the dictates of their own conscience. He said it had been a struggle even to protect that clause from being expunged from their records at the command of a selfish priesthood. He was now thankful he had been called to stand on a platform of Eternal Justice, where he could defend the rights of man. If he had done wrong, he was willing to be judged by a just judge. If the country were free from bigotry and priestly power, its hospitable homes could be equally enjoyed by all. Even now they were obliged to set themselves off and alone in order to secure the communion of spirit, and help work out a more favorable and better condition for the oppressed, and over-burdened, and suffering inhabitants of earth. He was willing to submit to a final decision, and as their time was limited, he would give way for his brother.

And Penn was again before the council, and said he willingly responded to the call, for he had the parchments with him to prove he had not departed from the law of justice in his earthly transactions with his fellow-man. Justice was the foundation of the religion of his people, and they look upon all as the children of one Creator who inherited the earth in common. He again claimed that his people were the descendants of Rachel, and he said if any of them had departed from the faith of their forefathers, he wanted them judged the same as others who worshipped the mammon of unrighteousness, and by their injustice had filled the earth with their abominations. As he retired the name Smith was called.

When Smith was next before the council, he spoke of his own sorrowful condition; said he was called to answer for a people who had been beguiled by the serpent, and was following after the kingdoms of the earth. He then acknowledged he had been intrusted with the spirit of truth, and should have been foremost in the work of building up the spirit kingdom among mortals. But, O, how sorrowful the thought he had surrounded himself with bad men who turned away from the counsels of spirit, and followed after the lusts and the mammon of earth, and who were still creating wrath for themselves and their followers! His only excuse in justification of himself and people was the example of leading men of a past age, whose records were still among his people, who had been taught to venerate and to believe that they had received Divine approval. He was willing to do all in his power in order to mitigate the evils that were still flowing from his own example. He asked for mercy, and prayed that his people might not be shut out of the kingdom of which he himself had so unfortunately proved to be unworthy. He admitted that the western mountains would be the only refuge of thousands that were born under the curse of a broken law that was still sanctioned by the leaders among those who had been his followers. He then withdrew.

And Miller was next before the council, where he was asked about being the leader of a sect who was deceived, and who had squandered away their earthly homes, and become a burden to society. He replied by saying that he was thankful for an opportunity to speak for himself and his people. He had been honest in his interpretation of the scriptures of a past age, and had been impelled to believe, by an unseen power, that the coming of the blessed Saviour with his holy angels to establish his kingdom with mortals was then near at hand. He then thought that himself and his people would be the first to receive them. He was glad his error was of the head and not of the heart. It was true they were in error, and had failed to comprehend the coming of the Saviour with his angels in spirit, and naturally had expected their appearance in materialized forms. He then said that his people had not been worshippers of the mammon of unrighteousness, and they would become coworkers with their Master in building up his kingdom on the platform of Eternal Justice. He expressed a desire that their errors might be forgiven.

Ann Lee was next before the council, where she answered for a sect known by the name of Shakers; and said she was glad she had been called to represent a people who had become tired of the corrupt and false condition of society, and had tried to purify their earthly surroundings. It was true they had suppressed the spirit that was intrusted to their keeping, and confined it to the narrow limits of their own order. And they had disobeyed the command to multiply and replenish the earth; but they had encouraged industry by their examples to others, and they had tried to establish justice in their intercourse in the business affairs of life. She asked that she might be judged in charity, and that her people might go out with the spirit of truth among mortals, and assist in building up the waste places upon the true principles of Eternal Justice. After saying she was the mother of a family of children, and had suffered from the injustice of others during the earlier part of her earthly pilgrimage, she also withdrew.

One of the Forest Maidens was the next in council. She had not come to make any excuse for her race, she had come to listen to the talk of the pale-face squaws and braves, and she could tell them that the spirit warriors of her race had been on their trail all over the lower hunting-grounds. She had many complaints to carry back to the Great Spirit about the injustice of his pale-faced children.

And India closed the session by invocation, again thanking the Great Spirit for the success of their labors during the past year, and asking for his continual blessing.

JANUARY 5, 1873. — After India's invocation to the Great Spirit, asking that all might have wisdom and strength sufficient for their labors, he said that Columbus and Williams, with others, had been called in order that each one could have an opportunity to answer for themselves.

When Columbus was next before the council, he was asked why he interested himself in the discovery of the continent of America and the final destruction of its native inhabitants, by the introduction of a race who disregarded their rights? He replied by saying, at the time he was a poor man, a native of Italy, and for thirty years he was impelled by an unseen power to start out in search of another continent; the vision was constantly before him night and day, and it seemed impossible for him to disregard the call. He travelled from city to city in search of aid, telling of his vision only to be laughed at by others, until the good queen Isabella of Spain, through sympathy in his undertaking, inspired her husband the king to assist with means in order to procure a scanty outfit for his voyage; and when he finally got under way, there were but few that cared whether he ever returned. He moved on into an open and unknown ocean, with the vision still before him, impressed with an inward faith that he should find a new continent, inhabited by a race of human beings then unknown to the civilized world. He had pushed along and overcome every opposing obstacle until the vision of his soul was finally realized. He found a new and fertile country inhabited by a race of human beings simple in their habits, but spiritually developed and kind to each other, as they looked up to the Great Spirit as the Creator and Author of their blessings. If he had done wrong by his obedience to a power that he could not dispel, he desired to be forgiven; and he also claimed that he had already been made to suffer from the injustice and wrongs of his own countrymen, who had preferred false charges, and had him imprisoned, in order to gratify their avarice. He then spoke of the changing cycles of time, and of the important results flowing from his discovery of America.

Then Williams was the next one in the council, and said he had not been called to answer in behalf of his own people, for they had already been well represented. It was concerning his former residence in the colony of Massachusetts, and he was ready and willing to answer, for it was known that he had to flee from the colony in order to escape from the tyranny of his persecutors; and he was persecuted on account of his religious opinions, for he believed then, and he still believed that the natives they had found in peaceable possession of the country were the rightful owners, and that justice required that their rights should have been respected. It was owing to the fact that he was impelled to advocate their rights from a natural sense of justice, that he had had to flee in order to protect his life. He asked that the noble red men, who received him and gave him protection, should be remembered for their humanity and suitably rewarded; and that the inhabitants of that land where he had found protection, and still had an interest, should be acknowledged, and made foremost in the light of the new dispensation based upon the broad platform of eternal justice; and that all who had wronged him by their selfish zeal might be judged in charity, for he had nothing charged to their account. All, so far as himself was concerned, had long since been forgiven. He then expressed his thanks for the notice he had received, and retired.

St. Patrick was next before the council, and said he was called, not to answer for the people of his own country, but to say a word or two in behalf of his countrymen, who were now residents of America. He would say, if the people of his own nationality had been taught to reverence him as the patron saint of their country, it was not his fault, for he had instructed them, when a frail mortal among them, as best he could, by the light of the spirit given to him. But it was his desire now that one and all should lay aside their idols, and turn away from their earthly principalities, and look to the living Spirit to guide them in the ways of truth, and up to the platform of eternal justice, where they would learn to venerate the blessed Saviour for his compassion for the race, and worship the Great Father for his untold blessings. He well knew his countrymen had been kept in ignorance of the living truths from the blind zeal of a selfish priesthood, and he prayed to the blessed Saviour that they might be enlightened and judged in mercy. He expressed gratitude for the attention his countrymen had received before the council, and withdrew.

And Metamora was again before the council, and said Red Jacket, Tecumseh, and their warriors were with him, and they had come to the wigwam to listen to the talk of the pale-face braves. He told them it was their avarice that sent them in search of new continents, and not the Great Spirit. If they had been directed by the Great Spirit, they and their race would have learned to have dealt in justice with their red brothers, who had come to the great council to demand that justice should be extended to the balance of their race; and the hatchet should never be buried again until their rights were restored. He had talked with the Great Spirit in the upper hunting-grounds that very day, and the Great Spirit told him to go to the council and charge his white brothers with their covetousness and their injustice, and tell them they had forgotten the Great Spirit, and had turned to the worship of the gods of Mammon. He told them how his red brothers had met them with open arms, and fed them from their baskets, and taken them into their wigwams for protection, and their only reward had been their base ingratitude. He asked them how they could expect mercy when they had shown none to their brothers; they had driven the red man's race from their hunting-grounds, and shot down their squaws and their helpless pappooses in their own wigwams, like fiends destitute of human sympathy, and he would never be satisfied until justice was restored to his race, and their lower hunting-grounds given up to the true worshippers of the Great Spirit. Metamora and his race were on the war-path.

One of the Forest Maidens was next before the council, and she had brought up to the platform many of the children she had gathered up in the wigwams of the pale-faces since the last council, where they had no fire to keep them warm, and nothing to prevent their starving. "O, see, Great Judge, how many there are: ten times ten, and ten over,—all without fire or food." She had put her hand on their little hearts, and stopped their faint pulsation, and had brought them up to the Platform of Justice to be warmed. If she had done wrong, they must tell her, for there were many more among the wigwams of the poor pale-faces where there were neither blankets nor bread. The Great Spirit would hear the squaws cry when they had no bread for their pappooses.

And India closed the session by another invocation to the Great Spirit, again asking for his continued guidance and care.

JANUARY 8, 1873.—After India's invocation to the Great Spirit, he said Morgan was before the council, and would have an opportunity to speak; after which they should commence the examination of the records of the Israelites; and he retired.

When Morgan was next before the council, and asked why he had exposed the secrets of an association of men that were following the light of the ancient mysteries, he said it was gratifying to have an opportunity to defend his action before the great platform of Eternal Justice, and would say that he had had a desire to attain to a knowledge of the living truths, and that no Order, controlled and sustained by the powers and principalities of earth, had any right to limit or suppress the aspirations of his spirit. But he was even now ashamed to admit that he had been a coward during his connection with the Order, and had failed to tell all that he knew of their evils or its effects. It was known by every intelligent member that they had fallen from the high calling the Order once occupied, and had broken the connection with the celestial Lodge by turning away and disregarding the call of the living Spirit; and they were using the symbols once held sacred in their struggle after the Mammon of unrighteousness. He said he had been impelled by an unseen power to expose the iniquity of the Order, and he still thought he had done right, for no true man could remain bound up by an order where all drank from the same *skull-bone* with a brother whose hands were stained with his brother's blood, after the time had arrived for them to take down their *cross-bones*, and acknowledge that all were the children of one and the same Creator, and learn that they must deal justly with each other. If there was any brother in the spheres who refused to meet him on the *square* and give him the hand of fellowship, he could remain behind; he desired to prevent no one from pressing on towards the *living temple*. He had suffered, and was willing, if necessary, to suffer more, if by his suffering his brother found rest. After again expressing his satisfaction for the opportunity to speak, he retired.

Then one of a tribe of Pequots was before the council, where he had come in order to represent the one known in history as Adam, and believed by some of the inhabitants of the present age to have been the first man created. But he could answer for himself and the tribe of his age that they had no history of Adam and Eve, or any knowledge that any such parties had ever had an existence. His own tribe had wandered away from the land of their forefathers, and finally become the residents of an unsettled but beautiful and fertile country. It had been formed by the receding of the waters, and produced spontaneously all that was necessary for their earthly existence. It was truly a land that flowed with milk and honey. They had been wandering many years in search of their new home through a barren and to them an unknown country, and the older members of the tribe had dropped off one by one in the wilderness, until at last all records of the country they came from, or the route they had travelled, were lost. But their descendants remained in their new home, and for a time were contented and satisfied with their earthly condition. The animals were tame and confiding, and all things seemed to partake of the harmony of universal nature. In the twilight of the evening, spirit messengers mingled and commingled with them about the doors of their rustic cabins. It seemed as though they had been led by a band of celestial messengers from their wandering in the wilderness into their new and fertile home. And as they increased in numbers, many became discontented: they wanted to go and come as the spirits around them did, in order to be satisfied. Such was the natural condition. It was not the beginning of creation, but the commencement of an age or cycle of time. And as the tribes increased in number, their worldly wealth increased, and avarice soon found a resting-place among them; when the herdsmen and the tillers of the soil disagreed and engaged in bloody conflicts, and the spirit of peace and truth departed. He said he had been shown that the first inhabitants on this planet had entered through a narrow passage in the east, and had long inhabited that hemisphere, without knowing of any other continent. The next entered through a narrow passage in the west, and had long been a distinct and peculiar people. The next entered through a narrow passage from the north, bringing with them the evidence of civilization from beyond. They had cattle and all kinds of goods, and travelled a long way before they made a settlement. The people who entered from the south were divided; and as the country changed by the receding of the waters and the natural action of the sun upon the land, they increased rapidly in numbers, but had no knowledge of each other's language. He said the people known as worshippers of the sun, spoken of in the Hebrew records, were the people that came from the southern hemisphere, and that the tribes on the American continent, who used the bow and arrow, were the descendants of the tribe of Nimrod, one of the wandering tribes of Israel. After saying he would be ready and prepared to answer, if any inquiry should seem necessary, he retired.

One of the Forest Maidens was next before the council. Said she had come to the wigwam of the pale-face squaw on the lower hunting-grounds of the red man; she was glad the Great Judge was listening to the talk of the pale-faces, for they had much to do in order to make restitution to their brothers. Much sorrow and much suffering would come to them in judgment for turning away from the covenants and commandments of the Great Spirit, and disregarding his great law of Eternal Justice.

And India again closed the session by invocation to the Great Spirit.

JANUARY 12, 1873. — After India's invocation to the Great Spirit, asking for wisdom and strength sufficient for their investigations, he said it was possible there would be more or less contention about the ancient inhabitants speaking through mortals of the present age in their own familiar language; but he said they had interpreters, and had schools in spirit, where they had been instructed the same as the dead languages were now rendered into the English, and as witnesses of a foreign language were examined in courts of justice through an interpreter. He then said that Seth, Enoch, and Noah were the next to be examined; and then withdrew. After which —

Seth was next before the council, and spoke of the habits and customs of the tribes during his own earthly experience. He said the country was fertile, and the tribes divided by different pursuits. Some tended the herds and flocks, and others cultivated the soil, while many formed centres of trade, where the accumulations of industry were bartered and exchanged. Many of the tribes were selfish and quarrelsome, and often broke up and wandered into other sections of the country, where they would settle down and renew their labors. And at the time of his own experience the tribes had become numerous in different settlements over the continent; they had no books or schools of instruction, and no records or history of their forefathers; their form of worship was the communion of spirit, and they had a covenant given by spirit that taught them by signs and symbols of their duties in life and of the resurrection, — which had become an established order among the leaders and representatives of the tribes; and, as far as he knew, there always had been sages and seers among them, who were instructed by the ever-living Spirit. He was pleased to know he was remembered; he would stand a witness for the tribes of his own age and generation; and then gave way.

Enoch was next before the council, and said, so far as he knew, all that his brother had related was true. He then said that the tribes were designated by the name of their leaders, which were often retained through many generations ; that the tribe of Cain was known as tillers of the soil, and that of Abel as herdsmen ; and their frequent quarrels, often ending in the shedding of blood, had brought them into notoriety. There was no truth in the stories of the historians that men lived at that age longer than at the present, only as they were represented by the names of their tribes. It was reported that he had walked and talked with God, and that he was, and then that he was not, for God took him. He said he had walked and talked with spirits, and the highest spirit was God ; that, when he was done with his physical body, he left it, as others had left their own, in obedience to the natural law; and when the tribes listened to the voice of the ever-living Spirit, and obeyed the law of justice, they were blessed; when they turned away and corrupted themselves with the evils of covetousness they were soon overwhelmed by their own abominations, and devastating wars, with flood and famine, cut them off from the face of the earth. He was pleased to know that he was still remembered, and would stand as witness for his tribes.

Noah was next before the council, and was glad of an opportunity to confirm what his brothers had said, and should avail himself of the offer presented in order to say a few words in his own behalf. Said he knew of no flood during his day and generation, unless it was a flood of ignorance and selfishness among the tribes. He thought the story of the Ark must have originated in the imagination of the historian, for the only ark he had the credit of building was the ark of the covenant, and that was a box which contained the symbols of their Order, which conveyed to them a knowledge of their immortal home, for they were overshadowed by the angels as they entered into the Holy of Holies. He said the story incorporated in the Jewish history of his planting a vineyard and getting drunk on the wine had done him and his posterity great injustice. Much of the time, with its events, during his age was not recorded ; he had no doubt the Hebrew historian had thought to cover it up with his story about the flood. He then said their lands were fertile, and the tribes had made rapid increase. Although they had no knowledge at the time that any other continent was inhabited, what was true of them was also true of the settlements of other continents. When the tribes obeyed the covenants, they were blessed, and when they turned away and followed the crooked path, it led them on to destruction. They had been told in his age they would return to the earth in spirit, and talk with mortals, and he was glad the Ancient of Days had come when the law of justice would be re-established. After a few words with his own tribes, he retired.

One of the Forest Maidens was next before the council. She had come from the upper hunting-grounds of the red man to tell the pale-face race of the love of the Great Spirit, and how they had brought sorrow and destruction upon themselves by their covetousness and by their injustice, and by their disregard of the Great Spirit's Law of Eternal Justice. And India again closed the session by invocation to the Great Spirit.

JANUARY 15, 1873. — After India's invocation to the Great Spirit, once more asking for wisdom and strength in order to govern them aright in their council, he said Abraham, Isaac, and Jacob were present, and would answer; whereupon he retired.

Abraham was next before the council. He said the historian had made sad work of the records of his age, for there was no truth in the stories about their having so many wives; they had bondmen and bondwomen that were bought of the wandering tribes in search of new homes, and it was the children of the bondmen that went out from their camps and formed settlements of their own. They had followed the customs of their fathers, and obeyed the same unwritten law, and worshipped the same God, in obedience to the voice of the Spirit. They had flocks and herds, and cultivated the soil, and manufactured their own goods, and lived in tents; and when the lands became exhausted in one section, it was their custom to move into other fertile localities ; and for many centuries the tribes were contented and satisfied with their blessings, as they were taught by the Spirit that when their earthly pilgrimage was ended they would be gathered home to their fathers, and be at rest. It was their custom to offer oblations to the Great Creator from the first-fruits, in thankfulness for his blessings. And it was true, at a time when he was agonized in mind from a dereliction of his duty, he did make an offering of his son for a sacrifice ; and the offering was accepted, and an angel sent to stay the sacrifice. The time of the gathering up had come, as they had been foretold. And he rejoiced that he had been called to stand up for his own tribes. After which —

Isaac was next before the council. He and his people had followed the examples of their fathers; they obeyed the same covenants, and partook of the bountiful blessings that flowed from the same living Source. The lands they cultivated were fertile, and his people were frugal and industrious in their habits, and their daily wants were well supplied. Their handmaids manufactured cloths for their own apparel, and exchanged with wandering bands from Arabia and Chaldea, who carried their goods on the camel's back. Said they had neither books nor schools, and no written records; the leading events of the age were kept on scraps of bark in marks and signs that had never been truthfully interpreted. Their habits and customs were the same as those of other tribes who inhabited new and fertile countries. When they obeyed their covenants, and followed the light of the Spirit, they were blessed; when they turned away and corrupted themselves with their own selfish abominations, they received their reward. And he was thankful that he could stand in his own place and answer for his tribes; for the time had arrived for the children of the bondwoman to be gathered together and acknowledged, and to prepare to enter the promised land above their earthly Jordans. And he gave way.

Jacob was next before the council, and said he would stand for his people, for they had drawn from the same well that supplied and quenched the thirst of their forefathers, and that well was a knowledge of the true God, who had watched over and blessed them with the communion with the spirits of just men made perfect by a resurrection from the corruption of the flesh. And they had the covenant made with their fathers, whose signs and symbols brought them into union with the ever-living Spirit, and taught them their duties to each other. It was the children of the servants and the bondwoman that wandered away into forbidden paths, and through ignorance and vice fell from their high estate, and covered the land with their abominations like the waters of a flood. He rejoiced to know the birth of a new era had arrived, when the people should have a flood of knowledge that would lead them to the living temple, where the tribes of the bond and of the free would mingle together. He said they had no authentic records for many generations from his age to that of the Jews, and the historians had covered it up with many incredible stories: they could answer for themselves; he was called to answer for his own people.

Then one of the Forest Maidens was before the council, and told how she had followed the trail of the old patriarchs in their wanderings over the eastern continent; she found they had been well supplied with the wampum they took from the land of their forefathers. She told them the effects of their many wrongs were still felt by the tribes on the lower hunting-grounds. And India closed the session by invocation to the Great Spirit.

JANUARY 19, 1873. — After India's invocation to the Great Spirit, he said the statements of Moses and Aaron would next be in order; whereupon he retired.

And Moses was next in council, where he said it was true he was the lawgiver to the people of his age, and was endowed with the living Spirit to lead them from the bondage of ignorance and oppression, away from the Pharaohs and taskmasters that oppressed them, in search of a land of freedom which should always flow with milk and honey. He taught them the covenants of God made with their fathers, and the commandments given through him on the mountain. When they obeyed the covenants and commandments of God, they were overshadowed by the Spirit and led into paths of peace. Many of his people were stiff-necked and rebellious, and turned away into crooked paths, and corrupted themselves with their own abominations. They set up statues and images of their own "dumb gods" that could not speak, and fell down and worshipped them. They surrounded themselves and their gods with the mammon of unrighteousness that brought their own destruction. It was of heavy and grievous burdens the people complained; it was through prophet and "seer" they were warned by the living Spirit to turn back and forsake their evil ways, and obey the commandments of God. It was the same with his people and their forefathers as it was with the people and their forefathers who were led by the Spirit of God to the American continent, where they could establish a government and enjoy their freedom. Their constitution was the covenant they made. Who had obeyed it? How had they treated the people they found in the country that was intrusted to their care? And had they listened to the Spirit of God that was speaking to them on the mountain, and in the bush, and through the mouths of his "prophets" and "seers"? Were not they still worshipping the idols and images they had set up to be the gods of the earth, although they had received the Law, and the covenants and commandments that were given to his people, and would be judged by them? And that might explain the cause why fire and floods and famine were fast devastating the land, and the cry of suffering that returns in answer to the broken law! He again spoke of the self-will and stubborn condition of his own people, and then gave way.

And Aaron was next in council, and said he was intrusted with the ark and covenant of their forefathers, and assisted in teaching the tribes the rites and ceremonies of the Order, which brought them into union, and taught them of their duties to each other, and of a reunion beyond the veil to meet with their fathers and be at rest. And all that gave heed to the voice of the Spirit, and obeyed the covenants and commandments, received the promised blessings. It was his duty to present as an offering of the tribes a gift of their first-fruits to the Great Creator, as a token in remembrance of their many blessings. It was also the duty of the priesthood of the Order to attend to the sanitary affairs of the tribes, and, when necessary, to heal the various maladies. All that obeyed enjoyed the blessings. But many turned away and followed after their own evil doings, and they set up images and dumb idols to worship, and corrupted themselves with earthly mammon that perished, until the cry of suffering from the oppressed brought the judgments from the eternal world that follow the broken law. And he withdrew.

A Forest Maiden was next before the council. She had listened to the talk of the braves, and knew well the cause of their many sorrows. Her tribe and their forefathers had obeyed the voice of the Great Spirit, and when their hunting was finished below, the Great Spirit called them up to his upper hunting-grounds. But still the cry of oppression and of suffering is heard from the pale-face race, and again the race of the red man is on the war-path by the command of the Great Spirit, to re-establish his Law of Eternal Justice, and they would guard the wigwam of the white squaw.

When again India closed the session by invocation to the Great Spirit.

JANUARY 22, 1873. — After India's invocation to the Great Spirit, he said Joshua was then waiting in order to make his report, and withdrew. And Joshua was the next in the council. He said it was true he was the chosen leader of the tribes after the death of Moses, and in about eight months they crossed the Jordan, and entered the promised land. The tribes they drove out were idolaters who refused to worship the God of Israel and obey his commandments; for it was over four hundred years from Abraham's reign to that of Moses, and the tribes had accumulated fast. Many had turned away from the covenant of their fathers, and become the worshippers of unknown gods, and set up governments of their own; while those who followed the ark, and listened to the voice of the Spirit, were the true worshippers of the God of Israel, and had no doubt, although they had many trials and hardships to endure, they would finally inherit the promised land. They were compelled to prohibit the communion with familiar spirits, for they spread conflicting statements among the tribes, and created discord and trouble in the camps. He then said Moses talked to the God of Israel on the mountain through the Spirit, as he himself was then talking before the council, and that all high mountains were frequently enveloped in clouds. At the time it was said the sun and the moon stood still, there might have been an eclipse; but, so far as he knew, there was no violation of the natural laws. Many of the habits and customs of his age had been magnified in order to suit the demand of the age that followed. It was true they cut the foreskin, but it was for a sanitary purpose: it prevented disease among the tribes, and had long been the practice. The spirit that he consulted spoke through Miriam the prophetess, who sat in the inner temple in the Holy of Holies, where the leaders of the covenanted people were permitted to approach, and inquire of the spirit during their search for the promised land. He then retired.

One of the Forest Maidens was next before the council, and said she had come to the wigwam of the white squaw, and had listened to the talk of the old brave who was good; but he and his tribes had been mistaken. She then pointed to a panorama of Africa, and to one of China, and showed him where his forefathers had crossed and entered their Garden of Eden, that had long since been covered up by the flowing of the mighty waters. She told him the race of the red man were inhabitants of the same lower hunting-grounds long before his race had left the homes of their forefathers. She told him that Moses, whom they had started out from his little boat on the water, had been cruel, and made laws for the people that were oppressive and that he himself never obeyed. She told him the stories of their evils and their abominations, which had been recorded and handed down to posterity as sacred, and which told of their wrangling and fighting, and corrupting themselves with their many wives and concubines, with the shameful accounts of strangling their offspring, had covered the lower hunting-grounds with crime, and the blood of their many victims was crying to the Great Spirit for justice. She then withdrew.

And again India closed the session by invocation to the Great Spirit.

JANUARY 26, 1873. — After India's invocation to the Great Spirit, he said Deborah, Abimelech, Ruth, and Samson were the next in order. And as he retired —

Deborah was before the council, and acknowledged she had assisted the covenanted people in their wars on the tribes that inhabited the surrounding country; but said she was deceived by the leaders, who claimed that all such wars were sanctioned by the God of Israel. It was their custom to exclude females from what they called their sacred covenant, in order to keep them in ignorance that they might more readily make them the slaves of their tyrannical power. The spirit within told her such things were wrong, but they were sure to crush it out, or make it subservient to their stubborn wills. There was not a time from Seth to that of Abraham, or from Abraham to that of Moses, that a woman was admitted into the mysteries of their sacred order, unless it was to deceive her that her offspring might be a charmed leader for the purpose of keeping the iron yoke on the necks of the people. She told them they had been crafty and cunning: they sent out their spies filled with deception, to hunt out other tribes who were trying to live in peace, and who could look up to the heavens above and see the same symbols they had made a mockery of in their pretended holy order, when they sent out their fighting bands to slay and lay waste, and commit unlawful and unholy abominations all over the land, while they lived on what they extorted from the industry of others, and satisfied their unholy desires with the bondwomen and the virgins saved from the slaughter among the surrounding tribes. She rejoiced to know the time had come when she could stand up in judgment against them; and as the Spirit had prophesied through her in their camps on the plains of Palestine, she would prophesy again they would have to return and undo their evil work, and cleanse themselves of their many abominations, before they could return and stand by the side of the fair daughters of Israel, who have found the living temple of the true God above their earthly Jordans. She then addressed a few cheering words to her companions, and retired. And —

Abimelech was next before the council. He remarked there was but little he could say in justification, for the prophetess had told the truth; said they were called upon to be leaders of a people in an age when they were ignorant and full of superstition, and he was compelled to do as the leaders had done before him. What he had done that was wrong he had many times regretted, and he asked that he might be judged in charity. If it was to go back and assist others in a work of restitution among mortals, cheerfully he would accept the duty assigned to him, for his sorrows had long been burdensome to endure. And he withdrew.

When Ruth was next before the council, she said that injustice had been done to her mother as well as herself in the records of the Israelites that were still among the people. There was no truth in the story about her gleaning in the fields of Boaz, or of her crawling around his feet on the threshing-floor. Her mother was a Moabitess and a relative of Boaz, and had a business transaction with him about her land at the time they were made so conspicuous by the historians. Their manner of living was similar to that of the poorer class of the present age: they were scattered about the neighborhood, lived in tents or cabins, and cultivated the soil from which they obtained their living. They had neither books nor schools of instruction, were often taught by spirit through many media, when their arbitrary rulers would permit the people to hold communion with spirits. It was a common opinion in her age that when they left the mortal body they would be reunited with their friends in spirit and be at rest, although they were treated as menials and inferiors by the males, and never intrusted with any of the mysteries of the ark of the covenant. She had been called a " gleaner," and she should continue to glean until her sex were redeemed from their long and unjust degradation. She then gave way. And —

Samson was next before the council, where he also complained that many of the stories told about himself had been greatly exaggerated; said he was a strong man by nature, and he was also a media through which spirit-power was often made manifest; said he was something of a wag, and delighted to be among the lower orders of the people, and tell them incredulous and foolish stories in order to excite their curiosity. There were times when they got into a row, the spirit would come upon him, and he tore things up; but it generally left him exhausted and frothing at the mouth. They put out his eyes in order to destroy his mediumistic influence; for the leaders were envious and jealous of all power they could not control for their own selfish designs, in order to perpetuate their rule over the people. Said he had been in many a row among the inhabitants of the earth since his own release from his body, and he was glad the time had come for a settlement.

One of the Forest Maidens was then before the council, and in beautiful language reviewed the history of the age of which they had been speaking. She told them they should have trusted the mighty power and the love of the Great Spirit made manifest through his blessings that were everywhere bestowed upon his children. They had turned away with ingratitude, and wrangled and fought with each other until the lower hunting-grounds of the Great Spirit were soaked with the blood of their victims; and they had thought to appease his anger by their bloody sacrifices to the gods of their own wicked and foolish imaginations. And such things are still called sacred, and are taught to the Great Spirit's pale-face children. She then told Deborah and Ruth to go with her, and they should sit upon the platform of Eternal Justice, by the command of the Great Spirit, in judgment upon all who had degraded and deceived them. She then told Abimelech and Samson to gather up their scattered tribes, and go back and use the power they were intrusted with and abused, to tear down the false temple, and destroy the records of their unholy and their evil abominations, that were still corrupting the tribes on the lower hunting-grounds. And India closed by invocation to the Great Spirit again with thanks for his continued blessings.

JANUARY 29, 1873. — After India's invocation to the Great Spirit, he said Samuel, and Saul, and David were next in order, and would have the opportunity to make their own statements. As he retired —

Samuel, the seer, was before the council, and told of his own experience with the tribes of Israel. He said the covenanted people were instructed by the Spirit; and when they were obedient to the voice of the true Spirit, they were led into pleasant paths; but as many turned away and had other gods to worship, they were brought into frequent conflicts that ended in the shedding of blood. The wilderness through which the covenanted people had to pass typified the general ignorance and superstition of the people of that age, that covered the land as they wandered about the country in search of new homes, while their disregard and disobedience had caused them much suffering. When he anointed Saul to be their king, he had forebodings that evil would be the result, and it proved to be the cause of much dissatisfaction, although many of the incredible statements that had been incorporated into what was called the "sacred records" never had any foundation in truth. They consulted with the spirits the same as the people of the present age, only it was considered more sacred, and generally controlled by the leader. He himself was a "seer," and foretold many of the evils with which the people had already been afflicted. And he gave way.

Saul was next before the council, and said it was true Samuel did anoint him king, or a leader of the tribes, in accordance with the custom of the age; but he soon joined in with the rabble, who wanted a stripling of a boy anointed in his place, and said the tribes were idling away their time, running about after "seers" and "soothsayers," a-trying to find out what God wanted them to do. He tried to stop it, and prevented their running after such things as much as possible, for he thought he was competent to manage their affairs without running after the God of Israel every day to see if he was satisfied. But the more he opposed, the stronger was the dissatisfaction, until it seemed as though all the spirits from the infernal regions were let loose, and they finally succeeded in dragging him down, and putting the stripling in his place. He said David was crafty and artful, and when it was noised around he was to be their king by the command of their imaginary god, it gave him great importance among the tribes. And he (Saul) had made a decree that the man who should capture two hundred of the Philistines, and march them into the king's camp, should be entitled to one of the king's daughters, when David by stratagem deceived them, and marched them in, and secured the prize. He said the evil spirit that tormented him was his knowledge of their hypocrisy, and the envy and the discord by which he was surrounded; and when he went to the prophetess called the Woman of Endor to inquire of the spirit, and Samuel made his appearance, he knew then his time was up, and he might as well quit. There was no truth in the unnatural stories incorporated into the old records; the same natural laws that control now controlled in his day; all that seems unnatural should be disregarded.

And David was next in council, where he also complained of the injustice he and his fathers had suffered from the falsifying of their records. He was a leader of the covenanted people, and had been faithful in the discharge of his duties, as he was taught by the Spirit and by the records of his forefathers. It was the tribes that disregarded the teachings of their holy covenant, and went into forbidden paths, that had covered the land with their evil doings. His people had been traduced, and the ark and covenant, and the symbols of their sacred order destroyed, until they were compelled to protect themselves with the "hod" and "trowel" of a common tradesman. The stories about their many wives and concubines were not true: they had been incorporated into their history by the rulers of a later age, who had turned away and disregarded the teachings of the Holy Spirit, and followed after the gods of the earth, and corrupted themselves with their own abominations, and with the perishable and transitory things of time. The temple he had instructed his son to build typified the celestial temple not made with hands, which they had hoped to find when they crossed their earthly Jordan and were gathered home to their fathers. There was still a remnant of his people who had been faithful to the covenant made with their fathers; and although they had been driven from their homes, and their holy temple destroyed, they had not been deserted by Israel's God, who would yet gather up the lost and scattered tribes, where they could sit down in their promised land with Abraham, Isaac, and Jacob, and be at rest. He then retired.

And one of the Forest Maidens was in council, where she spoke of their evil doings. If their records had been falsified, why hadn't they all been to work to blot them out, and put an end to their unholy teachings, that were still corrupting their pale-faced brothers all over the land? She had followed in the trail of their many evils that were sanctioned by the leaders of the tribes as by command of their God of Israel, until the wail of sorrow from the suffering pale-faces had disturbed the harmony of the upper hunting-grounds; and she had come to the council to say that the Great Spirit had never sanctioned any of their many wrongs that were handed from tribe to tribe, who knew not what to do. And India closed the session by invocation to the Great Spirit.

FEBRUARY 2, 1873. — After India's invocation to the Great Spirit, he said that Solomon and Nebuchadnezzar were next in order, and, after a few encouraging remarks, retired. After which —

Solomon was next in council, where he confirmed the history of his being installed in power after his father David's death, and fulfilled his instructions about the building of a temple that was dedicated to the God of Israel. It was a magnificent building, and in keeping with the order given to their fathers, which was handed down from generation to generation with the ark and covenant, and with a history of their wanderings, which had then become sacred. He said Hiram, his master workman, was a true brother, skilled in all the arts of his time, and the report of his being slain by a conspiracy of the under-workmen was not correct. There was a conspiracy, as the temple was nearly finished, among the under-workmen, who were anxious to know where the instructions were given that had resulted in the erection of a grand temple which displayed the symbols of their "sacred order;" for none but himself and Hiram, and one or two others, were permitted to enter the inner temple, and approach the Holy of Holies, where the voice of the Spirit gave instructions through the high-priest, who alone was permitted to enter. They were advised of the conspiracy by the Spirit, and placed an under-workman on guard, in Hiram's outward apparel, who was slain, and the insurrection subdued, and Hiram returned to his friends.

Hiram was not a son of a widow, for his father was living, and master of the "arts" he had imparted to Hiram. Their order was sacred: it was given from God, through his spirits, to their forefathers. And when they obeyed the voice of the Spirit, they were directed aright. And when a brother met his brother around the ark of the covenant, or before the horns of the altar, and upon his bended knees acknowledged his transgression, and asked to be forgiven, what true brother would refuse the hand of fellowship? How could he expect that God would ever forgive his own transgressions, if he refused to forgive his brother, and bade him go his way and sin no more? He acknowledged to his sorrow that he disregarded the warning voice of the Spirit, and followed after the evils and the vanities of the world; for he was left in his youthful inexperience, surrounded with wealth and power, and, tired of the uneasy and dissatisfied rabble that were ever around him, longed to be away where he could be at rest. He said the women that were now called his concubines in what was called the " sacred record " were the media of his day, through which the Spirit spoke to mortals. He thought it too sacred for the common herd, who was too ignorant to comprehend their teachings; and he had them gathered up and provided for at his own expense, where they were free from want and not corrupted. But after the novelty of the grand temple had passed away, and they neglected the teachings of their holy covenant, and satiated themselves with the vanities and follies of the world, the Holy Spirit was withdrawn, and they were left in Egyptian darkness. And when he turned again and would have given his kingdom for the Spirit, he sought it in vain. He then withdrew.

Nebuchadnezzar was next before the council, and ready to answer. He then said it was true he did go and clean out their holy temple, and they had turned him out to feed on grass in what they had called a " sacred record," in order to pay him for his trouble. He had found the wealth of an empire piled up in one magnificent building, which they called " holy," while the people in all the surrounding country, who were also the children of God, had been impoverished by the extravagance of their leaders, and were found starving for the common necessaries of life. He thought it was time that some one was found with humanity enough to go and clean out their sacred temple, and scatter its untold wealth among the suffering people. He felt justified in what he had done, and, if it was in his power, under similar conditions, he would do it again; for there was no necessity of any such extravagance in order to teach the people of the wonderful works of the Great Creator. The sun and the moon with the stars in the glorious heavens above were constant witnesses of his everlasting power, while seed-time and harvest should have taught them of his love, by the provision made for their daily happiness. He then said the temple was a grand display of workmanship, and that no description he could give would do justice to it; for there were many rooms they failed to open, and in one, two of his men were deprived of their lives; which intimidated the balance, and they fled in fear. He himself fell to his knees, imploring for mercy, asking, if he had done wrong, to be forgiven. At the time he was king, Babylon could command about forty thousand warriors. But most of the foolish stories that had been handed down from one generation to another were nothing but fictions of the age, gathered up and called "sacred," in order to suit the demand of the credulous. The vision shown to him in his dream, and the interpretation given by Daniel the "seer," had in part been fulfilled. He was dethroned, and turned out to wander like the beasts of the field, shorn of his power. Many kingdoms and cities have gone down, and many are soon to follow, and the majesty and power of the Eternal One acknowledged by his earthly children. Then he retired.

One of the Forest Maidens was next in the council, where she replied, and told of the fearful mistake they had made by their cruelty and oppression, for they had crushed out and destroyed the freedom of the tribes when the lower hunting-grounds belonged to the Great Spirit, where all were equally entitled to their daily blessings. But the avarice and the injustice of the leaders, and the stories about their wrangling and fighting, with their many told evils, which had been handed down from tribe to tribe and from generation to generation, had covered the hunting-grounds with the blood of their brothers that was now crying to the Great Spirit for justice. She then retired.

India closed the session by invocation to the Great Spirit.

FEBRUARY 5, 1873. — After India's invocation to the Great Spirit, he said Hezekiah and Confucius would speak, and after his usual encouraging remarks, retired.

And Hezekiah was before the council, and said he was the acknowledged leader of the tribes that followed the covenant made with their forefathers about one hundred years after their temple was sacked by the Babylonians under the command of Nebuchadnezzar. The temple had been plundered and desecrated by the common rabble, who knew nothing of the teachings of their holy Order. He had their abominations removed, and re-established the priesthood, and renewed the law and order among the tribes. The temple was consecrated to the God of Israel; but none but the worthy were permitted to partake of the rites and ceremonies connected with their holy covenant. They had signs and passwords for their own protection; and he knew of only twelve that were found worthy to enter the inner temple, and approach the Holy of Holies beyond the veil, where they listened to the voice of the Spirit. He said the tribes of his age were a wandering, dissatisfied class of people, never long contented with their condition, and their laws had to be severe in order to keep them in subjection. The priesthood were servants of God in fellowship with the covenant, and subject to the call of the people to look after their sanitary condition, and when necessary to "heal" their infirmities. He thought the remnant of the Judaites who were still faithful to the covenant of their fathers would soon return to Jerusalem, and rebuild their holy temple, and once more inhabit the plains of Palestine. After expressing his gratitude, he retired.

And Confucius was next heard by the council. He thought the accounts of the Judaites and their forefathers, which they had presented in their own behalf, were quite consistent with their faith; but if they had known of the wonderful and mighty works, and of the love of the Great Father, they would never have imbrued their hands in his children's blood. They had desecrated the earth the Great Father had given them and their children for an inheritance with their unholy wars and their many evil abominations. The Great Father's holy temple was at all times within their view high in the beautiful heavens above them, where they could not destroy it; but they could deceive the children intrusted to their care by their unholy devices, and put heavy burdens upon them too grievous to be borne. He told them to look, and he would show them the country their forefathers once inhabited, and where they had learned to love all of the Great Father's children; for they knew how to appreciate his many blessings. He then showed them a walled city with its temples, and told them to observe the little band of pilgrims who had emerged through one of the open gates. "Follow them now through the desert and across the sandy plains; see where they build mounds to commemorate the memory of the ones the Great Father has taken to his Upper Home. Now, after long and tedious wanderings over barren plains and sandy deserts, you see they have reached the water, and as you look beyond, you see the beautiful land, with its fruits and flowers enticing them to try and reach it. Behind them is a forest, and they are now preparing bark to form into boats. See how they are tying it together! And now you see again some of the boldest of the little band are in the boat, making their way across the water; and as you look you may see them land, and to all appearance they are delighted with the prospect. And now look again: you see the night approaches; but another little boat has been prepared, while more of the pilgrims are in it you see crossing over the water. O, yes, they are females, and the wives of those who before had reached the shore. They are anxious to be with their husbands, and as you watch they gain the land, and meet their loved ones. And now again, as we look, the morning has dawned, and a storm is troubling the water; but still the travelling pilgrims wait for tidings from those from whom they had parted. They have fears about their safety; but they wait; and as they wait, a thick fog is settling down that shuts out the distant landscape; and, as you look again, the pilgrims are travelling on to the northward. But as the smile of the Great Father returns and the fogs dry up, you may find your Adam and Eve in their beautiful Garden of Eden; and, as we take a little time to investigate, we shall find it was in reality an earthly paradise, for they found in abundance the good things the Great Father provides for his earthly children. And as we follow the little band of wayfarers in their new home, we find they are blessed with an increase, and their children's children multiply, and the Great Father was not angry. But as we follow them, we find that avarice has found a place in their Eden, and they are no longer satisfied in their beautiful homes. They wandered away in by and forbidden paths, and corrupted themselves with their many evils, until by wrangling and fighting, and by their discontent with their unholy wars, they cursed the earth with their covetous abominations, while the blood of their suffering and starved victims is still crying for the Great Father's law of Eternal Justice.

"Now look again, and remember what you see. In yonder beautiful paradise are growing all things that the earth produces that were intrusted to your care. You see its crystal fountains, with its golden arbors laden with festoons of variegated flowers; and there you see little children in every direction, diverting themselves with innocent amusements. They are the little waifs that your unholy abominations during your earthly lives cast out from their mother's womb before its time; but the Great Father, in his love for all, has gathered them up and provided for them in his paradise above. No wonder you shiver with affright! But you can't go where they are until you go back and undo your work, and make restitution, and cleanse yourselves from your evils. And you must suffer, as women had to suffer in travail, before you are made clean." And he withdrew.

One of the Forest Maidens was next before the council, where she said the old brave who worshipped the Great Father had told much truth, and it would be well for them to heed it, for the Great Spirit was not pleased with the condition of his pale-face children on the lower hunting-grounds. The Great Spirit had sent her race to see what his pale-faces were doing on the red man's hunting-grounds. "O hear, Great Spirit, they have stained thy beautiful white mantle with the blood of the victims of their cruelty, while the cry of many is heard who have no wigwams, no bread, and no blankets to make warm! O, Great Spirit, listen to their sorrows, and lift up thy great arm in anger, for many are starving and are freezing all over the hunting-grounds; and no one obeys thy great law of Eternal Justice on the lower hunting-grounds among the pale-faces."

And India again closed the session by invocation to the Great Spirit.

FEBRUARY 9, 1873. — After India's invocation to the Great Spirit, in thanks for his continued blessings, he said that Ezra, and Nehemiah, and Esther were next in order, and would be present and make their statements. And he retired.

Ezra was before the council, and said he was priest and scribe under the law of Moses; that he was in command of the covenanted people after their return from their Babylonian captivity. But, as a general thing, the kings who held the temporal power cared but little about the counsel of spirit, unless it could be used in order to strengthen their own dominions. The tribes were a wandering, discontented class, many of them inclined to be idle and easily discouraged; and as he thought it required stringent laws in order to govern them, the law and the commandments given through Moses were read to them in their assemblies. It was true the customs of his age and time, connected with their form of worship, seemed trifling; and in some sense they were; but then, he said they had a trifling class of people to instruct, for they were stiff-necked and rebellious, as well as superstitious, and constantly wandering off into surrounding evils, disregarding the warning voice of the Spirit given through covenants and commandments and through the mouth of the prophets. It was the same with them as they found it at the present age: how few of the people give heed to the warning voice of the Spirit that has been heard throughout the land, telling all to turn from their evil doings, and again obey the laws of God! He felt to rejoice that he had been called to stand up for his people. It was true the time had come when the God of Israel would set up his kingdom so long foretold, when the principalities and powers, with their earthly temples, would crumble away before the great law of eternal justice.

Nehemiah was next before the council. He confirmed the statements of his brother-prophet, for he also had been a teacher of the people, who had always disobeyed the voice of the Spirit, and turned away, and set up images of their own, and fallen down to the worship of other gods. Their temple was broken up, and the symbols of their holy order were carried away and desecrated; but they worked hard to have it rebuilt, in order to re-establish the covenant of their fathers, where they could approach the Holy of Holies, and listen to the voice of the Spirit, which led their fathers from the wilderness of doubts and fears over the Jordan and into their promised land. True, many of the fables of his day had foolishly been incorporated into the "sacred records." In order to judge of their age, we must put ourselves in their place. Life was a warfare, and the spirit rebelled against its earthly surroundings. All who obeyed the warning voice escaped the errors and the evils that end in sorrow. But the people of every age have gone into forbidden paths, and we see your own is no exception. They are building temples, and setting up images, and are divided and wandering away, and worshipping the gods of their own imaginations; they heed not the voice of the Spirit that is speaking to them, as it did to us on the mountain and in the "bush;" they will hear if it tells them how to increase their mammon of unrighteousness; but when it tells of their home above, and of the law of justice, they turn to their earthly idols. He then gave way. And—

Esther was next before the council. She was pleased that the time had come when she could stand and speak in behalf of her sisters of Israel and of Judah; and she asked that her name be stricken from the "ancient record," and that of her sister — the noble Vashti — replaced where it belonged, and from where it had been unjustly removed by the caprice and tyranny of her lawful husband. They had ascended in spirit above the skull and cross-bones that their earthly brothers put up to affright them, and who at last had found themselves without a password. She told them of their pride when surrounded by earthly power, and of their inhumanity to the mothers who had travailed in pain in order to give them an existence, and had watched over and cherished them when in their helpless condition; and how with ingratitude they trifled with, and corrupted and set aside those given for companions. She told them their sisters had been initiated into a sphere where they had been taught more of the justice and love of the Great Father; and when they returned to the earth, and made restitution, and purified themselves from their many evils, they would get the password to come up higher.

One of the Forest Maidens was next before the council. She had come to the wigwam of the squaw from the upper hunting-grounds of the red man, to listen to the talk of the pale-faces. If her skin was copper-color, it was pure, for she had never partaken of the evils the pale-face braves, in their struggle for power, had scattered broadcast over the lower hunting-grounds of the Great Spirit. She asked them where the temple was they built by putting many burdens on their brothers, and then shut them out by their unholy craft, and by passwords and by signs a favored few could enter in, and feast upon the first-fruits of the land; while your priests, in mockery to the Great Spirit, were burning incense to your unknown gods, and keeping the people in bondage. She told the fair daughters of Israel and of Judah, who had been trifled with and kept from their proper positions, to sit upon one corner of the great platform of Eternal Justice, and wait until their brothers cleared themselves from their unholy abominations. She told the braves to study their craft well; when they got the password from the Great Spirit, who was the Master Workman, they could take down the cross-bones they had put up to frighten others, and come up higher. She then withdrew.

India closed the session by invocation to the Great Spirit.

FEBRUARY 12, 1873. — After India's invocation to the Great

Spirit, he said three of the scribes were present to give an account of some of the ancient writings. And as he retired —

One of the ancient scribes was before the council. He had come to answer for the Book of Job, and said the object of the writing was to teach the tribes of his day the conflicts of the spirit with its earthly surroundings, while by its personality was intended to represent the various demands in the human organization. It was common for man to complain of his condition, and compare it with that of others, and often say, If such a one had been differently situated, he would have done no better than those who had come short of the object they had desired to attain. It was a common thing for the spirit of envy and discontent to enter in and disturb the harmony and the happiness of many families. Sickness, common misfortunes, disturbance in the business affairs of life, with loss of property and the breaking up of familiar ties, had caused many to fall, as Job did in the fable, from their high estate, and express similar doubts of the goodness of God. He said the phraseology of the poem had been somewhat altered, and it had failed to convey to the minds of the people what had been at the time desired. He then expressed his gratitude, and withdrew.

And another scribe was then before the council, and said he would answer for the psalms and spiritual songs that had been ascribed to David. He stated that many of the scribes of his time were "seers," and gave vent to their spirit visions in songs of praise adapted to the wandering condition of the tribes in search of their promised land. They had the ark and the covenant made with their fathers, and they remembered the promise made to Abraham and Isaac, and their souls were full of devotion to the God of Israel, who had watched over their forefathers in their bondage, and led them away from the taskmasters who had oppressed them; and as they moved along the plains and valleys, and camped by the side of beautiful waters, and could see their flocks and herds increasing, could they do less than remember the High and Holy One for his untold blessings? and they clothed their thoughts in devotional songs for the tribes to sing his praise.

Another of the scribes was then before the council, and said he had come to say he was a "seer" as well as scribe, and had clothed the thoughts and sayings of Solomon, and other men of age and experience, in language, in order to guard the youth from entering into the by and forbidden paths in which others had found to their sorrow disease and moral death. And why shouldn't the young be warned in order to escape, for no language could portray the suffering transgressors had to endure. It was the language of spirit to mortals to save them from the chastening rod of a broken law; and as he was the instrument through which the young and the unexperienced of his age were warned to flee from the evils by which all were surrounded, he would still cry aloud, for they found the mark of the beast in every land, and her ruined victims still lay helpless by the way, although the crumbling cities with their fallen images and ruined temples should be a warning to others; while the cry of suffering again coming from every quarter should teach the young of the present age to beware and not trifle with the immutable laws or covenants and commandments of God.

Then one of the Forest Maidens was next before the council. She told the scribe that some of his teachings had been good, but the avarice of his race, which they had shown by their wranglings and fightings and their unholy devices, had filled the hunting-grounds with much suffering. She had come to say the time had now come when such things must be removed from what was still called a "sacred record." And the pale-face race must understand that such things were never sanctioned by the Great Spirit. They had been tracked from the home of their forefathers across the water, and into their earthly paradise, which by their own evils was soon turned to what they have called Hades. And they had been followed up and down the beautiful earth in the valleys and by the rivers, and everywhere their trail was found. They had stained the earth with the blood of their brothers, when they should have been taught by the changing seasons that the Great Spirit was good to all, as the beautiful heavens above gave evidence of his mighty power; but they had disregarded the Great Spirit, turned away from the light given through prophet and "seer," and worshipped their earthly gods, until the hunting-grounds were full of evil, and the cry of suffering again was calling for the great law of Eternal Justice.

And India again closed the session by invocation to the Great Spirit.

FEBRUARY 16, 1873. — After India's invocation to the Great

Spirit, he said the next three books — Jeremiah, Isaiah, and Ezekiel — were the work of "seers" and scribes, and that Daniel was next in the order. And after his usual encouragements, he again retired. And —

Daniel was next before the council, where he said he had been a "seer," and often had visions as he lay upon his couch in the still of the night, that foreshadowed approaching events. When Nebuchadnezzar demanded the interpretation of his own vision, he was much disturbed and troubled in mind, for it was matter then of life or of death; and after many nights of fear and anxiety, the dream and its interpretation was made plain to his vision: he was shown that the empire would be divided, and the king dethroned and turned out to roam like the beasts of the field, shorn of his temporal power; the gold and the silver, the brass and iron, and the clay represented the kingdoms and the principalities and powers of the earth that would fade away before the final establishment of God's eternal kingdom represented by the little stone that was cut from the mountain. When he gave the interpretation to Belteshazzar, who saw the handwriting on the wall at the time he was revelling with his princes and their wives and concubines, and desecrating the vessels taken from the temple Solomon dedicated to the God of Israel, he was shown the time had come for the kingdom to be broken up and divided between the Medes and the Persians. And as the temple built by Solomon as directed by spirit was to teach them of the temple above not made with hands, and as they had to cleanse themselves from their earthly abominations before they could enter the Holy of Holies, that was in the inner temple beyond the veil, in order to enjoy the communion of spirit, so the present inhabitants of the earth must learn they are living in earthly temples surrounded by everything that was represented in the temple built by Solomon. And if they desired to enter the temple that is eternal, they must cleanse themselves from their earthly evils, and listen to the voice of the Spirit in order to get the password that opens the door beyond the veil. And as the temple built by Solomon had to be cleansed, after it was desecrated, before the Spirit could enter and hold communion, so the Book that has been handed down through the generations who have been taught to worship and call it "holy," and who have looked to it for light as the covenant tribes did to their temple, would also have to be cleansed of its errors, and the stories of all the earthly abominations the Nebuchadnezzars and the Belteshazzars had foolishly incorporated among its sacred pages. He then spoke of the closing up of the present cycle of time, and of the pleasure he had experienced in again speaking to mortals, and withdrew.

Parson Brown was next before the council. He had come to express his gratitude in behalf of his people as well as himself for the privilege they had been permitted to enjoy in listening to the explanations given by the representatives of a past age, in which his people had been much interested; and he was satisfied that many things so long a mystery to his own mind had been satisfactorily explained; and they were ready now to do all in their power in order to remove the cloud that still obscured the minds of mortals. And after again expressing his thanks, he retired. And one of—

Everett's New York boys was before the council, and told of the rapid progress made in their school; said the boys like himself had been with the leading men, who now felt an interest in their welfare, in every city, and had showed them how the poor people were compelled to live, and also the reason there were so many thieves and paupers. They had been to Washington, and left some to look after the Credit Mobilier thieves. It was a busy time with them, and they were setting traps that would expose more of the big thieves who were robbing the people. He said the little thieves and beggars, in whom we had taken so much interest, all sent their love, and would do all in their power to assist each other.

One of the Forest Maidens was next before the council. She spoke encouragingly to the leaders of the tribes who had been called to answer for their evil doings, and clean the records they had left, that were full of stories about their wranglings and their fightings, and their many wrongs, that all knew were not sacred. She told them their temple with its holy order had been misunderstood, and they used the light that was given them to increase the burdens of the people. She told them the Temple of the Great Spirit, that overshadowed the lower hunting-grounds, should have taught the pale-face race of the Great Spirit's power, and of his goodness, and of the duties they owed to each other as they travelled over the lower hunting-grounds.

And India closed the session by invocation to the Great Spirit, expressing thankfulness for his continued blessings, and asking for wisdom to guide their labors.

FEBRUARY 19, 1873. — After India's invocation to the Great Spirit, he said some of the ancient prophets were present, and would be the next to speak. As he retired, the prophet —

Hosea was before the council, and said he was used by the Spirit to instruct the tribes and warn them of the effects that would follow their evil doings. When they lived in peace, and dealt in justice with each other, it was well enough with them; but they were not contented; they would turn away and follow after the abominations of the age, and often get themselves into trouble. The tribes were ignorant, and superstitious, and selfish, and, right or wrong, followed the dictation of their leaders. They were warned by the Spirit of the judgments that would come upon them for their disobedience, and often did suffer from the fearful calamities sent among them, when they would turn from their evil ways for a time and listen to the counsel of spirit, and do better, and for a time peace and quietness would prevail. But, as a general thing, they preferred to worship their images and their dumb gods, that could not reprove them for their evil doings. But when the cry of the oppressed was again heard, God sent his spirits, who through prophets and "seers" gave warning of the terrible sufferings they were bringing among the tribes by their own wickedness and their disregard of the law of justice.

Joel was next before the council. He also had been, like his brother Hosea, sent among the tribes, an instrument through which they were warned by the Spirit to turn from their evil ways, and learn to deal in justice with each other. They were told to obey the covenant of their fathers, and turn away from their idols; but they were a stiff-necked, rebellious race, and would not obey the voice of the Spirit, which had led their forefathers from their Egyptian bondage into the pleasant and fruitful valleys along their earthly Jordans; but they had turned away and followed after the gods of their own evil imaginations. When they felt the chastening rod of the God of Israel, they did repent in sackcloth and ashes, but in their prosperity they turned back to their earthly idols. He said he was glad they had been called, for they could hear him speak through the mouth of another, as the Spirit had spoken through him to warn them of the terrible chastening that would follow their transgressions. And as they had long wandered up and down their barren and forsaken country, where their towns and villages and their idols lay in ruins, they could count their loss for turning away from the voice of the Spirit of the God of Israel.

And Amos was the next one in council. He had been a prophet, and felt a desire to again speak for his people, for they had wandered into many forbidden paths, and had sat in sackcloth and ashes, with their harps hung upon the willows, waiting for the voice of the Spirit to again lead them from their bondage; for they had travelled over and over their own once fertile and beautiful country, and knew well the cost of their own evil transgressions, for their sufferings had been long and terrible to endure. He was the one of his age through which the Spirit warned the tribes of the chastenings that would follow the broken law; and many a time it would come upon him in their camps; and although he knew not at the time what was said, when he awoke to consciousness he found himself exhausted and the tribes flat upon the ground, a-wailing over their transgressions. He said it was the work of the scribes of the camps to gather up the sayings of the Spirit, and clothe them in the language of the age: and he did feel to rejoice that he could now stand before the platform of Eternal Justice, a living witness of the truths advanced by the ever-living Spirit.

Obadiah the prophet was the next before the council, and said that but little space had been assigned to him in the old records, and he should not have much that seemed necessary to offer for the instruction of the tribes of the present age, of the warnings, and of the fearful judgments of the God of Israel that had come to his tribes, for their transgressions had been realized, and they and the desolate and barren condition of their once happy country were a standing witness of their mistakes when they turned away and disregarded the warning of the Spirit that watched over and led their forefathers from their Egyptian bondage. He thought the past should be a warning for the present tribes, who had turned away from the covenants of their fathers, and were building temples, and setting up images of their own to worship, surrounding themselves with the gods of the world, and again disregarding the voice of the ever-living Spirit. He thought the present age corresponded with that of his own, for the Pharaohs and taskmasters are still oppressing the people, and their wail of suffering again ascended to the God of justice, who had sent his spirits to give a warning to the people to escape the terrible judgments that must follow their transgressions. And when their temples and their images, their towns and cities are mouldering in ruins, they will remember in sorrow, as his people had, the warning voice of the Spirit. He then withdrew.

And Jonah the prophet was next before the council, where he said it was true that he had performed the part of a coward, and tried to escape the fulfilment of a duty he had been directed by the Spirit to accomplish. He was told to go to Nineveh, and warn the people of the fearful judgments of God that awaited them if they did not abandon their wicked ways. But instead of doing as he should have done, he made an effort to go another way, for he engaged passage on a vessel that was bound for Tarshish, but was soon after overtaken by a terrible storm. It was true he did secrete himself through fear, but he was not asleep, for he felt condemned for trying to shirk the performance of his duty. He said the master of the vessel treated him with kindness, and directed his men to make for the shore in order to land him; and the more they tried, the more the elements opposed them. But as a final result, he promised his God, if he would get him to the shore alive, he would go to Nineveh, and obey his command, when the feeling came upon him that his life would be spared, and he went into the water without fear of danger; and the storm abated, and he was taken to the land without the assistance of any kind of whale. But said it was a marvel to the inhabitants how he got to the land, which was no doubt the origin of the fish story. He obeyed the command, and went and warned the inhabitants of the city, who for a time repented of their transgressions, and were warned by the Spirit, and the terrible judgments that finally completed their destruction were for a time delayed. It was said he was angry because the city was not destroyed at the time as the Spirit had prophesied through him, but then he had had no knowledge of the people's repentance, and had been himself of a selfish nature. If he had done wrong, he asked to be forgiven. He thought the story about the gourd was like that of the fish, and most likely had originated in the fruitful imagination of the historian. Nineveh was then a walled city of wealth and importance, and was finally overwhelmed in its wickedness, and destroyed. He was satisfied from observation there were plenty of Jonahs among the inhabitants of the present age.

And one of the Forest Maidens was next before the council.

She had come from the upper hunting-grounds by the command of the Great Spirit, to listen to the talk of the pale-face braves. She told the old braves their tribes had been troublesome, and created great suffering on the lower hunting-grounds; and while the Great Spirit was good and sent his blessings for all the pale-faces, they built big storehouses, and shut up the fruits intended for the Great Spirit's children, while many were crying for bread. The Great Spirit says to the red man's race, "Go to the lower hunting-grounds, and see about the distrust and the complaint among the pale-faces." He gives them plenty for all, and why should the cry of want and starvation come back to disturb the upper hunting-grounds? They go and tell of their avarice and injustice. The Great Spirit says, "Go gather them up: they are unworthy to remain longer on the hunting-ground." And she would tell all she had heard. And India, as usual, closed by invocation to the Great Spirit.

FEBRUARY 23, 1873. — After India's invocation to the Great Spirit, again asking for strength in order to sustain their labors, he said the business of the session would be to call the leaders of the tribes, as each branch was called, to place themselves around the platform of Eternal Justice. But the one who had represented Adam would remain uncalled, until after the Great Media and his disciples had made their statements. And again asking for wisdom and strength to guide them, he withdrew.

And Seth was called. He responded by saying he felt grateful for the privilege of again taking his place as leader among the tribes he loved, and whom he had tried to guide as well as his poor frail human nature permitted. He spoke of the covenant they made with the High and Holy One, who inhabits eternity; said he had listened to the voice of his Spirit, and had tried to obey its teachings. He then gave an expression of his gratitude.

And Enoch was next called. He was gratified to know he was remembered, and he would take his place at the head of his tribes. Said he cheerfully joined with what his brother had well expressed, and that he had tried to do his duty. If he had failed, he hoped to be forgiven. And he withdrew.

Methuselah was next called. He said he had been a leader and a representative among the tribes, and had done what he could in order to keep them in the strait and narrow path that led to the promised land by the light of the covenant made with their fathers. They had all been poor, frail mortals; and when they had wandered into forbidden paths, they had suffered; and he prayed that all might be forgiven, and then cheerfully stood in his place.

And Noah was next called, and he was ready to take his place among the tribes; and as he built the ark that saved the records of their covenant from the fire and the floods, the wars and tumults their transgressions 'had brought among them, and had preserved it from the flood of ignorance that followed and covered the land, he was willing to assist the tribes of the present age in building another ark in order to save their covenant from the general destruction their own abominations had brought among them. Said he was thankful a remnant of his race was saved.

Abraham was next called. He said he was happy to again take his place at the head of the tribes; that he had tried to teach by precept and example obedience to the teachings of their covenants with the God of Israel, who had watched over them in their fruitful homes along their Jordans and Palestines. If they had waited and sorrowed, he knew they would again hear the voice of the Spirit telling them to take down their harps, and come up together and unite in a new song of redeeming love. He had always prayed that their human frailties might be forgiven, and he did feel to rejoice.

Isaac was next called. He was ready to take his place, and responded to the remarks of his father Abraham; said he tried to be faithful to the tribes intrusted to his care, and teach them in the laws and the covenants made with their fathers. He then said he would answer for his son —

Jacob, who stood ready at the head of his tribes in order to take their place among their kindred, and said that Elijah and Elisha had come up and taken their places, and there was a general shout of joy again sounding in the camp of Israel. He then withdrew.

And Moses was next called. He was ready to respond. He had come with his people, and they were ready to take their place among the tribes of Israel. Said he was zealous in his command over them, and had tried to make them obey the covenants and the commandments of his God. If he had been tyrannical in his administration of the laws, it was owing to his human frailties. They were a self-willed, stiff-necked people to manage. He rejoiced that the time had come when they could once more hear the Spirit's call to prepare themselves and get ready to enter the promised land, which they had now found was above their earthly Palestines. After giving them instructions, he retired.

And Aaron was next called, and was also ready to respond. Said he was a teacher and a healer among the tribes. He had tried to fulfil his duty in order to increase their spiritual growth, as well as heal their earthly maladies. He was thankful to be remembered, and would take his place among them. If he had erred in the performance of his duties, he asked to be forgiven in consideration of his human frailties, and withdrew.

And Joshua was next called. He cheerfully responded he was ready with the tribes intrusted to his charge. He said they were ready to take their place among the mighty hosts that were gathering together and chanting a new song of praise to the God of Israel for the place assigned them around his platform of Eternal Justice.

Deborah was next called, and said she was thankful she had been remembered, and she was willing to forgive her brothers, owing to their earthly imperfections; said she had been gathering together her frail sisters, who were driven from their camps in disgrace, who had decked themselves in scarlet in order to attract the travellers in the crooked and forbidden paths, and who at last had been cleansed by the waters of affliction, and had heard the call of the Spirit to prepare themselves for a new start in search of their promised land.

Ruth was next called. She sanctioned the remarks of Deborah, and said they had been taught by their fair sisters of the Gentile race, who had gathered up their own frail ones who had been wandering in sorrow and affliction, and had brought them up and clothed them in new garments. She then said they had been out and called in the long-lost ones who in sorrow had been driven from their own camps, and there was a general rejoicing among the mothers of Israel for the lost ones returned.

Samson was next called. He said he had not been of much importance among the tribes, although he had attained a notoriety on account of his being a strong man. He supposed he was a channel through which the power of spirit was often manifested; and if there were any more temples to be pulled down, or gates to be carried away, or Philistines to be slain, he was ready and willing to engage, and was pleased with the place assigned to him among his people.

REVELATIONS.   93

Samuel was next called. He said he was glad he had been remembered, and his people were ready to take their place, for it was truly a time of rejoicing and of happiness for the long scattered tribes of Israel and of Judah, who had renewed their songs of thankfulness and praise at the call of the Spirit. And he was ready to perform any duty the God of Israel, whom he had tried to serve and obey, now required of him. Said they would stand in the place assigned to them around the platform.

Saul was next called. He also was ready with his tribes. Said he had done the best he could in order to protect them; he was glad to be remembered. They would stand in their place, and be ready at the Spirit's call.

David was next called. He responded by saying he was ready to take his place among the tribes of Israel, whom he had loved as they followed him in search of their long promised land. He regretted his mistake in his anxiety to build an earthly temple, but he had learned by his affliction that the only temple the High and Holy One had required of his "earthly builders" was the temple of the physical body. How much superior it was to the one they built with wood and stone! for while the one was transitory and had long since gone to destruction, the other was reproducing, with its feet established on the foundations of the earth. Its head was the Holy of Holies inhabited by the living Spirit. How they had trifled with it in their wrangling and fighting; how they had broken them in pieces in their struggle for earthly power! But they had done it in their ignorance and in their mistaken zeal. And long and earnestly he had prayed to the God of Israel that they all might be forgiven; and surely it was with feelings of everlasting gratitude he responded to the call of the Spirit, and was prepared with his tribes to stand in their places around the platform.

Solomon was next called, and he also with his people was waiting to stand in the place assigned them, and then said he felt his own unworthiness as he stood among them stripped of his earthly power; and he asked them where was all the glory of their costly temple which they had built in untold splendor, with its golden candlesticks and its vessels of gold and silver, with its ornaments and jewels and precious stones? All had long since disappeared, and he had stood shorn of his power, and the humblest one among them as they roamed over their barren fields, and watched the mouldering fragments of their temples and altars, waiting for the rebuilding of their earthly temples. Oh, yes, he saw it now, they had mistaken the promise; the temple they should have found was in the spirit kingdom, and their promised land was beyond and above their earthly Jordans. Yes, he had seen the temple in all its grandeur, but he himself had no part in its erection. And he stood without, with his arms akimbo, with no password to enter. He then freely forgave Nebuchadnezzar for the destruction of their earthly temple, and said he would wait, with one foot upon the platform of Eternal Justice, until the Spirit again gave the sign.

Nebuchadnezzar was then called. He responded by saying he had come with his people, and stood ready to represent them before the platform of Eternal Justice; said he did not ask to step on to it; and if the golden candlesticks and vessels of gold and of silver, golden urns and cups, and ornaments of ivory, and precious stones, that he took from their earthly temple, were wanted, he could not bring them, for they were exchanged for food in order to feed the starving thousands that were impoverished by the foolish extravagance displayed in its erection. He said he was ready to go and assist in cleaning out other temples, which had caused the sighs and groans of the burdened masses for the aggrandizement of the few who by signs and passwords could enter and revel at the expense of the toiling and starving millions. He felt grateful to the High and Holy One to know the time had come for such things to have an end, and he would wait and take his chance of getting on the platform some other time.

And Hezekiah was then called. He and his people were ready to take their place among the assembling tribes of Israel and of Judah, for he had tried to be faithful to them when he was intrusted with authority. And he had them instructed in the covenants and commandments, which they still believed were sacred. He was glad of his call, and pleased with his reception among his tribes. Ezra and Nehemiah, and the author of Job, who had been "seers" and scribes among the tribes, were ready again to take their place, and right glad to be engaged again in the great work of eternal compensation.

Esther was next called. She was pleased that she had been remembered. She was united with others, and working for the restoration and the elevation of their sisters to the position the God of Israel placed them, upon an equality by the side of their husbands and brothers around the great platform of Eternal Justice.

Jeremiah, and Isaiah, and Ezekiel, and Daniel were next called, and were ready to take their places among the tribes. And as the Spirit had spoken through them, and warned the tribes of the judgments they would suffer in compensation for their evil transgressions, they would now prophesy through others, and again tell of the sure and terrible judgments that will find out all who disregard the covenants and commandments of the God of Israel, and turn away from the warning voice of his Spirit.

Belshazzar was next called. He said he was a witness to the fulfilment of some of their prophecies, for he had wandered up and down the earth in sorrow for his transgressions. He knew he had abused the power with which he was intrusted, and he felt, as he approached the platform of Eternal Justice, that his punishment was just. He was glad to be remembered by his people, and had often prayed that his errors might be forgiven.

And when the following number of the prophets, and "seers," and scribes were called, and responded by saying they also were ready and waiting to take their places, Hosea, Joel, Amos, Obadiah, Jonah, Micah, Nahum, Habakkuk, Zephaniah, Haggai, Zechariah, and Malachi. each one had been obedient to the call of the Spirit, as had. been witnessed from the various manifestations. Many of their sayings and writings had been misinterpreted and misunderstood from the general ignorance and superstition of the age that followed the terrible judgments of God sent among the tribes of Israel and the tribes of Judah in compensation for their evil doings. And as they had been called, they would form a band and stay among the people, and speak through the mouths of others as the Spirit spoke through them, and warned them again of the judgments they were fast bringing upon themselves by their disregard of the great law of Eternal Justice.

One of the Forest Maidens was then present. She said she had been sent from the upper hunting-grounds to be a witness of their condition. She was glad to see them gathering up in order to make another start in search of their promised land. She told them there were some of their tribes they had not found, but the Great Spirit had sent for them. "See, here they come: they are the old, gray-bearded prophets who told you the Great Spirit was a god of justice who would punish you for your evil doings, that fire and flood, that pestilence and famine were the reward of all nations who disregarded the Great Spirit's law of Eternal Justice. See the marks of the stones and the missiles which you hurled at them as you drove them from your camps and villages out into the caves of the mountains! Come up, old braves,—your new garments are ready,—and sit down upon the platform of Justice; and your scars will soon disappear after being examined; while Israel and Judah can sit upon the steps and wait until the Great Spirit look and see if all be on the *square;* then they may get the password to come up higher into the new and ever green fields that never perish, and where the temple of the Great Spirit is eternal." India again closed the session by invocation to the Great Spirit, with gratitude for continued blessings.

FEBRUARY 26, 1873.—After India's invocation to the Great Spirit, once again in acknowledgment of his protection, he said the evening's session would be occupied by Confucius, in order to complete their arrangements for the investigation of the Second Covenant. He said the mother of the One we called the Nazarene, and his reputed father Joseph, would be present and give in their testimony before the council. When, after again asking for strength and wisdom sufficient for their labors, he retired, and the familiar voice of—

Confucius was again heard by the council. He gave expression to the pleasure it afforded him of again being present, and told them they had Israel and Judah on the one hand, with the Christian dispensation on the other. He then addressed a few pleasant words of recognition to the band of reformers, and asked them to step up and be seated on the platform of justice, for it was long enough and broad enough for all who had worked for the elevation of the Great Father's oppressed and starving children.

He then turned to the leaders of the tribes of Israel and of Judah, and wanted to know if they were satisfied of the perishable nature of all their earthly glory; and then spoke of their barren fields and dried-up Jordans, of the ruins of their towns and cities. He asked them where their earthly temples now were, with their images, and then told them they purchased the vengeance of the Great Father, who heard the cry of his children, whom they oppressed when they forgot the Living God, who made the heavens above them, with the beautiful earth which they had polluted with their unholy devices; for they had set up gods of their own, which they had called on to sanction their cruel and bloody wars; and when their oppressed and suffering people tired of their unholy abominations, they had their prophets who could pretend to call down fire from their angry gods, in order to frighten and keep them in subjection; for their gods were like themselves, who revelled in blood and carnage until they lost the higher aspirations of their nature; and every tribe had a god of its own. He told them they disregarded the covenants of their fathers, and had turned away from the commandments that were given to them from the mountain by a high order of spirits; and that the Great Father could have loved them all, had they lived up to the principles which they were taught by covenant and by commandment. He told them their records contained a history of their evil doings, which had corrupted the generations down to the present age; and that the Great Father, or Jehovah, or Almighty God, or by whatever name known, who was pure and holy, could never sanction such unholy deeds. "No, no!" They must go to work, and dig up and uncover their crimes, for the Great Father has ordered all things to be exposed, and be ready for the judgment. "Now go with me," he said, "and we will follow this poor laborer crushed with heavy burdens. You see he has been carrying brick and mortar for your temples. Now see, he is met at the door of his humble tent by his faithful wife and their little ones. And what has he got to refresh and strengthen his weary body? You see nothing but a little bread and water. And as he partakes of it in sorrow, and his children nibble their dry crusts, he curses the Great Father for the conditions that surround him, for he has been told of the wicked revelry of the king and his courtiers. Now we will have a look at the king's table. Here, you see, is beef and mutton, and here is fish and fowl, with fruits of every kind, and wines of various flavor. Here is all of every variety the Great Father in his love has provided for his earthly children; but you see they have been hoarded up for the few who never labor. But, in mockery to the one they call "God," they make laws that crush the toiling millions and keep them in bondage. And yet you had every imaginary blessing, even to the communion with spirits. But you was not satisfied: you still wanted and asked for a Messiah. Now go with me, and look again. You see by the side of a hill a deserted cave, or hovel, where wayfarers have stopped to rest their weary limbs; and as you enter, you see by the light of a single candle a woman in travail. Now see, a child is born: it is the temple of the Great Father's earthly builders. And now, as you look again, you see the pure Spirit from the Great Father comes down to inhabit the new-born temple during its earthly pilgrimage." He then gave directions about the continuation of their work, and retired, when—

Wesley was next before the council. He remarked that he got as close to the Good Father as he could, in hopes that he might attract his attention. He said he was persevering when in his body, and he found the law held good. He thought the present inhabitants were covered up with transgressions. He thought the flesh would have to be cut from the bones in order to find the spirit. He said he had been familiar with the communion of spirit when in his body, and had given what he could to his people; that he had stood and talked to them until his clothes were wet with perspiration: but he was hidebound, and covered up with foolish creeds. If he had done any good during his earthly life, he did not know where to look for it now; but said he was delighted to have an opportunity to express his present opinions, and withdrew.

And one of the Forest Maidens was next before the council. Said she was sent from the upper hunting-grounds of the red man's race to the wigwam of the white squaw, to listen to the talk of the old braves. She was pleased to meet with Israel and with Judah, who had gathered up their wandering tribes by command of the Great Spirit. She told them the promised land they had so long been looking for was near at hand. She told them to look, and she could show where their forefathers started from. "Now you see a little band of pilgrims, with their forage bound to the backs of a lot of asses, which were then in use for carrying burdens. Now you may see them resting in a grove by a stream of water, where the squaws with their pappooses are seeking rest and nourishment. But yonder in the distance you can see a cloud of dust, and under it is an army who are seeking the destruction of the wandering band of wayfarers. See them look into each other's faces in affright; and as they gather their little ones, and flee into the forest in different directions, and are still waiting to be united." She then retired. And India closed the session by invocation to the Great Spirit.

MARCH 2, 1873.—After India's invocation to the Great

Spirit, he said that Mary and Joseph were present, and would make their own statements. And as he retired —

Mary, the mother of Jesus, was next before the council, and made the following statement. She commenced by saying that after the death of her father, her mother was left without means for her support, and she procured a situation in the temple, where she was instructed in the duties of a priestess who had to look after and assist in the care of the afflicted. It was an order or sisterhood of that age, whose office was considered sacred among the people. It was at the time when there was a general commotion among the opposing sects at Jerusalem, and the people had lost the light of the Spirit which was taught them through the covenants made with their fathers, while many denied of there being a resurrection of the spirit. It was evident at the time that some change was expected in answer to the general demand; for they had turned from the light, and were fast going into mental darkness and evil. Such, she said, was the condition when it was given out in the temple by the Spirit among the priesthood of the covenant, that an earthly temple must be furnished by earthly builders; that a pure spirit from the higher spheres could be reincarnated, to work through mortals for the building up of God's eternal kingdom in order to increase the happiness of his earthly children. She said the demand at the time appeared to be rational, and she consented to be the earthly recipient of the heavenly blessing. She knew the one assigned to be a partner of the consummation to be pure and devotional, while her own soul went up to God in thankfulness for his protection; and she knew of no law but that of obedience to the command. But afterwards, when she was conscious of being *enciente*, her sorrows began to multiply, for she was a poor girl, without influential friends, and knew she must soon be cast out of the temple, for the law of the Jews was severe, and had it been known, both must have been put to death.

The story of her being overshadowed by the Spirit, and of the child being holy, was advanced by the priesthood; but it gave her no relief, for she knew the people would not believe it, and she would have to bear her affliction alone. But she said it was soon arranged in the temple that she should have a husband who would watch over and protect her from the scandal that otherwise seemingly must follow; and accordingly the priesthood made arrangements with some of the order outside of the temple, where soon the needed one was found ; and she was married to Joseph, who fulfilled the obligation as a sacred duty, destitute of feelings so desirable in order to secure earthly happiness. She went to his home at Nazareth, where he owned a small house, and was by occupation a carpenter. She said Joseph was a good man, but was dependent on his daily labor for their support; and as he meditated on his condition he seemed crushed in spirit, and he finally decided they would leave their home at Nazareth, and go to Egypt, he thinking at the time he might put her away and be freed from his obligation. But he had dreams and night-visions that disturbed him, and they were told by the " seers " of the Messiahship of her son before his birth, although neither of them could seem to comprehend it; and, after wandering about the country, camping in the beautiful groves and by the streams, and the time was drawing near for her expected maternal relation, they concluded to retrace their lonely and sorrowful way back to their disconsolate home at Nazareth; and after many days of weary toil, when within three miles of their home, she was in travail, and compelled to stop in a little deserted cave by the hillside, where she remained alone until Joseph hastened to the village and procured the assistance of a midwife. On their return in the shade of the evening, her child was born. And when she was told it was a male child, her spirit was strengthened within, and she seemed to realize that there was truth in what had often been foretold. And after they were removed to their humble home, as he grew in stature he developed many peculiarities. He was often self-willed, and showed but little feeling for his reputed father. When they worked together, they often disagreed, and Joseph would send him home, where he would say he knew how to do the work better than that man did. And he finally told her that Joseph was not his father ; said something within had told him so. He would not go to school; he seemed to know what the books contained better than the teacher, and was often reputed to be quarrelsome. He showed remarkable spirit power among his playmates. When a boy he would prostrate them on the ground, and to all appearance they were dead. But when he desired to restore them, by the force of his will and the motion of his hand, they had to arise at his command. She said the first time he went to Jerusalem with them he was about fourteen years of age, and he seemed to be angry at the display of wealth and extravagance.

He disputed with the scribes at the temple, and told them that such a display was wrong when so many of the people were in want of bread; it was a sacrilege. His remarks were sure to attract attention and draw a crowd about him, for they were of a nature far beyond one of his age. And as he advanced in years, he seemed to comprehend the object of his earthly mission, and often spoke to her about it. She said they were poor and attracted but little attention, independent of the radical remarks and other peculiarities of her son, who was about twenty years old when Joseph died and left her with three other children. Jesus was a common name of that age. He was distinguished from other boys of the same name by his being called the "carpenter's son." He showed but little attraction for her, and the other children said he had the work of his heavenly Father to do; and as he advanced, it seemed to absorb most of his attention, and he was beginning to make many enemies by his bold attack on the priesthood and others in power who had departed from the light of the spirit; and for about two and a half years after he had chosen his disciples he was all the time among the people, teaching them of the heavenly kingdom, and healing their diseases, over which he had wonderful power. She said the earthly experience of her son as well as her own was sorrowful after his labors and sufferings, which had been but little understood. He came to her in spirit, and had been all that a loving son could be to a mother. She had no knowledge at the time what was done with his earthly body after it was taken from the tomb. She knew it was not resurrected to a newness of life, for she had seen him in his spirit form, and was satisfied. Said she had found full employment among the suffering ones of earth since her own transition, and it would be far more pleasing to her if those who profess to venerate her memory would devote the time to ameliorate the sufferings of the tens of thousands of her sorrowing earthly sisters. After saying she would answer whenever she was called, she retired. And —

Joseph, the husband of Mary, was next before the council, and made the following statement. He commenced by saying that it was true that Mary and himself had a lonely time during their earthly pilgrimage together, for neither of them could comprehend the mystery of God making itself known to mortals. And he found himself in a position, although voluntary, in which he had found that duties were required of him to fulfil he was poorly qualified to sustain; and he also knew how the jeers and scoffs of his comrades would be hurled at him as the dupe of some designing priest. But he loved the Order, and he felt there must be something sacred in connection with it, and that it was his duty to fulfil the obligation he had taken upon himself. Notwithstanding he felt crushed in spirit, and it made their home one of sorrow, for he was poor, and had to sustain his family by his labor, in an age when all of the laboring mass were poor. But developed in spirit and full of devotion, still they could not comprehend God or the manifestation of his Spirit; they could not comprehend there was an individualized spirit resurrected from the material body at the time of dissolution, and was still among them; neither had they been taught of a spirit-home above their earthly Jordans. After their return from Egypt and the birth of Jesus, as had been related by Mary, nothing of much importance transpired. There was no truth in the story about the slaughter of the children by order of Herod; but the wise men who it was said had seen the star in the east, were the Chaldean astrologers who had foretold the birth of the child Jesus, and of the results that would follow. He said they did come to their home and saw the child, and left them material aid; and the boy, as he grew up, had many peculiarities, as related by his mother. He was of delicate form and quick of comprehension, and was of a thoughtful and melancholy turn of mind, and seemed to comprehend that his life was to be devoted to the elevation of humanity. He was adverse to manual labor, and impulsive and restless under restraint; and as he grew to manhood he gathered about him a multitude of the so-called lower orders of society, and went out in opposition to the established customs of the age; and he soon fell a sacrifice to the bitter hatred of the priesthood that was then in power. After his crucifixion, the officers of the guard set a watch at the tomb where the body was lying, for they expected his disciples would endeavor to take it away; but in the quiet of the night the guard was overshadowed by the Spirit and made for the time unconscious, when all that was mortal of the mangled form was taken by the power of the Spirit to its final rest. After saying he passed out of his earthly form about twelve years prior to the crucifixion of Jesus, and was a witness in Spirit of the closing and sorrowful scenes then connected with his earthly mission, he withdrew.

An ancient Hindoo was next before the council, and made the following statement. He said he was permitted to listen to the reports made by the other two, for the man they had been talking about had at that time created some interest among his countrymen, and they felt an anxiety now to hear something about it again, for they had found out that the images they had been taught to worship had no power in spirit, and as yet they had not found out who to look to; said the god, wherever he was, had been good to them, but they could not see him. It was evident he sent good things to all of his children, but as yet they had not found out where to look in order to find him. He then expressed the gratitude of himself and his countrymen for the opportunity of furthering their investigations. And India again closed the session by invocation to the Great Spirit.

MARCH 5, 1873.—After India's invocation to the Great Spirit, again thanking him for his wise protection, he said Peter, and James, and John were the next in order to make their statements. And as he retired—

Peter was the next before the council, and said it was true he was one of the twelve who formed the little ragged and despised band who followed after and listened to the heavenly teachings of the one they called their Master. He had been a fisherman by occupation, and their habits of life were simple. As they sat in their boats on the beautiful waters, watching their nets and lines, by which they obtained their scanty living, what was more natural than that they should desire to learn something of the beautiful heavens above them, and of that wonderful and mighty power that upheld and sustained them, and had surrounded all with terrestrial beauty? And when they found their Master, endowed as he was with a capacity to teach them of a home in spirit in his Father's kingdom, where there were mansions for all of his earthly children, and who himself devoted his time in healing their infirmities and trying to ameliorate the sufferings of afflicted mortals, who were cast out and left forsaken and broken-hearted, no wonder the sorrowing ones followed after him and listened to his voice, as they partook of the bread of life which he broke, as he gave them freely to drink from the well of "living waters." It was true their Master was bitter in his anathemas against the systems that sustained a bigoted priesthood, and built up an aristocracy among the few that crushed the rights and liberties of the people; and he told them their earthly principalities would perish, and also their temple, represented the idols they were teaching the people to worship, when they should have taught them of the "temple not made with hands." It was their custom to go into the outskirts of the city of Jerusalem and the surrounding villages, where the common people would assemble in crowds, and gladly listen to the heavenly teachings of Jesus. Many times the excitement was great, for the people left their employment in order to follow their Master, and be themselves witnesses of his wonderful power; and many times they were forced to flee for their lives from the opposing force, led on by the craft that was always bitter with their persecution. At times, when the excitement was great, they returned to their occupation, and waited until the Spirit would again call them to their work among the people. Many times their Master, whom they loved, would sit by the stream, tired and hungry, and weep over the condition of the multitude, and the hardness of the hearts of the Pharaohs who kept them in bondage, for they were constantly watched by the spies of those in power, who sought in every possible way to deprive them of their freedom; and they were often hooted at and stoned, and driven from the little towns, for fear the people would leave their employment, and assemble where they could be taught by the living Spirit. He said they kept no record of their labors, and the only key intrusted to him was the key of knowledge, which had opened the way to his "spirit home" in the Great Father's eternal kingdom. After saying he would be at all times ready to answer his call, he retired. And —

James was next before the council. He had also been a fisherman, and was one of the twelve who were witnesses of the cruel treatment and the sufferings of Jesus, whom they delighted to call their Master; and they left their nets to follow him, for he taught them of heavenly things. His teachings were new and soul-inspiring, and the hungry multitude from every quarter gathered together to be fed with the bread of life. And as he taught them of the living temple above, and healed their physical infirmities, they found the living Spirit, and did rejoice; while those in power were waiting for a Messiah that would crush their national foes and strengthen their temporal power, those who turned away from their Master's heavenly teachings, and scoffed at him and his humble followers,—he who in the height of his terrible anguish prayed to his heavenly Father that they might be forgiven. He then turned and asked those who had crucified their Messiah if they were ready to listen now, and go at his second call; and told them they had looked many times, since they had been surrounded with the ruins of their desolate towns and cities, for the meek and forgiving One whom they cast out and crucified when trying to teach them of their spirit home. But they did not want to know; they had other attractions. So they nailed him to the cross, between two thieves of the lowest order. He told them to be on the watch for the call of their Messiah at this time, and be ready, or they might be left again. He said they had no authority from their Master to establish any church, and that they left no such authority; for they were taught by their Master, and by the Spirit after their Master's ascension, that all were heirs to an immortal life, and were entitled to the common blessings while preparing for an entrance into the Great Father's eternal kingdom. He then said it was true that the earth did quake at the time of the crucifixion, and the powers of the earth were shaken; the sun was darkened by a cloud, and the walls of the temple were rent; and that after the body was taken down from the cross, it was wrapped in linen and laid in the tomb, where an armed guard was stationed by the authorities to watch; but during the night the scene was changed, for the angel band who had watched over their Master terrified the guard, and removed the mortal part from their sight. And when his crucifiers, who were ever on the watch, returned, they found the guard was shaking with affright, but could give no account of what had transpired. But he himself, and his brothers, with many others, afterwards had abundant evidence of their Master's presence with them in spirit, and then knew that he had triumphed over the powers of darkness, and was satisfied. He then retired.

And John was next before the council. He confirmed what his brothers had stated, and said he also had loved their Master when he was with them in his earthly form, and had been blessed with his confidence and love in return. He thought there was no necessity of his repeating what his brothers had told; but he would say, as they had carefully inspected the present condition of earthly affairs, they found it the same as it was when they were witnesses of their Master's labors, when he was trying to give to the people a knowledge of their "spirit home," above the transitory things of time, in the eternal kingdom; while the leaders, now as then, had surrounded themselves with their earthly principalities, and had determined not to be disturbed, and were building costly mansions, and revelling with the things of time, and cared nothing about the things that belong to eternity. And as others had arrived upon the field of action, and found that worldly wealth secured place and power, they commenced the struggle with a disregard for the rights of the multitude whom God had created with a love and desire for the enjoyment of his blessings. But avarice had been the evil spirit which had robbed them of their earthly enjoyments, and deprived them of a knowledge of their heavenly home, and filled both worlds with sorrow, and left them in their worldly pride clinging to their earthly gods. Happily for himself and his brothers, they were fortunate enough to be found among the multitude, and were not troubled with the mammon of the world. A desire had naturally grown with them to know something of the world beyond; and when they found their Master, and heard him explain the mysteries of the ages, and show how spirit and matter were combined, they gladly followed him, and were blessed; for he taught them as they witnessed the manifestations of his power among the thousands of the poor and friendless, who were ever anxious to hover around him, where he cast out and healed many of their earthly afflictions, with their evil thoughts and passions, which have always been born with the flesh. And the multitude did rejoice when they found a Saviour, who could awaken new thoughts and desires as he taught them of heavenly things, while those of the little band whom he had chosen to be his witnesses, after being cast out and rejected by those in power, when driven by envy to their quiet forest retreat, would sit around him by the hour as he taught them of his Father's spirit kingdom; and it did seem as though the heavens were opened, and they could comprehend more of the mighty works of the High and Holy One who inhabits eternity, and they were encouraged to persevere with their Master in his work for the elevation of suffering humanity. He knew they were cast down and sorrowful at the crucifixion, but then they were soon restored by the presence in spirit of him they loved, who again and again inspired them to hold out to the end, with his assurance that he would be with them, which was true; for when their earthly pilgrimage was ended, he met them on the shore of the "ether" world, where he had shown them the untold splendors of his heavenly Father's eternal kingdom; and after travelling through the spheres, and sitting down together, joyfully contemplating its magnificent works, the Father told them he had other children that were asking for light in the darkened sphere below. He then remarked that they (the apostles) left no written record of their earthly labors; said the modern Church had followed nearest to the forms of the temple-worshippers among the Jews. Their Master's mission was to teach of a resurrection of the spirit from its earthly form, and of its final home in the eternal world; and those who desired to attain a home there would have to abandon their earthly idols, and gather up a knowledge sufficient to light them on the way. After saying he would respond whenever he was wanted, he retired.

And one of the ancient Hindoos was before the council, where he made the following statement. He told them that he had been in the spirit sphere about two thousand years, and that his people that were with him a long time ago had made the discovery that the earthly idols they formerly worshipped had no power in spirit; they were supplied with the necessaries for their sustenance, but had no knowledge from whence it had come, for as yet they had seen no god. They had watched the "dumb idols" which they were taught to worship, a long time after leaving their earthly bodies; but they found they were made hollow, and what things the people gave to them to appease their supposed anger, the priest who was in charge, often, by putting his hand in a hole he could open behind them, got them out, and carried them away in a bag. He said they had waited a long time, and had finally concluded that it was not right to have the people deceived. They wanted to teach their people that God was a spirit, and not angry when a storm disturbed the atmosphere, but that it was intended to purify the elements that sustained their earthly existence. Said their Hindoo children were attending the school that was established in spirit; and when they were sufficiently instructed they would go and mingle with the Hindoo children in their own country in every family, until they were familiar with their friends in spirit. He said teachers had been sent to them in their spirit sphere, who had taken them from their earthly idols, and had gone back with them to the time when man first desired something to venerate, — when their natural wants were supplied by an unseen power for which they were anxious to repay with gratitude. And they were a queer-looking people, and had awful-looking gods whom they had worshipped, so it was evidently not wrong for them to go to their idols when they had nothing higher to venerate. But they still thought it was wrong for the priest to deceive their earthly friends about their " dumb idols; " said his people were pleased to listen, and would come again.

And India closed the session by invocation to the Great Spirit.

MARCH 9, 1873. — After India's invocation to the Great Spirit, he said Magdalene and Paul were the next to make their statements, and after his usual encouragements, retired.

And then Magdalene was the next in council, where she said it was well known she was a native of the village of Magdala; her name was Mary, but from habit her friends called her Magdalene, to distinguish her from other Marys, Mary being at the time a familiar name among the people. She unfortunately inherited a feeble and diseased constitution from her parents, and was afflicted with what the physicians of the present age have named the " St. Vitus' dance," which often resulted in her losing the power of speech. It was about the time that Jesus of Nazareth commenced his labors among the afflicted, and had acquired great reputation for His wonderful power over the various kinds of maladies the poor were suffering with; and through the intercession of her friends she applied to him for help, and in three days' time, through the wonderful effects of his healing power, her bodily affliction was removed, and she was finally restored to health. It was then a common opinion among the lower orders of the people that all physical afflictions were caused by an evil spirit. It was thought when a bodily infirmity was removed, that the evil spirit, or devils, or demons, were cast out. She said she was thirty years of age at the time she recovered her speech and was restored to health by the healing power of her Saviour, and she had never ceased to love him for his compassion among the poor and sorrowful ones by whom he was daily surrounded; for he devoted his time to the healing of all without money or price, and after healing their infirmities, he taught them the way to their heavenly Father's eternal kingdom. It was his increasing fame that brought the people from the surrounding country with their afflicted friends whom he had healed and restored to sight, and that excited the envy and the hatred of his persecutors, who had sought on every hand for some charge which they might prefer against him for a violation of the Jewish laws. His terrible anathemas for their injustice which had caused great suffering among the people alarmed the high-priests and the rulers who were fearful of losing their power; for he had foretold their nation's calamities, and of the destruction of their temple, which in judgment would follow them for their evil doings. It was soon after that they condemned him to an ignominious death, and tried to make him carry the cross, an emblem of their cruelty, to which they had him nailed. And it was then that his little band of followers, as well as herself, were overwhelmed with affliction at the crucifixion, although with her clairvoyant sight she could see the bright band of angels that came to assist and strengthen him through the terrible ordeal; and when it was done, she saw the heavens open and the band reascend back to their heavenly kingdom. Although as yet she had not been permitted to enter that bright sphere, the sight of it had never departed from her memory.

She said it was on Friday that Jesus was crucified, and after the cruel sentence was finished, the body was taken from the cross, washed and anointed, wrapped in clean linen, and laid in a new tomb and covered with a stone which was afterwards sealed. The following morning she was the first at the tomb, for she had loved the One who had taught them of heavenly things. She found the stone had been removed, and the body was gone; but she soon after saw him in spirit, when he spoke to her, and she knew his voice. The other Mary spoken of as having been at the tomb was the mother of one of the disciples. It was a sorrowful time for his little band of devoted followers; but he often met with them, and encouraged them during their earthly pilgrimage after his crucifixion. She then withdrew.

And Paul, the apostle of the Gentiles, was next before the council, and made the following statement. He said there were only about one hundred and thirty of the followers of Jesus left at the time he got his commission; they had dwindled down by persecution and death; and he was then on his way with authority to arrest them, when Jesus stopped him in his mad career, and authorized him to go and promulgate the everlasting gospel of a risen Saviour to the Gentiles. It was the Jews who professed to disbelieve what he had told them after he was stopped persecuting the little band of humble followers of Jesus. But he himself knew what he was about, and he had tried to fulfil the mission which he had received from his Master with fidelity and truth. And although the records of his labors had often been mutilated, altered, and misrepresented, there was still enough to show that he had no authority to establish churches, or to build temples, where the people would continue to worship Dagon and Diana.

He then directed his attention to the hosts of Israel and of Judah, who had been gathered around the platform of justice. He explained the spirit covenant made with their fathers, and spoke of the covenants and the commandments given through Moses, and of their loss by their disregard and their turning away from the celestial teachers. He showed them that Jesus of Nazareth was the Messiah for whom they had asked; but they mistook his glorious mission, and cast him out and crucified him. "You wanted an earthly king who could increase your earthly glory: his work was to fulfil the law given to you through Moses, and establish the covenant of love, and set up his spiritual kingdom on a platform of justice that would have been respected and become universal among the nations of the earth. He had illustrated the works of the Spirit by his own labors of love among the poor and the forsaken ones you had cast out, and who were suffering with disease and with poverty in the hovels and by-ways of all your surrounding towns, where he found them and healed them, and then told them of the mansions in their heavenly Father's kingdom. But your envy was aroused: you could not receive him in his meek and lowly condition, so you crucified him and lost him, while in spirit he turned to the Gentiles in order to complete his work. But you may have the offer again to accept him for your king, and we shall see now if you are willing, while we again turn to the Gentiles, and see what they have done with our Master's gospel of peace and love which was intrusted to their keeping.

"Why, what can be the meaning of all this vast multitude who have been gathered up around a platform of Eternal Justice? What! all belong to the Gentile race? Yes. Why are there so many poor mothers in rags, with children in their arms who have starved for nourishment? Heavenly Father, what an army of the fair daughters of earth all branded with the mark of fornication! And here again, — why, what a vast multitude of little ones! and all branded with the mark of thieves! And what do you say, — you had to steal or starve, and that you have got a school now, where you are instructed? Well, here again are all the 'old folks' gathered together and happy, and who have been your saviors. And here, as we look again, we see the great platform of Justice, which has been established with those of every nation and of every color, who have been gathered around it, waiting for the humble Nazarene to come and pronounce his blessing."

He then told them the first covenant which Jesus came to fulfil and establish, was a communion with spirit; but the Judaites by their own neglect had failed to comprehend it, and rejected and crucified their Saviour, and continued to worship their Egyptian gods. And the second or gospel covenant, which he was commissioned by the risen Saviour to give to the Gentiles, was also a communion with spirit; but the Christian Church had likewise failed to comprehend it, and had cruelly cast out and crucified Jesus the second time, while the Pharaohs were building temples, and setting up their earthly images for the suffering and oppressed people to worship. But the fishermen and the beggars have again heard the call of the spirit, and have joyfully received and are waiting for his kingdom. He then said the Essenes of his day were a fraternal brotherhood who had held communion with spirit outside of the Jewish Church, and of which he was a member. It was established by the Israelites, and sanctioned by Solomon in the building of his temple. They had symbols for instruction, and signs and passwords for self-protection. His own symbolic teaching was addressed to the brotherhood to confirm the truth of a resurrection of the spirit, which was the everlasting gospel of peace and love he was authorized to deliver to the Gentiles, for which he was now called to witness. As he retired,

One of the ancient Hindoos was before the council. He remarked that he was allowed to come for information, expressed great pleasure at knowing he had found an idol that could speak and tell them about a spirit-god; said they had watched over their dumb gods of the earth a long time, but had found out they had no power; and they had also failed to find out where the god was that had so long sustained them. They were called "heathens," and they were permitted to attend the council in order to acquire more knowledge for the purpose of instructing their own countrymen. He confirmed the story told by one of his people, about the Hindoo priests having bags in which they carried away the treasures the people had given to appease the anger of their earthly gods.

When India closed by invocation to the Great Spirit.

MARCH 12, 1873.—After India's invocation to the Great Spirit, he stated that Pilate, who consented to the crucifixion of the Great Media, was present, and would make his own statement; after which, if there was time, others might have an opportunity to speak. Once more rendering thanks to the Great Spirit for continued blessings, and asking for wisdom and strength sufficient for their labors, he retired.

When Pilate was next before the council, where he related the following in connection with the condemnation and crucifixion of Jesus of Nazareth. He said the laws of the Jews were severe, and in that case intensified by the hatred of a jealous and corrupt priesthood. He then spoke of the labors of Jesus among the outcasts and lower orders of the people, by whom his merits were appreciated, and where it was evident he was accomplishing a great amount of good. It was the growing popularity resulting from his labors of love and sympathy with the afflicted that hastened his destruction; for the crafty priesthood was aroused, and they sent out their minions to hunt him down, and wherever they found the little band, they were hooted at and made the butts of falsehood and slander, and often stoned and compelled to flee to the forest for protection, with no one who had courage to assist, owing to the crafty and the cruel power then at their command, by which they had managed to keep the people in ignorance and bondage. No wonder he sorrowed and wept over their fallen condition, when he knew that all were his Father's children. He had love and compassion for all; but he rebuked their selfish wickedness, and despised their show of pomp and wealth, for he knew it had all been wrung from the sinews of the oppressed and afflicted multitude, which he had found in every direction about the city. It was his labors and his compassion that were fast arousing the people to a proper sense of justice. He then turned to those who had demanded the death of an innocent man, and told them they well knew their craft was in danger, and they cried the louder, demanding that Jesus should be crucified. "When I told you the man was innocent, that I could find no charge against him worthy of death, you still demanded he should be crucified. When I was still anxious to save him, and offered you Barabbas, who was a criminal, in place of Jesus, you still cried, 'Crucify Jesus.' I then said you were condemning an innocent man, and washed my hands of the crime, in your presence. Your reply was, 'Let his blood be upon us and our children.' And now again, before all the assembled hosts who have been gathered around this great platform of Eternal Justice, I acknowledge my sorrow for the part I performed, and humbly ask to be forgiven. If there is anything I can do in order to blot out the stain, I shall gladly comply, for there has been no time during all these long centuries, when I could forgive myself for submitting to the terrible crime of shedding the blood of an innocent man. But your Jewish and priestly bigotry was excited; his love and compassion for the afflicted, and his wonderful power to heal their maladies, had made you mad, and you nailed him to the cross, the most ignominious death your cruel laws devised. You tried to make him carry the cross on which you nailed him, but his delicate frame was unequal to the task. After satisfying your thirst for his blood in his expiring agonies, he asked, not to be relieved, but that you might be forgiven, and receive the heavenly truths he had faithfully been trying to teach you." — He then affirmed that the heavens were darkened, and the earth shook to its centre, in evidence of the terrible crime that was then committed; and they well knew the guards they stationed at the tomb to watch the lifeless form were overpowered with affright at the appearance of the angels, and could give no account of what had become of the body, or of how it was taken away. " But you still suppressed the truth, and deceived the multitude, in order to keep them in bondage. Thousands did believe in the divine mission of Jesus, but the terror of your cruel laws prevented a public manifestation of its truth. — And now, as we turn again, we have another manifestation of the same craft, in a new form among the Gentiles. They have built up their temples in order to hide away the living Spirit, and keep Jesus still nailed to the cross for the purpose of perpetuating the bondage of the people ; and by the same priestly craft, in order to hold their cruel power, they crucify anew the sons and daughters of God. They invent engines of destruction — the rack and the screw, and all manner of devices — whereby quivering and bleeding forms have been torn asunder; and all to gratify their thirst for power. But the time has now come for a settlement, and you must hunt up the mangled forms of your bleeding martyrs, and bring them forth, for their Heavenly Father has called for all, and he has every name written in the Book of Life." He then withdrew.

One of the Hindoos was next before the council, and said he was pleased with what he had seen. His people were gathering up in spirit in order to make a move, but they had no knowledge of where they were going. They had looked a long time for the Great God, but could never find him. He said they had been taught by their Koran to look for a great star-spirit that would come to them and swallow up their gods of silver and gold, of brass and iron. He thought it might be the star-spirit would gather up all that were attracted to his brightness, and they would become a bright star; while others, who preferred the gods of gold and silver, would remain behind, and be a dark star. His people in spirit thought the Great God must have wonderful power in order to have so bright an eye. They thought all should be kind to each other, in order to look up to the Great Eye and not feel ashamed. He then told them they need not sneer at his people for worshipping their idols, for they wanted to show their gratitude to something in return for so many blessings; and they had not broken their images in pieces as they did the speaking god that came to them. He thought the reason their priests were so greedy was, they knew it was time for the star-spirit to swallow up the dumb gods; and so they were trying to get all they could before he came. And —

One of the Forest Maidens was the next before the council. She told them she was sent by the Great Spirit to assist others in gathering up the scattered tribes of Israel. She then addressed Israel and Judah on one hand, and Gentiles and pagans on the other. She told them of the closing cycle that was near. "The Great Spirit say, Go down and gather up my pale-face children on the lower hunting-grounds, and then tell him why the cry of sorrow has come to disturb him. Great Spirit says he gives plenty for all his children, and he must know why they don't get their supply." As the Great Spirit looked, and she looked too, it was found that "some of his children have big storehouses and much wampum, some have none; some have much blanket, some have none. When we go tell Great Spirit some of his pale-face children have no fire to make warm, many have been frozen, and many too go dead with hunger, Great Spirit say, Much wrong; go gather them up; no have such things much longer." And she would away to the upper hunting-grounds, and tell all that was said in the council.

And India closed by invocation to the Great Spirit.

MARCH 16, 1873. — After India's invocation to the Great Spirit, he said that Barnabas and John were the next in order to give their testimony. After giving his usual instructions, he retired. When —

Barnabas was the next before the council, and spoke of his labors with Paul in his mission to teach the Gentiles the gospel of a risen Saviour, and of peace and good will to man. He said Paul was educated, and had high views in regard to his duties, and kept himself away from the little band of the early followers of Jesus that remained about Jerusalem. But after he was sent to Paul, and there was an understanding that all their labors were directed by the same spirit, Paul entered the work without hesitation, and by the outflowing of the Spirit convinced many of the truth of his glorious mission, which was to teach the Gentiles of a resurrected spirit that was immortal. He then said the Jewish Church and those that worshipped at the synagogues were bitter in their opposition to the lowly followers of their Master, after his crucifixion, and many that were satisfied of the divinity of his mission were afraid to acknowledge it. But as the disciples persevered in their work with the Spirit, and the evidence continued to multiply by various manifestations of their power over the afflicted condition of the unfortunate, thousands did believe, and made public avowals of their faith in the presence of the rulers of the synagogues. He stated that much of their labors were with an Order who had faith in the communion of spirit, which was taught through the covenant made with the ancient patriarchs, although, from the frequent disturbance and the chastenings that followed, the light had departed. But many were anxiously expecting the Spirit's return, and gladly listened to it through the promised Messiah. All such received it, and again rejoiced in their lonely march during their earthly pilgrimage. But he said the communion of spirit was again lost by the brotherhood, for as the worldly church increased in power and wealth, they increased their terrible persecutions, until the Order was again broken up and the Spirit departed. He then said there was no necessity of his extending his remarks, for we had the evidence with us on every side, from those who still cast out, and persecute, and crucify the Spirit. And he retired.

John the apostle was again before the council. He commenced by addressing the assembled hosts of Israel and of Judah. He reminded them of the mistake they had made when they rejected and crucified their offered Messiah, and of their long and lonely wanderings in their barren and deserted country. He spoke of the perishable nature of all earthly principalities, as witnessed by the mouldering ruins of their own cities and temples. He then told them to look, and, pointing up through an opening in the spheres, he showed them a beautiful plain with a temple, surrounded with the children they had parted with by their wrangling and fighting during their earthly wanderings, but who had been gathered up and provided for by their Heavenly Father, who has mansions for all. "But in order to attain those mansions, you must obey the teachings of Him you crucified, and purify yourselves from your earthly abominations, and become as innocent again as little children. Now the scene is closed, but you can get yourselves in readiness, for the humble Nazarene has come again with power to establish his Father's eternal kingdom; and you will have the offer once more to receive, or to again reject him." When, after a few pleasant words of encouragement, he again retired.

One of the ancient Hindoos was again before the council, where he gave a statement of the pleasure his people enjoyed from the many strange scenes that were transpiring. They had been a long time looking and trying to find out where the great God had been staying, but it seemed to. be impossible for them to find out. They were very soon satisfied, after leaving their earthly habitations, that they had been deceived by the priests who had taught them to pay their devotions to the dumb gods, for it was very evident, if it hadn't been for the treasures they gave to them, the priests themselves would soon have found some other earthly gods to worship. They were delighted with the opening that was shown them up where the children were kept. He thought, if God was a spirit, and he sent a little spark of his bright spirit down into the earthly bodies, where it staid until it was worked over and over, and made them all bright before he let it come back, his people would be satisfied, for their chance of getting back to the true God was as good as any other's. He thought, if those Judaites, that were often among the people of his country to fight, had not killed the god that was evidently teaching them about the home of the Spirit-God, he would have given the same kind of instructions to the people of his country, who would have been taught not to give all their treasures to their earthly idols which it seemed were only used to support a profligate and idle priesthood. As the Hindoo retired,

One of the Forest Maidens was the next before the council, and said she had come from the upper hunting-grounds of the red man to speak to the many tribes of Israel and of Judah, who have wandered many moons on the lower hunting-grounds in search of their promised land. She told them it was the call of the Great Spirit for the Eleven to gather up their scattered tribes, and be ready to make another move. The Great Spirit was speaking to his pale-face children, and all must obey his voice. And she would away from the wigwam watch-fire back to the upper hunting-grounds.

And India again closed the session by invocation to the Great Spirit.

MARCH 19, 1873. — After India's invocation to the Great Spirit, once again asking for wisdom and strength sufficient for their labor, he said Demosthenes was present, and desired a few moments' attention. And he again retired.

When Demosthenes was the next before the council, where he made the following request. He said he had come to ask for help in a battle where the weak and helpless were struggling with an earthly principality whose leader had been wounded in the hip, and who was marshalling his forces and making a wilful effort to crush out the freedom of speech and also that of the press, and by priestly array extinguish the voice of those who would expose their evils, their wickedness, and hypocrisy with their creeds and dogmas with which they have kept the race in bondage. And after saying that he was thankful to know that he could make his appeal to a band of spirits who had sanctioned the formation of a platform of Eternal Justice, he well knew his appeal would not be in vain. He then gave expression to his gratitude, and withdrew.

And Anna Ora, a Greek slave, was the next before the council, where she made the following statement. She said it was the custom during her earthly pilgrimage for the tribes to make war on the surrounding tribes, and when victorious, they selected the young and helpless of her sex, and kept them for their harems, and then sold the balance of their captives for other kinds of slavery. Those sent to the harems were compelled to submit to any kind of exposure their brutal masters demanded, and were often required to follow them in their pursuit of other conquests. Their terrible hardships often crushed out all human feelings, when they retaliated by destroying the lives of their masters. Her mother was captured, when she was in her childhood, by the Turks, and sold in bondage. She said Pythagoras was a teacher in the country where she was during her earthly pilgrimage, but the people had no knowledge of the communion of spirit, and were taught to worship dumb idols. She said their experience in their spirit sphere had been also one of fear, for when any change was coming to them, they were expecting to be captured and be again confined to slavery. She then retired.

And a woman whose lot was cast among the Turks, was next before the council. She made the following report in regard to the inhabitants of her country during her earthly pilgrimage, where all the people in the common pursuits of life were kind and faithful to each other, obedient and full of love for their parents; for then they had no knowledge of any other creator. They found the sex about equally divided, which had naturally taught them the marriage covenant. And as their unions were from natural attraction, they were blessed with healthy offspring and were happy in their domestic relations. But it was different with those who had power and wealth, for they never seemed to be satisfied; and it was with them as it has been in all ages — their many evils in the end secured their own destruction.

She said she had been happy with her parents and friends in their spirit sphere; but there seemed to be a gathering up among them at present, although as yet they had not been informed of what was expected would be the result. She was pleased with the opportunity of again speaking through the physical organization, and she thought it might be possible they would be permitted to return to the people of their own nationality, and teach them of the immortal spirit, and of its resurrection, and lead them above the transitory and perishable things that surround them to their spirit home, where the long-lost and forsaken ones would again be united in much happier unions. She then expressed her thanks, and retired. And the next was —

An ancient Egyptian "seer" before the council, where he answered by saying he was glad the time had come which was foretold in his age when they should return to the earth and again converse with mortals; and they had waited and wandered in spirit, and longed for the time to come; and now it had come, when they should see of the salvation of which they had been foretold, — when the High and Holy One would manifest his power and love to his earthly children, and raise them up from their darkened earthly condition to a knowledge of their home in spirit. And as he could look about him and see the gathering up of the numerous tribes who had answered to the call of the chosen ones, sent to lead them away from the dark and forbidden paths in which they all had wandered, he was thrilled with amazement as he contemplated the various manifestations of the power and love of the great Creator. And once more he would send out his voice in renewed warning to the inhabitants of the earth to forsake their evil ways, turn back and commence a new life, obey the covenants and the commandments of God, and listen to the voice of his Spirit, and shun the downward paths that lead to sorrow and to destruction. After an expression of his pleasure, he said if his own people had obeyed the warning voice of the ever-living Spirit, they would have been nearer to the eternal kingdom. When he retired, and —

An ancient Hindoo was next before the council, where he had come in order to see what he could learn that might be of use to his countrymen. He told, as others had, about their earthly idols, and was anxious to learn something about the great Creator, and for what purpose so many were gathering around their former leaders. His people were pleased with the bright things which had already been shown, and they were trying to get up and look over and see where the greatest of all lived. They had commenced a pyramid of their own countrymen by standing one on the other; he thought there would be enough of their own to reach up where the top one could see. They wanted no nation to assist, for fear they might be called away, and all their labor be lost. They were watching and listening to all that was said. He thought the old Egyptian could tell who built the pyramids in his country; but his folks didn't know what the squaw that had the bow and arrows was talking about when she told of the Great Spirit, and of the upper hunting-grounds. He thought they had better use language that all could understand.

And one of the Forest Maidens was next before the council, sent, she said, by the Great Spirit from the upper hunting-grounds of her race, to tell of his mighty power and of his love for his children. She was glad to see Israel and Judah gathering in their scattered and wandering tribes in order to follow the spirit to the lands which they had found were above their earthly Jordans. She and her sister squaws were sent by the Great Spirit to look after and report the condition of his pale-face children on the red man's lower hunting-grounds, where they had found many suffering and crying to the Great Spirit to protect them from the avarice and the injustice of the pale-face race. " Great Spirit say, Squaws go mark the wigwams' doors, and let my warriors know who and where to find all that have disregarded the laws of Fternal Justice." She then withdrew. And India closed the session by invocation to the Great Spirit.

MARCH 23, 1873.— After India's invocation to the Great Spirit, he said Aristotle's statement was next in order. He then retired, and —

Aristotle was before the council, where he made the following statement in connection with his former records pertaining to the laws of maternity ; and said he was anxious to have it understood he was still satisfied with the accounts he left concerning his investigation in that direction ; and would further say — confirmed now by continued research in spirit — that it was wrong for females of delicate health and feeble constitution to accept of the sacred and responsible duties connected with the maternal relations, and that healthy and strong females should only become the mothers of three or four children, with a vacancy of two or three years from birth to birth, in order to attain that necessary perfection so desirable to insure happiness. And furthermore he wanted it understood by all that the birth into spirit-life from the physical was just as natural and controlled by fixed and unchangeable laws ; and if parents desired happiness, and desired, as all parents should, to entail happiness on their offspring, they must conform to the immutable laws of the Great Creator. No one could plead ignorance to the laws, for all know that effects follow causes, and they could see the effects of the parents' transgressions visited upon their helpless and suffering children all over the Christian world ; and it was reasonable and natural to know how that a spirit born from a diseased and sickly physical form must necessarily for a time partake of its earthly condition. He then remarked that he had found every requisite facility in spirit necessary for the furtherance of his philosophical researches. And, after expressing thanks for the pleasure of again speaking with mortals, he retired.

And one of the mothers of ancient Rome was next before the council, where she expressed the pleasure that herself and people had found in the present call or quickening of spirit. She then told of their condition during their earthly pilgrimage. She spoke of the care Roman mothers had manifested in watching over and guarding the marriage covenants of their sons and daughters, that no inharmony might enter that would blight the physical prospects of their offspring. She then spoke of their own progress in spirit, and said if it had been retarded, they had found the primary department what they themselves had been instrumental in making it. She then spoke of their gratitude to the high controlling power who had permitted them to witness the gathering up of the scattered tribes of the Pagan and Gentile nations, and then withdrew.

When one of the Hindoos was the next one in council, and said he was permitted by those in charge to come and speak in order to satisfy his people, who were anxious to find out something about the Great Creator, for they had finished the pyramid they were building, and four of their people had looked over from the top, and were told to go back and read the law in the Koran, and they would find that all who tried to get in were thieves and robbers. He said they had seen the star-spirit spoken of in their Koran, but he had not said anything to them; they thought he was pleased, for he looked good-natured. And another one had told them to have all their things in moving order, for soon they would have to go up higher. He thought the people who had bows and arrows had belonged in a country away beyond Asia Minor, for they had seen people that looked like them there since they inhabited their present spirit home; and said the mound and pyramid builders were ancient tribes who built them for landmarks, and put their Korans in them in order to know where they belonged when they returned to inhabit the same part of the country.

One of the Forest Maidens was the next before the council. She had come to speak to the many tribes of the many nations the leaders of which the Great Spirit had ordered to gather around his great platform of Eternal Justice, where all were asking the way up to the Great Spirit. She told them the Great Spirit was good, and loved all his children; but they had encumbered themselves with their many evils, and forgotten their relationship to the Great Spirit and his home in the upper hunting-grounds. They had found much suffering and many evils, which they inherited, and which they had willingly entailed upon others, although they had often been told that all were brothers and belonged to the Great Spirit.

And India closed the session by invocation to the Great Spirit.

MARCH 26, 1873. — After India's invocation to the Great Spirit, giving renewed thanks for continued blessings, he said the present session would be devoted to the children, and that all those who had left their earthly forms in their childhood would pass before the council in review, headed by their teachers. And as he retired —

Miss Landon with her band of juveniles was among the numerous gathering, and she was before the council and made a few remarks. Said she felt unworthy of the privilege that had been assigned to her to speak in the presence of the assembled nations in a spirit sphere where the great law of eternal justice was now established; said she would willingly be clothed again in the mortal, and pass through another pilgrimage in compensation for the great pleasure the present gathering had given to her, as she was given now to comprehend its truth in all its grandeur, where the children of all nations who had been protected by their Heavenly Father's love, were again allowed to be represented in childhood in order for each anxious mother to recognize her own. And, as they came from their celestial paradise with flowers prepared to greet the weary wanderers of a lower sphere, who could measure the depth of gratitude that was flowing from each mother's heart as she clasped in her arms again her long-lost treasure! She said that her own heart yearned in her earthly life, where she found no counterpart; but in God's paradise of love, among the children intrusted to her guardian care for instruction, every desire in her nature had found compensation. And now let the mothers of every nation and tribe unite in an anthem of praise to God for his redeeming love, while the children prepare their triumphal arch for those who come from a higher sphere to instruct and assist in the final establishment of the great law of Eternal Justice. After expressing renewed thanks with heartfelt and grateful emotion for the part intrusted to her, she retired. And next —

An angel of light was before the council, and in beautiful words addressed the assembled tribes of Israel and Judah, and also the Gentiles as well as the faithful Pagans, whom he said, in their sincerity in their worship, had in confidence bowed down to their harmless idols.

He then told them all to look up through a grand archway then opening in the spheres above, and listen to the anthem going up to their heavenly Father's throne, in gratitude and love for the work already accomplished in successfully establishing the great law of justice in a darkened sphere of spirit, where all had awakened to a knowledge of their spirit resurrection. For the temple not made with hands in the kingdom above is now before you, while the bright inhabitants of the celestial spheres, who have never yet visited the earth, are looking down with wonder and delight as they join in the anthem of praise to the Great Father of all who has accomplished the work. And now he would ask them how the grand work they were permitted to witness had been established. Israel and Judah had both refused to accept it. Judaism, over eighteen hundred and forty years ago, cruelly rejected and cast out their Messiah. The Father sent them to teach them what Israel had failed to comprehend, from the law and the prophets or the covenants of the patriarchs, that the promised land was in spirit above their earthly kingdom; "and when the lonely one you crowned with thorns and crucified in derision wept for your blindness and prayed that you might be forgiven, he turned in spirit to the Gentiles to assist him in the accomplishment of this his glorious work. And now let the Gentiles answer for the earthly principalities and powers they have built up in the place of this their accepted Master's eternal kingdom, and for the condition of humanity intrusted to their charge through his gospel of peace and good will to all then made manifest through his resurrection, and through what has now been accomplished, as you are witnesses of the great joy of the lost and forsaken ones that have been gathered up and clothed and made happy. No wonder you are looking with amazement on a work of such transcendent glory, and ask yourselves how has the work been done. Wait and watch, for further developments are near at hand." He then addressed a few chosen words of encouragement to all who had been engaged in so grand a work, and retired. And —

One of the Hindoos was before the council, where he told

of his people's delight at what they had been permitted to witness; but they were startled with surprise at the sight of so many children with such untold quantities of beautiful flowers. They had watched the triumphal arch that led to the sphere above, and saw many wonderful things; but the spirit who had last spoken had escaped their observation, for while they were all looking in one direction, he must have got in possession of their speaking goddess in some other way. They were satisfied from what they had seen and heard that the Spirit God must be their Father, and they were going to ask him to let them go to their own countrymen, and tell them of all the wonderful things they had seen; and if it was consistent and possible, they would make their dumb idols speak, and tell of the glory and power of their Great Spirit Father. He thought the Great Father wouldn't be angry with them for giving their treasures to their idols, for the priests that had carried them away had never told them of a Spirit Father. His people in spirit were anxious the Father should send some one to teach them, but thought they had been deceived so many times they wouldn't know whom to believe.

One of the Forest Maidens was the next before the council, where she told of her race who had been sent from their upper hunting-grounds by the Great Spirit to report the condition of his pale-face children, who had taken the lower hunting-grounds of the red man's race. She had come to the wigwam of the white squaw and the brave, where the council-fire of the Great Spirit was bright. She had listened to their talk, and was glad the time had come for the gathering up of the scattered tribes who had long wandered in darkness. She told them the Great Spirit loved all his children, and it was not his fault they had turned away from the light of the Spirit, and disregarded his covenants and commandments given by prophets and seers.

When India again closed the session by invocation to the Great Spirit.

MARCH 30, 1873. — After India's invocation to the Great Spirit in memory of his continued blessings, he said two ancients — one a Jew, and the other an Egyptian — were next in order. After his usual good counsel and encouragement, he retired. When an ancient Jew, who gave the name of —

Nathaniel, was the next before the council, where he related something of his earthly pilgrimage; said he was a descendant of the tribe of Judah, and a leader in the brotherhood or fraternal order since called Essenes, who kept the covenants and the commandments given to the ancient patriarchs, who were persecuted and cast out of the Jewish church by the priesthood. His people had heard the call, and had gathered up in order to take their place among the scattered tribes, for they were told the Ancient of days would come, when they should all be gathered together, and speak, and mingle again with mortals. And he was rejoiced to know he had been found worthy to stand up and represent his people in testimony of the things which had been so long foretold, although they had wandered and waited in their deserted and barren country, watching for a change to come. And now they had turned to their Messiah, and had found he was the Jordan and the Palestine that led them to the promised land, where they should find the Great Father's temple built without hands. He was glad he had waited with his people, for they were all willing now to follow the voice of the Spirit, and come up and take their place among the lost and scattered tribes of Israel and of Judah, and follow the lead of their promised Shiloh, who at last had opened the way to their heavenly Father's eternal kingdom. He spoke again of the terrible persecutions of his people, who had held to the faith and were looking for their promised leader, while the Judaites had held to the earthly church, which had departed from the faith, and finally rejected and cruelly crucified their promised Messiah, but who had paid for their blindness through ages of darkness and suffering, waiting to hear his voice again. Now they have gladly heard the call in spirit, and are gathered together, uniting in songs of joy throughout their camps, anxiously waiting to see the glorified One they crucified. After addressing a few remarks to his own people, he retired. And —

The ancient Egyptian was next before the council, and said his people had answered the call of the angel of time, and had come up to their place among the nations, who in truth were being resurrected from the fear which had surrrounded them all for ages. The mystery of the past was fast dissolving, and the bodies they had embalmed to await their call in spirit would not be wanted, for they now found living bodies through which they could talk with mortals. He then said his own pilgrimage in an earthly body was after Abraham, in the patriarchal age, and before the time of Moses, who was a leader among the covenanted tribes. His own nation, the Egyptians, in his time had made great advancement in all the arts of that age, the records of which had been lost, owing to the wandering and wayfaring habits of the tribes, and much time with its events had disappeared from mortals. But the recording angel would have the account right in spirit, where everything must take its proper place. The mounds and pyramids contained the records of different tribes, who had left them for landmarks, in order that each might claim their own. The laws among his people were based on the great law of justice, and rigidly enforced. Whoever disregarded and violated the law was embalmed at the public expense, without a head, that others might take warning. They built no prisons, and had no criminals supported by the public, to demoralize the industry of the people. Their women were noble and true wives and mothers, and were satisfied with their natural position; they looked to the sterner sex, who then had not forfeited their manhood, for protection. They had no "media," who held communion with the inhabitants of the invisible world, to which they looked for light; but they had attained to a high order of human development, and were impressed through the brain, as their inventions and scientific attainments had already substantiated. More evidence of their early national progress would come to light through the spirit development of the people of the present age; for they were a set of diggers, and they would continue to dig until the hidden mysteries of the past had all been explained. He said it was the custom of his people, when the last one of a tribe or family was embalmed, their treasures went with the body in order to prevent the evil of covetousness among them.

One of the Hindoos was next before the council, and said his people were progressing in spirit, for they had been interested observers of all that had transpired. He then related the following incident of a party of them who were in search of the Father. And when they could go no further, they called to him as loud as they could call, and then asked, if he couldn't come to them himself, wouldn't he please send them some one that could teach them and tell them what to do? They didn't have to wait long before they observed that some one was coming who overwhelmed them all with affright;

and when the One drew near, they fell with their faces down, as they had been taught to do before their earthly idols. But soon they ventured to look, and a bright spirit, who was smiling, spoke to them as it moved around; but they were still fearful that it belonged to some other nation, and if it was injured, they would certainly get in trouble. But soon other spirits appeared that were like their own countrymen, and told them not to be frightened, for they could tell them what to do, if they were so anxious to find the Great Father. They were then satisfied with the promise; they returned, and should tell of their progress hereafter through their speaking goddess. As he then retired—

One of the Forest Maidens was the next before the council, where she had listened to the talk of the old braves, and was glad the time had come for them to gather up their tribes, in order to learn more of the goodness and love of the Great Spirit, who had sent out the red man's race from his upper hunting-grounds to follow the war-path of his pale-faces, and point out all who have treated the Great Spirit with ingratitude, and their own brother with injustice; "for the Great Spirit has again inquired about the condition of all of his pale-face children." After which, India once more closed the session by invocation to the Great Spirit.

MARCH 31, 1873.—After India's invocation to the Great Spirit, he said the spirit band had assembled to commemorate the events of the last quarter of a century; and among other things he spoke of the radical change in the minds of men, as an evidence of the power of spirit over matter, as one thing after another had been removed which had delayed the union between spirits and mortals. He then spoke of the tiny rap brought to notice in the humble home of the Fox family, at Hydesville, in the State of New York, where the mind of the child was impressed by spirit to answer the rap they made through matter by the snap of its fingers, and from that to the A B C of the English language, which was a triumph in spirit that was sent up in gratitude to the Great Spirit, that reverberated with renewed joy from sphere to sphere. He then said, as we were witnesses in the flesh of the mighty changes that were transpiring, we might be assured the work of reform would never cease until the covenants and the commandments were re-established, and all had a knowledge of their birthright. They felt to rejoice that by the sanction and help of the Great Spirit they had been successful in their united labors in lighting up a dark sphere in spirit, where they now had established the great platform of Eternal Justice, around which the nations of the earth were then assembling, each and every one in their own order. And after expressing gratitude to the Great Spirit, who had sanctioned and sustained them in their labors, said he would retire; and then John, known as the "revelator," would be present, and review their work.

And John was next before the council, where, after speaking of the magnitude of the work, and its wonderful success, he turned to the vast assembly, and commenced the following review. He first spoke to Israel and Judah, with their numerous tribes. He told them the apostles, of which he made the twelfth, had been directed to take their seats on the platform of justice which had been established; around which they had been called together, and could view the scenes which he was allowed to present before them. "And now, as I draw the curtain in this direction, you can all see — but for a moment — up into the paradise of God's love, where all the children that were cast out and lost from their earthly life are gathered in by their heavenly Father, where they have been reared up in purity and love. Look, now, as you see them change from childhood, — as they take the place assigned them with angels and archangels among the heavenly hosts; while here we have another scene, of children all dressed in blue. See! they are the little ones of every nation, that have been gathered up in spirit from their lost, and abandoned, and neglected condition during their unhappy experience. Yes, they are the children of the poor, from the highways and the alleys from every town and city. Some left their little bodies in the prisons, and some by the roadside, for the want of bread and clothing. You can all see how much they were left to suffer by their little careworn faces. But here they have been gathered up and clothed, and have a school provided, where they are taught the immutable laws of the Great Creator. Now, here we have another scene; all this vast assembly of females dressed in blue were abandoned and deserted, — sent into the dark sphere in spirit, with the brand of their misfortunes impressed upon them; but here they have found saviors who have gathered them up and clothed them; while here, in the next scene, are the men who were their companions in crime. You can see they have all suffered for violating God's holy laws; but they have been gathered up and taught their duties to each other. Now, here is another sight: all these were the victims of oppression from injustice and poverty; they were sent in disgrace from your prisons and your guillotines; and you that were their trusted guardians have been their murderers, terrible as it may seem! While here in the background is another vast assembly; they were once your honored clergymen who professed to teach others from their so-called 'holy records,' the way to the Great Father's eternal kingdom; but we all can see they haven't been able to find the way themselves. Look, now, as I raise the veil and show you the kingdom, you are thousands of millions of miles away from, you can for the moment see the beautiful 'throne,' where the Great Father and his Son whom you did profess to follow, are in union in their great work for the elevation of humanity.

"Now, then, you that professed to be authorized teachers of this vast assembly of God's children, answer this question: Who gave you the authority to teach them of an angry God, who was their creator, and of an endless hell, where all but a chosen few would forever be in torment? O, you needn't open your Book: we know what it should teach. Now, all that have taught the people the everlasting gospel of a spirit resurrection, and of a spirit kingdom where peace and goodwill would be the heritage for all. can now come forward and step up on to this platform. What! not even one starts! Well, then, all who have alleviated the afflictions of the widow and the orphan, clothed the naked and healed their maladies, comforted the afflicted, and administered to those in prison, can step on to the platform. And O, can it be possible that none claim the right? Well, then, now we will show the mangled forms of your martyred brothers, who have come from under the altars to accuse you; while here also are your engines of torture; and here is a body provided for this occasion. Now take it up, and place it in that machine of your invention, and show all the hosts of the heavenly spheres how you mangled your victims in your 'holy zeal' for earthly power. O, you did do it yourselves, you say. Well, then, call out now your menials that you employed to do it for you — and you are 'the ones.' Well, place that body in that machine, and fasten the legs and arms as you have so often done. O, yes, all can see the cruel sight. Now, take hold of that crank, and tighten the chains on your helpless and suffering brother, and let all see the knives penetrate his quivering and mangled form. See his eyes start from their sockets, as the limbs are torn asunder!— Yes, you tremble; and no wonder, for your unholy deeds have filled the earth with fear and suffering; and still you are our brothers, and we pity you. We have got no engines of torture here to increase your sufferings, but as yet we can't receive you. Your hiding-places in the dark sphere have been lit up by the labor of others, and you have no longer any place for seclusion; and your judgment is to return to those who are still under bondage from the effects of your own evil abominations, where you must work until the last remnant of your suffering victims is forever emancipated from the earth, *which you are not to touch, but must remain suspended between that and the heavens above you, until your work has been accomplished;* and then, and not till then, can you be received into the heavenly kingdom. And now, behold, is another scene. Here we have the soldiers who in affright have been sent headlong into the spirit sphere from bleeding bodies that were torn asunder in the rage of battle, where brother has been made to war with brother in the terrible strife. Mortals inaugurate to secure the perishable things of earth. And here again, as the veil is drawn aside in this direction, you see the horses ready for their riders, that will now go forth to the earth to battle with the powers of darkness. And here we have the 'old folks,' who have been gathered up and made happy; although they look amazed at the fearful scenes brought before them. And here come the representatives of a numerous and mighty race from a 'higher sphere,' that have never departed from the teachings of the Spirit; they have never been bound by any of your laws, or contaminated themselves with earthly principalities; but they looked up to the Great Spirit with gratitude, and worshipped him in purity and love. See, they offer to take the place of those who were judged to return to the earth, where they must labor until the records of their misdeeds are obliterated; but they offer to go in their place and accomplish the work for them. And here again is Israel and Judah with all their scattered tribes: but we don't pronounce your judgment — we leave that to the Gentiles. But I see the time approaching when there will be no more death; I see the physical gradually disappears, and the spiritual takes its place. I see a new heaven and a new earth, for the New Jerusalem, with its spirit-temple, ascending to the place assigned it by the Great Creator; while the action of the water on the surface of the earth, as it comes in contact with the fire beneath, will cast up new continents where spirit will individualize matter through its own wonderful laboratories up to man." Whereupon, after a few words of instruction as well as encouragement, he retired. And —

One of the Forest Maidens was then before the council. She had come to the wigwam of the white squaw to listen to the talk of the old braves. She was pleased to see all the wandering and scattered tribes brought up at the call of the Great Spirit. Her race had come down from their upper hunting-grounds, and would assist in removing the many stains from the long trail of the pale-faces, which had caused much sorrow. She could see signs in the east and in the west, and signs in the south, that would soon make great commotion among the pale-face race that had turned away from the covenants of the Great Spirit, and from his law of Eternal Justice.

After which, India made a few encouraging remarks, and then closed by invocation to the Great Spirit.

APRIL 2, 1873. — After India's invocation to the Great Spirit, once more acknowledging their dependence on him for strength in the prosecution of their necessary labors, and asking for wisdom sufficient to guide, that their work might be approved, he said Calvin and Bullard were next in order to make their statements, and retired.

When Calvin was then before the council, and again affirmed that when he seceded from the Church of Rome, and proclaimed the doctrines of the atonement through the death of Jesus, with a burning endless torment for unbelievers, he was conscientious, and thought he was doing right. He knew then the Church which he left was a corrupt and cruel power, and was destroying human life with her engines of torture and her inquisitions, in order to augment her power and influence over the people. It was his honest opinion that all transgressors deserved to be punished, and according to the way he had been taught to interpret the Scriptures of a past age, he felt sure at the time that the condemnation of the unrepentant was unavoidable; but as soon as they were satisfied of their mistake, they had gladly been at work in spirit, in order as fast as possible to remove the errors they had inculcated from the minds of mortals. He was also permitted to say the clergy, since the Reformation, were not included in the judgment already pronounced; for when they were arraigned, a year previous, and shown their errors, they had gladly accepted of the opportunity offered to them to commence a work of reformation, and they had found their labors in that direction the past year had proved to be a strong argument in their favor. But he said it was still true that the present advocates of the doctrines of the Church of Rome were now working with all their cunning tricks in order to get the political control of the North American continent. He said they were holding nightly councils, and had telegraphic communications with Europe, in order to further their present designs; but he could say with great pleasure that arrangements had already been made in spirit that would result in their final disappointment. And he retired.

Then Bullard was again before the council, where he also confirmed the statement of his brother Calvin. He said that for a time they were all shaking for fear they wouldn't be able to pass the dreaded judgment; but, happily for them, they found in One a mediator who had prevailed in their behalf, and they were allowed to continue in the work of restitution which they had got thoroughly organized; and he was sure no effort would be spared on their part until the desired work was accomplished. He was well aware the place for his labors was dark, and had long been cemented with the ecclesiastical magnetism of the Church of Rome; but he knew the connection was broken, and that light would flow in until the eyes of the mentally blind were opened, and all could see and acknowledge the grandeur of their Saviour's labors. He should stand by his own flock until they realized the truth of the everlasting gospel, and acknowledged the resurrection and the communion with spirits, and their final gathering up in the everlasting kingdom as the grand consummation of the labors of the One they had all professed to follow. When, after speaking of local affairs in connection with his old western home, he retired.

One of the ancient Hindoos was next before the council, where he expressed gratitude for himself and for his people for the pleasure as well as the knowledge they had already received. He said he could distinguish, among the different tribes that had come, the ones that formerly often made war on the Hindoo people. It was true, when they were successful in their battles, they thought their gods were pleased, and they never failed to make them rich with the things they captured from the tribes of other nations; but they had long since learned in spirit that such things were encouraged by the priesthood, who had the care of their gods, in order to delude the unsuspecting people. He was in hopes the time would soon arrive when they could enlighten the people of their own country in order that such cruelty might cease to have an existence, and the dumb idols so long used to deceive them be thrown out of sight.

And India closed the session by invocation to the Great Spirit.

APRIL 6, 1873.— After India's invocation to the Great Spirit, he said the people known with us as Mormons, or "latter-day saints," as they had been called, would be the next in the order of investigation. He then retired.

Smith, known as the Mormon leader under its first organization, was before the council, and said that he himself and his followers were arraigned before the platform of Eternal Justice, in judgment before the assembled nations, for the errors and the evils they had entailed upon their deluded and unhappy followers by turning away and disregarding the communion of spirit intrusted to them as the humble followers of Jesus their Saviour; but he was satisfied, however great had been his own humiliation and suffering, that the judgment would be right, for they were intrusted with a work designed for the elevation and salvation of the race from the degradation of their moral death. It was well known by those who stood as their accusers that they were intrusted with the communion of spirit, and with the gifts of healing and speaking the languages of the different nations, as well as that of prophesying; and, notwithstanding all this, they fell from their high calling, and failed in accomplishing the grand work which was intrusted to their care, and at last taken from them as unworthy, and given to others to finish. No one could tell how great had been his sorrow as he had waited for the judgment, for they grieved away the Spirit, that would have guided them aright, by their own degraded and selfish evils; and when they turned to the ancient recorders of Israel and Judah for light, it only increased the burden of their afflictions. He said he was aware of the wrong he did, but, unfortunately for him, he had surrounded himself with bad men who finally secured his fall.

And then Pratt was the next before the council, where he remarked that he had nothing to say in justification of their failure to accomplish a great work which was intrusted to them; they had fallen from their high calling by giving way and partaking of the errors and evils around them. They knew of their mistake when they lost the communion of spirit with which they had been blessed until they disannulled the covenant they made by their disregard of the commandments, and the spirit departed and left them shorn of their glory. But still they were loath to give up their earthly power, although they knew they had forfeited their trust and were unworthy; and not until they were cut off by untimely death, and found themselves naked in spirit, could they realize how great had been their failure. And as they were now arraigned around the great platform of Justice, and could see what had been accomplished by the labor of others, they felt the more keenly what they had lost, and would cheerfully comply with whatever judgment was assigned to them, in order, as far as possible, to make restitution. He then addressed a few consoling words to his brothers in their affliction, and told them they would profit from their past experience, and this time they would be faithful in whatever was intrusted to them in order to be accomplished. Then he withdrew.

And John the "revelator" was again before the council, and there said that he himself and his brother disciples had come by the direction of their Master, who himself had come to judge the "quick and the dead," but who had assigned to him and his brothers the duty of sitting in judgment on the Mormon leaders, who were intrusted with an important mission, which they felt grieved to know they had utterly failed to accomplish; for he himself was one who with many others in spirit were sent to them to assist them in their work of establishing a platform of justice in order to build up the spirit kingdom among the inhabitants of the earth. But as they had failed in the grand mission, and given up to the control of the powers of darkness, and given place to their own evil desires, their judgment was to return to their earthly scenes, where they must continue to labor among its deluded inhabitants until every evil resulting from their own disobedience was forever eradicated from the sphere of mortals; and then, and not till then, they could return to the platform of Eternal Justice, and once more receive the hand of "true fellowship." He told them he was truly sorry for them: they all felt a deep regret for the errors they had committed, for it was true all were brothers; but the time had come for the gathering up, and all would be judged in accordance with their deeds, whether it was for their good or for their evil. He then once more gave encouragement and counsel to those engaged in the finishing up of the work, and retired.

When one who had been with others who had suffered was next before the council, where she said, she, with a numerous band of the Mormon children, had come as witnesses to accuse those who had but just received their judgments. Her band were the representatives of many children that were cast out from their earthly lives, the result of some of the evils inculcated by the "latter-day saints;" but they were permitted by their Heavenly Father to leave their paradise above and return to earth to those who should have been their guardians, and where they would assist them in their noble enterprise in exterminating the many evils that have so long afflicted mortals. They were witnesses of the work that was already accomplished in the dark sphere of spirit, where the great law of Eternal Justice had been established; and they wanted a part in finishing the work, where Judgment with Charity would finally incorporate the great law of Universal Love with suffering humanity. As she then retired —

One of the ancient Hindoos was the next before the council, where he spoke of the children, and said they all had flowers they brought with them from what was called their paradise above, and had built up a grand pyramid with a different kind of flower which represented the people of every nation. He thought it was a magnificent display of their superior cultivation. He also remarked that those who had to go back in order to clean themselves looked rather sorry, but then it was kind in their children to offer to go and assist them in their labors; and said no doubt it would in the end alleviate their suffering. His own people were all a-doing splendid; the star-spirit had been among them again, and given instruction in regard to what they must do in order to be ready to go higher up in their long search to find the Great Father. As he then retired —

One of the Forest Maidens was the next before the council, and she had come to represent the numerous race of the red man. They had come by direction of the Great Spirit to be his witnesses at the gathering up of the many nations and tribes, at the great council of the Great Spirit; and many of his children were ashamed, as they gathered around the Great Spirit's platform of Eternal Justice, where they could see that they had not dealt with justice when they were on the lower hunting-grounds the trusted leaders among the Great Spirit's pale-face children. She then withdrew.

And India closed the session by invocation to the Great Spirit.

APRIL 9, 1873. — After India's invocation to the Great Spirit, again asking for wisdom and strength to assist them in their labors in order to have them approved, he said Confucius was present, and by request of the assembled tribes would again address them. He then withdrew.

And the good Father Confucius was again heard by the council, and said he had then come to answer the desire of the many who were anxious to know what had become of the people shown to them a-travelling north at the time they left their companions, who found their Eden over the water. He would now inform them they were a band of pilgrims who had left their homes and their friends in China, and persevered in their travels through the deserts and barren plains in search of unknown lands, not knowing where they were going to form a settlement. But after their separation, where further communication for the time was suspended by a heavy rain and the dense fog that settled on the water, and after waiting two days without tidings, they started in hopes of finding an opening that would take them to their friends' in some other direction. "But as we follow them north, we find that the waters prevented their further union, and they continued their travels until they found a fertile and beautiful country beyond the northern icebergs, where they have become a great and a prosperous people, as you see them represented here in spirit, and as you know the desire has gone out among the nations who have fitted and sent out different expeditions, expecting to find them. And now, as we turn back, we shall find the pilgrims that were then left in their beautiful garden, where they were happy and increased in numbers, from your Cains and Abels, down to Enoch, — who, it is said, was a just man, who walked and talked with God, — and Methuselah and Seth, with all their descendants down to Noah, where the historians have introduced a flood in order to destroy them; but you see they are all here gathered up, and represent many of the different nationalities and tribes, who are here to establish their one common origin. Here you see the red man with his numerous descendants, who have ever been true to Nature, and worshipped the Great Spirit manifested to them through the mysterious and wonderful works everywhere seen around them, and who now stand in spirit nearest to the Great Father, uncontaminated with the mammon of unrighteousness with which so many are scarred. They are the tribes. with their many descendants who followed a stream that led them to the gold fields of the western El-dorado, where they remained uncorrupted with the principalities of the earth. And here are the tribes with their descendants who have become pale in the face through the corruptions of the flesh, who first led the way to South America. The earth then was more level and fertile, with less water upon its surface. And as the tribes separated and formed settlements in different localities, it was often centuries before they would know of each other's nationality. And here now we have the confiding Hindoo, with his numerous descendants. who have bowed in reverence to their dumb idols in order to satisfy their veneration. And you now see all the tribes represented who have been called up before the Great Father's platform of Eternal Justice, where all his children can establish their relationship to each other, and prepare to go nearer to Him." When, after instructions concerning their investigations, he again retired, and —

One of the ancient Hindoos was then before the council, where he expressed his satisfaction with what he had then heard, and told of the progress his people, who had been called "heathen," were making. He spoke of the wonderful scenes that had transpired since they had all been called up together. He said each nation, or class, was kept by itself, and each class had chosen one of their own in order to represent them in the council; and when any charge was made that was wrong, any one who could refute the statement held up a hand, and then the opportunity was given in order to set them right in their investigations. His people were thankful for the kindness they had received, and would show their gratitude by giving more strength to their speaking goddess.

One of the Forest Maidens was next before the council, where she had come to listen to the talk of the old brave who was wise, for he had long been in council, and who worshipped the Great Father. She and her race were the children of the Great Spirit, who had sent them from their upper hunting-grounds to work with his pale-face children, who had never practised his law of justice and of charity with judgment and love for all. When they learned the Great Spirit's laws, and obeyed them, all the pale-face race would see the mistake they made by going into the by and forbidden paths that led them away from the Great Spirit, who had ever provided for his earthly children.

India closed the session by invocation to the Great Spirit.

APRIL 12, 1873. — After India's invocation to the Great Spirit, he said Maroni and John were the next to speak; when, after his usual instructions, he retired.

When Maroni was then before the council, and told them that he had wandered up and down the earth for many centuries to witness the fearful struggles for temporal power among the aspiring leaders of men, with no power to remove the cause of human suffering. No human imagination could ever realize his unhappy condition. Thirty-five hundred years ago, he was one of a tribe who then inhabited the North American continent; they had wandered away from the home of their fathers, and disannulled the covenants made with the patriarchs that taught them of a Father's home above, and went out in order to build up principalities of their own, where in their prosperity they forgot the great Ruler among the nations of the earth, and by their disregard of his just laws soon found themselves overwhelmed by a terrible destruction in the midst of their own foolish and evil devices. But time and again their descendants would forget the chastenings of their fathers, and pursue the same unwise and selfish counsels, only to be again overtaken and punished by the judgments that would follow their own evil doings. And such had been the experience and the history of his race for ages, as they had wandered up and down in spirit, suffering and sighing over their perishing and crumbling earthly principalities, which by their own disregard of the covenants of God they had entailed upon their race. But now their sighing was turned to joy, for they had found the great platform of Eternal Justice, where all could sit upon a common level and once again review their former relationship; and where each one could sit and judge himself, and not be the judge of his brother; and where no one could complain of injustice; but where justice and charity, judgment and love, would triumph over the power of darkness; where the Great Father and Creator of all, and Jesus the saviour and brother of all, would be known and acknowledged and adored by all and by every race. As he then retired, the

Apostle John was again before the council, where he made a few remarks to the assembled tribes, who had been assigned each nationality a place by themselves on the platform of justice, where for a short season they would be permitted to remain undisturbed in order to sit in judgment on themselves preparatory to their entering a higher sphere. He told them it was a glorious sight, and one they had worked long and patiently in order to accomplish, assisted and sustained in their labors by the angels of the higher spheres. He told them in the centre of the great platform were seated the prophets and seers who had been faithful in their labors for all; and there was Jesus, who in compassion for suffering humanity volunteered to lead them up to his Great Father's eternal kingdom, and who had willingly and patiently endured the terrible ordeal of the cross that He might show them his triumph over death and the tomb. " While here is the little band that He had then gathered around him, who had witnessed his terrible sufferings, as well as that of his glorious triumph, and who might now lift up their heads with joy, as every tribe and every nation gladly bowed their knees in gratitude, and acknowledged the purity of our Master's heavenly mission." He then remarked that other plans had failed to accomplish the grand work, and mankind in their mental blindness had clung to their earthly kingdom, which they had built up through avarice and human bondage, in their cruel struggle for temporal power. " But when the present council assembled in spirit, despatches were sent from sphere to sphere, and the dark sphere had been awakened from their long sufferings, and gathered together, where the result is now before you, where all are sitting upon the platform of Eternal Justice, and judging themselves as they contemplated the wonderful power and the boundless and endless love of the great Creator. And their earthly brothers have already heard the sound, and are reaching up and asking for more light in order to dispel the darkness and the doubts that surround them." After assuring them of the reality of the beautiful scene before them, he retired. And

One of the ancient Hindoos was then before the council, where he made a few remarks to his own people, and then said they had taken their place on the platform where they were preparing to go with the other tribes, and that his people would take the lead headed by their bright star spirit, who was going to show them the great Father. He said the bow-and-arrow girl was there with her race, and wouldn't speak. India closed the session by invocation to the Great Spirit.

APRIL 16, 1873. — After India's invocation to the Great Spirit, he said John would again address the assembled tribes. After which Martha would have an opportunity to speak. When, after his usual instructions and encouragements, he withdrew, and the

Apostle John was again before the council, and said he had come in order to make a few remarks to the tribes of Israel and Judah who were sitting in judgment on themselves upon the great platform of justice; and then called to their minds the terrible conditions they had left behind, which their own children had entailed from age to age down to the present time. He spoke of the present sufferings among mortals resulting from the false institutions which they themselves had sustained. He then spoke of their leaders and representatives who had been sent back to assist in breaking up the powers of darkness that cling to their earthly principalities. What if suffering and sorrow did prevail for a time? was it not that justice should again be recognized, and the spirit kingdom established where all would be taught the way from their transitory and perishable abode up to the great Father's eternal kingdom? He told them they knew well how much they had lost by their disregard of the prophets and seers which had been given to instruct them. And Jesus their Messiah they had rejected and crucified; turning again from the heavenly, they had clung to their earthly kingdoms; while the Gentiles had also rejected and cast out the Spirit, and are again crucifying the body in order to build up and strengthen their earthly power. But the time had come and the call gone forth, and all must answer, for the Book of Life was opened. "And as you go forth to do your work, see that the naked are clothed and the hungry fed from the bountiful provisions the Great Father has made for all; see that the prison-bars are broken, and that all are made free; for such has been the order. The work must be done, and but little time is given for it all to be accomplished." After a few words of encouragement, he spoke of Martha as one of the little band who had been a witness of the sufferings and persecutions of their Master, and then retired.

Martha was the next before the council, where she said she was a witness of the teachings of Jesus; and the gathering up of the nations and tribes, now having its fulfilment, was all foretold by their Master when he was with them in his physical form. Said she was one among many others that left their homes and friends in order to be near to him and listen to his heavenly teachings. He told them of his Father's eternal home, and of his mansions, and of his love for all of his earthly children; but the Jewish priesthood then in power was strong in its opposition, and treated Jesus and all that followed him with contempt. But she said he often told them the scene would be changed when he returned with all the angels to establish his Father's kingdom, for then those who rejected and cast him out would realize their loss, and repent in sorrow, and gladly receive him; when the little band who were then the chosen witnesses of his sufferings should be with him, and witness his glorious triumph over the powers of darkness; when all the nations of the earth would be gathered together in judgment. She then spoke of the success of his labors in establishing the great platform of Eternal Justice in Charity, Judgment, and Love, where all had bowed in humbleness before him, and with feelings of everlasting gratitude acknowledged the divinity of his earthly mission. She then spoke of the wrongs he patiently endured at Jerusalem; said he was pure and sympathetic by nature, and full of love and compassion for the poor and afflicted, and devoted much of his time in teaching them, as well as healing their various maladies with his wonder-healing power. He was severe in his denunciations of the Jewish Church and its false systems, which had caused much human suffering. And at the time of his crucifixion the sun was darkened, and the earth shook to its centre, and thousands who before had scoffed at and rejected him, believed and acknowledged he was their Messiah. She then spoke of their own dejected and sorrowful condition until they fully realized the glory of his triumphant resurrection, when they knew, as he often told them in spirit, they would partake of his joys. She then spoke of the many changes, and of the similar conditions by which we were now surrounded, and then retired. When —

One of the Hindoos was next before the council, and said he was permitted to come with his girl; and then he related the following story about the girl that was with him, and was to have been his wife if the gods hadn't taken her away. After she was gone, he was unhappy and wanted to go himself, when, in about three years, the gods were good, and relieved him also of his body. But he was disappointed in spirit, for his girl didn't come to him, and he didn't know where to go to find her. After many conflicts with himself, he was of the opinion she had gone, and cared no more about him. In a long time after, when overburdened with sorrow, one of his countrymen came along and asked him what was the matter, and why he was so unhappy. He thought he would keep his own secrets, so he made him an evasive answer, when his countryman looked at him sorrowfully, and after a while told him he knew what the matter was; but, as he hadn't given him a sensible reason, he disappeared. After that, he felt worse than ever, and he began to regret that he hadn't given him a civil answer, in order to have found out, if he could, what he had known; and for a long time he was left to himself, to fret over his lonely and unhappy condition. But finally the same spirit found him again, and found him willing to inquire about what he knew; and they sat down together, and had a talk. His spirit friend then told him about his girl, and asked him if he hadn't thought more of her than he did of the gods, and if that wasn't the cause of his trouble, and then told him he would take him where his girl was, if he was still anxious to see her. When he knew by his answer he wanted to go, they started, and were two days in getting to her home; and it seemed as if they were drawing near to the place where they would have to cross over the water. But it all disappeared as they entered the place, where he found his girl surrounded by a beautiful home, with everything they could desire, and she was happy to see him. And when he asked why she hadn't come to him in his sorrow, she answered by saying it wasn't proper for her to be looking for him among his male companions, who would have said she was a foolish girl, and would have taken the liberty to have made improper remarks. She told him it was proper that he should have been notified of her present home by one of his own sex. If he still loved her, now they had got everything they desired fixed up to please them, and both felt happy, it would be best for them to take hold of hands, and go and ask the Great Father if it were right that they should be united, and if he was willing for them to remain together. They both thought now there would be no objection; but should there be any, he would come and let us know. And then —

One of the Forest Maidens was next before the council. She had come to the wigwam of the white squaw to listen to the talk of the pale-faces, and she was glad to know the tribes had gathered up at the call of the Great Spirit, who had sent her race to the lower hunting-grounds once more to pitch their tents among the Great Spirit's pale-face children; and the red warriors were again on the war-path, and were looking for all who had so long dealt unjustly with their brothers. "Great Spirit say to his many red squaws in their upper hunting-grounds, Squaws, go mark the wigwam-doors of my pale-face children, who by their avarice and their injustice have disturbed the hunting-grounds with their crimes and with the cry of want and of suffering; let the red warriors know where to find them." And India again closed the session by invocation to the Great Spirit.

APRIL 20, 1873. — After India's invocation to the Great Spirit, and after giving instructions, he said Webster would first be heard, and would designate who should follow. He then withdrew.

Webster was again before the council, and said he was authorized to make a proposition to his red brothers, in order, if possible, to settle their claims for the great injustice the American people had inflicted upon them and their race. It was true the North American continent belonged to the Americans and their red brothers and their descendants, who should have lived together in peace and good fellowship, and developed the wonderful resources of the country. He also acknowledged the injustice with which they had been and were still treated by their white brothers; but he was authorized and instructed to give up the possession of the lands, if their red brothers would pay for the improvements and be satisfied; when the American representatives present acknowledged the offer to be just, and were ready to accept it.

But Metamora, who spoke for his race, said his red brothers were willing, in consideration of the spirit-knowledge imparted to all the Great Spirit's children through the assistance of their white brothers, to relinquish their claim to the land, and when justice was established with the remnant of their race on the lower hunting-grounds, they would bury the hatchet, and sit down with their white brothers near to the Great Spirit, and smoke the pipe of peace.

Webster then remarked that he had long foreseen the terrible conditions that would in the end submerge the country, and had tried, when with us in his body, to pursue a more reasonable course, in order, if possible, to avert the impending evils; but his timely efforts had been misconstrued, and himself cast out by his countrymen. Nevertheless, he still proclaimed the principle of "No north, no south, no east, no west:" and the law of Eternal Justice should be administered to all. The black man's race had enough to reach them the helping hand, but no one had spoken for his red brothers, or had given them the hand of fellowship, neither had any one. in Congress asked for justice for the red man's race. After a few pleasant words, he introduced his friend by the name of Hill, and again retired.

And one who gave the name of Hill, of New Hampshire, was next before the council, where he said he felt a just pride in having the pleasure of speaking, and he should endeavor to be brief. He then spoke of the lamentable condition the country was in, and of the burden of taxation of which the people complained, which was the natural result that flowed from avarice and injustice. He then adverted to the habits of the American people, and said they had been but poorly instructed, for they were all taught from their childhood to love and worship Mammon instead of the commandments from the Great Creator. It had been the universal practice of the parents to tie it to the necks of their children, for them to look at and handle before they had learned to talk. He thought it was nothing strange they parted with honor and everything sacred in order to obtain it. The schoolboy was told in every lesson to aspire after wealth and position by following the examples of others who in the fearful strife had attained it. Such things were wrong, and had corrupted the minds of the people until the cry of wrongs and of injustice was heard all over the land; and the people had forsaken the wise counsel and were overwhelmed by their own corruption in their struggle for wealth and power. He then said that he had been a Democrat when Democracy demanded justice for *all*. He still loved his country, and wanted it represented by men and not by the lovers of Mammon. When, after speaking of their combined and successful labors in spirit, he said he was pleased to stand with his countrymen who had rallied around the new platform of Eternal Justice, where they had renewed their covenant to labor for the emancipation of the race. He then retired.

A woman who gave the name of Bean, was the next before the council, where she said she was a native of Florence, in Italy, and was by favor permitted to speak. She gave expression to her gratitude for the opportunity, and spoke of the wonderful work already accomplished through the successful labors of those who had the work in charge. She then spoke of Israel and of Judah, with the many tribes gathered about them; and then of Egypt, and Africa, and China, with their untold numbers gathered around them, all waiting for the order to move from the one who was their leader. She then spoke of the sages who had united in the accomplishment of the great work; spoke of the one at their head with a red signet that united him with the Great Father, as an evidence that they had triumphed over the powers of darkness; and through Justice and Charity, Judgment and Love, the kingdom would be established with mortals. She again gave evidence of her gratitude, and then retired.

And one of the Hindoos was next before the council, where he expressed his gratification, and said his folks were going to have a place by themselves, and they were making arrangements about how nice they would have it prepared. He thought it should be a grand chair, with a canopy over it, for the Great Father to occupy when he came to see them. The great star-spirit had told them they were all the children of the Great Father; and now they were anxious to go where they could see him, and know they could all be his children and be nearer to him.

After which India, as usual, again closed the session by invocation to the Great Spirit.

APRIL 23, 1873.—After India's invocation to the Great Spirit, he said Washington was present in order to speak; that Arnold would be the next one heard, and would state who was to follow. When, after again expressing his thanks for what had already been accomplished, he retired.

And Washington was again before the council, where he remarked that it was with feelings of more than common gratitude in which he availed himself of the present opportunity in order to say a few words in the presence of the former representatives of his country, who had gathered around the great platform of Justice. He had long reflected on the present degenerate condition of the people of the beautiful country of which he had been called the "father," and he was pleased to see around him again good and true men — the men who stood firm in the day of trial, and defended their country from the aggressions of foreign despots and taskmasters that their children might inherit the greatest of all blessings — freedom. He then thanked the Great Father of all that they had been permitted to realize in what had been their country's failure; and as they united in their labors in building up their new America in spirit, it was founded on the imperishable foundation of "eternal justice for all." He then told them that what they had to do in order to rectify their former mistakes should be done, and that, too, without unnecessary delay. They all knew that chastening was sent in mercy that a great good might have its birth among mortals. After saying that Arnold, who had been put upon the record as a traitor to his country, had sought for a time to say a few words in his own behalf, and as it was unnecessary that he should prolong his own remarks, he would give way. And —

Arnold was the next before the council, where he said it was with feelings of everlasting gratitude he accepted of the great favor awarded to him in order to speak of his own misfortunes before his countrymen, who had rallied around the new platform of Eternal Justice, where he desired to say a few words in his own behalf, for he, too, had been a victim of false education. He was taught in his youth to worship the Mammon of the world, and in the day of his trial, with his human weakness he had bowed like others to the gods of the earth. He then said that with his love for money he had acquired the pernicious habit of gambling, and often resorted to it with a desire to strengthen his fortunes in order to command respect. He said it was true he was found wanting in the hour of his trial, and had been arraigned time and again by his country, who had called him a traitor. And he would say now, if the elements were in his nature, that his Creator had used him for a warning to others that the principles of human freedom might be the firmer established among his countrymen. Unfortunately for him, his propensity for gambling was strong, and he gratified it with those who sought the destruction of his country's freedom; and at the time of his fall he followed the fortunes of those who had put the temptation before him, and who treated him as a companion as long as his money lasted; but when that was gone, he was left to reflect upon the terrible disgrace he in a day of trial by his own weakness foolishly fastened to his name. And none but his Creator could ever know the extent of his sufferings and of his fearful humiliation in having to flee from his comrades that he should have protected with his life in the hour of danger. And though he failed and fled in the hour of his trial, he would now ask what those who remained had got to boast of, for it was well known all their institutions were a failure. Notwithstanding he had been held up as a warning for the benefit of others; every "department" now was full of traitors, while avarice and injustice, with crime and human suffering, were daily increasing in every town. They had failed to build on a sound foundation, and they too were now humiliated and mortified by seeing all their boasted institutions fast fading away.

He then said he would willingly return with others, and assist in the work of establishing the foundations on the solid and substantial platform of Eternal Justice for all; and when that was accomplished, and not till then, they might ask to be forgiven. When, after once more expressing his gratitude for the opportunity of saying what he had, he remarked that a tried and faithful armor-bearer was then waiting to speak, and he would retire. When the —

Baron Lafayette was the next before the council, where in beautiful language he portrayed the grandeur of the expansion of the individualized spirit as it unfolded in the sphere above, and was conscious of meeting again, face to face, with the loved ones it mingled with during its earthly pilgrimage. He then spoke to Washington in regard to the glorious destiny of his country; said it had been shown to him when they were struggling together in order to free it from the grasp of foreign taskmasters. He was then shown that it would be the country where the angel world would reveal themselves to mortals. He told him it was under the forest-trees, where he so often knelt down in supplication to his heavenly Father for blessings for his earthly children that were then struggling for the priceless boon of freedom. And as he was again permitted to meet with them as they had gathered together on the great platform of Eternal Justice, to renew their covenant with Charity and Judgment and Love combined, they would complete the work. He then told them of what he was shown when they were struggling for their country's freedom. He said he had retired to the favorite tree to meditate on what then seemed to be their apparent helpless condition, and he saw the heavens above him opened and the angels were gathering together, when he heard a great noise as it were "the rushing of the mighty waters," and was told it was the gathering in of the peoples and nations of the earth, who had been called up by the angel of time to answer to their names recorded in the book of life. And what he was then shown, which had seemed like a vision, was now having its fulfilment. He then told Washington that he himself must have had visions of his country's coming glory, for he had often made remarks which have since proved to have been prophetic. And now they all had a realizing sense of the scenes of the past in what they could behold around them; and they should be thankful to know they had a part in the great drama that was gathering the nations of the earth together where one language and one spirit were uniting all the Great Father's children; so let those who have been assigned to labor with mortals persevere in their work until the law of justice is established, and then Charity and Love will reign triumphant over the beautiful plains of earth as they now do in the spheres above. After speaking of the great pleasure the present interview had given to him, he retired.

One of the Hindoos was the next in council, and again told of his own people's pleasure in what they were hearing from others; and the star-spirit had been teaching them that all nations were the children of the Great Father, who was their Creator; and as they progressed into a higher knowledge of his mighty works, they would understand that all were brothers, and the discordant elements in their natures would disappear when they would stop their wrangling with each other and live as brothers should live together in peace. The bow-and-arrow girl had said that in two moons they would all move up nearer to the great Spirit-Father; and when they found out more about him, one of their people would come and let us know.

One of the Forest Maidens was next in council, where she said she had come to the light where the camp-fire was kept burning, where she had listened to the talk of the pale-face braves; and she was glad to hear them acknowledge the power of the Great Spirit, who had sent out his red warriors to find out the trail of his pale-face children that so long had disregarded the Great Spirit's law of justice. She then spoke to Israel and to Judah, with their many tribes they had gathered together, and were anxiously waiting for the promised land they had wandered far from during their long pilgrimage on the lower hunting-grounds, where they cast out the spirit and turned away from the One who had told them his Father's eternal kingdom with its many mansions was above their trifling, perishable, earthly principalities. After which once more India closed the session by invocation to the Great Spirit.

APRIL 27, 1873. — After India's invocation to the Great Spirit, he mentioned the names of Bennett and Greeley, and of Webster and Choate, who were present in order to speak at the present session; and after a few cheerful remarks he withdrew.

Bennett was then before the council, and remarked that he was gratified to have an opportunity to speak in the presence of so many of his old friends who had gathered around the great platform of Eternal Justice. He acknowledged he had been short-sighted and strongly prejudiced in his opinions during his earthly temptations; and he had advanced the interest of men as well as of measures not calculated to enhance the public good. And, so far as he himself and his paper with its influence were concerned, he was willing to return and labor with mortals until the effects of his own errors which he had so willingly made public were, if possible, removed from the minds of his countrymen. What if it did disturb the business affairs of their friends? They all knew its object was to promote the general good. And the work must be done. And, so far as he himself was concerned, he desired to make a specialty of the terrible crime of adulterating and poisoning the wines and other liquors used as a beverage and for medicinal purposes by all nations. He wanted those who had reflected upon the evil to join in the work, and they would stir up the minds of mortals until the great crime was better understood and abolished. All knew of the terrible sufferings of the confirmed inebriate, and they knew that wines and other spirits, when pure and properly used, were no injury to the health or the public good, but were useful and should be protected. He knew, and his friend Greeley well knew, the amount of crime and suffering propagated among mortals by the deception and the false statements of those who adulterate and control the markets; and they had both failed to speak, when they had control of the press, on account of the wealth and power of those engaged in the traffic. But now they knew of the evil and its fearful consequences, and had no excuse, and he should never be satisfied until the crime was forever abolished. He would leave the subject before the platform for further consideration, hoping that others would realize the need of some change. He regretted that a subject of so much importance had not received his attention during his earthly pilgrimage. But so far as he himself with his press had failed, he desired, where it was possible, that he might be forgiven. He expressed his pleasure for the present interview, said his friend was waiting to speak, and he would retire.

And then Greeley was again before the council, where he remarked, it was true they could see the results of their errors and would gladly unite with others in the work of eradicating their unfortunate effects among mortals. And he was glad to be united with those in spirit willing to engage in so good a cause, where, if he had failed to be president of his country, he was satisfied he was now in a position where he could do his country more good, and as he had been somewhat identified with the farmers, he should continue to advocate their rights until they were strong enough to stand up and protect themselves. It was their industry that created a large portion of their country's wealth, as well as the food for its inhabitants, and it was their right to make and execute the laws that controlled it. He said it was well known that politicians, with other non-producing classes, were not wanted in the commercial centres, and the time had arrived when they must find homes on the public domain, where by their own industry they could soon learn to procure an honest and more independent living. He had made up his mind to stand by the farmers of his country, and hereafter it should be his pleasure to protect and advocate their rights, and all who would, could have the pleasure of going with him. When, after a few pleasant remarks connected with local affairs, he gave place to his friend, who had been a farmer.

And Webster was next before the council, where he spoke of the changes that had been introduced among the people since his own pilgrimage among mortals. Then the farmer was considered the main support of the country. The towns and cities were small, and all the people had some kind of honest employment. Every family had its garden, with a cow and pig to look after, and the people were then uncorrupted and contented and happy. But now, he said, how sad the change! Avarice and pride with their demoralizing effects had already corrupted every department of trust, and nothing but the chastening power of the great Ruler among the nations could ever bring the people to a realizing sense of their fallen condition. He had found the farm during his own experience the safest place to protect and secure the happiness of himself and family, and he should go with his friends and stand by the farmer. After expressing his thanks, he retired; and then —

Choate was the next before the council, where, after expressing his gratification for the present opportunity of meeting with his old friends who were again prepared to renew their labors, he said he had decided to go with his brother Bennett and defend the people by exposing the curse entailed upon them and their children from the adulteration and the poisonous mixtures with which corrupt and unprincipled men have supplied the markets. He said the prohibitory question had been, and was still, agitated until the country, to the shame of humanity, was overrun with inebriates. The excitement had foolishly been prolonged until the schoolboys were affected by the contagion and had gone to drinking the poison and destructive imitations with which every market was readily supplied, and had become drunkards before they arrived to manhood. Such unjust abominations were wrong; and all knew who had sanctioned the new covenant, such things were not tolerated by the great law of Eternal Justice. When, after a few encouraging remarks in connection with their labors, he retired.

One of the Hindoos was the next before the council, where he made a few remarks concerning his own people; said they were pleased with the privileges which they had enjoyed, and were making rapid progress, and were anxious to learn all they could. He then spoke of the ancient tribes that were still gathering in, which none of his people had ever known or heard of before. He said they looked to be very old, and were creating great curiosity among the other tribes. He then spoke of one of the bow-and-arrow girls, who worshipped the Great Spirit, who was waiting to speak; and he would retire, and the next time another one of his people would tell us of how fast they were learning from the teaching of their great star-spirit.

One of the Forest Maidens was next before the council,

where she had come to listen to the talk of the braves, and tell them by the command of the Great Spirit of the much suffering of his pale-face children all over the lower hunting-grounds, where the tyranny and oppression, and the great wrongs of those in command, had reached the sphere of the Great Spirit, who had said to his red warriors, "What means this cry of sorrow? prepare for the war-path;" and who said to his red squaws, "Go mark the wigwam-doors where the cry of suffering is heard on the lower hunting-grounds." And she came to the wigwam of the white squaw, where the council-fire was bright, and had listened to the much talk of the white braves, who had told of the many wrongs of their pale-face brothers; and she would away and tell the Great Spirit of the work of his pale-face children. After which India closed the session by invocation to the Great Spirit.

APRIL 20, 1873.— After India's invocation to the Great Spirit, once more acknowledging their dependence, he said Red Jacket and Tecumseh were present, and would next be heard; and then retired.

Red Jacket was next before the council, and again spoke in behalf of his race. He told them to go with him to the far western mountains, and see their hiding-places, where they had been compelled to skulk away to avoid the tyranny and oppression of their white brothers, who with authority had driven them from their hunting-grounds and their fishing-streams, by the Great Spirit given, away into the cold and barren mountains. The avarice of their white brothers had taken all, and nothing was left the descendants of the red man but starvation and death. O, you need not point to your scarless veteran, who, you say, was sent here by the treachery of the red man. The Great Spirit can show a thousand to your one who have been sent here by the deceit and the treachery of the pale-faces, who are now telegraphing from city to city, and making preparations for exterminating the last remnant of the red man's race from the hunting-grounds where the bones of their forefathers have been desecrated by the avarice and the many evils of their pale-face brothers. Red Jacket and his red brothers have worked with you here, and they have worked with your media on the lower hunting-grounds of the red man, in order to build up your great platform of Justice; but Red Jacket can't sit down with you here until justice is extended to the balance of the red man's race on the lower hunting-grounds. So you must see to it, and remember that Red Jacket and his braves are again on the war-path. They had dug up the tomahawks once more, and if the balance of their race must be exterminated through the covetousness and the injustice of their pale-face brothers, every town and every city on the lower hunting-grounds of the red man shall waste away like the burning flax in the mighty winds of the Great Spirit. When, after a few words of instruction to his warriors, he retired.

The old chief Tecumseh was next in the council, where he said that justice must be established on the lower hunting-grounds, if it had to be done through suffering; for all the rights of the red man's race had been disregarded by their white brothers. They had driven them from their forests and from their beautiful lakes where game and fish were always bountifully provided by the Great Spirit for the subsistence of his red children. It was known that the many crimes of demoralized pale-faces had time and again been charged to the race of the red man, and his squaws and their children were driven from their homes, and were dying daily of starvation, authorized and sanctioned by the white man's government. Such inhumanity could no longer be endured; the camp-fires would be put out, and their pale-face brothers would be made to feel in their own homes the many wrongs which they had inflicted on the race of the red man, and they would learn that the Great Spirit had not forgotten his great law of Eternal Justice. Before another moon the red man's race would be on the war-path. He again referred to the terrible sufferings of his race, who had been hunted down like the wild beast of the forest to satisfy the avarice of the white man, and retired.

A Modoc squaw, with her pappoose and others of her tribe, was next presented to the council, where she said four moons past, when the Great Spirit's white blanket covered the hunting-grounds, they were driven away from their camp-fires by the pale-face soldiers. They had no blankets and no fire to make warm, so they all sung the death-march; and the Great Spirit took them home to his upper hunting-grounds. She said they suffer much with cold and with hunger; but the pappoose no cry for fear the pale-face find them. And the Great Spirit was good. He sent them in a vision, and made them warm, and they all wake up in the upper hunting-grounds, and find everything necessary to make them comfortable and happy. She then told of her brave, who was among the red warriors on the lower hunting-grounds, where she had been every day in order to see him, where he was driven by the pale-face soldiers, and had no much to eat. That very day she had seen him eat the bark of a tree to appease his hunger. She was shown that in four moons her brave would come to her and their pappooses; and she would have a couch prepared for him, and would make him happy. She then told them the pale-faces were no much good to her people; they no let them fish and hunt where the Great Spirit gave them fish and game for the red man's squaw and pappoose; and white man no give Indian much for his furs. Indian no have much to eat, no have much blanket to keep warm. Squaw go naked, pappoose cry for bread; red braves get angry, say paleface thief no good on the red man's hunting-grounds. She then, after answering a few questions to those who had gathered about her, told them to go to their countrymen on the lower hunting-grounds of the Great Spirit, and teach them of the great wrongs their race were inflicting on the children of the red man, driving them away from their beautiful foresthomes. As she then retired —

A woman introduced herself to the council by the name of —— Gray; said she was a former resident of Boston, and had been in spirit-life about seventy years; and she regretted to know our country had made such havoc of their glorious opportunities; but now the cup of their iniquity was full, for the time had come when they must reap the reward of their evil doings. She was a witness the statement of the children of the red man of the forest concerning many and terrible wrongs was true. She said their interests had been shamefully neglected by the people's representatives, while bad men, instigated by their covetousness, had robbed them of every right, and coarse and brutal soldiers in the government employ were still hunting them down and driving them from their forest-homes like the wild beasts of prey. The suffering the representatives of the people, by their disregard of the great laws of justice, had, from time to time, entailed upon the wards of the nation, was fearful to contemplate; but God was just, and his law of compensation was doing its work, and the powers of darkness would give way before it. She was pleased with her opportunity to make a few remarks; and said those of her sex who had been engaged in the good work of building up the great platform desired to be remembered; and as she then retired, one of—

The confiding Hindoos was next before the council, and told how finely they were getting along. Said the great star-spirit had given them the box which had formerly been intrusted to the other tribes. He described its appearance, said it had handles, and was carried by four men. It had been in Egypt and in Arabia, and was known by all the ancient tribes. His people did not know what was in it, for they had not looked; but they had dressed it up in beautiful external apparel, and had a gold cloth to cover it; and the star-spirit had told them, when they all started to go to the Great Father, his people should take the lead and carry the box in front of the other tribes.

One of the Forest Maidens was next in council. She had come from the upper hunting-grounds to the council of the old braves, where the red warriors had gathered, and asked that justice should be extended to the balance of their race, where the cry of their many wrongs has gone up to the sphere of the Great Spirit, who has seen with his great Eye the many sorrows his red children have had to endure from the avarice of their white brothers, who have built their wigwams high, and want much wampum. White man's storehouse large and full of the good things the Great Spirit give for his earthly children. White man have all; red man nothing. Great Spirit send white blanket to cover the lower hunting-grounds; white man stain it with the blood of the Great Spirit's red children. Squaw and pappoose come to the Great Spirit with no blanket, with no bread, with no fire to make warm. Great Spirit call all his red warriors, and say, "Quick, go find the pale-faces that make such work as this, and fetch them up here." You see where they can stand by the platform of Eternal Justice, and learn more about the Great Spirit's children on the lower hunting-grounds that were once covered with the numerous race of the red man.

India closed the services by invocation to the Great Spirit.

MAY 4, 1873.—After India's invocation to the Great Spirit, he spoke of the prevailing habits and customs of the present inhabitants, who, in their thirst for the Mammon of the earth, had ransacked the continent, cut down the forests, and dug up the soil in search of hidden treasures, regardless of the rights of the red man's race, until their wrongs had reached the throne of Justice; and the Great Spirit had opened the book of life, and was calling the nations to judgment. He then remarked that Parker was present, and would be the first to speak, after which Pierpont would follow. He then withdrew.

Parker was again heard in the council, and said he had come with his friend, who had been relieved from his labors in connection with the Banner, where he had been faithful in the work of establishing the truth of the communion of spirit with mortals. And he felt a pride in having the privilege of introducing his brother to his friends and coworkers on the great platform of justice, where he would receive the hand of fellowship, and hear the welcome benediction of "Well done; for you have been true and faithful to your trust, and can pass higher, and enjoy the fruits of your earthly labors; for the dark pall that has covered the sphere has floated back, and here justice has been established, and here the tribes and nations of the earth have gathered together, where each claims its own. No wonder, brother, you shrink back in astonishment at the magnitude of the work accomplished. But as you gain in strength, more light will be given to you, that you may penetrate and partake of the glory and of the grandeur and beauty of the scenes, as the mysteries, one by one, will disappear above the darkened sphere of earth." He then introduced his friend and brother, by the name of White, as one who devoted his time and means in order to advance the work of restitution. And after a few words of encouragement as usual, he retired.

Pierpont was then again before the council, where he expressed his pleasure in meeting his brother White, where they could show him what had been so successfully accomplished in spirit, while he had faithfully battled for the truth among the bigots and scoffers of earth. He told him the dark sphere in spirit had been removed, and a platform of justice established by the assistance of two who had retired where order prevailed, and had patiently sat with them, night after night, and year after year, until the work was finished. Here you will see schools have been established where the lost and forsaken ones of earth have been gathered up from the dark sphere and instructed in the duties of life, and told of their eternal home, and who are now laboring to ameliorate the condition of others. And here you will see that all nations have answered to the call of the angel of time, and each one has taken its place in its own order, as their names were called from the book of life. And here are those who have now come to thank you for your labors in their behalf, and as you grow stronger from the sympathy and the love of those who will gather around, you will soon be able to comprehend more of the endless and boundless works of the great Creator; and as the evening has been devoted to the pleasure of giving you an introduction to others engaged with you in your earthly labors, here you will find many who are now prepared to greet you. After speaking of their amazement at the grandeur of the scenes they had witnessed, he expressed his thanks for the privilege of being present, and retired.

One of the chiefs associated with the band of spirits who held communion at the Banner office was the next in council; and said he had come with his tribe to give his white brother a welcome to the upper hunting-grounds of the Great Spirit. He knew the brave had been good to the red man's race on the lower hunting-grounds, and he would take him to their upper hunting-grounds, and give him strength, and then he would see and comprehend more of the grand works of the Great Spirit.

After which, an Irishman was next in council. Said he had come, with many others, in order to acknowledge their gratitude to their friend for the knowledge of the communion of spirit imparted to them and to many of their countrymen through his faithful labors. He had broken the shackles of error and superstition, and helped light up "the purgatory" that held them in bondage. And as they drew nearer to the blessed Jesus, "their Lord and Master," they felt grateful to their brother for his labors in their behalf.

One of the Hindoos was the next in council, where he said he could show the man what had been done for his people, and how they had been told about the great Father, and had given up worshipping their earthly idols, for they had found a speaking god. And the great star-spirit, which their Koran had told of, had been with them to instruct them about the Father, and had given them a box to have in their possession, and had told them when they went to the Great Father, the Hindoos should take the lead of all the nations and tribes, and carry the box at the head of all the great, grand army. He told him they had been back to their people and showed them the star-spirit that would take them away from their idols; and then told him they had discovered that the people where he had come from had their earthly gods that were fond of gold. It seemed as though it had always been that way with their own gods. And when there was a storm or an epidemic among the people, the gods were sure to be poor. And then those fellows that had them in charge told the people the gods were angry, and must have more of their gold and silver. And it often took all they could get to keep them satisfied. Well, here are more of your friends waiting to speak with you; and here is the bow-and-arrow girl with all of her tribes, and he would have to go. After saying " Good by, mister man; when you have more time, we will show all the nice things sent to us by the Great Father," he retired.

One of the Forest Maidens was next in council, where she had come from the upper hunting-grounds, and told them the Great Spirit was ever near his children who worked in order to establish his great law of Eternal Justice. She then said the white brave who had been shown the platform where his friends had gathered in council was well known, and she had brought him a commission from the Great Spirit, that would authorize him to return to the lower hunting-grounds with authority to renew his labors, and complete the work of establishing Justice and Charity, Judgment and Love. Then all would know the Great Spirit, and be contented and satisfied, and cultivate the beautiful lower hunting-grounds of the Great Spirit, and partake of his daily blessings. And then again, as usual, India closed the session by invocation to the Great Spirit.

MAY 7, 1873. — After India's invocation to the Great Spirit, he said, owing to unfavorable weather, the session would be short, and occupied by the women; and, as he retired, —

Mrs. Townsend was the first in council, where she gave a statement of the surprise and the joy they had experienced in seeing the ancient tribes gathering together. She said it was the consummation of a glorious work which they had not anticipated. She spoke of the old folks and their happiness in their new apartments. She spoke of the children, and of their schools, and of their progress, and of the great pleasure all enjoyed who had a part in the accomplishing of the work. When, after her usual encouragement in connection with their labors, she said her sister Fuller was also present, and anxious to make a few remarks. After again expressing her gratitude, she retired.

Margaret Fuller was the next in council, where she remarked that although they were present at every session, it was pleasant to have an opportunity to speak, and said they were more than thankful for the varied scenes they had been permitted to witness, by the gathering in of the nations and tribes, each in their own order, where many things that were written but not understood had been represented to the satisfaction of all. Said no language could ever portray the grandeur of the wonderful scenes to mortals. She then spoke of her friends Mrs. Greeley and her husband ; also of Mr. White, recently of the " Banner," and said they were greatly astonished to see what had been accomplished, and were anxious to convey a knowledge of the scenes they were permitted to see back to their earthly friends; said the time was fast approaching when there would be an inquiry and a demand for such information by many who had turned a deaf ear to the voice of the Spirit among mortals; for all things in spirit were now working together in order that it may soon be accomplished. She then expressed her gratitude for the privilege of being one of the many engaged in the work, and said one of the old mothers was anxious to say a few words, and she would retire.

One of the old folks was the next in council, where she said her name was Wright, and her husband's name was George, and that they were natives of New Hampshire. She then told of the happiness of the old people in their new apartments, where they were forming a new acquaintance, and telling of the many incidents which happened in their youthful days, and where the children from the schools now often came among them and read selections from the books given them to study, which embodied the experience of the teachers of other planets, which had proved to be very interesting to the old people. She spoke of the old ladies who had an opportunity of speaking, and said they sent their regards, and were anxious to be remembered, for we could never realize the change in their condition, or tell how lonely they had been when no one had taken interest in their welfare. After expressing her gratitude for what had been done, she said her George had come with her and was waiting, and she would retire.

One of the confiding Hindoos was next in council, and he said they were getting everything fixed up in splendid order, and more things had been given to them that belonged to the box which the star-spirit had given to them. And there was a book "and a crook," with a compass and a square, with four dresses, which had belonged to the box. And there was to be an investigation, to know why the symbols had been desecrated, and why the knowledge they were intended to convey to the people had been neglected and lost. He said all the tribes who had had the box and symbols in their possession were cited to appear with their witnesses, and be ready to answer for themselves. They were told the book contained information in regard to their spirit-home, which was given when the covenant was made, and should have been taught to the people, and he guessed the Great Father was going to find out why it hadn't been done. He then said the girls with the bow and arrows, who told about the Great Spirit, were all busy looking after and assisting in the arrangement of the other tribes, and would speak through their goddess some other time. He then retired. And India closed the session by invocation to the Great Spirit, once more asking for strength to accomplish their labors.

MAY 11, 1873. — After India's invocation, he said it was arranged for the purpose of giving Ames, and Brooks, and Chase an opportunity to speak. He said it was also now in order for each nationality to make provision for their own people around the platform, and that Pilate would speak first in behalf of the Jews, after which the others would have an opportunity to speak. He then retired.

Pilate was again before the council, and said he felt a pride as well as a pleasure in being called to represent those with whom he mingled during his earthly trials. He told them to put aside all doubts and fears of the past, and enter into a fullness of the spirit-blessings again offered to them; for it was true Jesus of Nazareth, whom they rejected and cruelly crucified, was their true Messiah, who had come again, and had opened the way that would lead them up to his Father's kingdom. He warned them not to be left behind the second time; but let all the fair daughters, with the wandering fathers and sons of Israel and of Judah, tune up their harps and be prepared to join the innumerable hosts, as tribe after tribe are called, and again take their place in their march for the promised land. After speaking of their own loss in rejecting their promised Shiloh, and of their national destruction which followed, with their doubts and fears and their many sorrows in spirit, waiting for the fullness of time when He would again return with power to establish his spirit-kingdom, he said the time had come, and they had all bowed in gratitude, and had acknowledged the magnitude and the wisdom and the triumphant success of the humble Nazarene's " glorious mission." The time had come when the principalities and powers of the earth would again be shaken; and he thought their own blindness and suffering, with their national destruction, should be a sufficient warning to others not to disregard the voice of the ever-living Spirit, and then be rejected and go, as they did, blind and headlong into darkness, with sorrow and national destruction, and no one to lead or relieve them. He once more spoke of his gratitude for the present interview, and retired.

After which Chase was before the council, and told of his surprise in finding himself in spirit surrounded by so many of his old friends, and many he had once thought to be his enemies. It was now beyond his comprehension. And there was Brooks, and there was Ames, who had been hunted through their last session at Washington by a nest of vipers in human form, who were ever ready to sting with their poison venom those whom they could not control. He then spoke of his own condition. He had entered the spirit sphere with no preparation, naked and helpless, without knowledge of where he was going; and if it had not been for the friends who had come to his rescue, he knew nothing of what would have been his condition. He thought it was strange so much had been accomplished, and nothing said about it among mortals. The opportunity given him in order to speak had increased his strength and renewed his faith, and he should ever feel grateful; but the grandeur of the scenes in spirit was more than he could realize, for it still seemed to him like a vision. But as their time was necessarily limited, he must give place for his friend.

Ames was the next in council. He confirmed what his friend Chase had said, for it was true all three of them had been called up in the presence of a large assembly; but whether it was in order for a final settlement of the Credit Mobilier, or for something else, he could not say. But it was true he had showed them up at Washington, and made an *exposé* that was evidently needed for the good of his country, and for which he had nothing to regret, but was glad the duty had seemingly fallen to his lot. He then spoke of their reception in spirit, and said as yet it was entirely beyond their comprehension, for it was unexpected, and something for which he had made no provision. But the old and true patriarchs of their country had met them and given them a cordial reception;

and, so far as he himself was concerned, he was truly happy to realize he had made the change, and he was ready to engage in any enterprise calculated to benefit humanity. He was pleased with his opportunity to speak, and desired to communicate again, after he had had more time in order to look about and become more familiar with his change. When, after expressing gratitude, he retired.

Brooks was the next before the council, and made a few remarks. He thought it was unaccountable, for he could not comprehend the wonderful change through which he had passed; but stated that when he first awaked to consciousness he was alone, and he looked about himself and tried to realize his situation, when the thoughts that had been the last were the first to make their appearance, and as he was sitting in what seemed like reflection, he heard a voice say, " Brooks, didn't you do the best you could, under the circumstances by which you were surrounded?" and he answered, "Yes, he thought he had, for he couldn't see that he could have done any different;" when gradually the mist that had surrounded him seemed to disappear, and he could see the shadows of forms as they appeared in the distance, evidently moving towards him; and soon the charm was broken, and the "mystery of mysteries" solved, for he was greeted by his friend who had been dear to him, and who he knew had long since passed beyond the transitory things of time. He then expressed his thanks for the unfolding of another mystery, in the great privilege he had been permitted to enjoy by speaking through the vocal organs of an earthly form. He then retired.

One of the faithful Hindoos was the next in council. He told of the progress of his people; they were gaining fast, for the star-spirit had been with them again, and had told them more about the Great Father; and they were getting anxious to go and see him. He then told of many things in connection with their present arrangements in spirit, and said the men that spoke last were as much amazed as his people were when they found the great star-spirit.

India again closed the session by invocation to the Great Spirit.

MAY 16, 1873. — After India's invocation to the Great Spirit, he spoke of the return of another birthday of their media, and again thanked the Great Spirit for the wisdom and strength which had sustained them the past year, and for all that had been accomplished. He then stated the programme for the present session; said the relatives by family ties, as well as all in spirit who had been enlightened and benefited by the labors of the band, would form on the inner circle in spirit, and all others would then form as by order of creation, each nationality by themselves; and then a brother of their media, who stood next by birth, but was removed from the scenes of earthly life during his infancy, would speak first; after which Miss Landon, one of the teachers in the children paradise, would be present with the children as they passed into the new temple and under an archway of beautiful flowers, while in the temple would be found everything the planet has thus far produced for the children's inspection. Said they were still called children, for they had entered their paradise during infancy, and had retained their confidence and purity. And then, as all were waiting, he retired.

The brother referred to above was then before the council, where he spoke of the beauty of their home in a higher sphere, where kind teachers had always been near in order to cultivate their minds and explain the mysteries of the wonderful things developing in the Great Father's kingdom; spoke of their pleasure of being present where they could witness the gathering together of the nations, and tribes, and families of the earth. He said the changing scenes produced by the labors of the band had given a pleasure never anticipated; spoke of his pride in having the privilege of speaking through the earthly organism of his sister in the presence of his own companions, and said they had brought many flowers, which they had been taught to cultivate in their spirit gardens in order to commemorate the return of his earthly sister's birthday. He then spoke of their happiness, as they had often been permitted to meet and mingle and scatter their flowers among the old and weary ones that were coming up, in order to cheer them on the way; and after speaking of the kindness and the love of their teachers and guides, he left his love for his sister and earthly friends, and then gave way for another.

Miss Landon was again before the council, where she was evidently much affected by the magnitude of the scenes around her. She first spoke of the vast numbers of children who had been cultivated and instructed in the paradise of the Great Father's love, and of the great pleasure they enjoyed in meeting and mingling with their friends, and scattering their beautiful flowers among the weary and tired ones who had long wandered in the sphere of earth. She then spoke of the labors of the band, and of the great interest presented in the changing scenes during the past few months; and as they had witnessed the gathering in of the vast nations and tribes who had inhabited the earth, and had listened to their wonderful accounts, they could only marvel at the continued evidence of the magnitude of the mighty works of the great Creator. She then appealed in beautiful language to the different nationalities of both color and condition who were gathered together in spirit around the great platform of Eternal Justice, where one spirit and one language had taught them they were all the Great Father's children. She then asked them if it was possible to ever realize the debt of gratitude they owed the One who had been their saviour. And after giving expression to her own grateful feelings, said some of her school-children who were relatives of her earthly sister were anxious to say a few words on the return of the birthday; and after desiring that she herself might be remembered, she retired.

And Alwyn, and Anna, and Frank, and Fanny, each one in their turn had the pleasure of making a few appropriate remarks on the event of another birthday.

Another relative from the same school, by the name of Ella, said she had come with the others, and all had fetched substantial tokens of their love from their own handiwork to commemorate the event that would be laid up in the new temple which they now had the pleasure of passing through to await the new birth into the kingdom which they had patiently helped to establish. She then spoke of their happiness, and said the children from their schools were distributing their flowers among the old people, who seemed to grow younger as they enjoyed the sport. And as she retired, one of the —

Forest Maidens was then in council, and said she had come with her race, who were sitting in their canoes listening to what the pale-faces had to say. She then spoke of the mighty host who had assembled together as an evidence of the power of the Great Spirit. But her people had put out the camp-fires, and were sitting in sorrow for the injustice the balance of their race had to endure, which the Great Spirit had permitted to remain on the lower hunting-grounds. Her people were many in numbers, and they had many complaints to make of the great wrongs of their pale-face brothers, and they had gathered up in council, and put aside the pipe of peace, and were sitting together with their blankets over their heads, asking the Great Spirit for justice for the remnant of the red man's race.

One of the Hindoos was the next in council, and told of the progress of his own people since they had found out the Great Father was a spirit; and he thought they were about ready to make a move in order to get nearer to him. The star-spirit had been teaching them many things that were interesting, and they were all anxious and willing to learn. He then said the bow-and-arrow girl would not speak, for they had put out their lights and gone out; but he couldn't tell where they had gone, unless it was to look after their pale-face brothers.

And India closed the session by invocation to the Great Spirit.

MAY 18, 1873. — After India's invocation to the Great Spirit, he said Scott, and Prescott, and Cooper were the ones designated in order to speak at the present interview; and after a few remarks in connection with their labors, he retired.

Scott was again before the council, where he spoke of the injustice the race of the red man had had to endure, as well as those still remaining in the western mountains, where they were driven by the avarice of the land-sharks, whose aggressions had caused much of the trouble of which his red brothers had complained. He said the government hirelings had been sent among them, and they were shot down in their defenceless condition like the beasts of the forest, until all they had not killed had been driven from their homes to suffer. He wanted it proclaimed by those in council on the new platform that the rights of his red brothers must be protected; and if the policy of extermination is still pursued, let it cost enough in order to be a warning to other nations and peoples not to disregard the great law of Eternal Justice. He spoke in cheering terms of the progress of the work, and said the boys who had rallied around their new standard would see that it was not disgraced. After speaking of the pleasure they experienced from witnessing the varied scenes among the gathering tribes, he retired.

Prescott was the next in council. He told of the pleasure it afforded him to be remembered by his countrymen who had assembled on the broad platform of justice, around which the nations of the earth were gathering. He thought it a great privilege to have an opportunity to speak through an earthly form to those still wandering on the shores of time, and encouraged his friends in their work. He loved the law of justice, and would do what he could in order to have it successfully acknowledged among those they had left behind. Said he was afflicted, when in his earthly form, by the early loss of his sight; but he found by persevering he had made the ear do the work of the eye, and had given his thoughts through the pen, and left in book-form much that was valuable to his countrymen. And he would volunteer to go with others and assist in the work to enforce the law of Justice, with Charity and Judgment, until the law of Love became universal. When, after a few pleasant remarks for the encouragement of all in their work, he said he was formerly a resident of the historical town of Salem, Massachusetts, and knew something of the mystery that had formerly been connected with the communion of spirits; and as he retired —

Cooper was then in council, where he said he had devoted his time to a search after knowledge, and had been the author of a number of books during his earthly trials; and he was also pleased with an opportunity of meeting with so many of his old friends among his countrymen who had assembled around a platform where justice had been established in spirit, and he was ready to assist in its enforcement among the inhabitants of the earth; and he was truly sorry, so far as his own country was concerned, that it had been so long disregarded. He felt grateful for the opportunity of again using the vocal organs of an earthly tabernacle, and would cheerfully engage in the work for the amelioration and the elevation of mortals who were looking for, and anxiously asking for, knowledge.

McCarty was the next in council, and said he had been permitted to come in order to speak a few words in behalf of the people of his own country. And he then urged his countrymen to persevere in the enforcement of the great law of Justice which he said had, as a recognized principle, too long been disregarded among the inhabitants of the earth. He entreated his people, by the love they had for the blessed Jesus, who had died for them on the cross in order to lead them to his heavenly kingdom, to press on, be faithful in their work, and never tire until the principalities and the powers with their earthly kingdoms gave way for their Master's heavenly kingdom. Then would Justice have a place among mortals, and Charity, with Judgment and Love, do its work.

After expressing his thanks for the great privilege extended to his countrymen, as well as himself, he retired.

A Hindoo was the next in council, and there spoke in behalf of his own nation, and said they would turn away from their earthly idols as soon as they were taught about the great star-spirit. He then said the bow was a symbol in the covenant the star-spirit was teaching his people, and that was the reason the bow-and-arrow girls always had the bow in their hands when they came to the council to speak. He thought that was the cause of the Christians telling about the rainbow in their Koran, for they had no doubt forgotten the explanation that was given when the covenant was made. But as the bow-and-arrow girl was waiting to speak, he would go, although he thought, if she had a mind to do it, she could tell all about it.

One of the Forest Maidens was then in council, where she had come from the upper hunting-grounds by the command of the Great Spirit, who had been told of the many wrongs the race of the red man endured, on the hunting-grounds below, from the avarice of their white brothers who had driven them from their wigwams, where their sufferings from starvation were known. And she had come to the great platform to demand, in the name of the Great Spirit, that hereafter the pale-face race heed well the Great Spirit's law of Eternal Justice, in all their transactions with the balance of the red man's race.

And India closed the session by invocation to the Great Spirit.

MAY 21, 1873. — After India's invocation to the Great Spirit, he said the present session would be devoted to a review of the children's school, and some of them would have an opportunity to speak, in order to give some evidence of their rapid progress. When, after speaking of the success of their labors in spirit and of the untold pleasure it afforded, he retired.

One of the children by the name of Zask, of New York, was before the council, where she said that her own sorrowful experience was the same as that of thousands of other poor children in every city. She was neglected in her poverty until shame for her own naked condition departed, and she soon became familiar with the nakedness of others who were deprived of sufficient clothing to cover their bodies, and their natural feelings of shame were turned into hatred with a desire for revenge on others that were living in extravagance and luxury on every side; and after a few years of sorrow in their conflict with poverty and crime, they were sent untimely from the physical plane to the spirit world, where they found themselves in the same condition, full of envy and self-will, with a natural hatred for everything around them. Such she said was their condition in spirit when they were found by those who had proved to be their true friends, for they had gathered them up, and cleaned and clothed them in suitable apparel, and had shown further interest in their welfare by establishing schools where they were all organized in classes, where the neglected ones, without regard to condition or color, were now being taught by competent teachers a knowledge of the Great Father and his immutable laws, now manifested in the unfolding of all things that surrounded them, and also of their duties to each other, who were all children of the same great Creator. She then spoke of their wonderful improvement, and of the kindness and patience of their teachers in their efforts to overcome their former bad habits. But they were happy now, and the number of their classes appeared to be endless. She had no doubt they would cover the planet, for they could be counted by millions, while many of the children who had never known their earthly parents before had now been permitted to see them. And all had been told of the One who said, Suffer little children to come unto him, and forbid them not, for of such was the kingdom of heaven. She then spoke of their love for the one they called their earthly mother, who had let them come, time and again, to tell of their sorrowful condition before they were gathered together and their schools established. She then retired.

The next before the council was Reade, of New York, who confirmed all his schoolmate had said, and then gave a vivid description of his own sad experience among the humble and degraded poor. He portrayed the present condition of the poor children in every city, as had been witnessed by the thousands whom the poor boys had taken with them in order to show all how the poor were degraded and had to live in every town and city. And, without regard to the feelings of those who had assembled to witness their present exhibition, he told them how the continued neglect of the suffering poor drove them into crime from their childhood, and it was no wonder that life and property now had no earthly security. He was thankful to the good missionaries who had found them in their nakedness in spirit and had clothed them, and were teaching them of their natural rights. He thought if others had to suffer from the effects of their own neglect, the fault was their own; and they had better hunt up those in poverty and want, whom they had failed to give instruction and find something for them to do. He spoke of the kindness of their teachers, and of the interest manifested by those who had returned with them to the prisons and to the scenes of their former poverty-stricken homes. After expressing his gratitude for their change, he retired.

The next one before the council was a colored girl, who said she had formerly lived among the slaves of one of the southern plantations, where bad treatment and ignorance had made her like a wild hyena, and that was her condition when she was found in the spirit; but the kindness of her teachers, with their good counsel, had learned her to overcome her faults. She was happy now with her schoolmates, who were all treated alike and taught the same lessons without regard to color. She was pleased with the privilege of speaking, and said she desired by her good behavior to be worthy of all the kind treatment she was receiving; and, after expressing her gratitude, she retired.

Miss Landon was again before the council, where she spoke of her own experience as a teacher among the little ones who had passed to the higher life during their infancy. She said it was a great pleasure for them to come with their flowers and mingle in the schools with the children whose earthly conditions had been sorrowful. She expressed great pleasure in witnessing the wonderful change in their present condition. She also said they had found much enjoyment, and they loved to go among the aged of every condition, and distribute their celestial flowers, and cheer them on their way in their advance to the higher spheres; for it truly was a pleasure to those who had been neglected and deprived during their earthly trials, to be gathered up in spirit, where they are now clothed as well as instructed and made happy. And she instructed the children under her own care from the paradise of God's love, as they mingled with the others, whose care-worn faces still showed signs of their earthly sorrows, that they should make no distinction on account of color or condition, for all were the Great Father's children, and all equally entitled to his blessings. And after speaking of her own gratitude for the place she had been called to fill, she again retired.

The next one in council was a Jewess, who said she was permitted to say a few words in behalf of those of her own race who had been gathered up in spirit, where all were instructed in the same language in the great law of Eternal Justice. She felt to rejoice that her sisters of Israel and of Judah had been permitted to cross the waters where they could mingle with their sisters of other nations, where by the same spirit they could learn of their Messiah's heavenly kingdom. She felt a gratitude, she said, that was impossible to even express, as the wonderful scenes were conveyed to her mind; and, after expressing her thanks for the privilege of speaking, she retired.

One of the Hindoo children was the next in council, where she said she had come to answer for their class in the school where all the Hindoo children were progressing. She recited a very interesting composition as an evidence of their improvement, and said they were all delighted with the kind attention given to them by their teachers; and, after saying her people all thanked us for the privilege allowed to them in order to speak, also for the interest taken in their welfare, she retired.

The next one before the council was one of the Indian children, who told of the interest that was now manifested in their welfare by all the teachers of the schools, where they were teaching them that all were the children of the Great Spirit, and that the people of every nation and color were taught the same lessons in the same language; and they were also told that the Great Father and Great Spirit and Great Creator were all the same, whose great wisdom and power were everywhere made manifest by the wonderful and grand developments of all things around them; while they were much gratified with an opportunity of going to school, and said they were making rapid progress as they committed to memory the lessons given to them by their teachers; and they loved the good pale-face children now, since they had been taught that all nations and tribes belonged to the Great Spirit.

When India again closed the session by invocation to the Great Spirit.

MAY 25, 1873. — After India's invocation to the Great Spirit, he said the present session would be devoted to an organization of all the nationalities brought up at the present closing cycle, and it would include all represented by what was called the Bible history of creation, and that Elijah, one of the old prophets of Israel, was first in order, after which others would follow. Said they would defer the coming Wednesday evening session, and they would have everything in readiness for the following session; and then spoke of the opposing forces with which they had had to contend during his experience for the past eighteen years, and of the pleasure it afforded them in knowing they had been successful in their labors in spirit, and had triumphed over the power of darkness. Said the inhabitants of the earth were already feeling the change that was fast coming around by the wasting away of their present institutions, and as the old passed away, the new would be received, and the law of justice acknowledged. He then withdrew.

The next in council was Elijah the prophet, who spoke of the present gathering up of his people as a consummation of the visions of which he had long ago foretold, and for which he and his brother prophets had often been stoned and driven from their camps. But now the fullness of the Gentiles had come, and he who was their Leader had returned again, after being himself rejected, and cast out, and crucified by those who did not know him. But now, after wandering'and waiting in sorrow, all were glad to hear his heavenly voice, and were ready to accept and honor him as their true and only Messiah, who had come again to offer them the heavenly kingdom. And he counselled his people to see to it that none of the tribes of Israel or of Judah were this time left behind. He knew they had been rebellious and unforgiving; and they had suffered, and that should be a warning to others not to cast away the Spirit, or trifle with the God of Israel. He told them of the mistake they had made hunting up and down the earth expecting to find the promised land that was far above their earthly Palestines, and urging them all to be prepared, and for each séction to obey those found worthy to lead them. He then spoke of their improved appearance and of the sparkling of their eyes as they now united in their new songs of praise for the return of their long-lost Messiah. And after referring to the fullness of his own gratitude for their blessings, he retired.

The next before the council was an Irish prophet, who said he had come from his loved country with a commission in order to represent his own people in the gathering up of the nations of the earth around the great platform of Eternal Justice; and he exhorted them all to be prepared to follow the lead of the blessed Saviour whom they had professed to love, but of whom in reality they had known so little. They all knew now that their purgatory was forever closed, and they had nothing to fear, and must soon remove the principalities of earth, that were the stumbling-blocks in the way that prevented the progress of humanity, and turned them away from the communion of spirit that told of the heavenly kingdom of their Lord and Master, who voluntarily suffered upon the cross that he might triumph over the power of darkness, and open the way from the mortal and perishable things of earth to the imperishable and eternal kingdom, where all would partake of his glory. When, after telling them not to be laggards in their part of their Master's work, but have their lamps filled and ready, he retired.

One of the Hindoos was the next in council; and he had come in order to represent his people. He said they were all ready, for they had gathered around the box that had been intrusted to their care, and that was placed upon the platform of Justice by direction of the great star-spirit, who had also commissioned him to say that all the nations and tribes who had never been intrusted with the covenant would now have the privilege of forming on the same side and next to his people, and all the nations and tribes who had the covenant, and turned away and disregarded the teachings of the Spirit, must all form by themselves on the opposite side of the platform, and all the nations and peoples who had the gospel of a risen Saviour, and had used it in order to build up their earthly principalities, must now go and take their place by the side of those who had disregarded the covenant; while the Chinese and the older nations were gathered up together, and had a place by themselves. And the bow-and-arrow girls, with all their race, were stationed next to the great star-spirit. After telling about the anxiety some of the tribes manifested in regard to the box intrusted to his people, and the great pleasure it afforded them, he retired.

One of the Forest Maidens was the next in council, where she had come to stand for her race, who were many, like the trees of the forest. She told of the mighty power of the

Great Spirit everywhere manifested by the boundless and endless blessings bestowed upon his children. Yes, they loved the Great Spirit, and had returned to the platform where Justice had been established, and they would re-light their camp-fires and be in readiness to obey his command, for the time had come when justice must be established among the pale-faces on the lower hunting-grounds. She then spoke of the many nations and tribes who had answered the call of the Great Spirit, and gathered around his great platform of Eternal Justice, where Israel and Judah, with their many tribes, were again listening for the voice of the Spirit to lead to the promised land, which they had found was above their earthly Jordans, where they had long been in bondage. She then told of the red warriors, and the many archers of the red man's race, that were ever ready to obey the Great Spirit's command. And India closed the session by invocation to the Great Spirit.

JUNE 1, 1873. — After India's invocation to the Great Spirit, he said they had finished the work of gathering up the nations and tribes in spirit, and were then ready for the great Media to come and review their labors, and give further instructions. He then said the one we called the "healer" would take control, and give further instructions in connection with the present session. He then retired.

The familiar voice of the "healer" was the next heard in the council, where he expressed his amazement at the grandeur of the scenes before him, and said no language was sufficient to convey to mortals, in order for them to comprehend, the magnitude and the glory of the things which he was then permitted to behold in spirit. It was the gathering in of all the wandering and scattered tribes of Israel and Judah with their different nationalities, who were now resurrected and brought up to meet the Gentile nations around the great platform of Eternal Justice, where they were waiting to hear the voice of the blessed Saviour, who was present with his twelve apostles; and each one was assigned his place. He then said it had been appointed for John to first make a few remarks, after which the blessed Jesus, who had come in the clouds of the heavens with all his holy angels, would take control and pronounce the judgment. He then withdrew.

John the seer, and one of the twelve, was again before the council, and remarked it was truly a glorious consummation, and one they had long desired to see accomplished, when their Master would sit in his chair of justice, in his spirit-kingdom, and be acknowledged by the nations and tribes of the earth who had answered to the call of the gospel of the communion of spirit, as they gathered from a resurrection to the judgment. Yes; truly it was a scene that was worthy of contemplation, for it was as long and as broad as the planet from which the black and the white, the red and the copper-colored races had come up, each nation and tribe in their own order, to bow their knee in gratitude and veneration to Jesus, whom they gladly acknowledged to be their Saviour, for they knew he had voluntarily been a martyr that he might triumph over the powers of darkness, and lead them away from their transitory and perishable earthly kingdoms. And well they might rejoice, for it was truly a fulfilment of the sayings of the past, for they had seen the angels of light descending and ascending, bearing the triumphant news of the birth of another kingdom. And there was a new heaven and a new earth, where Justice and Charity, with Judgment and Love, would do their work; and the heavens were opened, and the archangels had assembled to bear witness of the grandeur of the scenes before them, while anthems of praise were flowing from every nation and tribe, and from every camp, in order to commemorate the wonderful triumph of the meek and the lowly Nazarene. He then said, as no language was sufficient to portray in full all that had been accomplished, he would retire and let Jesus, their Master and Leader, speak for himself.

Who, after taking control, said it was true the kingdom was established and never to be destroyed. He then said that after many unsuccessful efforts, his Father told him to commence the work in the dark sphere connected with the physical plane, where the spirits still partook of their earthly condition. And many had been the sorrowful scenes through which they had had to labor, where unhappy spirits, fearful of the doom which had been impressed on their memories, would flee in terror from their sight, and hide away among the neglected and dark conditions they had everywhere found among mortals. But, he said, by untiring perseverance they had succeeded in lighting up the dark sphere, and, searching out the retreats of the lost and forsaken and sorrowful ones, had by kindness established confidence and trust, until they were instructed in the schools which they had organized in a knowledge of their inheritance to the higher and happier spheres in spirit. He then said that he first went to those who had professed to be his followers; but they had refused to receive him, and rejected and cast him out. Said he had been in their costly temples, where they professed to worship; and he had been in their palaces, and found them stored with every luxury that nature and art had produced; and he had been in the neglected hovels of the poor, who were cast out and denied the possession of their lawful inheritance; and he had been in their prisons, where their brothers and his brothers were chained to the rocks with their backs bowed down with needless and cruel torture, often in dark and loathsome dungeons. And such things were sustained and upheld by those who profess to be his followers, and who build their costly temples in which they offer their devotions to him and his Father for their daily blessings.

He then turned to the Jews, who were gathered before the platform of Eternal Justice, on which his disciples were seated, who were the witnesses of his cruel and terrible persecutions during their own earthly trials, and told them it was true he was poor and despised, and without an earthly father, when they cast him out and crucified him, and they all knew what had been the result. He told them he came to them in order to restore what had been lost, and that was the covenant made by spirit with their forefathers, and which was given in beautiful symbols, and taught them of a resurrection of the spirit to its immortal home in their heavenly Father's Eternal Kingdom; but they had lost the chart that opened the way to their spirit home that was above, while they had wandered in the forbidden paths, and built up for themselves homes among the perishable things of earth. "And where now is all your glory — you that have been kings and rulers over the nations? Have you been satisfied in your rambles over your barren fields, and among the crumbling ruins of your temples and your images? You would have done better if you had listened to the voice of the spirit that told of the promised land above, where the fields are ever green, where the temples never perish." He then spoke of their labors and of their triumph in the work of establishing the great platform of Justice, and it was as broad and as long as the needs of humanity. "And the first on my right hand are those who were cast out from the brothels and prisons of earth, and who have been gathered up from their friendless and sorrowful condition, and clothed and instructed in the natural laws of their heavenly Father. They can first pass on and enter the kingdom. And here next are the ones who have been called 'heathen.' They stand with the ark and covenant of symbols which were lost; but they have gladly received its teachings, and they too are now ready and can enter the kingdom. And here next are the poor mothers who were neglected and cast out with scarred faces and matted hair, and without rags enough to cover their nakedness, who still show the marks of their sufferings. And here, next to join them, are their children, who have now been clothed and schooled; and they, united, can pass on and enter together. And here on my left hand are those who made use of my name, and what they have called my gospel, in order to build up their earthly kingdoms, and have aggrandized themselves at the expense of their brothers. They can return back to the scenes they have left, and undo their work, and assist me in establishing the law of justice. And here are those who, to gratify their avarice, monopolized the blessings and increased their wealth by the toil and oppression of others, for their own selfish aggrandizement causing the unhappy and sorrowful conditions we have everywhere seen around us. They are now judged to return where they must visit the homes of the poor and the abodes of suffering mortals, and sit with them at their tables, and watch by them as they lie upon their pallets of straw where the mildew and filth are oozing from the cold damp walls by which they are often surrounded, and wipe the death-damp from their starved and emaciated brows, and take away their fear and prepare them for their birth into spirit life. And here are all who were intrusted with the covenants, and have made them of none effect. They too must return and form themselves into bands, and work diligently for the overthrow of the principalities and powers of earth that have been established through injustice, unbind and break the prison-bars, and set the captives free. See that quick work is made of it, and that justice is everywhere established, for we have those in the body who have been co-laborers with us in the work. And it must be finished, so that when they are ready to come, we may enter the kingdom together. And here too are our ever-welcome red children of the forest, who have never departed from the covenant of the communion of spirit, and who have ever lived near my Father's kingdom. They will be with us in council until all is finished." Then, after a few personal remarks, he retired.

One of the confiding Hindoos was the next in council, where he spoke of the pleasure and of the satisfaction of his people for the position assigned to them among the nations. Said they were proud of the box and the covenant, and symbols given to them by the star-spirit, who had told them about the Great Father; but he thought they would not stay in the Father's kingdom until the great star-spirit could go and stay with them. He then said, when the star-spirit was talking, all were listening in amazement, but they could not see him. But when he was again seated in his chair on the great platform, it was then that all nations and tribes were on their knees, and all held up their hands in acknowledgment of his just and righteous judgments, and all had volunteered to return and assist in the work until the great law of Eternal Justice was triumphant. And then he thought the Christians might obey the teachings of their Koran, and beat their swords into ploughshares and pruning-hooks, and all worship the Father under their own vine and fruit-tree.

India again closed the session by invocation to the Great Spirit.

JUNE 8, 1873. — After India's invocation to the Great Spirit, he spoke at some length on the present condition of human affairs, and compared it with the condition of the Jews at the time they rejected and cast out and crucified their Messiah. He said the conditions were very similar: the first had cast him out when in the body, and the other had rejected and cast him out in spirit; and he said the conditions that would follow would be much alike, and would end in the overthrow of our nationality, which had caused great suffering among the people from the increased burdens imposed by those who made and administered the laws. He then retired.

The one next in council said he was a Jew, and was a witness of the crucifixion, and familiar with the history of that age, and compared it with the present. He thought the Gentiles had no cause to complain of the Jews, for they had committed the same fatal mistake after an experience of eighteen hundred and fifty years. He thought the chastening of the Jews with the destruction of their earthly principalities, and of the small remnant that was left, and they scattered over the earth with no nationality, should be a warning to all other nations how they trifled with and cast out and crucified again the Spirit of the ever-living God. He then said their own sorrows had been terrible to endure; they had wandered and waited all the long years among their once beautiful but long since dried-up and deserted Jordans, waiting for their Messiah to come again and tell them of the promised land that was above. And they had taken up their harps, and had tuned them anew, and were glad to listen to his voice, and they were now ready and willing to follow. After expressing his gratitude for the privilege of being present in order to speak for his people, he retired.

One of the Hindoos was the next in council, where he told of the wonderful things that were fast taking place among his people; and he thought they would soon have them all looking after the star-spirit, and turning away from their earthly idols. He then said that he also was full of gratitude for the privilege of speaking for his people, and they would do all they could in order to give their little goddess, who had let them speak, all the strength they could during the coming week. He then retired.

One of the Forest Maidens was the next in council, where she spoke of the present condition of the remnant of her race, who had been driven from their wigwams, and from their fishing-lakes, and from the wild game in their forest-homes, by their pale-face brothers. And she would tell the Great Spirit of the injustice that was then being done to his red children, where some were already singing the death-song, who had been hunted down by the pale-face race, who had chained them together, and were driving them to their death as they did the beast to its slaughter.

India again closed the session by invocation to the Great Spirit, again thanking him for strength and for light that had resulted in what they had accomplished.

JUNE 15, 1873. — After India's invocation, he said there would be a gathering of some of the leaders at the present session for a business purpose, and that Everett and others would be heard, in order for the arrangement of their present work; and, after speaking of what had been successfully accomplished, and of the great pleasure it gave them in spirit, he again retired.

The next in council was Everett and Lincoln, with King and Booth, who all spoke with interested feelings in connection with the work that had been already completed; and they cautioned all to be aware, and not let sympathy interfere with justice as they mingled again with their earthly friends in order to finish up the work. They must see that all remained firm in spirit until justice was established among the nations of the earth, and though the principalities built up through injustice and oppression had to give way in order that all might be protected in their rights. They could remember what the Saviour had said, who had suffered for all, that "the work must be quickly done."

Booth then called their attention to a scene then presented to their view in the distance among the Israelites, where the Spirit was addressing them through one of their prophets, and warning them to turn from their evil ways, or sudden destruction would be their doom. "See, the elements are thickening around them as they gather stones to hurl at the faithful old prophet in order to drive him from their camps! and, as he retires in sorrow for their blindness, you see the storm breaks forth with fearful and terrific grandeur, and removes them from the face of the beautiful earth their unholy deeds had been desecrating. But here we still have them in spirit, where every one is a living witness of the power and the everlasting love of the Great Creator." When, after the usual expression of gratification over the results of their combined labors, and a few remarks in connection with their present duties, he withdrew.

One of the Hindoos and one of the Forest Maidens were in council, and had an opportunity of expressing their opinions and giving further testimony in connection with the affairs of their own nations and tribes, who had been gathered together with all the mighty host that answered to the call of the Angel of Time, and had come forth in order to take the place assigned them at the present closing cycle.

India, after a beautiful invocation to the Great Spirit in thankfulness for his many blessings, adjourned the session until the 22d of June, 1873.

When, after his invocation to the Great Spirit, he said, owing to the weary and tired condition of their media, they should have a short session. He then spoke of the changes that were transpiring among mortals that would awaken them to their condition.

One of the Hindoos and one of the Forest Maidens were next in council, where each one spoke of the change that had taken place among the nations and the numerous tribes in spirit after the judgment, and that many who were permitted to enter the kingdom had volunteered to return, and desired to remain with the others until their work was finished. The Hindoo said his own people were delighted, and they had sent ambassadors in spirit to the people of their own nationality that would awaken a new interest among the people about the star-spirit that was spoken of in their Koran. He thought they would soon be in condition to make their dumb idols speak with a living spirit, when the Christian would have to return and be a-looking after the heathen in their own countries. They had also decided not to leave the star-spirit until all had been completed.

India again closed the session by invocation to the Great Spirit, acknowledging their dependence, and asking for wisdom and for strength sufficient for their labors.

JUNE 29, 1873.—After India's invocation to the Great Spirit, he said that Confucius would occupy the time of the present session in giving the necessary directions for the further prosecution of their various labors. He then withdrew.

Confucius was again before the council, where he spoke approvingly of what they had already accomplished. He told of the labors of the prophets and seers, who had foretold of the glorious events which had already transpired. He spoke of the renewed happiness of the wandering pilgrims who had crossed over into the beautiful fields which the Great Father had provided for the grand reception of his wandering, wayfaring children. He spoke encouragingly to those whose work was not yet finished, and told them they must persevere, and they would finally be triumphant. He told them that the powers with their earthly principalities were already shaking upon their false foundations, while many who had again crucified their Saviour and scoffed away the living Spirit were already calling for the rocks and the mountains to hide them. He told them they had no occasion to delay their work, for the closing cycles of the past had shown, when mortals cast out the Spirit and clung to their perishable kingdoms, they only hastened their own destruction. And, after speaking of the magnitude of their work, and of its grand results when finished, he invoked the blessings and the protection of the Great Father on their renewed labors, and again withdrew.

India closed the session by invocation to the Great Spirit, once more asking that wisdom and strength might be given to them, sufficient for the full accomplishment of their labors, that in the end all might be approved. And, after a few words of instruction, he again withdrew; when from July to the following month of October various reports were made at the regular sessions of the council by many of the different parties who had been connected with their previous labors, as well as by many others who had been brought before the council, where each one made their own reports that were often of a desponding and sorrowful nature.

OCTOBER 26, 1873.— After India's invocation to the Great Spirit, he told the assembled host in spirit that the time had now arrived when there could be no further delay with their labors, for there was evidently no excuse for their earthly friends who had been warned time and again to turn from their evil ways, and listen to the call of the Spirit, that would have led them out of their earthly bondage; but the counsels of the Spirit had been disregarded, and they had turned a deaf ear to the warning voice, and were again struggling for the Mammon of unrighteousness, in order to perpetuate their earthly kingdoms, and must now be left to reap their own reward. He then said that Peter and John were waiting to make further statements, and retired, after his usual encouragement.

Peter, one of the apostles, was the next in council, and again confirmed the history of his Master's cruel sufferings and of the persecutions of his little band of followers, and then spoke of the changed condition that now surrounded them; said the key that was given to him opened the door into his Master's spirit kingdom; but all who had used the symbol in order to build up and strengthen their earthly principalities had found it had no charm in spirit, although many still kept it hanging to their girdles, in evidence of their earthly power, who had failed to open the door of the heavenly kingdom. He told them there was a lock their key had always fitted, and they could open the door and he would show them where it led. "O, you stand back with affright! Why, it only leads into the purgatory of your own making; but you may lock the door and throw away the key where it may never be found, for you have been saved independently of your own efforts; and when you have undone the work you labored so hard in order to establish during your earthly pilgrimage, you will get the key that opens the only door that leads to the Master's kingdom." After speaking of the wonderful change from the transitory and perishable to the celestial, where they had seen of his power and glory, he gave way for his—

Brother John, who was the next in council, and said he was glad the time had arrived for the opening of another seal, for he had looked with amazement and delight on the mighty hosts who had answered the call of the angel of time, and had gathered around the great platform of Justice, as they listened to the opening of the Book of Life. Yes, it was true, it was a calling of the nations together to judgment, and it was what they had looked for and expected at an earlier day; but, notwithstanding the time had been prolonged, the recording angel had been faithful, and every name was kept in remembrance until the coming of the bridegroom, in order to invite them to the marriage feast. And as the time for a closing cycle was at hand, and could not be delayed, he would give way for one who was a leader among the people of his own day and age. And then, after a few words of cheerful encouragement for all to persevere until they finished their work, he retired.

An old man, apparently crippled with infirmity, was the next in council, where he acknowledged he had been a priest of the Order among the Jews, who did persecute Jesus and his followers. And he had come in order that he might ask to be forgiven, and have some place where he could sit down and see Jesus once more as he passed by. He then said that he himself and his people had wandered up and down their forsaken country, but could find no rest. They had lain themselves down by the side of their once beautiful rivers, hoping to be washed away, and they had climbed to the tops of their highest mountains, and dashed themselves down headlong, praying for annihilation; but they had found it impossible. But, then, he knew he had hated the meek and compassionate Jesus, and he had exulted when the nails crashed through his hands. But, then, Jesus and his little band of followers were encouraged and sustained by the angels, while he and his people were surrounded by devils, and knew not what they were doing; and they were thankful even now to be remembered and called up in judgment, and would sit together in sackcloth and sorrow, and when Jesus passed by again they would beg to be forgiven. He then retired.

One of the confiding Hindoos was the next in council, where he told of the box the star-spirit had put into their possession, and how they had dressed it up and were now ready for in-

spection. He then showed them the temple of which the
symbols had given them instruction, and then asked them if
they could see any broken columns. He then showed them
the cherubim that overshadowed the mercy-seat in front of
the Holy of Holies, and asked them if they could see where a
piece had been broken from one of the wings. He said the
star-spirit had told him to ask the questions. He then showed
them the children that had been gathered up in spirit, where
they had been clothed and formed into schools. Then he
showed the women who had no husbands during their earthly
lives, and pointed to the clothing they had on when they
entered the spirit world; and also to the men in another
group, who had been their companions. He said all these
conditions had been taken into consideration by the great
star-spirit when he announced the judgment, and that the
twelve who were to judge the tribes of Israel were now ready
to complete their work. He then retired.

One of the Forest Maidens was the next in council, where
she told of the great love the Great Spirit had for all of his
children, and the many tribes of her own race that were then
working for the establishment of justice among the Great
Spirit's many pale-faces, who again had turned away from
the light and the love of the Great Spirit, and were wandering in darkness all over the hunting-grounds.

And then India closed the session by invocation to the
Great Spirit.

NOVEMBER 2, 1873. — After India's invocation to the Great
Spirit, he said that King and Pierpont, with others, would
again be in council during the present session. After a few
words in connection with their labors, he withdrew.

King was again heard in the council, where he spoke of the
results of their combined labors in spirit, and of the pleasure
afforded them all in what had been successfully accomplished.
He thought it would not be right for them to enter into the
kingdom to remain until they had done more in order to relieve the oppressed and suffering condition of mortals. Said
he could not help but feel his own unworthiness as he contrasted his opportunities in life with others by whom he had
been surrounded. He had had friends to strengthen and sustain him in his work, while others had struggled on alone and
friendless; and he thought it was in accordance with justice
that all who had toiled their way up alone without the help

and assistance of others, should be left to enjoy the kingdom, while himself, and others like him, should remain behind until they had accomplished a change among the suffering and forsaken outcasts of earth that would be sure to enhance their own happiness as they returned and mingled together with their Master in the eternal kingdom. He should ever feel grateful for what he had been permitted to enjoy, and for the privilege of expressing his opinion again in the presence of his earthly friends. When, after expressing his anxiety for the early triumph of their resumed labors, he retired.

The next one in the council was Pierpont, where he sustained the remarks of his brother, King, and said he should feel his own unworthiness if he had not in the last days of his pilgrimage in the flesh made some effort in order to strengthen and confirm the knowledge of the communion of spirits. He said that he had heard the voice and gladly held counsel with those who had passed on before him; and although he had been jeered, and called an " old fool," on account of his course, it had not disturbed him or deprived him of his happiness. He was thankful to know he had not turned a deaf ear to the heavenly messengers, for he had found them waiting for him and ready to cheer him on his way as he awoke to a newness of life above the dark, cold portals of the silent tomb. He was ready to join with all that would work for the amelioration and the elevation of the human race ; and they would continue the work until all were saved, and Jesus their leader could say it was finished ; and then they could all return and enter his heavenly kingdom together. He then expressed his gratitude for another opportunity of speaking, and again retired. When the friendly and familiar voice of

Paine was the next heard in the council, and said it was true that he was persecuted during his pilgrimage among mortals, and the light that was reflected through his organization was appropriated by others for their own special benefit, while he was turned out to be scoffed at by every bigot until many times he was friendless and without a home. And he could see no justice in their being delayed in their spirit progress, waiting for others who were still grovelling in their avarice after the Mammon of the earth. He told them they had all had their experience in the lower conditions of life, and he felt it to be their duty to press onward and upward, and if possible nearer to that great positive Mind that had brought them into existence. He was thankful for his earthly experience, and thankful for the opportunity to give expression to his present opinions. He then said, with expressive and beautiful language: "O, thou Son of Mary, I thank thee for all thou hast done for me and for suffering and fallen humanity." Saying he had often felt sorry for the bigoted clergy who had been his traducers, for they had found Jesus, whom they all profess to worship, still surrounded by the suffering poor who have been cast out and degraded by mortals. He then said the Hindoos had taken their place among the moving tribes, and would not be represented at the present session; but that Magdalene, who was a witness of the persecutions and the crucifixion of Jesus, would be the next to speak. And after expressing his thanks for his own opportunity, he again retired.

Magdalene was the next in council, where she spoke of the change that was taking place among her own people, and said she was ever willing to stand among them as a witness of the sympathy and the compassion of him who healed her of her earthly maladies. She told them they had seen him in spirit standing by her, with his hand upon her head, as a further evidence for those who had mocked and spit upon him and kicked him, as his frail body swayed under the heavy cross they tried to compel him to carry. She then told them she still could see those among them who had slapped her and her sorrowing sisters in the face, and told them to close their mouths as they spoke of the kindness and of the power of the One they had cruelly nailed to the cross. "Well, if the remembrance of your evil doings still makes you tremble with fear, O why did you come here to arouse anew the feelings of indignation? But look, you will see the One you crucified. And you have gladly acknowledged him to be the king of the Jews, also the King of kings in his glory." She then said that she had found her place near to their blessed Saviour in his kingdom, and she rejoiced to know that his great work would soon be understood, be acknowledged and appreciated among mortals. After speaking of the many evidences he gave of his divine mission to depraved and fallen humanity, and of their own terrible suffering after the crucifixion, and of their present happiness to know that fallen mortals for whom their Master suffered had cheerfully bowed and confirmed the divinity of His mission, she retired; and again India closed the session by invocation to the Great Spirit.

NOVEMBER 9, 1873. — After India's invocation to the Great Spirit, he said one of the Jews who had officiated in the temple at Jerusalem would give his own statement from the memory of events connected with the history of the great Media; and after a few encouraging remarks connected with their labors, he retired.

The next one in council was Hebus, who said he was familiar with the history of Jesus, whom they had called the Nazarite; and he had been a witness of the downfall and the suffering of the people of his nation for their blindness in turning away and disregarding the heavenly teachings of the One they crucified. They had all departed from the covenant and the counsels of their fathers, and were wedded to their earthly principalities, and could not endure the rebuke of the one who had been taught in spirit; for they could see the poor and the forsaken ones they had cast out of their synagogues gathering around him, and were rejoicing for the bread of life which was daily dispensed among them. He said he was endowed with authority at the time among his people, and he confirmed the statements others had made in connection with the birth and mission of Jesus, and of his crucifixion, and the persecutions and sufferings of his early followers, who held fast the communion of spirit. He was glad the Ancient of Days had come, and that the nations and tribes had gathered together and had heard the judgment announced in spirit. It was true their trials and sufferings in their fallen and lost and forsaken condition had been of long endurance, and he was glad to be remembered even as a witness of their own blindness. He was glad to see around him so many of those with whom he had been familiar during their earthly pilgrimage, and it was evident they would not reject the light which was again brought by the return of their lost Messiah. After expressing his gratitude, he said he would give way for one of the women, who was also a witness of the events of his own day.

The next one in council said her name was Elizabeth, and that she was a relative of Mary the mother of Jesus; and she also confirmed the statements in connection with his birth, and of his rejection by the Jews, who refused to acknowledge his divine mission, but cast him out and nailed him to the cross. She spoke of the mental darkness and sufferings that followed, and then prayed that the people of the present age could be warned in time, and not, like the crafty and self-righteous Jews, commit the same error and go willingly as they did into darkness and national destruction. She then referred to many incidents as an evidence of the similarity of the present closing cycle of time with that of the Jews. Both had lost the light of their covenants and were struggling to enlarge and strengthen their earthly kingdoms, while poverty and crime with their attendant sufferings were fast increasing. She hoped the nations of the earth would take warning, and turn back to the law and the prophets, and sit in sackcloth and repent of their evil ways. After expressing her gratification for what had been already accomplished, she retired.

One of the Hindoos was the next heard in council, where he said his people were about ready to move, and they had the box with the symbols, and should carry it in the front of the great procession, for the star-spirit had taught them that the light that was reflected from it would lead them into the Father's kingdom, and that was the reason it had been given to the nations who had lost the chart and had been wandering in their own darkness. He said one of the bow-and-arrow girls was waiting, and wanted to speak, and he would retire.

One of the Forest Maidens was the next in council, where she told of the mighty hosts of the red man's race, who had left their upper hunting-grounds in order to do the work of the Great Spirit; and they had gathered up the lost and scattered tribes who had long wandered in darkness and in doubts around their desolate and deserted homes up to the broad platform of Eternal Justice, where they had learned from the power given to the Great Spirit's central Son that they must remember hereafter the great law of justice in their dealings with each other in all of the hunting-grounds of the Great Spirit. She then retired.

India closed the session by invocation to the Great Spirit.

NOVEMBER 16, 1873. — After India's invocation to the Great Spirit, he said John the seer would first make a short statement, after which our friends — the "Healer," and Deepwater, also Shadow and White Fawn — each would have an opportunity to make their own statements. The four last-mentioned had long been trusted and confidential friends, who had been assigned duties to perform in order to assist and strengthen their media in the accomplishment of her part of the work, and whose familiar voices were often heard when the council was not in session. India then retired.

John, the revelator, was the next in council, and said that his present position was in part the result of his fidelity to the spirit during his earthly pilgrimage, and that they were finishing up the work that was then inaugurated through the mission of their Master's labors and sufferings. He told them that message after message had been sent to mortals, confirming the truth of the resurrection of the spirit; but owing to their dark condition of mind, they turned from the spirit and clung to their perishable earthly kingdoms; while the spirit turned away in sorrow, and patiently waited the further unfolding of events, until by the successful lead of Jesus their Master, whose labors in behalf of suffering humanity had never ceased, they had at last been triumphant, and the dark sphere had disappeared, and in its place they had the platform of Eternal Justice, where they now sat in council and listened to the reports of all who have been sent to investigate the various affairs of suffering mortals. When, after a few remarks connected with personal affairs, he again retired.

Our friend known as the "Healer," was the next in council, and said he had been among the inhabitants of the earth, and into all of their churches and institutions where they professed to be the followers of the blessed Saviour; but he said it was everywhere evident their professions were not true, for they had departed from the teachings of the spirit, and had cast it out, and were all following after the mammon of unrighteousness. He said they daily crucified their Master, and were wrangling and fighting with each other for more power, in order to build up and strengthen their earthly principalities. He had also been in their prisons, where the poor and the afflicted and the friendless were incarcerated — thousands after thousands who had been neglected and cast out by those in affluence and power. He had been into their insane asylums, where the obsessed were deserted and left to suffer. He then asked that a band of spirits might be sent with a special commission and with power to relieve those who had in their own terrible condition taken the control of the earthly forms of others. When, after a further statement of the craft and the deception of mortals in their struggle for the mammon of the earth, he retired.

Deepwater was the next in council, where he confirmed the "healer's" report, and further said that he had been among those who were called "rich," and found them in their affluence; and he had been with the poor in their afflictions, and found them neglected in their struggle for the comforts of life ; and he had found that among the wealthy the spirit had been rejected, and was only consulted with a view to obtain more wealth in order to build their storehouses larger. He had also been in their so-called temples of worship, that were dressed up in purple and gold, and found among them all the same effort in order to gratify their worldly pride. He had been in their council-chambers, and in their halls of legislation, and had found that craft with its many arts prevailed, and that justice was nowhere recognized in the business affairs of men. And after confirming the sorrowful condition of the neglected poor who had gladly received the spirit, he retired.

Shadow was the next in council, where she said the Great Spirit had given her a mission among the spirits of the air, and she was a-doing her work. She was familiar with the suffering among the pale-faces that was caused by injustice, and she thought it was time the Peters and the Pauls and the Nazarenes went to work and did something in order to change the condition. She should do the work the Great Spirit had assigned to her without fear, if she had to blow them all from their great platform of Justice. After telling of the many sorrowful scenes she had seen among the pale-faces, and that she loved to work for the Great Spirit, she left.

One known as White Fawn, was the next in council. She said she had been teaching her tribe in spirit how to cultivate fruits and flowers. She told of the kindness of the Great Spirit, and of how her tribe had improved, and had beautified their hunting-grounds in spirit through the knowledge they had obtained from the pale-face spirits. Said their home was near the paradise where the pale-face children were taught to cultivate flowers; and she had been permitted to visit their gardens in order to learn how to lay out and improve and beautify the homes of her tribe. She invited those in the council to go with her and see for themselves how much they had improved their upper hunting-grounds; and after saying she thanked the good pale-faces for letting her speak, she withdrew.

One of the Hindoos was the next in council. He said his folks were also thankful for the many favors they had enjoyed ; and when they found the Great Father, and were shown their place in his eternal kingdom, they would go to work and beautify it. He then said, as their goddess was not very well, he thought she must be tired, and he would go, and the bow-and-arrow girl would not speak until the next session, for they had gone with a commission to their red warriors that were on every trail on the hunting-grounds. India closed by invocation to the Great Spirit.

NOVEMBER 22, 1873.—After India's invocation to the Great Spirit, he said that Madison and Jefferson and Monroe would each one have an opportunity of making a few remarks. After which David would have a chance to make his report. He said it was desirable to have a short session in order to keep up the strength of their media, and he again withdrew.

Madison was then in council. He said he was thankful, as the war-cloud was again hovering over their country, to be present with so many of his former associates, and have an opportunity to speak through an earthly form in the presence of earthly witnesses; for it was still a pleasure to remember they had stood side by side in the defence of their country from the elements of foreign aggressors until freedom had its birth. And if those they had left behind in charge of the sacred trust had degenerated and forgotten its worth, and gone after their golden gods, he still rejoiced to know that the Power to whom they all belonged, although unseen, but felt and as yet but little understood, had given them their beautiful America in spirit; and they had been called together as upon the mountain around the great platform of Eternal Justice, and in the hearing of their earthly witnesses to renew their pledge and sign their names to a new constitution, which would proclaim to mortals the birth of the spirit to its immortal home. Such were his present sentiments; and as he did not wish to prolong the time that was ever precious in the work of freedom, he would give way for his brother Jefferson, who was always ready to defend the rights of man. He then withdrew.

Jefferson was the next in council, and said it was true he had ever tried to protect his countrymen from the encroachments of foreign aggressors, for it was evidently their intention to have strangled freedom at its birth; and if those they had left behind in possession of the priceless gift had become demoralized and unworthy, it was from their association with foreigners who had been permitted to participate in every department of the government. But he was thankful to know they had sent the "Chair of Justice" to Washington, and it would remain there until every form of injustice was brought to the surface, and received from the voice of every true American its just condemnation. He then said their country below had been flooded by the people of every nationality ever since the birth of freedom; and it was also true that, as soon as their flag was raised, they proclaimed the glorious truth of the freedom of every spirit to its immortal home. Here again came those of every nation, rejoicing and anxious to convey the tidings back to those they have left behind; and he was glad, and if it was the will of heaven for them to stand shoulder to shoulder, they would do so until their last enemy was routed, and had joined with them in promulgating the great and the glorious truth to the dark and craftbound and benighted world. After expressing his confidence in the successful accomplishment of their work, he withdrew.

The next in council was Monroe, where he expressed his satisfaction in the remarks of his brothers, and said he felt a pride in the privilege awarded to himself to stand with them, for he had also taken a part in protecting his countrymen in their constitutional rights, and it was a gratification to him to know that at last chattel slavery was acknowledged to be wrong, and had been expunged from the records of the States. But as they had had to struggle through much opposition in order to secure an acknowledgment of the rights of man to think and speak in his own behalf, so also had they found many opposing elements during their present labors in order to establish a knowledge of the birth of the spirit to its immortal home. But, thanks to that unseen power through whose agency they had been sustained and upheld, both at last had been accomplished, and that, too, in their own country; and now they had to stand up before the council, who had assembled on the broad platform of Eternal Justice as witnesses in the great cause of human progress, and he was pleased to see so many around him in spirit who had participated in the struggle for national freedom, and glad to know they could realize now that something had been accomplished through their labors; and they could contemplate the wisdom of that unseen power which moved upon them and their fathers in order that they might find a refuge on a continent where freedom could have its birth. Their country was now the home of the people of all nations, instigated by the wisdom of that same mighty power that a knowledge of a higher birth — the birth of man's immortal spirit — might become universal, and no longer be shrouded in darkness and doubt. And he would say, as they had again been called together and had rallied around the great platform of Eternal Justice, and renewed their pledges to uphold a new declaration of freedom, let them see to it one and all that their countrymen who had proved themselves worthy received a hearty welcome on their arrival in New America, and that hereafter they relax no efforts in their labors in order to remove every form of tyranny over the minds of mortals. He felt grateful for all that had been accomplished, and encouraged them to work on until the great truth was everywhere established, and all were permitted to partake of its blessings. He then withdrew.

One of our southern friends, who was known by the name of David, was the next in the council, and said his name had been called, but he was not ready yet to report. He had been out and had gathered up many things he was anxious to lay before the council who had built up the great platform of Eternal Justice; and he would soon make his report, and everything should be established; for thus saith the Lord, and so said he. He had been to Washington, where Justice was doing its work with those who had forgotten the admonition that "he who got riches not in the right was a fool, and should leave them in the midst of his days."

India then closed the session by invocation to the Great Spirit.

NOVEMBER 30, 1873. — After India's invocation to the Great Spirit, he said —— Henry, —— Calvin, —— Luther, and, if there was time, one of the ancient Jews would give in their reports; and then, after a few words of encouragement in connection with their labors, he withdrew.

Henry was the next heard in the council. He told them he was also thankful for the opportunity offered for him to stand in his place as a witness of the truth of the immutable law of progression, and he felt a just pride in being permitted to see so many of his countrymen gathered around him in spirit who had participated in their struggle for national freedom. He rejoiced to know they all could realize now that something had been accomplished through the combination of their various labors, as they contemplated the wonderful wisdom of that power that moved upon their fathers to find a refuge in a country where freedom could have its birth; and they could again see the America they had loved for its association with the name of liberty, flooded with the inhabitants of every nationality through the wisdom of that unseen and same incomprehensible power, in order that a knowledge of their higher birth — a birth of the individualized spirit to its immortal home — should no longer remain in darkness and in doubt. As they had been called to rally around the great platform of Eternal Justice, and had renewed their pledges to a new declaration that proclaims freedom for all the sons and daughters of earth, let them see to it one and all that their countrymen who were worthy, received a hearty welcome on their arrival to their New America in spirit, and that no effort should be relaxed until their descendants could sit down together in peace, in the full enjoyment of both temporal and eternal blessings. After which he expressed gratitude to the higher powers, and then withdrew.

Calvin was again in council, and said that since he was last before them he had labored diligently among the people for whose opinions and condition he was held responsible, and he could say, after a careful investigation, that their influence was dying out. He had stood by the side of the priest in his pulpit, and by his couch at night, and had impressed on the tablet of his brain a fear of the terrible doom he had pictured for others, until his features became distorted with affright, and they would try to hide away and beg to be forgiven. He said they had felt crushed since the spirit had been withdrawn, for they had deprived themselves of their last and only resource by turning away and disregarding its call; and they have asked to be let alone, and are satisfied with their present enjoyment in their earthly kingdom, and are willing to abide the consequences when they are called up in judgment. Then, after a few encouraging words to others who were in a similar condition with himself, he again withdrew.

The next one in council was Luther, where he made his report by saying it was true their followers had turned back, and were gathering up and looking after their earthly treasures; but as they were transitory and perishable, the darkness was fast gathering around them, for in their blindness they rejected the call of the One they professed to worship, who had come with his heavenly messengers to finish his work. But they had cast out all who had rejoiced at their coming, for they had brought them the bread of life that others in their pride had refused to receive, and again closed the door that shut themselves out of his heavenly kingdom. He confirmed the statements his brother had made, and said as time with them now was precious, he would not prolong his remarks, but would give way for their ancient brother whose history was known among the tribes of Israel. He then retired.

The next one in council, in the feeble voice of age, made the following statement. He said he was one who had prayed that he might obtain knowledge, when an angel of light stood by him, and told him to arise and go and warn his people to forsake their evil ways, and turn again to the High and Holy One, that the evil days would not come among them. He was affrighted, and started in order to flee away, but the angel stopped him, and told him of the fearful conditions that must follow the people's transgressions. He then pointed with his finger to the closing cycle of the birth of their Messiah, and from that down through the cycles of time to the present, when he would come in his power with all the holy angels, and set up his kingdom. He then said that he had wandered with his tribe up and down their barren and desolate country, heart-broken and disconsolate, earnestly praying and waiting for the time to arrive when they should again be called. And now, he said, with everlasting thanks to that Eternal Power who had not forgotten them, once more their time had come, and they were willing and ready to take the place assigned them. And, after speaking of the long vista of time through which they had waited in darkness and doubt and in affliction, he said, "O, brother of earth, stand up firm, and warn your own people in season, and tell them not to shut themselves out from the light of the Spirit, and so be compelled to wander in darkness and in doubts, and suffer as we have suffered!" He then retired.

One of the Hindoos was the next in council. He told them that his people wanted to keep the passage open for themselves, for they had many things of interest to report. He said the star-spirit had told them, when he returned to the people who professed to be his followers, and were worshipping him in their own respectful way, he had rapped and rapped and rapped for the hundredth time, but they did not know him, and they would not let him in; so he turned back and had set up his kingdom in the dark sphere, where they had to clean up all the filth and all the terrible conditions that were cast out by those who had professed to worship him. And the star-spirit now said, when they called to him he should not hear them. He said we would find in our Koran that when the rich man was told he must dispose of his goods and divide them among the poor in order to secure his passport to a place of rest, he turned away and was sorrowful, and was still looking after their promised Messiah's kingdom.

And India again closed the session by invocation to the Great Spirit, asking for wisdom and strength sufficient for their labors.

DECEMBER 3, 1873. — After India's invocation to the Great Spirit, again thanking him for the privilege of assembling in convention with mortals in order to pursue their labors, he said the present session was assigned for the reports of some of the women connected with the band, and that Mrs. Townsend and Mrs. Fuller, and Mrs. Washington and Mrs. Jackson, with others, if there was time, would have a chance to bring in their reports; and he withdrew.

Mrs. Townsend was next heard in council, where she said they desired to say a few words in connection with their present design, and, as they had finished up their part of the work in the dark sphere in spirit, they were ready to commence with mortals; and she told them, in order to be successful and make speedy work of it, they must go into every condition of society — go into the mansions of the wealthy and into the more cheerful homes of the middle and industrious classes, and more especially into the hovels where they would find poverty and suffering among the unfortunate and the poor who were deprived of the common blessings. And they must see to it that the great law of Eternal Justice was everywhere enforced; they must hold up and strengthen the weak, and teach the strong that all are entitled to the blessings freely bestowed by their heavenly Father, and from what they had learned in the dark sphere, where they had mingled with many sorrowful conditions, and witnessed the changes that had taken place. She felt that they were all competent for the work, but she warned her sister spirits of the terrible scenes they would have to encounter, and of the obstacles they would find in their way among mortals; but she knew they would persevere and finally triumph over every opposing force. Then, after expressing her gratitude for the perseverance of their earthly witnesses, and encouraging them to hold out until the work was finished, she gave way for her sister and co-laborer in their important work.

The familiar voice of Margaret Fuller was again heard in the council, where she expressed her gratification for the privilege of meeting with so many of her sisters who had come in order to renew their pledge to strengthen and sustain each other in the work that was now assigned to them; and she was satisfied they were no strangers to the suffering connected with the darkened and sorrowful conditions among the inhabitants of earth; but she thought, from the recent experience they had all passed through, they would now find it a pleasure to go among them and work for their elevation. And they would commence their work by going among those in affluence, and impress them to lay aside their costly apparel, and dress themselves in garments of less expense and more befitting their stations in life, and then take from their abundance and go among the sick and forsaken ones in their cheerless and desolate homes, and administer to their necessities; see that employment suitable to their conditions is provided, and that each one has a part to perform in the various duties of life, and that all partake of the Great Father's blessings. She knew from her own experience from what they had encountered in the dark sphere in spirit, that such a work would give their earthly friends an abiding happiness which they had never yet enjoyed. And they must also go among their weak and frail sisters of earth, and take them by the hand, and give them strength and fortitude in order to withstand the fallen conditions that surround them, — elevate them in mind, and lead them away from the haunts of vice and of shame, and see to it that such traps that have been set in every town in order to beguile the weak and the friendless, are no longer allowed to exist. She well knew many sorrowful scenes would be presented; but they must remember their leader in the work had set the example during his earthly pilgrimage, and he would strengthen and sustain them until all was accomplished. After desiring to be remembered to their earthly sister whose organism they were permitted to use in order to accomplish their work, she gave way for her sister Washington, whose labors among them, she said, had been of great value. She then withdrew.

Mrs. Washington was the next in council, where she gave expression to her pleasure for the privilege of being present with her sisters, who were still engaged in the good work, for she said they all loved their country and its inhabitants, which, in the changing scenes of life, they had been called to leave behind them. She said that a great work had been accomplished in the dark sphere, and their America, which had been dear to them during their earthly experience, was assigned to them in spirit, where they had all assembled around the great platform of Justice, and where each one renewed the pledge to work together and never cease their labor until the beautiful America, which they had left behind, was once again free, and free from the customs and the vices which to our shame had become prevalent from unnecessary contact with foreign nations. "Why," she said, "it was but a day or two ago that her George had remarked that it was impossible now to tell an American from a foreign prince, for each one has his gold-headed cane, and his fob chain, with his diamond pin, and other foolish and corrupting fashions that are eating out the substance and destroying the virtue and the happiness of the people." It was their intention to save us from the terrible condition into which we had blindly fallen, for they disliked to see their countrymen corrupted and their beloved America under the control of the people of other nations. She said the fathers of our country, who still loved freedom, had assembled around the platform of Justice, and had formed, and pledged themselves to, a new constitution for their America; and they had sent it up through the higher sphere in order to have it approved; and they were now ready to commence their work with mortals. Said she was pleased with the opportunity which had been provided for them to speak, and desired to be remembered to their earthly sister; said that George had expressed his gratitude to know they had found two of their country's children that were worthy and could be trusted with important and necessary messages in connection with the finishing up of their labors. She then said, as the time with them now was precious, she would withdraw and give way to her sister.

Mrs. Jackson was the next one in council, where she said she was also pleased with the opportunity of again being present with her sisters, and to know they had gathered together to organize for the purpose of elevating their earthly sisters, who had become weak and frail from their disregard of the precepts and examples of their grandmothers and following after extravagant and gaudy fashions and customs of other nations. She said that her Andrew, who a moment since was by her side, had remarked that the men they had left in trust with the freedom of their country had become as trifling and as frail as the women, and if there was not a change soon, all would be lost, and their country would be under the control of the peoples of other nations, for it was evident our statesmen had degenerated, for they were gambling away the sacred rights of the people with less forethought than might be found among a lot of country school-boys. Rights that were purchased with the toil and blood of their forefathers were disregarded and not appreciated. She said they would have their sisters of America, instead of idling away their time in the marts of trade, gazing through the show-windows at the extravagant and expensive robes imported from foreign countries, go among the linens and the ginghams manufactured by their own countrymen, and there select their dress-goods, and take them to their homes and make them up with their own hands, and then devote their spare time in elevating and ameliorating the condition of their less favored sisters. She then said that she was still strengthened by the firmness of her noble husband, and they would see to it that the extravagance and corrupting customs imported from foreign lands were put aside. After saying it was proposed that a woman of another country should speak, and she would withdraw and give her an opportunity, she left her regards, and retired.

The next one before the council said she was born in England, where the fathers of America had their birth. Her sister had been talking about the freedom of their country, and about the extravagance and the corruption of other nations; but she said that her country had never enslaved the African on account of his color, and it was well known their courts had imparted justice to all, without regard to wealth or station. She was willing all should enjoy their own nationality; and she thought where a prince had wealth and station that gave him power, he had a right to use it; and she thought it was enough for each nation to look after the weaknesses and the imperfections of their own inhabitants. It was but a narrow channel that separated the one country from the other, and but a short distance back to the time when the children of each country were playing together. After expressing her pleasure for the opportunity of meeting her sisters who were engaged in a good work, and for her own privilege of speaking, and for the favors her own countrywomen had before enjoyed in the council, she withdrew.

One of the Forest Maidens was next in council, where she said she had come from the upper hunting-grounds as by the Great Spirit sent to the wigwam of the white squaw, where the white sisters were talking about the freedom of their country, and she had come to tell them their country formed once the hunting-grounds of the red man, given to them by the Great Spirit; but when the white man's brothers, on the other side of the channel, asked for pay for the red man's hunting-grounds, then the white man drew his weapons, and fought with his white brother for what he calls "liberty." But when the red man drew his bow in the defence of his squaw and pappoose in his cabin, the red man found that justice dwelt not with his white brother. She then told them the parchments they had sent up were received in the red man's upper council, and signed, and they had carried them to the Great Spirit, who had approved them. And they now had lawful possession of the red man's lower hunting-grounds, and they must see to it that, through the bad seed that was sown, it was not rightfully inherited by the people of other nations. The Great Spirit had assigned them a country where the orange groves and the flowers are in perpetual bloom, and the red man's race was satisfied; but they had come to protect the wigwams of the white brave and his squaw, and their little boats were now moored by the willows, and the door into the council-room was their own private door, and they still loved our country, for it was the home of their forefathers. She then withdrew.

The next one in council was a Hindoo woman, where she said she had come by permission of the star-spirit, who told her to say that she was also one of their sisters. It was true the dumb idols they had looked to for protection hadn't learned them much; but she thought if they had had the Koran, that taught them how to live and about the gods that were above, she didn't believe they would have as much dirty work to perform among their people as the other women had been telling about. But the great star-spirit was teaching them in spirit what he had taught others through their Koran. She was glad to learn how to speak through their goddess, and she would go and learn to speak in the same way to the people of her own country, and said she thanked their goddess for letting her speak, and she felt grateful for the privileges her people had received in the council.

After which India closed the session by invocation to the Great Spirit.

DECEMBER 7, 1873. — After India's invocation to the Great Spirit, he said that Washington, and Calhoun, and George the Fourth of England, and, if there was time, others would be heard in the council the present session, and after his usual encouragements, he retired.

The familiar voice of Washington was again heard in the council, where he expressed his satisfaction in the work assigned to them, and advised a union in the present labors, and said the conditions that were unfavorable among those they had left in charge of the people's rights would soon be changed. Said he knew that much suffering had been entailed upon the people of their country from the development of institutions which they were instrumental in founding, and which time and further observation had satisfied them were wrong, and the privilege was now given them in order to undo their work where the effect had not been beneficial. He said they had been granted all they had any right in justice to expect, and he thought it their duty to make a permanent and substantial foundation in finishing up their labors among mortals. Such were his present views, and he was thankful for an opportunity in order to express them; and, as time was now precious again with them, he would not prolong his remarks. He would withdraw by introducing his friend.

Calhoun was the next one heard in council, and again made a strong appeal in favor of the opinions he had formerly advocated, and still thought, if the people of the other states had let the southern people and their institution alone, it would have been much better for their country. He then called to their minds many acts of aggression, from the eastern and the northern, as well as the western states, that had finally terminated in the terrible war which had devastated the whole country, filled it with widows and orphans, and generated a greater and more humiliating condition of slavery than had ever before existed among an intelligent people; and then asked them, if the system of servitude was wrong, why they had upheld it until it became unprofitable in the colder states? And why they sold their slaves to the southern planter, and then got jealous of his prosperity, and stirred up strife and hatred until war and its fearful results had made slaves of them all, and bankrupted the nation? He then called upon his brother statesmen, who had assembled together, to bear witness to the truth of his remarks; and then said, as their brother George from over the channel had been called on to make a report, he would withdraw and give him an opportunity.

George the Fourth, of England, was the next one heard in council, where, after a cheerful greeting with many of his friends whom he recognized present, he made a general statement of the fearful results that had been entailed upon both countries from the natural effects of their avarice, for they all had encroached upon the rights of each other, and warred with the people of other nations until the garments of both countries were dripping with blood, and their inhabitants were degenerating into classes of thieves and paupers. He said the outlook to him was fearful to contemplate. He could see no way they could ever atone for their national transgression; but they must look to the Most High for wisdom and strength, and rally around their countrymen, and work as they should have worked when they were the trusted guardians of the people; and in time the great law of Eternal Justice would be established among them. And, after speaking of our own country's degradation that must result from our amalgamation with the people of all nations, he said an old man, whose history was familiar among the Judaites, was present for the purpose of making his report, and, after expressing his own pleasure for his opportunity to speak, he withdrew.

An old man, apparently burdened with the weight of years, was the next heard in the council, where he told of the sufferings of his own people, and then said he was one who was sent by the Spirit to warn them to turn from their transgressions, and look up to the High and Holy One who had blessed them and blessed their fathers before them; but they, by their evil doings, had become unworthy of his daily blessings, and heeded not the warning, but followed after their unholy abominations until the earth cast them out as unworthy to encumber the ground they were polluting. And they had been wanderers and aliens in spirit, forsaken by the spirit of light that offered to lead them to their promised land. He had shown them the Messiah with the holes in his hands and side, and told them of the time when the Ancient of Days would return with his holy angels, and call the nations of the earth together in judgment. And now the time had arrived, and the Book of Life was opened in which the recording angel of time had kept the accounts of every one with a pen and with ink that never fades. And he asked them if they would look over the records of their strife and avarice, of their cruel wars and their fighting, and of their many evil abominations, the record of which was still corrupting mortals, and ever expect to be forgiven? He then said that the angels had worked and had waited in sorrow until the electric connection was made when they ascended again and the sound of joy reverberated through the upper sphere. But lo and behold! as they soon return, frail mortals have gone back after their earthly idols, like the dog to his vomit, showing the covetousness of mortals. He then withdrew.

The next one before the council was of Irish nationality, where he told of the changes that were fast approaching, and said it was good to be working in the vineyard of their blessed Lord and Master, who had come in power in order to establish his kingdom; and the nations who professed to be his followers had gone sadly astray, and he was aware that many disturbing conditions would have to be covered with the mantle of charity, for man in his worldly wisdom had for a long time entirely departed from the great law of justice. He knew the blessed Jesus had great compassion, and he had come to finish his work with mortals, and, indeed, great sorrow must be endured by all who had turned a deaf ear and scouted at their Master's call. He said he felt grateful for the privileges that had been extended to the people of his own country, as well as for his own opportunity of speaking, and should gladly unite in the work of cleaning out the purgatories that were among mortals. He then retired.

One of the Hindoos was next in the council, where he spoke of the improvements his people were making in spirit from their opportunity of hearing the accounts from all the Christian nations. He then told of the man who spoke through their goddess after Washington. His folks thought he must have been full of fire and tow by the way he made the others sparkle; but he said the star-spirit had put a lot of black men with woolly heads on the platform of Justice for him to see, and when he stopped speaking and looked up and found who were before him, he was surprised, and appeared to be frightened, but could find no place where he could hide. He then spoke of a people who claimed the box the star-spirit had given to the Hindoo nation; but they did not let them have it, and the star-spirit said they should have kept it when it was intrusted to their care, and not cast it aside as a thing of no value. Then the bow-and-arrow girl had come and wanted to speak, and he withdrew.

One of the Forest Maidens was next in council, where she related the many evils committed by the pale-faces who had taken possession of the lower hunting-grounds of the red man. She said the wail of suffering and of sorrow had gone up to the Great Spirit, and He sent out his red children to go and find out why it was so, and see what the complaints were all about. They had been among the pale-faces, and knew why they had stained their hands in each other's blood, and should return and tell all unto the Great Spirit, who had heard the wail of sorrow from the hunting-grounds.

And India closed by invocation to the Great Spirit.

DECEMBER 10, 1875. — After invocation to the Great Spirit, he said the present session would be appropriated to the hearing of the reports from the women; that one by the name of Lee would first report, after which Fanny Fern with others would have an opportunity. And after his own statement in connection with the good results of their combined labors, he again withdrew.

Mrs. Lee was next in council, where she said she was formerly a resident of Boston, and had given much thought to the unhappy condition of the affairs among mortals, and she was glad to meet with those engaged in a work of such needed reformation; she would return with them to their sisters of earth, where they would gather about the weak and the frail ones, and give them strength to see and arise from their terrible degradation. She told them there would be fearful things to encounter; but they must take courage from the example of the one at their head, who himself knew all and would give them strength for their work. She was pleased with the great privilege granted to her to speak through the organs of speech that belonged to her earthly sisters, and, as it was desired she should make her time short, she withdrew by introducing her spirit sister.

Fanny Fern was the next one heard in the council, where she said she felt a pride in again having an opportunity to speak. She encouraged her sisters in the work they were about to engage, and told them to persevere and overcome all national feelings, and work together for the advancement of one common humanity, for they all knew the frailties of their weak and erring sisters of earth, who must be strengthened and lifted up from their fallen and degraded condition and made to know there is a higher and a happier home for all.

They must go to them and stand around them day and night until they could make them feel there was something for them to do. She knew those in affluence would find a greater pleasure in putting aside their costly robes and, in a more becoming and less expensive apparel, devote much of the spare time to alleviating the sufferings among the poor and less fortunate everywhere found in the marts of trade, administer to their present necessities, and point the way to the higher and the happier condition of life. By so doing, the good work would never falter until all was accomplished, and the great law of Eternal Justice established on an everlasting foundation among the varied affairs of mortals. She then said her sister Webster was present in order to make a few remarks. And, after a few words in connection with the great pleasure they were permitted to enjoy in witnessing the unexpected and changing scenes presented to them, she withdrew.

Mrs. Webster was then before the council, and said she was also glad of the opportunity to be present with her sister, where she was allowed the privilege of speaking again through an earthly form; and it was her desire to encourage her sister spirits in the great work they were about to engage among those they had left behind them; for they still loved their country, and had sorrowed over the fallen condition of its inhabitants. They had felt the loss of confidence connected with the affairs of men before they were called from their earthly trust, and her Daniel, thought then, and still thinks, their troubles should have been settled in a more humane and honorable way. But affliction and sorrow had ingulfed the whole country, and they would work again to establish Justice and Charity in order to ameliorate the unhappy condition of their people; and she would have her sisters of earth return to the plain and frugal habits of her own day, when a narrow black dress and check apron, with handkerchief for the neck as white as the beautiful snow, were all they desired, but she said that wealth with its demoralizing tendencies had made fearful inroads. Both priest and people had turned away from the landmarks of their forefathers, and gone into the by and forbidden paths until pauperism and crime, disease and death, were at every door. After saying that a Chinese woman was present, who had been instructed in our language, and would make a few remarks, she left her regards for her little sister through whom she was speaking, and then withdrew.

The Chinese woman was then before the council, and made the following statement. She had come from the sphere of her own people in spirit in order to encourage her sisters of other nations and peoples to persevere in their labors for the amelioration and elevation of their earthly friends. She then spoke of the time when the people of her own country were blessed with the communion of spirit, and had daily intercourse with their loved ones who were called by the Great Father beyond "the veil of the flesh." She spoke of some who tired of their home, and wandered away in tribes and formed settlements on other continents, and how the light from the mountain-top was given to them through the commandments; but they continued to wander in doubts and fears, and clung to their earthly principalities. She told of how a high and pure spirit had volunteered to descend and take upon himself the external of the meek and lowly Nazarene in order to teach man in his fallen and sorrowful condition, and lead him away from the changing scenes of Time up to his Great Father's eternal kingdom. She told of how he was persecuted by the earthly powers, and was finally nailed to a cross and crucified, and cast out of their earthly kingdom; but he triumphed over the powers of darkness, and ascended above his earthly tomb, and again showed himself in the presence of many witnesses, and told them to persevere in the work of human progression. He pointed the way to their eternal home. She then said the sphere of her people in spirit was up towards the mountain-top, nearer to the High and the Holy One, where no one could enter until they divested themselves of their earthly trappings. The good father Confucius had been their teacher, and showed them the way to the Great Father's eternal spirit home. She urged her sister spirits, who had gathered around the platform of Justice, to pledge themselves to work for the elevation of their own countrymen from their dark and sorrowful condition. She then invited them to return with her to her country's sphere, and she would show them things to encourage and strengthen them in the work. When, after a few cheerful words, as well as thanks for the privilege and the pleasure of speaking, she withdrew.

The next in council was a woman of Irish nationality, with her children, where she said they had been all starved and sent to purgatory through the avarice of old England, and they were sent before the council to be the witnesses for the poor people of Ireland, who had suffered through injustice. She gave testimony that when they were starving by thousands for the want of something to eat, old England stowed away the food sent for the benefit of Ireland's suffering poor from America, until it was musty and sour, and then charged them their last penny for a wee bit that was not fit for the dogs to eat. She then showed the rags they had; they could not be made to cover their nakedness when they were cast out and sent to the purgatory in spirit. She asked if it was right for a people for whom the blessed Jesus had done so much, to be treating their own people in such a way. When, after expressing her gratitude for what the good spirits had done for her and her children in hunting them up in their purgatory, and cleaning them, and giving them garments that were fit to be seen in company, — she said the woman that was wanting to speak was sitting upon her feet awaiting, and she would go and give her a chance. She then withdrew.

One of the Hindoo women was next in council, where she stated that her people had sat and listened to the different accounts that were given in the council; and they had considered among themselves that a people who had a Koran, which had told them of a place above where the gods would receive and reward the good people, and of a place somewhere in which the bad people who disregarded the commandment of their gods, and disannulled the law of Justice, would and ought to be punished. Her people thought such cruel statements which had been made were not very respectable, and they had concluded in their minds it would have been better and more to their credit now if they had never had a Koran; for if they could not live in obedience to its teachings themselves, they ought not to have taught it to their children, for it was evident from their example to others they had never believed what they were teaching. And so the great star-spirit had told them, and he was now teaching them what had been taught others by the Koran; and they all loved the star-spirit, and obeyed his precepts, and followed his example. She felt grateful for the many privileges her people were allowed to enjoy, and said the bow-and-arrow girl was waiting, and she would retire.

One of the Forest Maidens was the next in council. She had come to the wigwam of the white squaw, where the camp-fire was bright, down from the upper hunting-grounds of the red man's race near to the Great Spirit, from where the wail of distress and of suffering caused by the white man's injustice to his brothers had come; and the Great Spirit said to her, "Go quick, and see if my earthly children are turning back into the snakes and the toads they come from, and why this darkness and strife has again covered the land." And she came as by the Great Spirit sent, and had listened to their talk; and she would return and tell him his white children had forgotten him, although surrounded with his daily blessings, and that avarice had taken the place of love, and that poverty and crime of every kind were fast covering the face of the beautiful earth in darkness and strife. She would tell the Great Spirit to withhold his blessings from this pale-face race, until they learned to deal in justice with each other. And as she retired—

India again closed the session by invocation to the Great Spirit.

DECEMBER 14, 1875. — After India's invocation to the Great Spirit, again thanking him for their daily blessings, and asking that wisdom and strength still be given sufficient for their labors, acknowledging the evidence of his power and his right to govern, and that his children should learn to ask and to be thankful for their blessings, he asked that their earthly witnesses might be kept from the cares and distractions, from the dissensions and the vices, among mortals, until all was finished and approved. When, after saying that Warren and Prescott and Booth would be present, and that they should commence the examination of the old records of the Israelites after Christmas, he again withdrew.

Warren was in council, where he said he was gratified with the opportunity of again speaking in the cause and behalf of freedom for his country. He then spoke of their conflict on Breed's Hill, and how he had sacrificed his life in his youth on the altar of liberty, that his country might be free from the demands of foreign taskmasters. He then told of the rattle of cannon, and of the smoke and the blaze of Charlestown, and of the red-coats that were sent in order to enslave them, but found good and true men who had pledged themselves to sacrifice all but their honor in the defence of their country's liberties; and although many good men fell in the struggle that followed, the result in the end was glorious. And he said they had again gathered together around the platform of Justice, and renewed their pledge to work once more in order to release their countrymen from their bondage, which had proved stronger and more dangerous to freedom than all the combined power of foreign despots. It was the bondage that wealth and fashion, craft and superstition, had engendered. When, after a few encouraging remarks to his brother soldiers in connection with their new order of battle, he withdrew.

Prescott was next before the council, where he deplored the demoralizing and fallen condition of their countrymen. He said that liberty was a priceless boon to inherit, and we should have considered its great cost, and not so foolishly squandered it away. He thought those who had been intrusted with the management of the good old ship of state, had sadly mistaken their duties, and instead of watching with a jealous care every sign of decay, they had gone out after railroads, and race-courses, and fast horses; while the good old ship had been left to rot in the water, and was creaking in every joint. He was thankful that the duty was again assigned to them to look after the unfortunate condition of their country; and they would see to it that a new crew was put in charge of the old ship, who knew how to cork the leaks and put it once more in good repair. And then, in a few appropriate remarks, he encouraged them all in their work, and said that light and strength would be given sufficient for its accomplishment. He then withdrew.

The familiar voice of Booth was once more heard in council, where he again reviewed the scenes presented before the great platform of Justice the past three years; and spoke in high terms of praise of what had been already accomplished; said soon the little bell would tingle, and the curtain would rise on another part of the great drama, when the tinkers at the head of Church and of State would drop their heads, and try to find some place in order to hide away in shame. He then spoke of his boy, and said he was then present, and well satisfied with the part in the great drama which he had been chosen to perform; said all were selected for a part, and should be prepared to answer the prompter's call. When, after his cheerful encouragement, he expressed his satisfaction with the progress of their labors, and withdrew.

One of the confiding Hindoos was the next in council, where he spoke of the things that had transpired among them during the past, and expressed his satisfaction with the remarks of the last speaker. He said his people would like to have him for one of their gods, and then said they were getting along in splendid order under the teachings and by the directions of their great star-spirit; but one of the bow-and-arrow girls had come again, and he would have to go. After saying they would do all they could in order to give their little goddess strength for her work, he retired.

One of the Forest Maidens was then in council, and said she had come from the red man's upper hunting-grounds by the command of the Great Spirit, to sit by the council-fire at the wigwam of the white squaw and the white brave, that she might listen to the complaints of the pale-faces who had trifled with the Great Spirit's law of Eternal Justice; said she knew the brave who had sacrificed his physical life in his youth in the maintenance of his country's freedom. She picked him up in her canoe, paddled him over the stream, and showed him where the red-coats were retreating; she then took him back to the old brave who had stood by his side. She was not surprised they now sorrowed over the fallen condition of their pale-face brothers who inherited the freedom that was purchased with blood; and she would away back to the Great Spirit, and tell him all she had heard said by the pale-face braves at the wigwam-council where the watch-fire was bright.

India closed the session by invocation to the Great Spirit.

DECEMBER 17, 1873. — After India's invocation to the Great Spirit, he said the present session was assigned to the old ladies who had gathered in commemoration of American independence, and of the event of throwing the tea into Boston harbor in order to oppose foreign taxation; whereupon he retired.

Those that were mothers at the time of the Revolution had the privilege of speaking before the council, where they expressed dissatisfaction with the fallen condition of their descendants, who had bartered away their freedom for the foolish and gaudy trappings that had been imported into the country. They told of the frugal and industrious habits of the wives and mothers who stood hand to hand with their noble husbands and brothers in the struggle for national liberty; and they had all met together on this the centennial anniversary to celebrate it with one of their old-fashioned tea-parties, and they would pledge themselves to work with their descendants until they felt again the spirit that moved their forefathers,

14

and make another rally in opposition to burdensome and unjust taxation. After speaking of their accumulating happiness in spirit since their new organization among the old people, the last one withdrew.

Miss Landon was present, and made a few remarks. Said she was permitted to enjoy the society of the old people who had assembled in order to commemorate an important historical event; she had come by invitation with the children who had brought flowers from their celestial sphere to scatter as they mingled with the aged in order to enliven and increase their happiness. She said the old folks, who appeared as natural as ever, were having a pleasant time, for they were still surrounded by the same conditions which they accumulated during their earthly pilgrimages. After expressing her gratitude for this renewed evidence of the Great Father's love for his children, she retired.

One of the Hindoos was present, and said that his people were also permitted to see and enjoy the old folks' celebration.

One of the Forest Maidens was next present to represent her race. She then said the Great Spirit had found the right material among the pale-face braves, who belonged to the noble mothers who were present, through which the spirit of freedom had its birth, and from that had come the knowledge of the higher birth of the immortal spirit that could now hold communion with those they had left upon the lower hunting-grounds, and tell of their spirit-homes, and point the way up to the beautiful stars that were jewels in the Great Spirit's crown; which should have long ago taught his pale-face children not to disregard the Great Spirit's great law of Eternal Justice.

India closed the session by invocation to the Great Spirit, again thanking him for his care, and asking for wisdom and strength sufficient for their work.

DECEMBER 21, 1873. — After India's invocation, he said that Parker and White and Wordsworth would report during the present session, and, if time permitted, others; and, after his usual encouragements, he withdrew.

Parker was the next in council, where he reviewed their labors, and expressed his gratification for what had been accomplished in spirit; said he had come to ask for more help in order to strengthen their force the coming year among mortals; and was thankful that he could get the necessary help now to finish their work without applying to the earthly powers. He said the halcyon days of the priest and the leaders of craft were about over, for the time was near at hand when they would have to lay aside their saintly robes, and come down from their high estate, and go to work among the suffering and starving people which their false systems and teachings had everywhere engendered. He gave encouragement to all engaged in the work of establishing the law of Justice so long disregarded in the affairs of men, and told them that with firmness and perseverance all would soon be accomplished. He then said the time was valuable, and he would withdraw and give place for his brother and co-laborer by the name of—

White, who spoke of his recent experience in passing from his physical to his present home in spirit; said his change was unexpected and sudden, but he had found the surprise on his part was natural and agreeable. He then spoke of his trying labors through the "Banner," given in order to instruct and enlighten humanity, who were asking for knowledge of the communion of spirit and of their spirit-home. He spoke of the chilling and disheartening influence he had been made to feel by the scorn and scoffs of the so-called Christian combinations, who profess to obey the precepts of the Saviour of man; but now he said he was receiving more than he could ever have expected, for thousands whom he had never known were flocking around him in spirit, and with outstretched hands were thanking him for his earthly labors. When, after expressing his gratitude, he retired.

Wordsworth, the poet, was present, and expressed his great pleasure of again having an opportunity of speaking, and he referred to the time when the inspiration of spirit guided his pen in the production of some things which still enlighten and cheer weary mortals on their way during their earthly pilgrimage. He said it was from the same great and inexhaustible fountain which had inspired the prophets and seers, the apostles and sages, of other cycles of time, that was given in order to warn them of the judgments that must follow the downward course their avarice and injustice were leading them, but all unmindful of the sorrowful scenes which the Angel of Time had already recorded, for what had been done before would again be repeated, and the same results must follow. After encouraging all in their labors, and saying they were for the improvement of mortals, he withdrew.

One of the old soldiers of the Revolution was then in council, where he told of their struggle with a foreign power that our country might be free, expecting that their children and their children's children would inherit the priceless boon of liberty. He said it grieved them in spirit to see how foolishly we had trifled away and sold our "birthright" for the trappings and gewgaws of foreign nations, who he said had already picked the last feather from our national carcass, and were now quarrelling among themselves over the bones. He was thankful for an opportunity of speaking, and was in hopes he might feel better about the sorrowful condition of his country after expressing his opinion. He then retired.

One of the Hindoos was the next in council, where he made a few remarks in connection with their own improvements; said his people would ever feel grateful for the pleasure they were permitted to enjoy in speaking and hearing what the people of other nations had said in the council. He described the operation; said it was like the telegraph, and everything that was said was put on their bulletin-boards, and taken from them to the people of every nation. He thought it was strange that every one who had spoken had some complaint to make about the condition of the people of their own country. His folks had come to the conclusion, from all they had seen and heard, that our progress was not very respectable for what had been called a great Christian nation. He said the bow-and-arrow girl was away with her tribe, and would not speak at the present session, for they had gone with a despatch to their red warriors.

India closed the session by invocation to the Great Spirit.

DECEMBER 24, 1873. — After India's invocation to the Great Spirit, he spoke of the sorrowful conditions that were fast increasing among the nations of the earth, and of the sectarian influence among the ecclesiastical associations of the day, and of the use they made of sacred things in order to build up and strengthen their earthly power. He then spoke of the terrible suffering of the millions who were neglected and forgotten, or cast into prisons and pauper institutions, and robbed of their natural rights. And after saying that Confucius was present and would give further instructions, he withdrew.

The pleasant voice of the good father Confucius was the next in council, where he spoke in beautiful and earnest words of the birth and labors of Jesus of Nazareth. He showed that the object of his mission was to unite the broken link between "spirits" and "mortals," who by their transgressions had lost the light that came from their loved ones who had stepped beyond the veil of the flesh. He spoke of the labors of Jesus among the poor and the outcasts, who were forsaken and despised by the leaders and by the bigoted self-righteous who were the representatives of the temporal power, and should have been the guardians and protectors of the people's rights. He spoke of his ignominious death upon the cross between the two malefactors, and of his triumph over the powers of darkness, as he reappeared in the presence of many witnesses who have borne testimony to the everlasting truth of the communion of spirit. He told of how He had strengthened and sustained his earthly followers, and then led the way through the dark sphere in spirit for all who had obeyed the covenants and were ready for the light; and how He had again returned with a countless host of angels, and by "rap and tap" and "tap and rap" around the altars of his professed followers had again and again given evidence of his presence in spirit, and had been once more rejected and cast out. But He would not be crucified this time, for his work was a-going on among the suffering ones of earth, and could not be stopped until justice was again established, and his kingdom of righteousness was revived and acknowledged by all. When, after his usual encouragement, he gave instructions in order for us to prepare to receive the statement that would be given by the leaders and guardians of the tribes of a past age, and then retired.

One of the mothers of Israel was the next in council, where she told of their wanderings among the valley lands along their beautiful Jordans, when surrounded by their flocks and herds, protected by those they loved; for they had enjoyed the communion of spirit, and knew when their friends were gathered home to their fathers, they would not be lost. But as the tribes increased, they went into forbidden paths, and the light of the spirit departed, and left them in the dark with nothing but the perishable things of the earth to sustain them. She then told of the demand that increased among the tribes for the coming of the promised Messiah, and how He did come among the meek and lowly ones of earth, who were rejoiced to hear his voice, for he told them of their Father's kingdom that was above their earthly Palestines.

But He was rejected and reviled by the high and self-righteous, who scoffed and sneered at him, and cast him out and nailed him to the cross. She then spoke of their national degradation and suffering which followed, and of their wandering and sorrow in spirit, shut out of the Messiah's kingdom.

One of the Hindoos was then present, and made a few remarks. Said the interest among them was increasing; spoke of the children from their paradise who had been among them, and had covered everything up with flowers. The star-spirit also had been telling his people how the children were taught to cultivate their gardens, and were instructed in the language of flowers; and he had told them about the Great Father, whom the bow-and-arrow girl called the Great Spirit. And as one of them was then waiting, he retired.

One of the Forest Maidens was then in the council, where she had come from the upper hunting-grounds of her race. She had seen the gathering together of the mighty nations and tribes who had answered the call of the angel of time, and were by the camp-fires around the great platform of Eternal Justice. She then bowed her knee, and called to her tribe to follow her example in evidence of the triumph of the one they called Jesus of Nazareth, whom they had known in his great mission to the lower hunting-grounds as the Great Spirit's central Son.

India again closed the session by invocation to the Great Spirit.

DECEMBER 28, 1873. — After India's invocation to the Great Spirit in thankfulness for his continued blessings, and asking for wisdom and strength sufficient for their work among mortals, he said, as they commenced on the old records, the first investigation would be from the reputed Adam down to Noah, and that different ones who were mentioned in the Bible history, who had been leaders among the tribes during that period of time, would be cited to be present and give an explanation of historical events which have been incorporated in their records. He said the examination would be in the presence of the twelve apostles, and that John would direct the evening's session. He then withdrew.

The next was the apostle John, who said their object was to throw more light over a period of time when the inhabitants referred to had kept no records, and, in fact, he said they had no knowledge of any other continent that was then inhabited, and they had found themselves in spirit mixed up and still in as much doubt as they had during their earthly pilgrimage; that Cain, Enoch, and Noah, with others prominent in the Bible history down to the time of the Messiah's advent, would be questioned, and that after that the apostles themselves would be the witnesses. Whereupon, after a few words of encouragement, he again withdrew. And —

Cain was the next before the council, where he made the following statement, and denied, so far as he himself was concerned, that he had ever slain his brother, Abel. He said that the tribes at the time of his earthly pilgrimage had become numerous, and had then spread over various parts of the country; that they had no tidings of their forefathers, and no knowledge of where they had come from, or of any other continent, and they naturally supposed the one they inhabited was the only one there was on the planet. He said they knew of no Garden of Eden, but they had a conscious knowledge of the home of the Spirit, and held communion with their friends who had passed beyond the veil, and were satisfied they had been gathered home to their fathers, where all would find rest. But as the tribes increased, and their interests became diversified, they were absorbed in worldly affairs, and disregarded the fellowship with spirit, and avarice soon shut out the light, and left them to wander in darkness and in doubts. The story about Cain slaying Abel was an allegory in its time, designed to show the condition between the tribes that turned away and corrupted themselves with their earthly idols, and those who followed the voice of the Spirit. Said they lived in tribes or families, and had flocks and herds, and cultivated the land similar to what the people do at the present age. The name of the founder of a tribe lasted through many generations; as that of the race of Cain, who were cultivators of the soil: or that of Abel, who were shepherds, with their numerous flocks. But then, as avarice and injustice increased, their troubles often ended in the shedding of their brothers' blood. He was pleased that an opening had been again made through which they could renew their communion with mortals, and said he would gather up information among his tribes, and report at another time. He then withdrew.

Enoch was the next in council, where he said he was the one

that was reported to have walked and talked with God, and that he was, and then that he was not, for God had taken him. He said it was true he walked and talked with spirits, and the highest spirit was God. He confirmed the report of Cain, and then told of the terrible sorrow experienced by all who turned away from the living Spirit, and bowed down to their earthly idols. The tribes had become numerous, and had wandered over the continent in search of their earthly treasures until avarice and evil had covered the land in darkness, which often culminated in a deluge of woe and of suffering that secured their own destruction. He rejoiced to know the time had arrived when the lost and scattered tribes were gathered together, and were willing now to hear and obey the voice of the ever-living Spirit. He was thankful he had been called to stand for his people, and would refresh his memory among them, and, if he could have the opportunity, would report some other time. He then retired.

Noah was the next one in council, where he said the condition of the tribes during his own physical experience was very much like that of the inhabitants of North America two centuries ago; said they wandered about over the different sections of the country wherever the leaders desired to locate, and it was a common thing to have a fight among the tribes in order to decide the right of possession; that all who disregarded the teachings of the Spirit were struggling to increase their earthly power. He said they had no records of the nationality or of the origin of their forefathers, or of any other continent, although it was common among the tribes in their wanderings to come in contact with those of another language. He then spoke of the ark that was intrusted to himself and others; said it was a box that contained the symbols of a covenant that was made with Spirit, which taught them of the change they were destined to pass through on leaving their earthly pilgrimage, and of their duties to each other in order to secure the communion and the light of the Spirit. But he said, as the tribes increased in power, they continued to increase in avarice, and their transgressions and evils covered the land in darkness until the Spirit, represented as a dove, could find no place to rest. Said he felt grateful for an opportunity to represent his people, and at the next session they proposed to commence the Bible record at the time of what had been called the "flood." He then withdrew.

One of the Hindoos was present, and said the wonder was still increasing, for the people that were called antediluvians were so mixed up together, they could not tell one from another. He said the star-spirit and Confucius had gone among them, and would soon have the tribes set right. After saying the bow-and-arrow girl would not speak, for they were again out with the numerous warriors of their race, who were on the trail of the pale-faces all over the hunting-grounds, he retired. India closed the session by invocation to the Great Spirit.

JANUARY 1, 1874.—After India's invocation to the Great Spirit, he said they had been directed to make short work of the old Bible records, for they had been altered over and over, and patched up so much, there was but little left that was of much object to preserve. He then made a statement to the effect that Shem, Ham, and Japheth were present, and would be allowed an opportunity to make their own reports; when, after the usual encouragements, he retired.

And Shem was then in council, where he said that himself and brothers were the sons of Noah, and they were instructed by the Spirit, with whom they held communion, to gather up their effects and prepare to escape from the fearful destruction that was fast overwhelming the tribes who had turned from the light of the Spirit, and were in fellowship with the gods of the earth by which they had been corrupted, and had followed after their own evil devices, until the land which they had long inhabited was again submerged in darkness resulting from the covetousness of the tribes. Such, he said, was his condition when his father with his sons and their families, with a few others who had been faithful to the covenant, were told when and where to go to avoid the evil days and the destruction that was fast approaching; and they obeyed the timely warning of the Spirit, and gathered up their temporal possessions, and found a home in a distant section of the continent, where they increased in numbers, and for a time lived surrounded with contentment and happiness, while the tribes they left were destroyed in the midst of their own unholy abominations, as others had been before them when they turned away from the covenants and the commandments of the High and Holy One, and worshipped their earthly idols; for it was that whenever they turned away from the light of the Spirit, their evil notions were strong, and they were soon left in their own darkness. They had no records, for none had been kept for centuries. They had no knowledge of the origin of their forefathers, or of any other continent, for the arts of reading and of writing were to them unknown; but their own experience was similar to that of the first inhabitants of the American continent; no history remained of them, or their towns and cities which had been overthrown and buried up in the general ruins their transgressions had brought about in the closing cycles of time. Still there is a remnant left that retain many of the ancient traditions of their forefathers, who followed the light of the Spirit. After saying he felt grateful to know he could be a witness for his people, and had mentioned about all that would be of much interest, and that he was anxious for his brothers to speak, for they all had a numerous posterity that were gathering about them in spirit, he then withdrew.

Ham was the next in council, and he confirmed his brother's statement, and then said they were directed to a fertile and healthy section of the country, where they were surrounded with their flocks and herds, and were blessed with a numerous posterity. He said it was their custom for the name of the leader or founder of a tribe to be retained for many generations; and although many hundreds of years had passed away which had left no reliable earthly record, every tribe was perfect in spirit, and had come forth at the call of the angel of time, and was found ready to take its place, for their father was faithful to the covenants with the Spirit, and his brothers had squared their earthly pilgrimage in compliance with the symbols that showed them the way to the upper temple. He was more than thankful for the privilege assigned him to speak, and wanted his brother Japheth to enjoy the same privilege, for he thought it would assist them in gathering up their tribes in spirit. Their posterity were numerous, and could be traced down to the tribes of the present age. He then withdrew.

And Japheth was the next in the council, where he confirmed the reports of his brothers; and then said it was true that a mighty host were gathering around them in spirit; but it had taken them a long time in order to clean up and be in a condition to answer the call, for too many of them had wandered into the forbidden paths while they were tenants of an earthly form, and had burdened themselves with the things that had brought them much sorrow. It was true they had learned through suffering the mistakes they had made, and were ready and willing to take their place among the assembled tribes. He then said it was with them as it had been with others before them, and to the sorrow of mortals was still the same, for the beautiful country where they had found rest for one or two generations was again overrun by the tribes of other sections, often speaking in a different language, where they bought and sold, and trafficked together, until avarice and injustice had done their work, when the light of the Spirit departed, and left them again in their own darkness to imbrue their hands in each other's blood, until the just judgment of the High and Holy One removed them again from the ground which in their selfishness they had polluted. After saying he felt grateful for the privilege of adding his testimony with that of his brothers, he withdrew.

One of the Hindoos was present in council, where he said that the covenant with the symbols of which they had been telling was the same one the great star-spirit had given to his people, and was teaching them from it what the other tribes had been taught before; and it was very evident that if they had attended to its beautiful teachings as they should have done, in place of leaving it standing around in the fields, while they were devastating the lands that sustained them by their terrible fightings with each other, they might possibly have been higher up in the Great Father's eternal kingdom. After speaking of the interest that some of the tribes manifested in the box the star-spirit had intrusted to his people, he said another one of the bow-and-arrow girls had come, and he would retire.

One of the Forest Maidens was the next in council, where she told of the numerous race of the red man, and of the kindness and love of the Great Spirit, who had bountifully supplied their wants when they inhabited the lower hunting-grounds. She had come from the upper hunting-grounds near to the Great Spirit, and had listened to the talk of the pale-faces, who in their avarice and injustice had forgotten the kindness and love of the Great Spirit, and in their wranglings and fightings with each other had seen much sorrow; and they were willing now to answer the call of the Great Spirit, who has sent forth his mighty warriors to awake and bring up his pale-face children, who have been worshipping their earthly gods, — where they could see how they appear, and where

the Book of Life has been opened by the command of the Great Spirit's Central Son.
India again closed by invocation to the Great Spirit.

JANUARY 4, 1874.—After India's invocation to the Great Spirit, he said the present session was assigned to the old patriarchs Abraham, Isaac, and Jacob. One object was to assist them in the arrangement of their tribes, that each one might have its proper place as they gathered up in spirit. After speaking of the surprise and pleasure the wonderful scenes were producing, he again retired.

Abraham was then in council, where he said it afforded him pleasure in having the opportunity of again entering into the Holy of Holies, where spirit could commune with mortals, for it was true the Ancient of Days had set, and the nations and tribes of the earth were gathered together in answer to the call. He had seen them coming from mountain and plain, and from the Jordans and Palestines of their own happy country; and his soul was again overflowing as he contemplated the compassion and the love of the great Creator, who had been his God and the God of his fathers. He then sent forth his directions for the numerous tribes who had looked to him as their leader during their long pilgrimage, and told them to gather around the great platform of Eternal justice, each tribe in its place, and there, after uniting in an anthem of everlasting praise to the Great Father, bow down in acknowledgment of his wisdom and of his compassion and love, and also of his justice; for he had fulfilled his covenant, and gathered them all into his great Ark of Safety, and had opened the way to the eternal city into the temple not made with hands. After saying he was so much overpowered at the grandeur of the scenes he had witnessed, he desired to say no more, and gave way for his son.

Isaac was the next in council. He said it was truly a grand consummation in the fulfilment of the promise made to his father; and as he had seen the scattered tribes coming from valleys and plains and from the mountain-tops, he knew the time had come for them to enter the Eden of their promised land. He then told his people to gather up each tribe in the place assigned to them, and then contrast the scene before them with all their barren and forsaken country, and their crumbling and wasted principalities, and then bow in humbleness of spirit, in acknowledgment of the wisdom and of the justice of the High and Holy One, whom they had disregarded by turning away from the voice of his Spirit, and becoming wanderers and aliens in the land of their fathers. He rejoiced to know they had not been forgotten, and they would join in the songs of universal praise for their deliverance from their earthly bondage. After saying he was ready with his tribes to take their place, he withdrew.

Jacob was the next in council. He said it was true he did turn away from the voice of the Spirit and from the covenant of the fathers, and found a home in a strange land. He had not been forgotten, for the same God who watched over and protected his fathers had protected him also and surrounded him with a numerous posterity; and he loved the lowing of his herds, and the blessings that the beautiful earth produced, and was satisfied; and he rejoiced to see the numerous tribes, as they gathered in from hill-tops and plains and from around the moving waters. If some were without the symbols of the covenant made with the fathers, without breastplate and girdle, they had received through birth an inheritance in the eternal city. They had waited long in order to prepare and purify themselves, and await the coming of the promised Shiloh, who was gathering up the lost and scattered tribes from the mouldering ruins of their earthly principalities, and would lead them up to the ever-green fields of the Great Father's eternal kingdom. He then said the grandeur of the scenes he had witnessed was beyond human comprehension; but he was thankful for the pleasure he had received, and appealed to the High and Holy One that sufficient strength be given to the little handmaid through whom he was speaking, that she might hold out until the work was finished. After saying that Joseph would report at the next session, he withdrew.

One of the Hindoos was next in council. He also spoke of the great interest manifested in the appearance of the various tribes, as they had been getting together from every quarter. He said some had the symbols of the covenant and some didn't; and it was by that the leaders knew where each tribe belonged. He thought most of them would be glad to find some place where they could have the box which the star-spirit had given to his people. He had only stopped a few moments to say his folks were well, and the bow-and-arrow girls were still on the war-path, and retired.

India closed the session by invocation to the Great Spirit.

JANUARY 7, 1874. — After India's invocation to the Great Spirit, again thanking him for all that had already been accomplished, and asking for wisdom and strength sufficient for their labors, he said Joseph and Benjamin would continue the report of the Bible history, and again withdrew.

Joseph was the next in council, where he spoke of the time of his own pilgrimage in the flesh, and said the accounts that had been incorporated with the records of the past age concerning himself and brothers had been exaggerated, although in the main the report was true. He then spoke of his visions of coming events, which often troubled his mind; and as he was in the habit of relating them to his father Jacob, it excited the envy of his brothers, and they sought an opportunity in order to get him out of the way, for they disliked his father's interpretation of what they called his dreams. But the results, under the providence of God, had placed him in a position where he was instrumental in doing much good among the suffering people. He said it was true they were a stiff-necked and rebellious race, with but little aspiration for the spirit, and were prone to disregard its counsel, but would wrangle and fight among the tribes about their earthly gods until the country which they inhabited was full of their abominations. Pharaoh and all his hosts with chariots and horses were ingulfed in a sea of mental darkness, and the tribes had scattered, and had wandered in the wilderness of doubts and fears, and through the red seas of their afflictions, down to the present closing cycle. He felt to rejoice that the angel of time had sounded the everlasting summons for all to appear around the great platform of Eternal Justice, where the seals of the past age were broken, and where they could bow their knee in gratitude to him who alone was found worthy to open the way and lead them from their earthly Jordans up to the promised land. He then told them it was the one who had been jeered and scoffed at and crucified, and who had penetrated through the darkened spheres of earth that He might plead in their behalf, and who had again returned in order to renew the covenant of his Father's love, and lead the wayward and weary ones of earth back with him into the Great Father's eternal kingdom. As he had seen them coming from the east and the west, from the north and the south, from mountainside and plain, every tribe in its own place, his own soul was overflowing with amazement and love at the wisdom and power of the Great Creator. He then said that he had loved his father and brother Benjamin, and they had had a happy reunion in spirit; and also his other brothers, who had been scattered, and whose posterity was still numerous among the tribes of the east. After an expression of thanks that a place had been found where the covenant of the communion of spirit could be renewed with mortals, and that his brother Benjamin was yet to speak, he withdrew.

Benjamin was the next in council. He spoke of the increase of his own posterity, and said they had been selfish, and in their blindness and want of comprehension in regard to the covenant with spirit they had clung to their earthly possessions. He felt grateful for the privilege of solving the great mystery, and rejoiced to know the time had come when the seals would again be broken, for the scales were falling from their eyes, and they felt their bondage to the transitory and perishable things of earth were fast drawing to a close. It was true their avarice and their injustice had caused them much sorrow which had been long and terrible to endure, and whatever could still be in judgment for them they were ready and willing to receive. He then said he would answer for his other brothers, whose numerous posterity had scattered tribe after tribe over the face of the earth, where they were still represented among the different nations. His brother Joseph and himself were the only legitimate children, and the bond of affection had never been severed between them. He then spoke of the grandeur of the scenes they had witnessed in spirit since the commencement of the present gathering together; no language could convey to mortals even a shadow of its magnitude, for they had seen the assembling hosts coming up from every quarter: it was tribe after tribe, and every tribe in its place and order; it was nation after nation, and generation after generation, who for century after centuries had left no earthly records; but they had heard the call of the angel, and were gathering around the standard of their promised Shiloh. When, with evident emotion, he again gave expression to his gratitude, and withdrew.

Thomas, one of the twelve who sat in judgment over the tribes of Israel, was then heard. He spoke to the assembled tribes, and told them of their wandering up and down the earth in their struggle and search for the Mammon of unrighteousness. He spoke of their barren and deserted country, and of the crumbling relics of their perishable kingdoms among their dried-up Palestines; and asked them if their earthly power and glory had satisfied them. He then pointed beyond into the ever-green and beautiful fields of the Great Father's eternal kingdom, and showed them the way they had delayed their happiness by their stubborn and their wilful unbelief in the teachings of their own Messiah. He then told them that he himself was a witness of the labors and of the sufferings of their heavenly Teacher, whom they did cast out and crucify, and blindly and cruelly imbrued their hands in his blood; and as he had contrasted all that his Master had done for them with the way they had repaid the sacrifice, he still felt that he ought not to forgive them, and he would not, until they could forgive themselves, and bow down in everlasting gratitude before the great platform of Eternal Justice, and acknowledge the grandeur of his Master's work. Then, after a few remarks concerning personal affairs, he resumed his seat.

One of the Hindoos was then in council, and again told of his own people's progress, and said the star-spirit was with them, and had been looking with compassion on the ones who had persecuted and crucified Him, for he knew how they had suffered for their own blindness. He said many had come to the star-spirit and asked permission to go back in order that they might tell their friends what they had seen; but the star-spirit would say, No, it was of no use, for he had often been himself and had rapped at their doors, but could not get in. And then he said they would sit down in sorrow, and sigh over the things that troubled them, and, it seemed, in some way they had to remember. He then gave way.

One of the Forest Maidens was next in council, where she gave encouragement to the tribes, and told them the Great Spirit was good, and that his great Eye, which surveyed daily the suffering condition of his earthly children, had dropped many tears in grief over their injustice. She said she once belonged to one of the scattered tribes on the lower hunting-grounds, but she had long since gone with her race up nearer to the Great Spirit; and she would return and tell of the many millions who had answered the call of the Great Spirit, and had turned away from the contention and the strife that still followed in the trail of their pale-face brothers.

India closed by invocation to the Great Spirit, again thanking him for his untold blessings, and for the success and the harmony connected with their labors.

JANUARY 11, 1874. — After India's invocation to the Great Spirit, he said the investigation of the Bible record would be continued, and that Moses and Aaron were present, and would make their own statements. He then said that the labor had become a necessity, for there were many billions of spirits who still looked to their leaders for light. And, after his usual encouragements, he again withdrew.

Moses was then before the council, where he said he had been called before the platform of Eternal Justice to answer before the twelve, who were appointed to sit in judgment over them, and they must give an account of the way they had kept and obeyed the covenants and the commandments which were given in order to instruct and guide them through the wilderness during their earthly pilgrimage. It was now his duty to take his stand upon the platform, where he would have to become their accuser, for they all knew they had been a stiff-necked and a rebellious people, who were constantly wrangling and fighting each other, and never satisfied with the counsel of God's ever-living Spirit that was striving to lead them through the red seas of affliction, out of the wilderness of doubts and fears, into the knowledge that their promised land was above their Jordans. They knew his station in life : he was the poor orphaned shepherd-boy, without friends to sustain and uphold him ; but God did appoint him to be their lawgiver and their leader; and they had wanted him to be their slave, for they were selfish and exacting in their demands, and could never be contented. He then asked them what had become of the covenant with its beautiful symbols that opened the way for the longing spirit to its immortal home, — from the ark in the wilderness during their earthly pilgrimage, to the temple not made with hands that was eternal; and what of the commandments that were given as by God himself from the mountain-top, that told them to turn away from their many evils and obey the law of Eternal Justice ? He told them their own records showed what they had done : they turned away in derision, and had disregarded the holy commands, and clung to their corruptible, earthly kingdom, until they were destroyed in the midst of their evil abominations, and they had found themselves deserted wanderers in spirit, outside of their promised Eden. He then told them it was not the time now to be a-wringing their hands in agony of spirit, for they had been warned of the fearful results of their transgressions, and knew that the judg-

15

ment was just. And he was glad the time for the closing cycle had arrived, for his mission with them was finished, and he could now stand among his own tribes. After speaking of his many trials that had been prolonged until he was worn out through the perverse natures and the mental blindness of those he had been appointed to lead and to impart instruction in regard to the duties of life, as well as a knowledge of their eternal home, he gave way.

Aaron was the next in council; where he gave testimony of his labors among the tribes. He then recalled their attention to their wilful blindness, and how he tried to teach them the ways of truth and righteousness; how from time to time he gathered them around the ark of the covenant made with their fathers, and then himself entering into the Holy of Holies, where the ever-living Spirit would address them in language appropriate to their fallen condition, until their stubborn necks would bow to the ground in sorrow for their transgressions; and still they would turn, and go into the by and forbidden paths. They well knew that they had been a stubborn and a rebellious people, and had disregarded the covenants and the commandments of God, and did violence to the teachings of his Holy Spirit, and had come short of their promised Eden. Their earthly principalities had perished, and the covenant intrusted to them—which they had disregarded—had been taken away and given to another people; and they were shorn of their earthly glory, and had found themselves still wandering and forsaken and in darkness. And he felt to rejoice that he could stand with Moses, who was appointed to lead them through the wilderness during their earthly pilgrimage, and who had now taken his place upon the platform of Eternal Justice, around which they had been called to appear, and where all must bow in honor to the King of kings, who left his high estate to be again clothed in the form of man, in which he was persecuted and crucified; but still he had triumphed over the powers of darkness, and opened the way to his Father's eternal kingdom; and he had again returned in spirit with power to renew the broken covenants, and call up the wandering tribes and nations of the earth in judgment. After speaking of their wanderings, and of their doubts and fears, and of their many sorrows over the transitory and perishable nature of their earthly kingdom, he withdrew.

One of the Hindoos was next in council, where he spoke of the improvement his people were making under the instruction given by the star-spirit, and said they felt sorry for the tribes who had lost their leaders, for they knew they were the ones that often came into their country and made war on them, to increase their earthly goods, which generally ended in great destruction and suffering. And his folks had come to the conclusion, if they had the covenants, and were taught by the Spirit that such things were wrong, the punishment they have complained about was nothing more than what was right; for it was evident, if they had thrown down their weapons of destruction, and stayed in their own country, they would have had much less trouble. And he noticed that many of them still cast anxious looks in the direction of the Box the star-spirit had intrusted to his people, and he had no doubt they were sorry they had so foolishly lost the light it had imparted.

India again closed the session by invocation to the Great Spirit.

JANUARY 14, 1874. — After India's invocation to the Great Spirit, once more returning thanks for his continued blessings, and asking that wisdom and strength be still given sufficient for the accomplishment of their labors with mortals, and after his usual counsel concerning the physical condition of the media through which they held communion, he said that Sarah and Hagar and Miriam were present, and would report during the present session, and then again withdrew.

Sarah was next in council, and remarked that she was glad the time had come at last when they were permitted to stand up and speak for themselves in regard to many things which had foolishly been incorporated into the so-called "sacred records" of their own age and generation; for the inhabitants of the present age were under a cloud of midnight darkness, and it was time for the light to dawn in order to save them from their own destruction. It was true many of the reports in the records concerning their own earthly pilgrimage had been greatly exaggerated, for it was a time when man controlled with despotic power, and everything had to yield to his will. Many things did transpire, under the providence of God, that seemed difficult to understand; but when it was revealed, it showed his wisdom and love for his wandering and wayward children. She then denied, and said the stories were not true that were told about the immorality of their women, for all had their sorrows when those they loved went into the by and forbidden paths; all had their earthly trials, and they had sighed, and waited in spirit, to hear the voice of the true Shepherd, who had come at last and called them together. And as she was permitted to stand on the great platform of Eternal Justice which he had caused to be erected, and, by the side of her husband, could see the gathering in of the tribes and nations of the earth, as they came from the east and from the west, from the north and from the south, and from every island and every continent, she had trembled with delight at the grandeur of the scenes; and she felt that she could with truth and sincerity forgive her sisters and forgive and forget all, if aught had been remembered of the past, and in confidence and trust bow before the twelve who were the witnesses of their promised Shiloh, who had returned to break the seals, and again remove the cloud, and call up the wandering nations of the earth to judgment. After expressing her gratitude and her satisfaction for all she had experienced in the past, she was ready then to partake of her lot in the changing scenes before her, and withdrew.

Hagar was the next in council, where she gave expression to her own pleasure, and said the privilege was granted to her to take her stand among the nations; and then said, if she was made to be subservient to the will of man during her servitude, and was then cast out, she was not deserted by her Heavenly Father; and as the time had arrived for her to stand on the great platform of Eternal Justice, where she could see her kindred and tribes gathering in from mountain-side and plain, hastening to surround her and call her "mother," she was satisfied. And if she had no man to stand by her side where he could partake of her blessings, she rejoiced that it was her privilege, and she was proud that she could be their leader; and as the Great Father had been bountiful in his blessings to her, all other Hagars, who had been cast out and were friendless, could fall in, and they would find protection under her banner, where they would all bow to the twelve and before the One who had gained the grand title of "King of kings," for they all had been clothed with the elements of mortals, and had themselves been persecuted, and could feel for others who have seen affliction. She then asked them where her dominions should be located, and was told up on the southern hemisphere. She thanked them; and after addressing the mighty host that was flocking to her standard in beautiful and appropriate language, she pointed the way, and retired.

Miriam the prophetess was then in the council, where she spoke of the condition of the tribes who were led by Moses. She said they were prone to wander over the country in search of new homes, and paid no respect to rights of possession of other tribes who had then formed settlements of their own in various places over the continent. The Canaanites and the Hittites, the Amorites, the Hivites, and the Jebusites, were the tribes and peoples who had established themselves outside, and were independent of the others who held to the communion of spirit or were known as the covenant tribes. She said the leaders who lived up to the requirements of their symbolic order, and who were permitted to enter the Holy of Holies, where they got instructions from the Spirit, were not always willing to obey the counsel they received. She herself was a media through which spirit communed with mortals. She was not a sister to either Moses or Aaron, only by fellowship in the covenant order which was established by spirit to open the way from the transitory things of earth up to the Great Father's eternal mansions. She said their own experience was similar to that of other people during their earthly pilgrimage who had formed settlements on a new continent, where avarice and the undeveloped condition of the tribes in their selfishness had caused them much suffering. Most of their own history had been clothed in unbefitting language. They had all had their experience with earthly things, and had waited long to be initiated into the celestial city where the great Grand Master sat in council. She rejoiced to know that one brother had been found who was worthy, and who had opened the way, and had built up the great platform of Eternal Justice, around which the nations of the earth were called up in judgment. She then asked for a corner where she could open a lodge and initiate her sisters into the mysteries of the Order, and give them the signs and passwords, that all might stand equal as they entered the grand temple above. She then spoke of the wonderful and incomprehensible changes that were taking place, and of her own pleasure for the opportunity of solving the mystery of the ages — the communion of spirit with mortals. After which, she withdrew.

Another of our Hindoo friends was the next in the council and again told of the wonders they were permitted to see and of the pleasure imparted from the reports the women made. He said the one who stood alone was surrounded with a mighty host, and she had shown many things that had never before been explained to them. He could not see where the end would be; but one of the bow-and-arrow girls had come with the representatives of her race, and he would go, and give her a chance to speak.

One of the Forest Maidens was next in council, where she told of the wail of suffering that had reached the ear of the Great Spirit, and had disturbed the quietude of the upper hunting-grounds. She had come with her race, who had once covered the lower hunting-grounds, to the council-fire at the wigwam of the white squaw, where they had listened to the talk of the pale-faces; and they had been on the trail of the remnant of the red man's race, who had fled to the western mountains, where they sat in sorrow and complained of the injustice and of the many wrongs done by their pale-face brothers; and they would away to the Great Spirit, and tell him all that had been said and done by the pale-face race that inhabited the lower hunting-grounds of his mighty red warriors.

India then closed the session by invocation to the Great Spirit, again acknowledging their dependence, and asking for wisdom and strength sufficient for their work.

JANUARY 18, 1874. — By direction of the council, this session was adjourned over until the 24th, on account of the health of the media; and after the proper direction was given in regard to health, the order was obeyed.

JANUARY 24, 1874. — This was a short session, under the control of our Irish friend known as the "healer." After his instructions concerning the health of the media, he said it had been arranged for three or four, who were then present, to make reports, and then withdrew.

The next in council was a mother with her three children, who reported that they had all been starved in one of the wards set apart for the accommodation of foreigners, on their arrival at the city of New York. The story she related before the council was heart-rending, and it could hardly be believed to be possible that such things were allowed in a Christian country; but she affirmed that her children were the fruits of a lawful marriage; and, although she had been poor, she had never disgraced her husband or herself and her children by dishonoring the marriage covenant. Her record was examined in the Book of Life, and the order was then given that suitable clothing should be given to herself and children to pass.

As she then passed on, two young women were the next in council, where, on examination, it proved they had been enticed from their homes and deceived by false representations, and both had got into trouble; when, by trying to hide their shame, they brought their physical lives to an end in an effort to destroy their unborn illegitimate offspring. They were told their situation had been reported and examined, and no possible excuse could be made in their behalf. They had intelligent parents and good homes, and had voluntarily broken the laws of the great Creator by their disregard of his marriage covenant; and they had also broken the laws of man; and they must go back and get the men who had deceived them. When they returned, the men were asked why they had perpetrated such great wrongs upon the young women, and they answered by saying they had loved them, and their misfortune was a natural result. But they were soon told their mistake, and that they had violated the great law of Eternal Justice by giving up to the control of their unholy and unlawful passions; that true love would always protect and cherish the mother and her offspring as the best of all the Great Father's blessings; and, owing to their transgression, they could not pass, for in the spheres beyond there was no marriage, and nothing impure was allowed to enter; and they must return and labor with mortals, whose sorrowful condition was the result of their disregard of the covenants and the commandments of the Most High given for their instruction and their happiness.

The next one present was a man at the head of his family, who had been residents of the north of Ireland, with a blank card in his hand. He was told at once to return and have his card filled out. And he retired.

The next were the parents who were looking for their child that had been taken into the school in the sphere beyond, where the child had been attracted and had come to meet them; but neither of the parents was prepared to go with it. The father had preceded by a few years the mother's arrival in spirit. They had lived in a discordant and unhappy condition during their earthly pilgrimage, and the mother and child were left unprotected and without necessary means for their physical sustenance. She had married another man, which had broken up the first covenant, but both had a claim on the child. The woman was asked if she had devoted a reasonable time to reflection and meditation after her husband was taken from her. Then he was asked if, upon his birth in spirit, he had visited his wife and child, and done all that was possible to ameliorate any of their sufferings. Conditions had been such that neither obligation had been fulfilled. The father was then asked if he was willing to go with the child, and let the mother remain behind. He readily answered that he would; but was told that was not the decision which had been recorded. The mother could go with her child, and he must return to his labor among mortals, and fulfil the obligation he had voluntarily taken upon himself, and he must work until the unhappy conditions his bad example had fostered were forever obliterated. He then sorrowfully returned.

The man with his blank card had returned, and was told his case had been examined during his absence, and they had found that when he had possessions of land and estates, with tenants and servants at his command, he had lived with his family in luxury, while many who were dependent and looked to them they had served for sustenance, were often left to suffer in want for the comforts of life. One of his boys, who unknown to his father had gone with his basket in the night in order to supply the wants of the afflicted, was furnished with a pass. The others were directed to return, and told they must labor for the elevation of mortals until all who had served them and had any just claims were satisfied.

JANUARY 25, 1874. — India was again present at this session, and after his invocation to the Great Spirit, he said they would continue the hearing of the leaders of the covenant tribes, and that Joshua, and Samuel, and Saul were the next in order to report. When, after his usual remarks in regard to the importance of their labors, he retired.

Joshua was then in the council, where he addressed the tribes of which he was appointed to be the leader. He told them of their wayward wanderings during their earthly pilgrimage, and of his own labor in their behalf; told of his efforts in order to keep them in remembrance of the covenants made with their fathers. He affirmed that he had been faithful to the great trust confided to him by his brother Moses, who had received the laws given for their instruction from the Spirit on the mountain; and he was a witness of his labors

and of his deprivations and sufferings when trying to lead
them through the wilderness of their earthly pilgrimage. And
after all their labors in order to remove their doubts and their
fears about their promised Eden, they would turn away from
the ever-living Spirit and follow after Baal with his dumb
gods of silver and gold, while it was true that he had led
them into the valley lands that were flowing with milk and
with honey. And they had wandered among the Jordans and
the Palestines of the beautiful earth, but they had never been
satisfied with the changing scenes of time. He felt to rejoice that the closing cycle had arrived when they had gladly
responded to the call of the Spirit, and were preparing themselves for the crossing of another Jordan, where they would
find their long sought-for promised land. After giving his
people instructions about their lawful position, he withdrew.

Samuel was then in council, where he spoke of his own experience among the tribes, and said it was true that he did
hear the call of the Spirit when he was a child, and that he
was satisfied to venerate and follow its counsel after arriving
to manhood. He had tried to lead his people in the straight
and narrow path that would have insured their happiness;
but Saul thought evil of him when he anointed David to be
their king, although it was by the direction of the Spirit, and
he obeyed the command. He told them he had watched over
them in their wanderings, and had felt their sorrows for the
disappointments they had brought upon themselves by going
into the forbidden paths; for they were always a-longing
after Baal who enticed them with his earthly images; but
they had counted their loss as they had sat in spirit, sighing
over their folly, as they had witnessed the wasting away of
their earthly kingdoms. He then spoke a few cheering words
to the mothers and daughters of Israel and of Judah, and told
them to hold up their heads and be comforted, for the time of
their deliverance was near at hand, and the voice of the ever-
living Spirit would again be heard calling them· from the
perishable, higher up into the eternal kingdom. He then
spoke of his gift as a seer, and of the great mystery of the
communion of spirit with mortals, which was the same in
every cycle of time; and said that much of their own history
had been misunderstood owing to the darkened condition of
the human mind, and that more light would finally expel the
darkness, and show that the tribes of his age were governed
by the same immutable and unchanging laws of the High and

Holy One who inhabits eternity, and whose imperishable temple above conveys a knowledge of his wisdom and power to his earthly children. After expressing his gratification for the privilege of again speaking through an earthly form, he withdrew.

The next one in council was Saul, who then addressed the tribes over which he was anointed king in compliance with the custom of the age, when they were pilgrims in the flesh. Said he knew that he had been tyrannical and overbearing when in authority among them, but that was his natural disposition, and all he had done he thought was for their good. He was pleased to be remembered in order to take his place, as they had again gathered together in answer to the Spirit's call to prepare to move to a higher plane more in unison with their advanced condition. If those they left behind complained of their imperfections, he would ask them if they had done any better: if they had kept the covenants and the commandments, and followed after the good which they had left for them; or had they too bowed their knee to Baal, and burdened themselves by worshipping their earthly gods? He said complaint was made of him for banishing the diviners from among his people; said he did so because he thought they were doing them no good; for he could not believe the Great Infinite Power, who had created and sustained them, and surrounded them with blessings, had anything to do with their avarice which was constantly encroaching upon the rights of other tribes, and getting them into trouble by their wrangling and fighting with each other. He felt to rejoice that the time had now arrived for them to see and forgive each other's errors, and sit down together and unite in an anthem of praise to the Great Father of all for the manifestations of his wisdom and love for his erring children. He then remarked that the evil spirit which was said had disturbed him when in command over his tribes, was his own suspicions in connection with the disturbed conditions of the tribes that surrounded him. After expressing his thanks, he gave a few encouraging words to his people, and retired; whereupon India again closed the session by invocation to the Great Spirit.

JANUARY 28, 1874. — After India's invocation to the Great Father, asking for the continuation of his blessings and for wisdom and strength sufficient for their labors, he said the present session was set apart for the women, and that Deborah and Hannah, Ruth and Abigail, and, if time permitted, Joel would make their reports. He then retired.

Deborah was next before the council, and said it was a pleasure for her to speak through the organism of another in the same way the spirit had spoken through her own physical organs. And as she was now permitted to take her stand on the broad platform of Eternal Justice, which had been at last erected over the darkened scenes of earth, she did rejoice to know the time had come for them to be resurrected in spirit, and gathered up where tribes and nations could take their place and prepare to enter their promised land; for they had long wandered among the decaying kingdoms of their earthly conquests, and had learned how transient had been their glory. And all who had turned a deaf ear to the ever-living Spirit, and had disregarded the covenants and the commandments of the High and Holy One given for their instruction, and had gone into the forbidden paths that had corrupted the earth with their evil doings, must return and labor among the tribes until the history of their terrible mistakes was blotted out from their national records. She then told the mothers of Israel and of Judah, who had been overtasked with their earthly burdens, to step forward, for the time had come for them to enter into the everlasting kingdom where they would find rest. Whereupon, after giving the others a few words of encouragement, she gave way for her sister spirit.

Hannah, the mother of Samuel the seer, was the next in council, where she spoke of their trials and sufferings; said she had been blessed with a knowledge of the communion of spirit, and that she obeyed the counsel she received, and dedicated her son to the service of the God of Israel, and sent him to the temple in his youth to be instructed in the covenants and the commandments given to their fathers; but when he arrived at manhood, and was invested with authority, he soon followed the example of other leaders of the covenant tribes who had thirsted for earthly glory. She then told them of their unholy deeds and of their wars, of the blood and carnage they had passed through, which was sickening to the sight of others. She told them of their struggles with the surrounding tribes in order to increase their power, and of the many wives they had used to bring forth their offspring to increase the number of their warriors; and of the judgments of God that followed the broken covenants, — how they had been left deserted and alone in their sorrow, and the history of their abominations that was still in the records they had sealed with the blood of their brothers, and corrupted and increased human suffering for century after century down to the present closing cycle. After telling of her own sorrows, she told them she wanted nothing to do with any of them: all she asked for was her children who were deserted and left with none but herself to protect them. She would join her sisters and pass beyond where none of their discord could ever enter. They who had been the trusted guardians of the holy covenants and the boasted leaders of the tribes could return and labor with their descendants until the records of their evil doings were blotted out and forgotten, and husband and wife, with their own true offspring, could come up and take their place on the platform of Eternal Justice in purity and love together. She then called their attention to the ark of the sacred covenant that was intrusted to their care, which in their struggles for their perishable kingdoms they put aside and abandoned. They now could see it on the platform guarded by the more faithful Hindoos, with the Messiah, who had stood by it, whom they had cast out and crucified. She then spoke of the twelve chosen witnesses who were then examining the testimony that was being offered in their behalf, that, if possible, some excuse might be found for their blindness. After expressing her gratification for the pleasure she experienced in speaking with mortals, she gave way for her sister.

Ruth was the next in council, where she addressed the assembled tribes, and told them of their condition when she was an earthly pilgrim among them; and she spoke of the change that had taken place. She and her sisters were now permitted to take their stand upon the platform of Justice, and claim equal rights with their brothers; and as they were kept in obscurity, and had to bear the burdens while wandering in the wilderness during their earthly trials, they were now permitted to take the lead, and would enter the kingdom before them. She told them when they had purified the records which they had left, which still bore testimony of their unlawful deeds, that were now a mockery and a blind guide among their descendants, and could look up and justify themselves for their many errors, they would be prepared and could come up and enter the kingdom in new and clean apparel, where they all could sit down together and unite in a new song to the God of Israel for his endless blessings, and for his wisdom and compassion for his wayward and erring children. When, after a few pleasant remarks, she said, as she had enjoyed the privilege of being with us to speak before, she would give place to another.

Abigail was the next one in the council, where she told of her own troubles and of her sorrows. Said she had been the wife of two of the famous leaders, but she did not know to whom she belonged, or whether in justice she belonged to either, owing to the unhappy and discordant condition connected with the strife and the confusion in their struggle for power during their earthly trials. She said many of her sisters had been the unwilling wives among ten or a dozen others claimed by one of the boasted leaders, and who were often left to suffer when most in need of protection. She was rejoiced to know the Messiah had returned and lit up their dark sphere, and built up the platform of Eternal Justice, where they were now permitted to stand, knowing they would be protected in their rights. She would not ask to enter the beautiful paradise beyond, whither her sisters were going, until she had returned and done something for the elevation of suffering mortals who were anxiously asking for their rights, and were casting from their records the evidence of their blind condition, and of the unholy abominations said to have been sanctioned by the God of Israel, and handed down as sacred by those who had disregarded the holy covenants and the commandments given to their fathers, which they have set aside and made of no account, until the earth was again covered with darkness and strife. She then said their work with mortals would not cease until the covenants were restored and their sisters protected in their marriage rights, and could stand equal with the one to whom they plighted their affections, that when the toils of earth were done, they could ascend together with their offspring, and receive the benediction of "Well done" from the angels. After saying she felt grateful for the privilege of speaking, for it solved the mystery of the ages, and would assist them in the arrangement of their change in spirit, she withdrew.

Jael was the next in council, where she said she had been granted the privilege of coming to speak, in order to set herself right among the tribes, by whom she was accused of committing a barbarous act, after enticing a wayworn warrior into her tent under the garb of friendship, when he was fatigued after the heat of battle, and in confidence had gone to sleep; that she had taken the spike from the door of her tent, and with a hammer driven it through his temples, and pinned him to the ground, and slew him. After relating her story, she confirmed its truth, and said if she had done wrong, she desired that she might be forgiven; said she was encouraged and stimulated by their example to commit the act, for they had wrangled and fought with the surrounding tribes to increase their power, and covered themselves with the blood of their brothers, until in their carnage and strife they had all become more like fiends than like human beings; and they had intensified their own inhuman and unholy deeds by saying it was the command of the God of Israel for them to fight their way and slay all who had the courage to protect their homes and their wives and children from the general slaughter. She thought she might have one consolation left, for if their records were true, they must justify her and her cruel act; but if their records were not true, let all look to it who have perpetrated and sanctioned the terrible falsehood, for it had been handed down from tribe to tribe, until age had made it sacred, and the nations of the earth by its sanction were still revelling with their hands dripping with their brothers' blood. She would take her hammer and nail, and go back to the earth, and remain there until all such false and unholy records were forever obliterated. After she had expressed her sincere gratitude for the privilege granted her in order to free her mind, she retired.

One of the Hindoo women was then in the council, where she said the star-spirit had permitted her people to be present, where they could listen to the statements of others who had been taught by the gods that could speak. She said the gods her people had worshipped did not talk. But they had bowed down to them in sincerity, and in a true desire to be good, and deal in justice with each other. She thought if her people could have had a covenant that taught them of a resurrection of the spirit, and the commandments which told them how to live in order to secure the blessings of the talking god, who had created them and brought them in communication with his spirit children, there would have been less complaint about injustice. But then, she said, it was not for her, who had no such advantages, to be speaking in that way before them. The great star-spirit was good, and was teaching her people in spirit the covenants and the commandments the other people had been intrusted with. And she thought they would soon be in a condition to return to the people of their own nation, and teach them about the speaking god, and how they could secure his favors by dealing in justice with one another. She then said she was much pleased that she could be allowed to speak, and that her people were all thankful for the great favor which had been shown in their behalf, and then retired.

One of the Forest Maidens was then in council, and said she had come to the wigwam of the brave and his squaw as by command, and she had listened to the talk of the daughters of Israel and of Judah, and she had followed in the trail of their many wrongs, which were still causing sorrow all over the lower hunting-grounds, while the cry had gone up to the Great Spirit, asking why a part of his pale-face children are revelling in luxury with his blessings, and the balance starving for bread. She then told them that if the Great Spirit should come to the earth in his power, he would burn it up in an hour. But He had sent out his workers, who were more numerous than the sands of seas, and brighter than ten thousand suns; their bows were strong, and their arrows sure; and all must stand before the great platform of Eternal Justice, until the wail of suffering caused by avarice and injustice ceased to be heard among the pale-face children of the Great Spirit, who were still desecrating the beautiful hunting-grounds of the red man's race by their many evils and their false professions of love for the Great Spirit's Central Son.

India again closed the session by invocation to the Great Spirit.

FEBRUARY 1, 1874. — After India's invocation to the Great Spirit, he said that David, and Gad the seer, and Nathan the prophet, and Solomon, would make their reports at the present session; and after a few cheerful words of encouragement, he again retired.

David was then in the council, and there said the time had arrived when he must make a true statement of his own management at the time he was their king and the trusted leader of the covenant tribes; and then said he must acknowledge before the platform of Eternal Justice, where all were called to appear, that he had deceived them, and had led them in the by and forbidden paths, contrary and in defiance of the counsels of the Holy Spirit. In his anxiety to increase his temporal power, he had unwisely followed the examples of the leaders before him, and turned aside from the covenants and the commandments given to the fathers, which he should have obeyed in order to insure their blessings. But he disobeyed the voice of the Spirit and followed after other gods — the gods of blood and carnage of his own creating. And he had long stood before them shorn of his power, and ashamed of his weakness in his struggle for earthly glory, when in his pride he had wanted to be great that his children might inherit his fame. And he had urged them forward in their battles — where they imbrued their hands in their brothers' blood — by falsely telling them it was the command of the God of Israel. He had trampled down the nations and tribes around them, and imposed unjust and burdensome taxes to increase his wealth, for he desired to build a temple that should far exceed all other earthly temples in splendor. He then said he had before denied the record that told of their many wives and concubines; but he could do so no longer, for to his shame he was compelled to acknowledge that the record in that was true. And as he could see them before him on the platform of Eternal Justice, he had no claim on either one, for he had disobeyed the holy commandments, and was cut off in the height of his selfish ambition, and it fell to his son to complete his plans, of whose history all were familiar. And he asked where was the temple and where was all their boasted earthly glory? It was for him, who had wantonly deceived them, now to leave them and return and labor for the elevation and the purification of others who have suffered from their examples. He said the sacred records would have to be purified from the history of their own evil doings; other temples and principalities would have to fall, and the covenants and commandments of the High and Holy One be restored again in their purity to the wandering pilgrims of earth. After a few personal remarks, he retired.

Gad, the seer, was then in the council. He also said he was called in order to stand as a witness of the abomination committed, in defiance of the counsel of spirit, by the leaders and the rulers of the people, who disregarded the warnings of the Spirit of the Most High, and when told of the fearful results that must follow their evil doings, they turned away in scorn, and did violence to those through whom the Spirit spoke in order to frighten away, and drive them to the caves in the mountains; and then filled their unholy "records" with warnings about the "lying spirits," called them soothsayers, and wizards, and familiar spirits, and cautioned the tribes to have no fellowship with them, knowing their evils would be exposed; and such things were still pointed out in order to frighten mortals. He said they perverted the counsel of spirits, and established their craft to frighten, to deceive, and rob the tribes; and when warned of their crimes and their effects, they had tried to make him falsify the spirit. But now he could rejoice, for the spirit had called them again, and they found themselves arraigned before the platform of Eternal Justice, where they could see the covenants which they had disregarded, and to their shame they had disgraced, taken from them and given to a more worthy people; and they could go back to their descendants who were still building temples and disregarding the covenants and the commandments of the Most High, and again scoffing at the voice of his Spirit; and they would have to labor until the history of their own evils was taken from the sacred record of the union of spirit with mortals before they could return with clean hands. After speaking of the hardships that the media of his age had to endure, owing to the covetousness of the rulers among the tribes, he gave place for his brother.

Nathan, the prophet, was then in the council; where he said he was one through which the spirit had made itself manifest to the people; and he was permitted to realize now as he could see the fulfilment of the wonderful things that were seen and foretold among the covenant tribes of Israel of the coming of the Messiah, who would take away their fears and lead them from their earthly Jordans up and into their long-sought promised land. He then said he had been shown in a vision, and they were told by spirits of the beautiful temple that lay beyond, and of the cherubim that overshadowed the mercy-seat; and they had copied from the description given, and built up their earthly temple through which by passwords and signs the leaders increased their power, and used it in order to deceive and enslave and oppress the people. And now they could see upon the platform before them those they had stoned and driven to the mountains for being the instruments through which they were warned of the terrible sufferings that must result from their fearful transgressions, if they did not turn back and obey the commandments of the God of Israel, who had told them of the Spirit's home that was above their perishable kingdom. After speaking of the fearful calamities that overtook the tribes for their wilful disobedience, he said they were punished by floods and fire, by pestilence and famine; many times whole nations were cast out from the earth which their evil doings were corrupting after turning a deaf ear to the warning voice of the living Spirit. And after saying that he was thankful for an opportunity of speaking to his people in a way the Spirit had spoken to them before, when they were pilgrims of the earth together, through his own vocal organ, he withdrew.

Solomon was the next in council, where he remarked, as they were now arraigned before the platform of Eternal Justice, it was plain to see the errors they had committed as they could see themselves stripped of their earthly fame. Said it was true that by his consent a costly temple was built, by which the wealth that had been gathering from the industry of the people for a century had been foolishly squandered in trying to imitate the imperishable and beautiful temple above. He was ambitious, and desired to perpetuate his fame among the surrounding nations. He wanted a place where they could deposit the Ark of the Covenant made with their fathers, that other nations might see and learn to worship. But, alas! his glory soon departed, and their temple with all their earthly principalities had crumbled away, and they were still left behind and had not accomplished what they had most desired. But he could see now, if he had used his wealth and station in order to have ameliorated the sufferings and elevated and improved the condition of his people, — if he had gone into their cottages and seen that justice had been extended to all, — he would have built up around him a living temple that might have been eternal. But, alas for him, he had failed! and the work was left for the promised Shiloh to finish, who left his high estate and was reincarnated in matter, and came up among the meek and lowly of earth, and partook of their afflictions. He too was tempted with wealth and power; but he could not be won, but passed through the silent tomb, and arose triumphant over the powers of darkness, and had opened the way to the Great Father's eternal kingdom, and had again returned to the darkened scenes of earth, and had now built up around Him a platform of Eternal Justice that could never pass away. After speaking of his own trials and temptations, he bowed an adieu to those upon the platform, and told the daughters of Israel and of Judah to pass on into the beautiful and pleasant fields that were in sight beyond, and he would return to the earth, and labor with mortals until the broken covenants were again restored : when he hoped that he might return and in justice claim his place among them. After expressing his gratitude for the courtesy which he had received, he retired.

One of the Hindoos was then in council. He also spoke of the condition of those who were once the guardians of the people, and said it was sorrowful to see so many of the great men losing their power. Some of them wanted to look into the box the star-spirit had given to his people, but they had not been allowed as yet to do so; said the star-spirit had sent ambassadors to his nation, and he thought now they would soon have an understanding of something above their idols. He was sorry for the man who had spoken last, for there was a time when he sent his ambassadors to all the nations for the silver and gold that was put into his temple. After telling about what they were going to do for their goddess who had allowed them the use of her vocal organs, he said the bow-and-arrow girls were still on the war-path.

Whereupon India again closed the session by invocation to the Great Spirit.

FEBRUARY 4, 1874. — After India's invocation to the Great Spirit, he said Bathsheba, and Vashti, and Esther, and one of the Hindoo women, would occupy the time of the present session. He then spoke of the work that was already accomplished, and of the pleasure it gave them in spirit, and said it could never be comprehended by mortals; but nevertheless the work would not cease until all was finished and the covenants were again established. And after his usual encouragement, he again withdrew.

Bathsheba was then in council, where she said she had sought for the present opportunity to speak in behalf of her son, for although he had built a temple, and had been intrusted with wealth and power, was he anything more than man, weak and frail, surrounded by those who would flatter, and by temptations that too often lead astray? She had known of his weakness, and she had prayed in agony of soul to the great positive Mind that he might be sustained, that he might be strengthened and stand firm in the hour of his trial. But he had failed, and turned away from the living Spirit of the High and Holy One of Israel, and revelled in the filth and dirt beneath. But she said there were many extenuating circumstances that must still plead in his behalf, for it was an age when many wives and children were a mark of distinction among the chosen leaders of the tribes. It was a custom that was handed down from tribe to tribe, and they had eaten and drank with it around them until none thought it a crime. She claimed that the wrongs and the errors committed by Israel were no excuse for the scattered tribes and nations of the present age, for they had been the recipients of more spirit-light, and should have forsaken the wrongs that bring sorrow, and held on to all that was known to be true and good. And with them such things were open and above-board, and no woman was thought to be degraded on account of the position she was called to occupy, where they all were provided for and partook of the common blessings. But now it was closeted, where they revelled in their filth in secret until the women were diseased, and then deserted and turned out to die, and to enter the spirit-sphere a friendless outcast. She knew her son had failed, and had come short of the promise; and they had sat in sorrow, and had suffered over their frailties. But if he was still to be shut out of the kingdom, she would remain out of the kingdom with him, and they would go and wander up and down the earth together. She then spoke of the darkness and sorrow that covered the people after their fall from the communion of spirit, and withdrew.

Vashti was the next in council, where she had come as a witness that she might assist in strengthening others to stand firm in the cause of justice and truth. She said it was true they had all had their trials, but what cared she for crown or kingdom when asked to purchase it by her own debasement as well as that of her husband, who first of all should have been her protector in the place of ordering her to exhibit herself for the gratification of men at a drunken banquet. She asked if they had nothing to do but to revel, as they often did, with wine and song, and with their wives and their concubines. "Why do I say *wives* in the place of *wife?* You well know it is because you made your unlawful wars on the surrounding tribes and nations, and made captive slaves of their women that you might fill your homes with their choicest daughters, whereby you could glut your sensual and sordid appetites until the nations of the

earth were filled with sorrow! What cared you for the poor
and suffering ones around you? Who among you taught
them of the resurrected spirit, or went to see if they were
supplied with even the common bread of life sufficient to
satisfy their daily hunger? But you could shut up the light
of the covenants made with the fathers, and guard it day
and night with passwords and with signs intrusted only to
the few, who by their cunning craft increased their power
that was used in order to build up their own principalities,
while poverty and suffering from your avarice and your
injustice were seen and felt on every hand." She said she
felt now that she was permitted to stand on the platform of
Eternal Justice, where her sisters were gathering up around
her, that she could not say enough in accusation against
them. It was true they had been gathered home to their
fathers, but they were found in the dark which they had
wilfully created; for they had turned away from the commandments and covenants of the Great Jehovah, and had
grieved away his Holy Spirit given them for a guide, and
shut themselves out of his eternal kingdom; and they had
shut themselves from the beautiful earth by their unholy
abominations, and were still groping about hunting after their
Egyptian gods, while she and her sisters, with the poor and
the deserted and friendless, had sat by the willows and wept.
She said she rejoiced to know that one was found who was
faithful and true, who was scattering away the dark mists of
earth, and was bringing up the nations and tribes in judgment. She then expressed her gratitude for the privilege of
speaking to her people, and said she would give place to her
sister who was chosen to fill the place which she herself did
refuse to occupy. She then withdrew.

Esther was the next in council, where she expressed her
pleasure that she had been remembered at the gathering up
of the scattered tribes; and as she was allowed to stand upon
the great platform of Eternal Justice before them, she felt that
she had no complaints to make, for her sister Vashti had already said all that was necessary in that direction. She said
it was true she was placed in a position during her earthly
pilgrimage which she had not sought for, and she had used
her influence as best she could for the purpose of improving
the condition of her people. She felt that the time had now
arrived when the daughters of Israel and of Judah could take
down their harps, and join hands with the daughters of Jeru-

salem, and go out together and work for the elevation of their earthly sisters, and then return to the twelve who sit in council, and receive the blessing of "Well done !" from Him who sits at the head, who has opened the way up to the house of many mansions. She said it was her desire that the old and the weary ones should pass in, and that the young and cheerful should go with them, and be counselled by their wisdom, while others who have trodden the wine-press before could return to the darkened scenes of earth, and labor with mortals until the light of the covenants and commandments from the God of their fathers was again restored, and their records purified from the history of their many wrongs; then return and join the loved ones, and enter the temple not made with hands, where, in a grand and glorious union, all could unite in a new anthem of praise and thanksgiving to the King of kings, who triumphed over the powers of death and Hades, and had opened the way to the Great Father's eternal kingdom. After a few pleasant remarks, she said, in answer to an inquiry about Mordecai, that he was her benefactor, and was a good man, and had arrived to great distinction as a chosen leader among his people. She then retired.

One of the Hindoo women was the next in council, and said it was a great privilege for her people to be allowed to hear what all the others had said, and it was not so very strange if they could turn away from their gods that could tell them of the beautiful things that were in store for those who proved true to the requirements of the covenants that were intrusted to their keeping, and then turn away and fall down and worship the Egyptian gods in order to satisfy the demands of the flesh. She thought, after all that had been said, it was no wonder the people of her country did not want anything more to do with them or their gods. It was evident, if her people had paid their devotions to the dumb gods, they could see they cultivated some sense of justice which they had showed in their daily intercourse with each other. She said the great star-spirit was teaching her people, and they tried to obey his instructions in hopes to receive his approbation. Many who had been prepared had already returned to the people of their own nation to impress the great truths which they had been taught upon the minds of others; and they were in hopes the time would soon arrive when there would be no more heathen with them, either in spirit or among their earthly descendants. She was thankful for the privileges her people had enjoyed; and as the bow-and-arrow girl had come, she would retire.

One of the Forest Maidens was next in council, and said she had come from the upper hunting-grounds where the Great Spirit sat in council. She had come to the wigwam of the white squaw, and listened to their talk, to learn why the lower hunting-grounds were again covered in darkness. She would away back to the Great Spirit, and tell him how all have turned away from the light of his covenants, and are following after the counsels of their earthly gods. "Why do you stand here shaking in fear of the power of the Great Spirit? Go back, and remove the heavy burdens you have left for others who have followed in your trail, and who are still in the wilderness and know nothing of the power and love of the Great Spirit. Remove from the records the history of your errors, and take away their fears, and lead them up to the living temple where the Great Spirit's central Son is waiting upon his platform of Eternal Justice in order to receive them."

After which, India again closed by invocation to the Great Spirit.

FEBRUARY 8, 1874. — After India's invocation, he said one of the sons of Solomon, his successor in command, and Elijah and Elisha, would give in their reports at the present session. He then withdrew.

Rehoboam was next in council, where he thanked the powers who had made the provision for him to speak to his people through an earthly tabernacle; and said it would be impossible for mortals to comprehend of its importance to them in spirit in assisting to arrange and establish order among the tribes. He said he was a boy of but little experience when placed at the head of an earthly kingdom; but he had ever been thankful to the Great Creator who had provided him with an earthly father that was worthy and had become celebrated among the nations for his wisdom, and who had built a magnificent temple in order to cover and protect the ark with the "sacred covenants" made with the fathers to exalt and perpetuate its memory among mortals. What if he had failed in the end, and did grieve away the Spirit from the Holy of Holies! He would ask, if at the time he was not earthly, and like others around him composed of earthly material; and if the earthly or material part of man had not always wrangled with the spirit for the gratification of its own demands? He then told his father to cheer up, for he had already suffered too much over his failure. He told him to let his former "smile" return again, for he had battled well with the elements that surrounded him. He had done all that he could to prepare for Him who was to follow, and who had finally triumphed over the powers of darkness, and had opened the way from the perishable to the imperishable and eternal kingdom, and had already awakened the scattered tribes and nations, and had called them to the judgment. He was aware of his own failure in many things, but that was between himself and his people and his Creator. He had faith to believe they could settle their own difficulties among themselves, and then assist in working out a higher condition for those they had left behind, when they could join hands and follow the Messiah, who had gained the crown with the grand title of "King of kings," into the beautiful fields that lay but a little ways beyond. After speaking of the grandeur of their work in spirit, and of the great interest they still had for mortals, he said Science must take more interest in the welfare of the race, and investigate the laws of spirit and matter, and build up a shield of protection around woman, who was in herself a "holy of holies," where matter and spirit were germinated into living forms. He said, although the Spirit departed from their temple where it could have more freedom, they had media through which it spoke, and they had seers and prophets who endured fearful persecutions from those in power, as the instruments through which the Spirit did warn them of the terrible sufferings that must follow their transgressions. When, after a few encouraging words, he withdrew.

Elijah, the prophet, was next in council, and said he was glad to be with us again, and was pleased to have an opportunity to speak to his people: and then told them of many things that transpired when they were pilgrims of the earth together. He reminded them of their being told that he would speak to them through an earthly organism, when the Ancient of Days would come and call them up in judgment. He then told them of their wandering in the forbidden paths, and of their going out and not returning, but being scattered among the tribes and nations. After turning away from the covenants of the God of their fathers, they had followed after and bowed down to the worship of Baal, and for ages had been slaves to the dumb gods of the earth; but naked and sorrowful they had returned, and were still anxiously inquiring the way to the promised land. He told them that he was old and weary when he left them, for they were always asking the way, but could never be satisfied. Time after time the spirit gave them counsel until his tired form was exhausted, and he would crawl away into some secluded place and wait until the spirit-band who watched over him could recuperate his wasted forces, while they were the ravens that fed him with living bread; and they would have fed and sustained you all, if you had heeded their heavenly counsel, and led you into the pleasant fields where the Jordans and Palestines are never dry, where the beautiful banks are green, and the flowers forever blooming. High in the heavens above is the pure and holy Spirit that has created and sustains you, and sent his spirit to guard and lead you through your earthly pilgrimage; but you could not be satisfied: you wrangled and fought and tore each other in pieces, urged on in your cruel work by the gods of your own creating, who were ever ready to do your bidding in that direction. But you have found they had nothing to give you, and you now find yourselves resurrected in spirit, naked and sorrowful, with nothing to show for your trouble. But upon the platform of Eternal Justice before you can be seen the ark with the covenants given for your guide, which you exchanged for your earthly gods, and which in your poverty now in spirit you have found guarded and protected by the people and tribes of another nation. When, after speaking of his own trials and vicissitudes during his experience among mortals, he said he was aware the time was near for his change from the mortal to the immortal, and he endeavored to get away by himself to his favorite retreat. But then his brother followed after him; and when away by themselves, a storm in the elements burst forth, in which there were heavy thunder with vivid electrical flashes, accompanied by wind and rain, at which time the spirit was on them both; and while his brother was entranced, he himself was taken away in another direction, and his spirit failed to make the usual connection with its physical body; and what his brother reported that he had seen was a vision of his spirit-birth. The reason they did not find his physical body was because they did not look in the right direction. He then said it was a terrible thing to turn away from the Spirit of the living God, for suffering was sure to follow. He trembled in spirit for the nations and tribes of the present age, for they occupied a similar relation to the people of his own age, whose long-sufferings for their wilful blindness had been terrible to endure. He thought he had said all that was necessary, and he would give way to his brother, of whom it was said before that he had received his earthly mantle. When, after a few cheerful words of encouragement, he again withdrew.

Elisha was next in council, and ready to improve his opportunity to speak to his people. He told them of their failures, and of their being dissatisfied and hard on him when he used to warn them of the sufferings they were bringing upon themselves and their children by turning away and disregarding the holy covenants made with the fathers, after the spirit had warned them to beware of the effects of their evils. He told them he remembered well how they had struggled and fought with each other to increase their power, and had often wanted him to acknowledge that their unholy deeds were sanctioned by the God of Israel; and they had tried to destroy him, and went after other gods of their own imagination that would revel with them in human bondage. He said that many things which they had claimed were sanctioned by the God of their fathers were not true, for the Great Creative Spirit that had given them seed-time and harvest never changed, and they were told He remained the same yesterday, to-day, and forever. And if they had obeyed the covenants given to the fathers, and the commandments Moses received upon the mountain, given for their instruction and sanctioned by the Most High, they would have obtained the blessing of an inheritance in the eternal kingdom. But they had shut themselves out by their evil and unlawful doings, and had wandered with their Egyptian gods in darkness. He was glad to meet them around the platform of Eternal Justice, which had been erected by others, where they were called up in the settlement of the great day of accounts. And as they had often made him prophesy when they were pilgrims of the earth together, he would now prophesy for them again that when their work was finished they would join hands and follow the lead of the true Shepherd who had opened the way into the Great Father's eternal kingdom, where all gladly acknowledged the marvellous manifestation of his wisdom, and of his justice and love for his wayward and wandering children. After speaking of the opening of the seal, and of the great pleasure it imparted to them in spirit, he gave them a few words of encouragement, and then withdrew.

One of the Hindoos was the next in council, where he spoke of the advancement his people were still making by their opportunity to hear the accounts that were made by the tribes of another nation; and then told of the mighty hosts that were passing through an archway that had been prepared for the purpose. Some were not permitted to go through, but had to return in order to finish something which they ought to have done before they came there. The great star-spirit looked pleasant as the tribes were passing through; only when some who felt unworthy to go would approach him, a-crying and begging to be forgiven, he would look sorrowful as he turned away his head and could not relieve them. He said his people had come to the conclusion that there would have been less complaint if the unhappy ones had followed the light in their Koran.

India closed the session by invocation to the Great Spirit, again with thanks for the approval of their labors, and also asking for strength and for wisdom sufficient for the accomplishment of the work, and that their earthly witnesses might be helped to endure the parts assigned them.

FEBRUARY 11, 1874. — After India's invocation to the Great Spirit, he said Rahab, and Jezebel, and Huldah, and one of the Hindoo women, would be heard at the present session, and then retired.

Rahab was then in council, where she said she had come to stand as a witness with the mark of the scarlet still upon her; and she then asked if she was not entitled to as much consideration as those who upheld and sustained her in what they knew was wrong and forbidden by the commandments. She asked why her house was set apart under a mark of disgrace, while those in command were allowed to have their wives and their concubines, and even then often deserted them and cuddled themselves away under her protection, and upheld and sustained her in a business they knew was forbidden and unlawful. Why did the holy men, who were sent out as spies, and who said they were directed by the God of Israel, come to her house for protection? And why, she would ask, did not the chosen leaders of the tribes, who had the ark with the covenants and the commandments that forbade such things, knowing it to be wrong and destructive to happiness, see and have it stopped instead of allowing it to go broadcast among the nations? Why was not a shield of protection placed around the marriage covenant sufficient to guard woman from all such unholy abominations? They had all suffered from its effects in spirit. She knew man had been gross and brutal in his nature; that he had taken woman in her helpless condition, and used her, and then cast her aside. The history of her wrongs was handed down from tribe to tribe, and from generation to generation, for the children had followed the examples of their fathers until the "scarlet mark" with its terrible fruit had filled the earth with corruption, and they were now called up before the platform of Eternal Justice, where they had to stand face to face with their judges. She wanted this thing to be settled; and she would take her stand by the archway upon the platform, where none who had known the law and broken it should pass until the crime that had caused so much sorrow and human suffering that its very name had become loathsome among the tribes was blotted out and forgotten, and woman again elevated and restored to her true position, where she was placed by the side of her husband in the Garden of Eden. She then expressed her thanks for the pleasure of addressing her people, and withdrew.

Jezebel was next in council, where she said that she also had charges to prefer against the chosen leaders of her people. She then told them how they had been deceived themselves, and had devoted much of their time in strife and human carnage in their anxiety to deceive others; and that often when they were smarting under the effects of their defeats, the gods whom they had appealed to for help were the spirits of the dark sphere, and were laughing among themselves over their misfortunes. And still they were never satisfied, but ransacked the country from island to continent, and filled it with strife and sorrow in trying to increase their earthly power, while the unprotected woman was cast aside, and, "Jehu-like," was trampled under their feet, and the poor and the helpless were left by the roadside to perish; and they were still goaded on by their imaginary gods until they thirsted for the blood and the spoils of their brothers, like so many fiends incarnate. She then told them that, as now they had been informed of the terrible effects of their evils, they should go to work in earnest, and see that its history was blotted out of the "sacred records;" and they should remember that the stain must be removed from the Most High by their falsely proclaiming that He had sanctioned their unholy deeds. It was true they had the covenants made with the fathers, with the Ark and the holy commandments, and they had toted them about the continent at the head of their mobs in order to terrify and intimidate the surrounding tribes that were trying to live in peace; but they themselves had never obeyed the heavenly counsels, and she rejoiced that a platform of Eternal Justice had been erected, where they were obliged to stand in order to expose their wickedness. She then gave them a few words of cheerful encouragement, and gave way for her sister.

Huldah was the next in council, where she confirmed the statements of her sisters concerning the condition of the wandering tribes, and said that from the time of the reign of Solomon's two sons down through the reign of all the kings, it was a perpetual scene of confusion and slaughter among the surrounding tribes; and from the time when the ark with the covenant was shut up in the temple the high Spirit departed and left them; and although many of the daughters of Israel and of Judah, and the daughters of Jerusalem, were media through which the Spirit spoke, it was seldom wanted, unless it could sanction the demand for power which had grown up among the leaders of the tribes. She said they had not attained to a knowledge of a resurrection of the individualized spirit which was afterwards made manifest through the mission of the Messiah, but they did know that a spirit spoke, and often called on it for counsel. But when they departed through their increasing avarice from the teachings of the spirit of justice and truth, the spirit of justice and truth departed from them, and left them wrangling and fighting with each other about their earthly principalities; and they soon turned away and lost sight of the promises of a heavenly kingdom. They had wandered and waited in sorrow for their blindness, in their dark and lonely condition in spirit, waiting for the second coming of the Messiah; but they had heard the call, and had gathered together the scattered tribes in spirit, and were preparing to follow Him who had also had his trials, but had proved to be the true Shepherd. When, after a few pleasant remarks concerning her own position as a media during her earthly pilgrimage, she withdrew.

One of the Hindoo women was then in council, where she spoke of the progress of her people in spirit, and said they had been talking among themselves, and had come to an understanding that the people of the other nations, who had so much knowledge and light to guide them, had evidently got strangely mixed up, and it seemed very sorrowful to hear so many complaints about their committing such great wrongs notwithstanding the light which was intrusted to them, which they had evidently used for their own destruction. It made the star-spirit look sorrowful to hear them talk of the struggles they had in order to obtain power as they seemed to call it, when it only increased their opportunities to do wrong, and to injure each other as it multiplied among their descendants. She said they were learning from the covenants which were intrusted to them, and they drew near to the great star-spirit, and loved to obey his precepts. After saying she was also very thankful for the privilege of speaking, she retired.

One of the Forest Maidens was in council, and said she had come from the upper hunting-grounds by the command of the Great Spirit, to listen to the talk at the watch-fire of the pale-face squaw and brave. She had heard the complaints of the fair daughters of Israel and of Judah, who knew the Great Spirit had never sanctioned the abominations of their fighting braves, who had filled the lower hunting-grounds with sorrow; and she would away back to the Great Spirit, and tell him all that was said around the platform of Eternal Justice; she would tell him the white blanket He sent down to protect the vegetation of the lower hunting-grounds was everywhere stained with the terrible crimes of his pale-face children. And as they had said that such things were in the records handed down from tribe to tribe, and sanctioned by the God of Israel — " now bring him out and show him, and let us see how he looks after being saturated with the blood of many victims." She said she liked the spirit which the pale-face squaws had manifested, and she would return and lead them back to the lower hunting-grounds, where the Great Spirit's archers had already been sent in order to clear up and remove the infamous charges that have been laid even at the Great Spirit's door by his wrangling and fighting pale face children. After which she retired.

India closed the session by invocation to the Great Spirit.

FEBRUARY 15, 1874. — After invocation to the Great Spirit, he said that Nebuchadnezzar, Daniel, and Belshazzar would be heard the present session; when, after his usual encouragement, he again withdrew.

Nebuchadnezzar was next in council, and said he was thankful for the opportunity of speaking, and he would say that during the interim since he was last before the platform, he had devoted his time to a thorough investigation of the affairs among mortals, and was well informed in regard to their present condition. He had been in their temples where they professed to worship God, and he had been in what they called their courts of justice, and he had found everywhere among what was called the leading class the same struggle for power; but the cry of oppression had not diminished among the laboring and industrious classes, who, since man's fall from a knowledge of the law of Eternal Justice, have had to bear the heavy burdens in every nation. As it was in the age when he was an instrument sent for the purpose of distributing among the starving people the untold amount of wealth which Solomon had foolishly squandered in the building of his temple, so unfortunately the same condition prevailed; for their costly temples were everywhere decked out in rich apparel. The ever-living Spirit has departed, and left them as it did their forefathers a-worshipping their Egyptian gods; for they had shut up the Holy of Holies, and kept under the wings of the cherubim for their own protection, until the cry of the suffering and the starving poor, who are the outcast victims of a designing priesthood, has again disturbed the harmony of the heavenly spheres. He then said he had been turned into the fields by the reports of designing men, who had falsified the records; but he was willing to take any place they had thought proper to assign to him among the suffering masses who were everywhere cast out with the dumb beasts to feed on grass, and wander homeless and friendless, and exposed naked to the dews of heaven, while the favored ones in power, who had grown fat upon the spoils, were still revelling at their banquets. He thought as he had been found worthy before to assist in distributing the wealth from their earthly temples among the suffering and starving people to whom it belonged, he should prefer to continue in that business until the law of Eternal Justice was once more established, and the pilgrims of the earth return in gratitude, and love and worship the true and ever-living God in his imperishable and beautiful temple not made with hands. After a few cheering words of encouragement in connection with their work among mortals, he withdrew.

Daniel was next in council, where he told them they would remember that he had labored not for worldly distinction, but had tried to live near to his God, and did listen to the voice of his Spirit, and was guided by the counsel he received; while they were witnesses of the fulfilment of many things given for their instruction which he had foreseen. He told them of the time when they would be resurrected in spirit, and called to stand before the bar of Eternal Justice to render up an account of their stewardship during their earthly pilgrimage, when they would regret they had turned away from the counsel of spirit, and disregarded the covenants and commandments from the God of their fathers. "But then you had your Jordans and Palestines, and you disregarded the promise of those that were above; but you have learned at your own cost the mistake you made when you turned and cast from you the ever-living Spirit. Where now are your temples you struggled so hard to keep? And where are your banqueting-halls where you revelled, while the poor whom you had robbed of their substance were starving for bread? You can now listen, for it has been assigned as my duty to meet you at this platform, and tell you that the inhabitants of the earth are still suffering from your examples; they have again turned away, and cast out the ever-living Spirit, and are worshipping their golden images and their Egyptian gods in their earthly temples; and you must return and undo your work. Now is the time when you are the ones to be scoffed at and cast out and driven into the mountains; for they will not receive you. But you must work among the temple-builders and in their banqueting-halls, as we worked with you when we were sent to teach you of your home above. And when your work is done, and the covenants and commandments of the Most High are again restored to his earthly children, you can return, and we will meet you at the platform of Eternal Justice, where you will be permitted to cross over and be at rest." He then spoke of the relative condition of the present inhabitants of the earth with those of his own physical age, and said that in many respects they were similar; but the present was held to be the more accountable in proportion as it was known they had had greater light. After speaking of the grandeur in spirit of the present closing cycle, he withdrew.

Belshazzar was the next in council. He also said it was a pleasure to him to have another opportunity of addressing a few words to his own people, for it was true they rejoiced to know the time had arrived when they could return and assist in the work of restoring the covenant among mortals. He thought there was but little to be said in their behalf. He spoke of the labors and precepts, and of the resurrection of the Messiah guaranteed to the world through the mouth of many witnesses. He spoke of one who was prostrated to the ground and temporarily made blind at the grandeur of the interview, and of the commission given that he should go to the Gentiles and proclaim the glad news of a risen Messiah, and of the general acceptance of the truth among the so-called Christian nations. He then said it was true his people had the covenants made with the fathers, and they had the holy commandments given to Moses on Mount Sinai for a guide for the people, but, owing to the terrible struggle for the temporal power that had increased among them, few could realize the truth of their divinity. He knew the present inhabitants of the earth were in a fearful condition, for they had rejected the Messiah the second time when he returned among them in the clouds of the heavens with an army of witnesses who had asked for admittance at every door; but they had been denied among all that had professed to be his followers, who were building temples in order to obscure the light, and strengthen their earthly principalities; for they still had their banqueting-halls where they revelled with wives and concubines, and drank their wine from gold goblets, in temples they have called "holy." It was well known they were tired of the wail of sorrow that has long flowed from the suffering masses of the people, and they would gladly return and assist in bringing to an end all such unholy abominations. He then spoke encouragingly of the progress of the work, and retired.

One of the Hindoos was next in council. He also spoke of their present labors; said the star-spirit was giving directions, and they were doing all they could to take away the fears, and establish confidence. He thought when every one got into their own place among the tribes, they would be contented and happy, and then mortals would most likely feel the influence, and it would be easier for them to keep the commandment — which the star-spirit had given for them — to love one another; and when that was obeyed, the trouble would come to an end, for the mouths of the hungry would be filled, and all would be satisfied with the blessings the Great Father had provided for his earthly children.

Whereupon India closed the session by invocation to the Great Spirit.

FEBRUARY 18, 1874.— After India's invocation to the Great Spirit, he said Cleopatra would be the first in order to report, and that she would state the one authorized to follow; and he withdrew.

Cleopatra was the next in council, and spoke of the pleasure it gave her as she embraced the opportunity of again speaking to her people through a physical form, and. she called to mind the troubles and trials they had experienced when they were striving and fighting for place and power; and how they were told by prophet and by seer of the coming of the last days, when they would be incarnated in an earthly form and talk with mortals. She told them they were taught by compasses and square, and by symbols, how to direct their lives aright, if they would draw near to the mercy-seat overshadowed by the wings of the cherubim; and how they had failed to follow the light, and had revelled in human blood and in carnage for power to strengthen their earthly kingdoms; and how they had failed and come short of the promise, and had wandered in Hades for centuries, sighing over the crumbling ruins of their perishable kingdoms, a-watching over their mouldering forms of earth, expecting they would be called to reinhabit them. She then recited the mission of their promised Shiloh around whom the nations were gathering; told of how he had left his Father's kingdom, and was incarnated in an earthly form, and grew up among the inhabitants of Jerusalem. She told of his triumph over the flesh and its lust for earthly aggrandizement; how he had passed the tomb and was triumphant over the powers of darkness, and passed through Hades with its many sorrows to the kingdom of light and love; and how he had again returned with an army of messengers of mercy, and had built up the platform of Eternal Justice, and rolled away the darkness which had so long entombed them. Their Hades had disappeared, and they were resurrected to light and to a newness of life ; and as they had witnessed the gathering up of the nations, as tribe after tribe had taken their place among their kindred, the prophecy that a nation should be born in a day was fulfilled. She then addressed one whom she recognized as Father Sadi. She told him he had loved his earthly possessions and his wealth, for they had given him power among mortals; told him of his camels and of his bags of treasure that he had stored away in his cave, thinking he would again inherit when he returned. " Poor old man, as you now appear with your white locks flowing about your trembling frame, the perishable earthly treasures you stored away can never be of use to you here; but come now and lean upon my arm, and I will assist you up one step, and point the way where you can yet earn treasures that will never perish." She then told them the promised land which they had sought was still beyond; but when they had removed the obstacles they left in the way of others, they would get the password to "cross over." She then spoke to her maids who had been faithful and still stood by her, and to the people who had looked to her for protection; said she had been educated amid strife for earthly power, in scenes of blood and carnage, and it was natural that she partook of its spirit; but they had learned to their sorrow of its terrible wrongs; and she would follow her Saviour in his work of mercy, wherever she could be useful in order to blot out the records of their errors, and help to restore to mortals the covenants and the commandments which to their great sorrow they had broken. She then addressed a few words to her Hindoo sisters, who had gathered around in order to listen to what she had been saying. She told them of how they had bowed down to their gods of wood and of stone, and of how they had enriched them with their treasures for nothing but fancied favors; and now had found that designing ones had enriched themselves at their expense. She then spoke to her red sisters, and paid them a compliment for their purity and the freedom they had enjoyed; said she would gladly join them in their earthly mission. She then spoke of her gratitude for the privilege extended to her, and of its great benefit to them all in their new organization in spirit. After saying it was decided that one of her pagan sisters should follow, she retired.

One of the Hindoo women was next in council, where she said it was true they had bowed in reverence to their dumb gods, and it was true that during their earthly pilgrimage they had had no one to teach them of their error. It was also true that her people had been taught the art of war by the example of the surrounding nations, who had the talking gods, whose records still showed they were constantly wrangling and a-fighting with each other. She said it was a great privilege the star-spirit had awarded to her people that they might be present and hear what the other nations and tribes who had such great light given to them would say; and they were glad to hear them acknowledge their sorrow for the course they had pursued in violating the laws. The starspirit had already instructed her people of its evil effects, and it was their intention to teach their own people to follow his precepts and examples, and obey his commandments. She then said one of the bow-and-arrow girls, about whom the other woman had spoken, was waiting, and she would retire.

One of the Forest Maidens was then in council, where she told them she had come from the upper hunting-grounds where the Great Spirit sat in council high above them and their earthly gods. She had come to the wigwam of the white squaw and brave, where the watch-fire was bright, and where the Great Spirit told her to listen to the talk of his pale-face children, and when they repent of their many transgressions, and turn back to the covenant and the commandments given to their forefathers, then let them return and renew the landmarks as by the Great Spirit given, — and take away the stumbling-blocks by which they have crippled their children, — and clear the way that all may know the road to the upper hunting-grounds. She would go from the terrible scenes of blood and carnage, and from the cry of suffering among the pale-face race now on the lower hunting-grounds, and when she had told the Great Spirit all, she would return with more of his archers to do his work. Then the pale-face squaw who stands high among her tribes, and who has worn the sceptre of her earthly gods, can go to the lower hunting-grounds of the Great Spirit, and finish her work. When it is done, she can return to her own place; for she could not yet enter the beautiful hunting-grounds of the red squaw, who had never broken the Great Spirit's law.

India again closed the session by invocation to the Great Spirit.

FEBRUARY 22, 1874. — After India's invocation to the Great Spirit, he said that Joel and Amos, Zechariah and Maccabæus would have a chance to address their people the present session. He then called their attention to the time and to the labor and patience that had been necessary in gathering them together, and of the time which had been allotted to them to repent of their transgressions and purify themselves from their sins in order to enter the promised land. And all who had been chosen leaders, and were faithful to their trust, would stand at the head of the tribes who had looked to them for counsel. All who had come short and been unfaithful must go into the ranks, and others more suitable to take the lead would be appointed; for they had been called to stand before the platform of Eternal Justice, and must all be prepared to deal in justice with each other before they could expect to cross over. After a few encouraging remarks, he withdrew.

Joel was the next in council, and expressed his pleasure for another opportunity of speaking to his people. He called their attention to the time when he was the instrument through which they were warned of the consequences which must follow their own disregard of the covenants and the commandments of God. He then counselled them to be vigilant in their organizations, and see that every one was in his own place and prepared to leave the wilderness of their Egyptian bondage, with their doubts and fears and their mental blindness, together with the real red seas of affliction which they had all passed through in their long search for the promised land; and as all that seemed necessary had already been said to them, he desired a few words with his earthly brother with whom they had long sat in council. He then asked what must be the condition of the people of the present age in comparison with those of his own when the line was drawn before the platform of Eternal Justice. He thought it was of the utmost importance that the subject be well considered, for the judgment was at hand and would not be delayed. "And, my brother, as you have been chosen and set apart to be a witness of the sorrows and the terrible sufferings that my people have had to endure for their blindness in scoffing at the spirit sent to warn them to turn from their evil ways, and forsake the alluring temptations of their earthly gods, and turn back in obedience to the commandments of the Most High, so be faithful, and tell your people of the conditions that are already among them. And when their time comes, as come it must, they will all know how well you performed the mission assigned you. And to you, and to our little sister, your handmaid, who has so faithfully performed her part, we shall forever feel grateful, and shall be with you to the end." After addressing a few encouraging words to his people in connection with their present work, he withdrew.

Amos was the next in council, where he addressed the people he was sent to rebuke for their transgressions. He told them they might remember him from the fearful judgments that followed, for it was near the closing cycle, when he was sent among them to warn them of the conditions they were bringing to themselves by their evil doings; and they were now called together before the great platform of Eternal Justice, which was as broad as the heavens, where each one of the scattered tribes had found its place among their kindred. And it was the work of the promised Messiah, who, in compassion for their blind and fallen condition, left his high and heavenly home, and was reincarnated in the flesh, and labored among the lost and forsaken and suffering ones at Jerusalem, — where he was cast out and crucified, but had triumphed over the darkness that long held the race in bondage, and made an opening through the dark sphere, which they had made by their blindness and their transgressions, back to the Great Father's eternal kingdom into the living temple. He then said, "O, my earthly brother, as you are the chosen witness of the present closing cycle of time, make a faithful record of the things that are given to you by the Spirit; for if the people of our age, who had the shadow only of the glorious truths that were afterwards made manifest, still were chastened for going into the forbidden paths, and have wandered for centuries in darkness, — O! what think you must be the condition of the people of an age who have had the gospel of the resurrection of the spirit, and of a risen and glorified Saviour who had cleared away the mystery which had entombed both spirit and matter, and returned among you to be once more rejected, after fetching with him your fathers and your mothers, your wives and your little ones, to be his witnesses where none but the poor and the forsaken have received him?" He said he had foretold the destruction that would overwhelm the Mammon-worshippers of his own age, who had forsaken the covenants of the Most High, and were revelling with the spoils of their victims. And he would prophesy that the temple-builders of the present age, who send their ships across the mighty waters for velvets of purple, and for gold and precious stones, to deck their shrines, where they assemble in troops to worship their Egyptian gods, will yet see them shaken to their foundations; and while their earthly principalities are crumbling, the poor and the forsaken, which they have cast out, will be gathered up and taught the covenants and the commandments, and the communion of spirit under the broad canopy of an imperishable temple not made with hands. He then addressed a few words of instruction to the tribe he represented; after which he expressed his gratitude for the privilege, and said it was of great importance to them in assisting to get their people in order, saying they should be with us in the work until the end; whereupon he retired.

Maccabæus was next in council, and also said he was authorized to take his place, although he did not know that his people cared to see him, for to their sorrow they had experienced the truth of all he had been sent to tell them. But then, he said, he wanted to have a little talk with his earthly brother. He wanted to say that he was familiar with the history of his own people, for he had followed them from their Garden of Eden, which was emblematic of the beautiful earth; he had followed them through the wilderness during their physical pilgrimage, and into the red seas of their afflictions when striving and fighting with each other. And he wanted it to be recorded as his opinion that, in accordance with the age of the planet and the light of the spirit which they were able at the time to comprehend, they did far better than the inhabitants of the present age, who had received much greater light through the teachings of Jesus the Saviour of man. They knew of his resurrection, and had long been looking for his return; and when he did return in spirit, and brought their loved ones with him, they had everywhere refused to open their temples in order to receive him, but still clung to their earthly principalities, and bowed in their worship to Dagon and Diana. "Remember now, my earthly brother, that you and your little handmaiden are the chosen witnesses of the present closing cycle. Mark the record, and stand firm until the end, and we will be with you. Desire not for worldly wealth, for it engenders covetousness and sorrow. Remember it, and put it in the record as our request. All that you need for your earthly happiness you will have." And when the great and the last commandment was obeyed, there would be none left to suffer. He then spoke of his pleasure for the opportunity he had had of solving the mystery of spirit communion with mortals, and retired.

India then closed the session by invocation to the Great Spirit.

FEBRUARY 25, 1874. — After India's invocation to the Great Spirit, he said there were a number of the mothers of Israel and Judah present, and would be permitted at the present session to make their reports. He then spoke of the satisfactory progress of their work, and withdrew.

Rebecca, the mother of Jacob and Esau, was the next in council, where she said her name had been called, and she was glad that she had been remembered. She spoke of the changing scenes, and of the trials they had all experienced; said many things were reported in the records of the past that her earthly sisters of the present age looked upon with dismay; but she and her sisters of their race and tribes were happy in their faith, and listened to the voice of the everlasting Spirit, and were anxious to be guided and governed by its heavenly counsels, and were willing to bear fruit for the building up of the earthly heritage. They were now gathering in and arranging their scattered tribes, and preparing their garments for going up nearer to the endless fountain of wisdom and love flowing from the Great Creator. She was thankful for the opportunity of saying a word or two through the organism of her earthly sister, and would like to prolong her visit, but as only a moment or two was assigned them, she would withdraw.

Rachel, the mother of Joseph and Benjamin, was the next in council, where she said it was true they were happy in the faithful discharge of their earthly duties, and if their sisters of the present age had aught to reflect against them, she desired they would consider the changes produced by the lapse of time, and then ask themselves where would have been the present tribes and nations of the earth if there had been no mother of Israel and of Judah. She was pleased to say that herself and her people were guided by the voice of the spirit of the God of Israel; and when they lived in obedience to its heavenly counsels, they were blessed and contented and happy in their lot. It was a pleasure to know they were still represented by their descendants among the scattered tribes of the earth, who were known by their plain and becoming dress, and who still listened to the counsels of the ever-living Spirit; and they were still contented with their lot, for they had been preparing for the coming of the promised Shiloh, around whom the nations and tribes were gathering, He having rolled away the mental darkness in order to take them nearer to his heavenly kingdom. She felt grateful for the privilege of saying a few words, but as her time was limited, she would have to give way for her sister, who was in waiting.

Abijah, the mother of Hezekiah, was the next in council, where she was pleased that she had been remembered among

her sisters, who were the mothers of the fair daughters of
Judah and of Jerusalem, who had all had their trials during
their earthly pilgrimage, and had been faithful in the discharge of their earthly duties, and had waited patiently the
quickening of the Spirit, preparing for the call of the angel
that would usher them into the nearer presence of the High
and Holy One who had created and sustained them. Said the
privilege given her to again speak with mortals was a new
experience, for which she would ever feel grateful, and would
give place for another sister, who was anxious to solve the
mystery.

Jerusha, mother of Jotham, was the next in council, where
she remarked that this was a glorious day for them, when
they could take their harps down from the willows, and unite
in the new song, while their scattered and broken tribes were
gathering in around the platform of Eternal Justice, each one
in their place, rejoicing as they received the light and the
love that were flowing down from the Great Father's eternal
kingdom. She was also glad to answer her call, and gave
way for another of her sisters.

Jehoadah, the mother of Amaziah, was the next in council,
and said they had clung to the covenants made with the
fathers, and had tried to follow the voice of the spirit whose
counsel led them into the paths of peace; but when they let
the spirit of discontent and of avarice come among them,
their peace and happiness soon disappeared, and discord and
destruction took its place. They had all had their experience
in battling with the perishable things of time, and would
gladly exchange for those that were eternal, and had long
been waiting and were ready for the place assigned to them.
She felt thankful she could be a witness of the opening of the
seals, and would give way for another of her sisters.

Zebiah, the mother of Joash, was the next in council, where
she remarked that the historians had made as sad a havoc
with their names as they had with the records of their earthly
pilgrimage; but they knew their place, and had gladly responded to the call, for they had been resurrected and quickened by the spirit, and had already commenced the work
required, for they were reaching up for the cloth handed
down by the angels, and were cutting and fitting and preparing their garments in readiness for the new birth that
nature was again bringing forth; and when it was finished,
their sisters of earth could unite with them in anthems of

thanksgiving and praise to the Most High. She then gave expression to her gratitude, and gave way for another of her sisters.

Hamotell, the mother of Zedekiah, was the next in council, and spoke of her trials and of her sorrows among others with whom her lot was cast; and said she had stood in her place, and done what she could for the building up of the earthly heritage of the Great Creator, and it was compensation to know that herself and her tribe were not forgotten: they were registered in the Book of Life, and had been called by the angel of time to come up and take their place again with their kindred, where, in a happy union with her sisters, they were preparing the new garments more suitable to their condition. After speaking of the grandeur of the scenes they were now permitted to witness, she withdrew in order to give place to her sister.

Ithalia, the mother of Ahaziah, was the next in council, where she addressed a few encouraging words to her people. She told them she had been nurtured amid the scenes of strife and human slaughter, and she had partaken of its spirit; and when called to take the lead, when they were pilgrims of the earth together, she was surrounded with darkness and trouble; but the unfolding events of time had softened its aspect, and she was thankful and ready to stand in her place. She gave way for her sister.

Judith, of Bethuel, was the next in council, where she spoke to her people of the changing scenes they had passed through, and said she had stood by the covenants and the commandments held sacred by their fathers. She looked to the God of Abraham, in faith believing that He was ever near, and able to protect her, for she had learned to see Him through the wisdom and love made manifest in his wonderful works; for whatever her eyes beheld gave evidence of the work of a Master Mind that was truly worthy of her highest devotion. She had come with her kindred in answer to the call, and they had taken their place where every link in the grand order of creation was perfect. And they were happy in arranging their apparel in order that they might soon be ushered into a nearer presence of the Great Creator. She was pleased, and should remember with grateful feelings her opportunity of speaking through the organism of her earthly sister, and then retired.

Jehosheba, the daughter of Joram, was the next in council,

and said she had found her place among the mothers of Israel, and was glad she could be useful in arranging the gathering tribes who had long wandered among the valleys and Jordans of Israel; and if all had not climbed to the mountain-top while travelling through the wilderness during their earthly pilgrimage, all had been useful in making up the great chain of life, and had cheerfully responded to the call in order to clean up and be prepared for the coming of the Bridegroom, whose light was already reflected among the nations. She was pleased that she had been remembered, and would give way for another of their sisters.

The Woman of Endor was the next in council, where she remarked that she was happy to respond to the call, where she could stand before the platform of Eternal Justice, that all might know the position she had occupied, and why she had been called a wizard and a witch. She then gave the name of Celia Celoia to her kindred, and spoke with the appearance of great feeling of the troubles and the trials they had passed through, and of the pleasure they now enjoyed, after the scales were broken and the seeming mysteries explained, and each one found themselves in their own place among the scattered tribes. She then spoke of her own condition when she was a media among them, and of the legions of the spirit forms of those thought to be dead, who often came up before her many times the trembling victims from their bloody battle-fields, who in their seeming wrath were ready to tear down the very heavens had it been possible; and time and again did she try to hide away in her sorrow, and pray to the God of Israel that she might be relieved from such fearful conditions; when the answer was returned to her to be patient and to hold them fast, and not let the last link between spirit and matter be severed. She was thankful, as she was now called to take her place among them, to know they could appreciate the position she then filled in the grand and mysterious work of the Spirit in organizing and individualizing through matter. She then said the time assigned for her present interview had expired, but she would return when she was called, and make further statements. After introducing her niece who had also been a media, she retired.

Prudence was the next in council, where she spoke of the things in connection with the trials and sufferings they had to experience in common with others. She said she was one of King Saul's friends; and she then called to him and asked him why he did not command her now to close her eyes and shut her mouth, and not tell of the many victims she saw in spirit that had been slain in their fearful struggles that he might retain his power. She then told them of the King of kings, who had built no perishable temples, and who struggled not for earthly glory,— who had meekly borne his heavy burdens that he might triumph over the opposing forces, and open the way from the dark and struggling scenes of earth to an imperishable temple in the eternal kingdom,— and who had returned and spoken the second time. And behold, both wizard and witch and familiar spirits come forth at his command, and stand before his great platform of Eternal Justice, where every one could know their place. She then expressed her pleasure for the privilege of speaking through another's physical organism, for she realized now how the spirit of another had formerly spoken through her own. She then retired.

Etheral, one of the daughters who had worshipped Baal-Beor, was the next in council, and said she thought there was quite as much sincerity in their worship of the gods they could see as there was with those who had worshipped the one they said could talk but they could not see. She thought the desire flowed from the natural development of veneration, and they had looked for some object to which they could pay their devotions in thankfulness for their daily blessings. She told them that the tribes who had professed to worship the talking God had often made war on her people in order to increase their wealth; and as they had continued to move along, each people on different sides of the Great River, she had not noticed any difference in their developments. Her people had been taught in spirit by the same Saviour who had opened the way for others; and they were thankful for the light which all had received, and were gathering up and preparing for their change. She was pleased to have an opportunity of speaking in order that her own people might understand the way the other tribes had been instructed; whereupon she withdrew.

One of the Forest Maidens was next in council, and told them she had come from the upper hunting-grounds of the Great Spirit to the council-fire on the lower hunting-grounds, where she had listened to the talk of her pale-face sisters who had been taught by the covenants and commandments of the

Great Spirit. Her people had been taught by the Great Spirit, who had told them not to strive for the perishable principalities that never satisfied, but look up to the beautiful heavens, where all was imperishable and emblematic of the spirit's home. Once, when they turned away from the home of the Great Spirit, and from the example of others were going after the things that perish, a bright spirit was sent to them, and in their affright they thought it was the Great Spirit's Son; and they turned back to him, and asked to be forgiven, and never after had they broken the Great Spirit's commandments. And now they were with him in the upper hunting-grounds of the Spirit. And again, when Israel and Judah's race turned away from the Great Spirit, and forgot his commands, and through avarice and strife were struggling for the perishable principalities of the earth, then again the Great Spirit sent his Son; and when he returned to the upper hunting-grounds, he said, "O Father, see I have been with my earthly brothers, and have been crucified! O Father, let me return, for they are now crucifying many others, and I will try and clear away the darkness that all may yet know Thee." And as I have found you gathering around the great platform of Eternal Justice, so called and built by the Great Spirit's Son, and as I have heard all you have said, I will away back to the upper hunting-grounds, and tell the Great Spirit, for I know He will be pleased. And when you have finished your labor, and come up as it were led by the Great Spirit's Son, then you will find out who we are, and know that your work is "well done" among the balance of the paleface race on the lower hunting-grounds.

After which, India closed the session by invocation to the Great Spirit.

MARCH 1, 1874. — After India's invocation to the Great Spirit, he said the gathering in under the second covenant the gospel dispensation would commence the present session, and that Joseph and Mary were present, and would make their statements. After speaking encouragingly of the work which had been accomplished, he again withdrew.

Joseph was the next in council, where he again spoke of his own earthly trials, and said it was true he was the foster-father of Jesus, and that he was now called with Mary his wife and their children to take their stand on the platform of Eternal Justice around which the nations and tribes had been gathered in spirit; and he felt that he was unworthy of the position which he was called to occupy. Said he was of humble origin, that he was poor and unlearned when chosen for an important work ; but said he had tried to be faithful to his trust, and had stood in his lot and place and done the best he could under the circumstances in which he was placed. He then called upon the angel band who had watched over and guided him during his wanderings with Mary the mother when in her travail, to witness his obedience to their instructions; and he asked that Jesus might forgive all that had seemed amiss, and give them a place near to him in his kingdom ; for he had been a witness of his sorrows and of his fearful sufferings during his earthly trials, when he was cast off and neglected even by those who should have been the nearest and dearest to him, but who could not and did not comprehend his grand and glorious mission. It had been his privilege in spirit to be near to him during his sorrows at Gethsemane and at the Cross, and he did rejoice when it was known that He had triumphed over the powers of darkness, and had ascended to mingle again with the heavenly hosts above. He then said, as he was called with his family to stand in their place as the humble Nazarites, the memory of the past was once more vividly brought to his mind, and he was too much overcome with amazement at the wonderful scenes before him to prolong his remarks, and he would give way for one who was a faithful companion in their sorrows as well as in their joys. He then withdrew.

Mary, the mother of Jesus, was the next in council, where she again spoke of her earthly trials and sorrows, and of her lonely and forsaken condition after the death of Joseph. She spoke of their fears of personal harm on account of the manifestation of spirit given through her son, and said he was opposed and seemingly deserted by those who should have been the first in order to have protected and sustained him; but all failed, owing to a want of capacity to comprehend and understand his mission. She then said the inquiry was often made by those who had been anxious to know where her Son was from the time spoken of when he was noted for his contention with the crafty ones at Jerusalem until he was again found with his disciples completing his work ; and she said he was with his parents at their humble home in their obscurity, poor and friendless, working for his daily bread, and developing up into the fullness of the glorious mission which he had come to fulfil, with none to understand or sympathize with him in his work; although he often referred to sayings of prophet and of seer who had foretold of his coming among them, and of the light which through him would be reflected among the nations. She said, as the time approached for the completion of his labors, the opposing elements were strong, and her own sorrows and fears were terrible to endure; that his brothers and sisters turned from him with fear, owing to the powerful opposition manifested against the ruling priesthood, who had crushed out and trampled under their feet the sacred rights of the people. But, notwithstanding, he went forth, and publicly proclaimed a free gospel for all, and was at all times, after he commenced the work, found among the sorrowing and the suffering outcast ones, a-healing their maladies and pointing the way to their heavenly Father's eternal kingdom. He publicly and fearlessly denounced the building of earthly temples as an extravagant and needless expense, and pointed to the heavens above them, the imperishable works of his Father, and worthy of their highest adoration; but his powerful manifestations of the spirit, with his fearless opposition to the avarice and the injustice of the rulers in their earthly kingdom, soon brought their power to work against him; and after passing through his fearful ordeal, he soon returned to her, and, with his hand on her head, spoke and told her to have no more fears, for he had triumphed over the powers of darkness, that he did strengthen her through the balance of her earthly pilgrimage, and had many times since taken her with him in his work among the spirits in the dark sphere. After encouraging words in regard to our own connection with spirit, she said her son was with us in our labors, and again withdrew.

One of the Hindoos was then in the council, and expressed his pleasure that his people were still permitted to keep their place by the sanction of the star-spirit through the investigation of the gospel dispensation. He then spoke of the disturbance and the wrangling that were still going on among the nations about their earthly kingdoms, and said it looked as if six of them would soon be fighting among themselves about their earthly gods, in order to find out which one of their idols was the best.

Whereupon India closed the session by invocation to the Great Spirit, again thanking him for the strength and for the wisdom which had sustained them all in their labors.

MARCH 4, 1874. — After India's invocation to the Great Spirit, he said that Mark and John the Baptist would make their statements at the present session as they continued the investigation; and after his usual encouragement, he again retired.

Mark was then in the council, where he said it was true that he was one of the chosen witnesses of the teaching and the suffering of Jesus their Master, and notwithstanding all the powerful manifestations that were given, they could not and did not understand and comprehend the law of the communion of spirit; but still they followed their Master in his labors of compassion and of love among the sorrowing ones with whom He devoted his time in alleviating their afflictions, and then pointing the way to their heavenly Father's kingdom. He said they were poor and ragged, and often hungry, and despised by the wealthy Pharisees, many times hooted at and stoned by the mob, which was instigated and set on by the fearful opposition and condemnation of the priesthood, until, tired and weary and forsaken, they could only find rest in the forest secluded from the habitation of man. And after all their trials and sufferings, and after the crucifixion of their Master, and his glorious triumph, they must still find the "Pharisees" in their earthly temples paying their homage to their Egyptian gods, while the poor are still despised and forsaken, and those who listen to the communion of spirit are cast out of their synagogues, and scoffed at with scorn. He then said it was unnecessary for him to prolong his remarks, for the truth of what he had said was familiar to all who had given heed to the signs of the times; and he would give way for his brother, who was another witness of the trials and persecutions and of the fearful sufferings of their Master in his labors of compassion and love in order to enlighten and elevate the race. Whereupon, after a few encouraging words, he withdrew.

John the Baptist was the next in council, and said he had come, not with flesh and blood, with his head under his arm, but in spirit form that was perfect and immortal; and he would take the stand on the platform of Eternal Justice, a living witness to the persecution, the bigotry, and the avarice and injustice of his brother man. He then said that the report of Jesus saying that He had flesh and bones after his resurrection was not true; but it was true that He did materialize and show himself to his disciples and to many others, in evidence of his grand triumph over the power that held the race in bondage. Many witnesses of the truth feared to sanction it, owing to the cruelty of the opposing power; for all who adhered to the truth of the communion of spirit were cast out of the synagogue by the ruling priesthood, and treated with contempt. He said the manifestation of the spirit among them was the same as it is among the people of the present age; but the truth had been suppressed and kept from the record. His own family, and that of Mary, his aunt, were hooted at, and the report that she had given birth to a child that was illegitimate was circulated and thrown into their faces in order to reflect on the evidence of the manifestation of the spirit; but in his retreat in the forest and by the beautiful running waters, He was not deprived of its presence; and when the people came to him and often desired it, He baptized them in the water, and told them to purify themselves, and obey the commandments, and the Baptism of the Heavenly Spirit would follow. He then said that his brother Jesus authorized the establishment of no church but that of the communion of spirit triumphant and everlasting; all others were perishable and belonged to the Egyptian gods. And he then called to him, and told him to remember all they once had to suffer from persecution, and to remember what others who hold to the covenant of the communion of spirit still have to endure; said he rejoiced to know the time had arrived spoken of by prophet and seer, when there would be a resurrection or a quickening of the spirit, and all would be brought into judgment. He then said the Essenes of his age were a remnant that held to the covenant of spirit handed down from the patriarchal age, and that the Aaron priesthood was typical of the resurrection and final triumph of Jesus over the darkness that had held the race in bondage. Whereupon, after a few encouraging words, he spoke in glowing terms of the end, and then invoked the Divine blessing, and retired.

One of the red men of the forest was then in the council, where he claimed an interest in the lower hunting-grounds of his race and tribe, and complained of ravages and the destruction the pale-faces had made in their struggle for wampum. He spoke of the beautiful rivers they had dammed up, and of the forests desecrated by their avarice, where the red man once loved to hunt for his daily food, and talk to the Great Spirit. He then told of the remnant of the red man's race that was driven from the hunting-grounds of their fathers, and
18

was then sitting in a distant land, cold and hungry, where they had been sent to starve by their pale-face brothers. He said the Great Spirit was not pleased with the Christian's god, and had sent his archers from the upper hunting-grounds in order to establish his law of Eternal Justice.

One of the Hindoos was next in council, where he spoke of the progress they were making from their present opportunity of associating with the Christians; said his folks had come to the conclusion that if the women should keep on singing and praying in the public streets, they would find out after a while where the " heathen" were in their own country; and they had also concluded that the men would not be pleased to have the women neglect their family duties, and stand around the street-corners discussing public affairs; thought the men had shown great weakness by their allowing such things to be possible. That was what the star-spirit had said; and he let them go everywhere among the Christians in order to see what they were doing, and why they neglected their own people to look after the affairs of other nations.

Whereupon India again closed the session by invocation to the Great Spirit.

MARCH 8, 1874. — After India's invocation to the Great Spirit, he said Judas and Peter were ready and would give in their reports at the present session; and after his usual encouraging remarks in connection with their labors, he retired.

Judas was the next in council, and there said he was called to stand as a witness in condemnation of all who had so unjustly condemned him for the part he was chosen to perform during the earthly mission of Jesus his Master. He said he had followed the trail of those who had claimed to be the disciples of Jesus, and found every temple and altar, and every pew they had, was made by the sale of his Master; for they had kept Him in every market-place, and sold him for the tribute-money they used in order to strengthen their earthly principalities throughout all the Christian nations, — where he had been up and down the isles of the temples which they had dedicated to the gods of their own imaginations, but where his Master was shut out in spirit and nailed up in form, and still used in mockery by those who knew nothing of the trials and sufferings in order to educate and elevate the human race. Said he had often heard the anathemas they had heaped upon his own head for the part he was called to act; and said it was true that it had fallen to his lot to carry the bag; it was true it was seldom they had much of anything in it, and he was necessarily disturbed about the means required to purchase sufficient food to satisfy their hunger. He then told them to prepare, and he would show them who the real Judas was. As he then opened a space and pointed, he said, "Now you see him:" it was that worldly Jew who clung to his earthly kingdom, and cared nothing for the imperishable kingdom of his heavenly Father. He was the Judas that entered in and had caused him to sell his Master; and none but his Master could ever realize how great had been his sorrow; but it was a part for which he had long since been forgiven. And as he was called to take his stand upon the platform of Eternal Justice by the side of his brothers, he was ready and willing to perform any other part that was assigned to him in the fulfilment of his Master's work. After saying he would ever be ready to answer when called, he withdrew.

Peter was the next in council, and said he was ever ready to appear in his place before the assembled nations and tribes, a witness of the trials and sufferings and the glorious triumph of his Master over the darkness and the ignorance and bigotry of both Jew and Gentile, which had bound them fast to their perishable kingdoms. He then spoke of his own labors in order to elucidate and explain the teachings of his Master among the people, and of the Baptism of the Spirit that would follow in order to quicken and prepare them for the ushering in of their Master's imperishable and eternal kingdom. He told them of their turning away from the light of the spirit, and holding on to their earthly principalities; how they had enlarged their storehouses, and ransacked the earth for the mammon of unrighteousness; how they wrangled and fought with each other to increase their power in order to build up their earthly temples, and deck them in costly and gorgeous array, and then dedicate them to their earthly gods, where a few of the chosen ones could sit in mockery to the living Spirit, while the millions were cast out starving for the common bread of life. He then spoke of the vision shown to him during his earthly pilgrimage, as it appeared like a great sheet held by the corners, and then filled with all manner of creeping things, in order to show their common origin, and teach all that what the Great Father had created should not be cast out to suffer and be deprived of the common blessings. He spoke of the work of Jesus their Master among the poor and suffering and forsaken ones at Jerusalem, where in compassion He had healed their infirmities, and then pointed the way to their heavenly Father's imperishable and eternal kingdom, and told them all that His Church was of the resurrected and ever-living spirit whose temple was everlasting, and when He was lifted up, He would draw all unto him. That the Rock on which he built was that of the Spirit, which was immortal; and the only key was the key of knowledge that opened the way from the dark terrestrial into the Bright Celestial Kingdom, where the Great Father had many mansions for his children. He then spoke of the mighty hosts gathered up around the great platform of Eternal Justice, where spirit and mortal combined; of the triumphant work of their Master. There was Gentile and Jew, there was Israel and Egypt, with their worn and weary tribes, tired of watching over the mouldering ruins around their earthly gods, who, quickened in the spirit by the call of the Angel of time, had gladly come forth to find their places, where they rejoiced to know not even one had been forgotten by the humble Nazarene, who had known of their burdens and sorrows as he labored with compassion and love that he might clear away the mental blindness which had kept them in bondage. He then spoke of the fearful and the long suffering the nation had to endure who had cast out the Spirit and turned away from the covenants and commandments of God, or who had used them to burden and oppress the people, by craft and injustice, in order to enrich and strengthen their earthly kingdoms. He spoke encouraging words of the work which had been accomplished in spirit, and said he would be ready to answer again, should he be wanted, and then retired.

One of the Hindoos was next in council. He said he was permitted to come in order to represent their own people. He spoke of their progress, and said the star-spirit was teaching them many things that would make them as wise as any of the other nations; he thought the Christians, who had shut out the spirits from their temples, could not keep the star-spirit out; for he had laid aside his brightness, and went in and out, and knew what they had been about. And the great star-spirit said he had been in all their places of public worship, and had found nothing but a formal show, where they assembled in order to gratify their worldly pride, for no people could have regard for him who neglected and cast off their own, which he had found homeless and friendless, suffering in neglect and poverty on every hand, notwithstanding they had many earthly temples where they assembled and outwardly professed to worship his Father.

Whereupon India closed the session by invocation to the Great Spirit, once more acknowledging their dependence for continued blessings, and asking for wisdom and light sufficient for the accomplishment of their labors for the elevation and improvement of spirits and mortals.

MARCH 11, 1874. — After India's invocation to the Great Spirit, he said that Mary Magdalene, and the wife of Herod, and Elizabeth who was one of the media of the little band that stood by the Great Media during his earthly trials, and one of the Hindoo women, would also have an opportunity to report during the present session. After which he withdrew.

Magdalene was the next in council, where she said she was ever ready to stand in her place upon the platform of Eternal Justice, and testify to the sufferings of the blessed Saviour, and his little band of devoted followers. She spoke of her own condition as an invalid, and how she was healed of an infirmity she had inherited, by the spirit-power of him they called "Master." She told of his trials and of his sufferings from the cruel treatment of his opposers. She told of his labors among the afflicted and sorrowing ones, who were cast out and neglected by those intrusted with power, which they used to increase the heavy burdens among the suffering people. She told them of the terrible agony in the Garden of Gethsemane and at the Cross, and that those who sympathized were driven by the scoffers into their secluded habitations to grieve and lament the loss of him who had been a friend in their affliction, and who returned to them in spirit, and told them of his triumph over death and hell which had held the race fast bound to their earthly kingdoms. She told them of the freedom and the beauty of the spheres beyond, and of his Father's imperishable and eternal kingdom, where they would be with Him when their earthly trials and sorrows were finished. Great, she said, had been their trials and their afflictions; but much greater now was their happiness to know and to realize the magnitude and the grandeur of their Master's heavenly mission; and as tribe after tribe and nation after nation, from isle to isle and from continent to continent, had been gathered around the great platform of Eternal Justice, where each one found their place among their kindred, they all felt to forgive and forget the trials and hardships which they had to endure. She then said that those who had sorrowed and sympathized with Jesus their Master during his earthly afflictions had found their place near to Him in his heavenly kingdom. And after saying she felt grateful for the privilege of again having the pleasure of speaking, she introduced Elizabeth as another media of the little band who was drawn by the spirit to be witnesses of their Master's labors, and again withdrew.

Elizabeth was then in council, where she confirmed the statement of her sister; said she was one of the women that clung to their Master, who taught them of heavenly things; that she was a media through which the spirit of Elijah the prophet often instructed and encouraged their Master in his labors during the terrible ordeal through which he was enabled to pass in order to enlighten and elevate a fallen race who had turned away from the spirit, and was using the sacred covenants to oppress the overburdened people to increase the power of their perishable principalities. She said He was of a sensitive nature, and felt keenly the sufferings of those in affliction, as well as the fearful opposition that met him on every hand; for there were but few who stood by to sustain him in his labors of love, owing to the power of the priests over the minds of those who administered the cruel laws of the Jews; for they stirred up every opposing element, and sent out their cohorts to watch, and, if possible, to prevent the fulfilment of His heavenly mission. She then spoke of their own trials and sufferings before and after the crucifixion, and of the joy of his returning, when He told them He had triumphed, and explained to them the freedom and beauty of the spirit spheres through which He had travelled; and told them to be faithful and keep the commandments, and when their earthly pilgrimage was finished, where he was there they should also come. She then spoke of the fearful calamities which soon overwhelmed the nation that rejected and cast out and crucified their Master, and of their longsuffering in spirit, — the result of their transgressions and their wilful blindness; and of the continued labors of their Master in order to clear away the darkness that held them, sorrowing over their perishable earthly kingdom, and prepare for a quickening of the spirit that would call them higher and release them of their doubts and fears. She then spoke of the powerful and convincing manifestations of the spirit that were given through their Master, and said the truth was not half told, owing to the opposition of those in power, although the evidence of his divine authority was free and open for all. After a few encouraging words in connection with the present closing cycle, she said the time for another pentecost was near at hand, and then withdrew.

The wife of Herod was the next in council, where she said her name was Laleial, and she was a witness of the fearful and terrible sufferings the Judaites as well as the people of the surrounding nations had brought upon themselves in their struggles for earthly power. She told of the desolation at Jerusalem, and of the barren and forsaken condition of the countries once inhabited by the Israelites, that were kept for a warning to the Gentile nations that they might not turn away and disregard the covenants and commandments of God given for their instruction. She then asked if the nations who had the gospel of a risen Saviour had done as well as they who had nothing but the shadow; and if the devastation of their countries with their principalities had become a waste and a reproach for their transgressions; and if their trials and sufferings had been terrible to endure, what could the Gentile nations of the gospel age expect? She then said they had come in order to warn us of the approaching judgments, for the seals must be broken, and the vials would be poured out among the nations that were still wandering in the forbidden paths, and dedicating their temples to their earthly gods. She then spoke of the Nazarene, and of His trials and sufferings, and of his labors in order to enlighten and elevate the nations; and said it would have been much better for them had they obeyed his instructions and been prepared to have received Him when he returned and stood at their doors and knocked. After expressing pleasure for the privilege she had enjoyed, she retired.

One of the Hindoo women was the next in council, where she spoke of the gratitude of her people for the privileges extended to them; said they had been instructed by the great star-spirit of things that appertained to their eternal welfare, — things of which they were deprived as a nation during their physical pilgrimage. She said they were taught not to be covetous, for they were not allowed to go away from their own gods and pay their tribute, and then render up their devotions to the gods of the other peoples and nations that were round about them; although it was often claimed that the other gods had given manifestation of having superior powers. She then said her people had talked about such things in spirit, and were satisfied, if they had paid their devotions to the gods that could not talk, they had done it in sincerity and with a pure motive; and they had concluded they would stand more justified in the sight of the Father whom they could not see in any other way than the people which had had such great light, and still turned away, or had used it to destroy each other in their struggles for temporal things. Said her people had not killed their gods, but had tried to do right as they understood what was right, and had obeyed the great law of justice in their transactions with one another; and the things the star-spirit was teaching them now it was their greatest pleasure to obey; and they trusted that when they were ushered into the presence of the great Father, they might all stand free from condemnation. After saying her people were all thankful for the great light they had now received, and were anxious to be remembered, and as the bow-and-arrow girl was waiting to speak, she would retire.

One of the Forest Maidens was next in council, where she reviewed the subjects which had been investigated before the platform of Eternal Justice. She had been sent as by the Great Spirit from the upper hunting-grounds of the red man's race, where all had sat in council; she had come to the watch-fire of the pale-face squaw, and listened to the talk of the daughters of Judah, who had gathered around the light of the Great Spirit's Central Son; and she had also heard the talk of the daughter who had bowed the knee in devotion to Baal; and she would away back to the upper hunting-grounds, and tell all to the Great Spirit, who had already sent His mighty warriors to look after the pale-faces on the lower hunting-grounds.

Whereupon India again closed the session by invocation to the Great Spirit.

MARCH 15, 1874.—After India's invocation to the Great Spirit, he said many of the people and tribes who had been gathered around the platform in spirit were without a leader, and it was desirable that one of their number should have an opportunity to enter the physical form, and learn the way to impress and control in order to impart the information to others who were to engage in their work with mortals. He said none could realize the fearful strain on both body and mind of a media, who was necessarily used for the accomplishment of such work, and that no earthly compensation could reward them for their service; but in spirit, where all things were known, all who have suffered in order to ameliorate the sorrows of others would receive their full reward. He then said that Mark, and Bartholomew, and Simeon were the next in order to report; and, after his usual encouragements, retired.

Mark was the next in council, where he spoke of his own knowledge of the labors and sufferings of Jesus, their Master. He told of how the lame were made to walk, and the blind to see, and that all that would receive were supplied with the bread of life, and partook from the stream of living waters to quench their thirst, — which was free for all, without money or price; and of how little He had been understood even by those who were chosen to stand by Him and bear witness of the trials and afflictions He had to endure in order to establish the communion of spirit with mortals. Said their Master was compassionate and forgiving, with a confiding and loving nature; that He was controlled by the Spirit when the anathemas were hurled upon those in power, who had built up their earthly principalities through injustice that had brought great oppression and poverty among the mass of the people. It was true they were poor and so-called illiterate fishermen; but they were chosen by their Master, and did testify among the people of the mighty manifestation of the power of spirit with which He was then endowed; and if He did not come down from the cross and destroy those in power, and set up a temporal kingdom as they desired and expected He would, He destroyed death and hell, and arose triumphant over the darkness of the tomb which had held them all in bondage; and He returned to them in spirit, and proved beyond all human doubts to the satisfaction of many hundreds what He had tried to teach them before, and encouraged them in the good work of extending the knowledge of the communion of spirits with mortals. And as they were fishermen, and were still permitted to stand by their Master in spirit, it was their pleasure to assist in drawing the "net" that was bringing all before his great platform of Eternal Justice, where with rejoicing they gladly acknowledge the grandeur of his heavenly mission. He then spoke of the pleasure they now enjoyed in being the witnesses of their Master's work at the closing of the present cycle; and, after a few words of encouragement, he retired.

Bartholomew was the next in council, where he confirmed the remarks of his brother, and said their trials and sufferings were severe, for they were ignorant of the law of spirit control, although their Master often told them that his kingdom was not of the earth and perishable, but of the spirit and eternal,—and that He had come to teach them of a union of the Spirit with mortals. But after all his labors, they were disappointed, for they had expected a temporal kingdom, where He would assert his power, and they should have the pleasure of seeing his triumph over all who scoffed and had cruelly opposed his labor of compassion among the sorrowing and afflicted people. But their Master knew the object of his mission with mortals, and patiently endured the fearful ordeal; and when He came to them after his resurrection in spirit, and encouraged them by the assurance that He had triumphed over the powers of darkness, and would draw all unto him in spirit, the beauty and grandeur of his Messiahship was explained; and they had more to encourage them through the balance of their earthly pilgrimage, for He was often with them to assist and cheer them along the way. And as they were now permitted to sit together on the platform of Eternal Justice, which had finally been established through the acknowledgment of their Master's triumphant labors, where they had witnessed the gathering up of the scattered tribes and nations in spirit, and where all had willingly bowed before Him, their joy was now complete, for they could comprehend something of the magnitude of His eternal glory. After giving expression to his feelings of pleasure for the privilege of again speaking to mortals, he retired.

Father Simeon was the next in council, where he testified that he had held communion with the Spirit of the blessed Saviour of man before he was reincarnated; and he told him He was going to be clothed in the flesh, and would be among them, and they would not know him; that He would be cast out and crucified by the Jews, who would refuse to receive him. He said his own spirit was in agony when the Spirit with which he had held communion was gone, and he could not know where to find it. He was full of grief, and could find no comfort. He travelled the streets of Jerusalem day and night; he went to the temple, and upon his knees before the altar he prayed to his God to give him back the pure Spirit which he had loved, for he could not endure to know He had been reincarnated, and was among them to be scoffed at and would have to suffer; and when he found the infant Jesus, he knew in spirit that it was the Spirit with which he had been in communion; and he did bless the child, and he blessed God who had sent Him to open their blind eyes and lead them up to his heavenly kingdom. He then upbraided the Judaites for their want of comprehension; told them they were stubborn and they were wilful; they let their Messiah go ragged and hungry; they had spat upon him, and they had stoned him, when He was doing all that he possibly could to convince them of his Great Father's love. They had called Him the leader of a ragged mob, when in love and in compassion for the afflicted He was healing their infirmities. "And you cast Him out and crucified him, after his coming to lead you away from the perishable things by which you were surrounded into his Father's imperishable and eternal kingdom; but you would not heed his heavenly counsel, and you have sat by the wayside and sorrowed; you have taken a long and circuitous road to get here. And here I stand one of many witnesses against you, and I am thankful for this opportunity to say what I have expressed, for I cannot yet feel to forgive you." After thanking those who were still pilgrims in the flesh for their attention, he said he would ask that their labors should be blessed when they were in accord with the law of justice, and then retired.

One of the Hindoos was the next in council, where he spoke of the interest his people had taken in the different statements which had reference to the great star-spirit; and said the old man who spoke last had but just come down among them, and was a white, pure spirit. He then spoke of a great celebration his people were going to attend at a place called the *Hub*, where the people were preparing for a great time over one of the Christian gods they were going to have lie in state. His people were going, for it reminded them of the times they used to have over their own gods, when they wanted a big show in order to get the people together to teach them to be respectful to those in command. They would take one of their gods, and dress it up in rich attire, and then place it on a platform on wheels with long ropes, so they could draw it around the market-places among the crowds of devoted worshippers; and often, when there was a shout, one or more would throw themselves under the wheels, and be crushed to atoms, believing, as they were taught by those interested in getting up the show, that they would be absorbed by the gods which they worshipped; and their friend would fetch more of their material wealth to satisfy the god when they came to offer up their devotions. He said they had been taught by the star-spirit that it was still the same thing everywhere among the temple-worshippers, for they all had their speaking gods, who stood up on a finely decorated platform, and all the heathen round about, who gathered together to pay their devotion, had to defray the expense of keeping up the show in order to be considered respectable. And if any were sick and poor, and did not go, the speaking god never went to see them; or, if he did, he told them their misfortunes were the result of their neglect to send their portion of tribute-money for the gods at the temple. They had been told by the star-spirit such things encouraged pride and idleness among the people.

Whereupon India again closed the session by invocation to the Great Spirit.

MARCH 18, 1874. — After India's invocation to the Great Spirit, he said that Martha and Mary, and a half-sister of Jesus, and Henriette Renan, would make their appearance, after which one of the Hindoos and one of the red man's race would occupy the time of the present session; and, after a few encouraging words, he again withdrew.

Martha was the next in council, where she spoke of the time when herself and sisters formed the little band of devoted listeners to the heavenly teachings of the blessed Saviour. She told of how they were scoffed at, and traduced, and cast off, on account of their appreciation of the teachings of their Master, who was meek and compassionate and sorrowful over the fallen condition of the people, who had turned away from the light of the Spirit given through prophet and seer, and were following after their earthly idols, and building up their principalities in pride and power, until no warning given by their Master could awake them to a sense of their national responsibility. She then spoke of their quiet and humble home, where her brother Lazarus, who loved their Master, and Mary their sister, often sat and listened to the beautiful descriptions of the heavenly spheres, which He would give after returnig tired and dejected from being repulsed and maltreated by those who had no desire to comprehend or appreciate His labors of love and compassion among those that were cast off and afflicted. She did rejoice to know that the time had arrived when they could all take their place upon the platform of Eternal Justice, where they would be honestly represented, and understood and appreciated in their true relation to each other; said she was thankful for the pleasure of speaking, and, as she had before enjoyed the privilege, she would not prolong her remarks, but would give way for her sister Mary, who was also anxious to speak through the vocal organs of their earthly sister. And, after a few words of assurance that their Master had come with power, and would finish his work, she retired.

Mary was the next in council, and expressed her pleasure for an opportunity of confirming the remarks of her sister. She then said that their brother was not dead, as had been stated by the historians; but he was in a condition that was now called a " trance;" and when their Master — as they had loved to call him, for He taught them of their celestial home — had returned, the spirit of their brother Lazarus was quickened, and his physical body was again restored. She then said their brother was what is now called a " clairvoyant media," and that he had often told of the beautiful things he was shown, which was explained to them by their Master who appeared to be familiar with the heavenly missions. And they loved him for his purity, and sorrowed with him in his afflictions; for He well knew all He had got to pass through in order to perfect the union between spirits and mortals, and lead them away from the perishable up to their eternal home; and poor, and despised, and rejected, and cast out as they were, they had saved from their scanty earnings little by little until they had enough to purchase the ointment with which they did commemorate their love for Him; for He had told them the time had come when He should leave the physical body; but they should not be forgotten when He returned to his Father's kingdom. And they were not forgotten; for He remembered and came to them in his beautiful and imperishable spirit form, and cheered them along on their lonely earthly pilgrimage; and when it was finished, they found their place near to their Master in the Great Father's eternal kingdom; and they had returned, and were all doing what they could in order to draw others up to his kingdom, where there was joy and peace in the Holy Spirit. After expressing love for the one through which she had been permitted to speak, she gave way for Hannah, the daughter of Mary and Joseph.

Hannah, the sister of Jesus, was next in council, where she said she had been permitted to come in order that she might make a few remarks in connection with her own knowledge of the trials and sorrows of her brother. She spoke of his early habits in his boyhood days, and said he was different in many respects from others of the family and from the associates with whom they assembled. She said He was thoughtful and appeared to be headstrong and self-willed, with magnetic force sufficient often to prostrate his playmates when they abused him. She said they were afraid of his power, for it often got them into trouble among their young companions. In his more thoughtful moods, he would talk about his heavenly Father, and about a kingdom that no one appeared to know about but himself. And once, when they were together where the people had assembled to listen to the reading of the Laws given through Moses, her brother took up the Book, and told the people it was not the law as it was given from his Father. He then read to them passages from the Book as he said it should be understood, and told them how they had altered it, and in apparent anger threw the Book to the ground and left them. When He was gone, the people murmured one with another and called her brother a law-breaker. She said the opposition increased until their family, being poor, was cast off and seemingly disregarded; and their poor mother, after her father Joseph's death, was left comparatively alone with her children in their sorrow. She then said it was about the time of the death of her father that the spirits got the control of their cousin John; and then he opposed the scribes and the Pharisees the same as her brother; and that had increased their troubles until her poor brother Jesus found no peace or comfort at home, for they could not understand the beautiful teachings of the Spirit, and they all opposed him; they had not comprehended the grandeur of the work He had come to accomplish. But as the time drew near when He would have to pass through the terrible ordeal, He came to them at their retired and humble retreat, and told them that his time had come, and of what he must pass through, and the desired object to be attained. He then bade them an affectionate good-by. She said he appeared so changed that she seemed to realize the truth of what he had told them, and she kneeled down at his feet, and earnestly prayed for his blessing: when He put his hand upon her head, and blessed her and her children, and promised them a place near to Him in his heavenly Father's kingdom. And she said it was a sorrowful time with them until after his terrible sufferings were closed, for it was true the earth did quake and was shaken to its centre during the cruel struggle; but when it was finished, they seemed to find relief. And He soon returned to them in spirit, called them by name, and told them of his triumph; and, after that, their earthly trials and afflictions were looked upon as a trifling affair in comparison with their assurance of again uniting with their brother in his immortal and eternal home. And when the time for their change did come, they found their place with him in spirit, as he had often told them, far beyond the comprehension of mortals. After speaking of her own grateful emotions on being permitted to witness the gathering up of the scattered tribes and nations and kindred of the earth in spirit around her brother's great platform of Eternal Justice, where they all bowed in acknowledgment of the grandeur of his earthly mission and of his glorious triumph over the power of darkness, she expressed her gratitude for the pleasure she had experienced in again speaking with mortals, and withdrew.

Henriette Renan was next in council, where she spoke of the pleasure she had experienced from her privilege of being present during the hearing of the reports connected with the ushering in of the gospel dispensation, for she had travelled over the country with her brother, where the scenes which have become so important transpired, and the history to her seemed to be familiar. She sat by his side on the banks of the Jordans and Palestines where the ancient tribes had wandered, earnestly in search of fragments of ancient history in order to finish his book, without knowing at the time that all with whom they so much desired to be familiar were gathered about them in spirit; and, although her brother was skeptical in regard to their present communion, he spoke to her in beautiful and prophetic language of the spheres which all were destined to inhabit. But she said their own interior musings were not put into the book, but they had cast him out as it were without it, although his historical writings were now doing a good work in breaking the shackles that had long held the mind in bondage; and she was preparing the mind of her brother for the ushering in of the higher light. Said she was delighted with her new experience of speaking through the vocal organs of her earthly sister; and, as she was promised that she should soon have an opportunity of speaking again, she would not further occupy the present time, but would give way for one of their Hindoo sisters, who was anxious to make a few remarks. And, after expressing her gratification, she retired.

One of the Hindoo women was next in the council, where she told of the pleasure of the people of her own race. Said they had cuddled up close together in order to get a good view of the family and friends of the great star-spirit. She said their present appearance on the platform was a great surprise, and every one was anxious to see them; and well, she thought, they might, for it was really a beautiful sight. She then spoke of the children; said they were dressed in gossamer, and sparkling belts that were brighter than the noonday sun; and, as they were gathered together, they all seemed to be very happy; but the tribes were looking with amazement, for they did not appear to know where the friends and relatives of the star-spirit had come from. She then said her people were preparing for the celebration of what was called in spirit an important event, for it was to commemorate the time of the star-spirit's return among mortals, when they were all notified of his presence by what was called the "raps." They had been informed by the star-spirit that was the way he had notified his professed followers when he returned among them with his angels in order to finish his work, and establish the great law of Eternal Justice; but it seemed that none of his own were prepared to receive him with his heavenly visitors when they stood at their doors and knocked. She said our Koran taught that if they knocked it would be opened, and if they asked they should receive; and they were going to ask the Star-Spirit if they could not have the same kind of dresses for their children which they had there seen upon the children of his own family relatives,— they wanted them for the coming celebration. She said they would take them off, and not have them soiled, for they did not think it proper for the children to wear their best clothes every day, for it soon had a demoralizing effect upon their young minds. They would ask, any way, and if it was right they would get them. Said she did not know of much of anything more she desired to say, and she would not take up the time, for the bow-and-arrow girl was waiting to take her place; and after saying she felt very grateful for the many privileges her people were permitted to enjoy, she withdrew.

One of the Forest Maidens was then in council, where she spoke of the wandering and scattered tribes that had been gathered together, and were then looking with amazement at the Great Spirit's Central Son, who had called down those of his first love who had assembled before them on his platform of Eternal Justice. And she had come to say to them all, notwithstanding the degradation and the reproach they had suffered when they were scoffed at and spat upon, and cast out, and cruelly crucified, they had all been near to the Great Spirit; while those who had been their persecutors had sat in darkness, and wept over the crumbling ruins of their earthly principalities, and had now been called forth by the order of the Great Spirit, who has sent out his archers to gather them up in judgment; and they must return and follow up the trail of their many wrongs, and see that the commandments and covenants of the Great Spirit were again restored to his pale-faced children, whom they had left in bondage, before they returned in order to take the place which they would have had on the great platform of Eternal Justice, if they had obeyed the laws of the Great Spirit when they were pilgrims together on the beautiful lower hunting-grounds.

After which, India closed the session by invocation to the Great Spirit.

MARCH 22, 1874. — After India's invocation to the Great Spirit, again thanking him for the past, and asking for wisdom to guide and direct them in their present labors, he said that Paul, and the Great Media, and one of the Hindoos, would occupy the session; and, after the usual encouragement, he withdrew.

Paul, the messenger to the Gentiles, was next in council, where he said they had made a thorough investigation of the gospel of a risen Saviour, which he did receive when on his way to Damascus, with authority from the high-priest at Jerusalem to arrest and persecute any of the little band of the faithful followers of their Master. And the result of their investigations was that they had found all those in power, who professed to be the followers of the humble Nazarene, in the same condition of mind the Jews were in at the time they cast out and crucified their Messiah; although he did come at the time foretold by prophet and by seer, they were not prepared to receive him and listen to his heavenly teachings; but they rejected and cast him out, and did all they possibly could in order to suppress the evidence that was given on every hand, and that should have satisfied them of the truthfulness and purity of his divine mission. But even so they found it at the present age with the Gentile nations, who have been looking for his return in spirit with the angels to finish his work, — when the Ancient of Days would sit, and the nations of the earth would be called together in judgment. But still they had wilfully disregarded the signs of the times, and turned the gospel of the communion of spirit from its original design, which was to teach the people of all nations of their immortal home; they have turned back to the perishable things of the earth, and are using the glorious gospel of "peace and goodwill to all" for the building up of a commercial religion in order to gather to themselves the mammon of unrighteousness, and have rejected and cast out and again crucified their Master, and persecuted and imprisoned those who have given heed to his call. He then said that those in spirit who had seen the evil effects of their false teachings had worked faithfully among mortals the past year, and their earthly principalities and powers, which they have built up and sustained through injustice, were already shaking on their sandy foundations, and the time would soon come when they would be crying out, and asking what they should do to save themselves from the terrible conditions with which they had become so covetously surrounded. He spoke of their labors and trials at the commencement of the gospel age, and said that Peter was not at Rome, and had no authority for the establishing of any church but that of the communion of spirit that was free for all; and also that he himself was faithful to the trust their Master confided to them, and that he went forth and promulgated the glorious news of a risen Saviour, which was the everlasting gospel for all nations, whose temples were imperishable and eternal in the heavens. He said it was true that they labored under difficulties and embarrassing conditions, for the people of that age knew but little of the birth of the individualized spirit that was immortal; and they clung with their animal instincts to their earthly homes, and scoffed and jeered at those who told them of an imperishable kingdom in spirit, where the Master, who had triumphed over the powers of darkness, had gone. And he said that mortals still complained that he had been sour and cross, and not without some reason, for he had labored with many bodily infirmities; notwithstanding he was of a sympathetic nature, and had worked for the good of all. But he believed then, and still believed, that the place for a woman's influence was at her home, where there should be purity, and where she could best use her divine gifts in the work of fitting herself and those intrusted to her care for their immortal home. But for the present, he thought, they should go into the streets and alleys in troops, and into every place where human suffering was fast increasing, and learn for themselves the fearful results that follow a disregard and a violation of the covenants and commandments of God. He then spoke a few cheerful words connected with what had been accomplished in spirit, and told us to be faithful and stand fast, and the work for the present cycle would soon be finished, and withdrew.

Jesus of Nazareth was next in council, and spoke of his trials and sufferings at Jerusalem, where he had labored in order to enlighten and draw them away from the transitory and changing scenes of time to the imperishable and eternal kingdom of their heavenly Father. He taught them the folly of striving for the things that perish at the expense of things that were enduring and everlasting; for they had turned away and fallen from the light of the spirit which had been given to mortals, and were striving through avarice and injustice to build up and perpetuate their earthly kingdoms, while the toiling millions of brothers and sisters, that were also the earthly children of their heavenly Father, were cast out and neglected, deprived of their natural rights, and left by their leaders in poverty and rags to suffer. He labored and sorrowed over their blind condition, that all might be elevated by his instructions. He had told them to seek for the higher light and they would find it, to ask and they would receive, to knock and it would be opened to them; but they turned away, and scoffed at and derided and disregarded his counsel; they cast him out and crucified him, and clung to their earthly kingdoms; while he prepared the way for those who did receive him, and returned to his Father's higher mansions. He left them the law and the prophets, with a new commandment that "they should love one another;" and had also left them the everlasting gospel that told of the open way that all might be prepared to follow; when again his Father had said to him, " My Son, take your companions, and return to my earthly vineyard, and see this time if my children are ready to receive you." Whereupon they all obeyed the command. And they had first visited what were now called the wealthy classes in every town and city, where they had found those in power, living in their palaces, and worshipping in their earthly temples; but they were not prepared to receive them. He said it was true they did not know them; but the spirits they found groaning under their altars were gathered up and taken to another sphere, and they again returned to them in anguish and anxiety of spirit, and stood around them by their altars and rapped; but they had found it of no use: they were too much absorbed in their schemes of an earthly commerce; they had no time to listen to the call, or give heed to the warning of the spirit. And they had left them with their mammon of unrighteousness, and went again among the fishermen, and among the beggars which they found in the streets, cast out to suffer, deprived, through the avarice of their wealthy brothers, of their share of the common blessings; and they had found them ready and anxiously waiting to receive them. " And, my earthly brother, you know how we have labored, for you and your handmaiden have been our earthly witnesses, chosen to sit with us in council, and keep a record of the reports that have been made, year after year, of the sorrowful conditions in spirit which have been truly represented. You know of the erection of the platform of Eternal Justice, around which the nations with their scattered tribes have gathered, and of our labors in the dark sphere, where thousands upon thousands of the spirits fled from us through fear, until their hiding-places had disappeared; and none but the Great Father in his love for his earthly children could tell how much they had sorrowed and suffered over their fallen and unhappy condition. Now, my brother, let us still work together, that all may be ready to enter in when my Father calls for my return. This is my ' second coming,' and my Father will not delay. The work must be finished. I cannot tell of the terrible sorrows that will befall those who have disregarded the call of the spirit; but I could describe something of the happiness and of the love and sweet union that will be universal when all are prepared to enter into my Father's heavenly kingdom." He again spoke of his own labors among the Jews at Jerusalem, to entice them to turn away from the things that were temporal, and hold to the spirit that was eternal. He said the judgments that followed their refusal should teach all nations the error they committed when they turned away from the law and the prophets, and followed after external and temporal things. It was true he admired the architects of the temples which had professedly been built for him; but when he had found so many of his brothers and sisters, being also the children of his Father, who had been cast out and were in poverty and rags, starving for the bread of life, He looked upon their temples, and upon those who stood up in them and professed to worship his Father through his name, in sorrow, and he had wept over them as he had wept in the Garden of Gethsemane over the blindness of the temple-worshippers at Jerusalem. Nevertheless, they heed it not, but are struggling on in order to increase their earthly stores, forgetting the admonition that was given, that " even this night thy soul may be required of thee." " And now, my earthly brother, with your handmaiden, my earthly sister, stand strong through the darkness that is fast approaching, and my spirit shall be with you. Remember that nothing but the veil of the flesh is between us; but of the day and the hour knoweth no one, not even the angels, — but my Father only, — when it will be said, It is finished; the Bridegroom is ready; let the guests into the marriage-feast, and close the door." He then said it was his desire and constant prayer that all might be ready; he would soon be with us again; but this was the last time he should come as the humble Nazarene. And after a few words of encouragement, he again withdrew.

One of the Hindoos was next in council, where he expressed much pleasure on his own behalf, and spoke of the gratitude of his people for the privileges they still enjoyed; for they all could hear the star-spirit talk when he was speaking through their goddess; but they could not see his star. He then spoke of the great celebration they were preparing to attend, and thought, when that event transpired, the starspirit might show himself to them all in his brightness. After saying that the bow-and-arrow girl was not going to speak, for the star-spirit had told them they must be saving of the physical strength of their goddess, they were rejoiced to obey the command, as they were anxious about the heathen among the Christians, and he retired.

After which, India again closed the session by invocation to the Great Spirit.

MARCH 25, 1874. — After India's invocation to the Great Spirit, he said Sapphira and Priscilla would report, after which one of the Hindoo and one of the red man's race would occupy the balance of the session; and, after the usual encouragement, he retired.

Sapphira was the next in council, where she said she had come this time with the intention of telling the truth. And she went on and related the circumstances connected with the history of Ananias and Sapphira spoken of by the author of the Acts of the Apostles; and said the report was true that her husband did dispose of his estate, and they had made it up between them to apply a portion of the amount they had received for the benefit of the association known as the "early followers of the Saviour," who had taught them the communion of spirit, and with whom it was their intention to join; but they had carefully reserved a portion of the amount in order to provide for themselves in case they failed to harmonize with the association. They could withdraw, and would have other means to supply their necessities. She said their sin consisted in the deception they used in proposing to enter the association without full faith in the manifestation of the Spirit of God, and telling a falsehood in connection with the amount which they had received; and the Spirit, which searches and knows the secrets of all hearts, knew their deception, and made an example of them for the benefit of others, and to keep the association, that was then pure and good, free from the corrupting influence of avarice. She said they had no call to go: it was an affair of their own choice; and if they had told the truth, they would have had no trouble. But they did not tell the truth, and they had found themselves lonely wanderers in spirit, where their sufferings and sorrows had been long endured, and where it had seemed as if everybody they met had known their failings; and it had seemed as if the memory of their faults, which they should have to overcome, would never depart. She expressed her gratitude for the privilege of confessing her sin before the assembled nations, who had been gathered around the platform of Eternal Justice; and she desired that herself and husband might be forgiven. And she would ask, if it were possible, that the blessed Saviour would give them something to do in the work of establishing his kingdom. After again expressing her gratitude, she withdrew.

Priscilla was the next in council, where she related things that were in connection with her own experience among the early followers of Jesus, and also that her husband and herself were first awakened to the truth and magnitude of their Saviour's earthly mission through the manifestations of the Spirit given by Paul, who at the time was known to them, and was called by the name of Saul; and who was a bold and fearless advocate of the everlasting Gospel that told of a risen Saviour who had demonstrated by his own triumph the immortality of the race, and proclaimed peace and good will to all. And they had long since become tired even in their spirit-sphere of the foolish accusations that were still hurled upon the heads of the little band who was then the earthly branch of the spiritual church inaugurated by the Saviour himself, that was in communion with the church that was triumphant; and all knew they were pure and good, and satisfied with their daily blessings; for they were taught by those who had passed beyond the vale of the evils that had been engendered from avarice and from the lust of the flesh that were transitory and perishable and not satisfying to the demands of the spirit. But when they met together in their humble way in order to counsel and strengthen each other, Jesus and the prophets were with them to aid and assist in their work of charity and love ; and they had to heal the sick, and cheer up the broken-hearted, and strengthen the weak and the afflicted, who were tormented by their opposers on every hand. And often in their public assemblies, where the poor would gather in order to be healed of their maladies, and be taught by the Spirit of things concerning the law, they would be set upon and broken up by their mortal enemies, instigated and often led by the priesthood who were bitter and unforgiving in their hatred, — when théy would scoff and hoot at them, and throw stones at those assembled and engaged in the work of ameliorating the suffering condition of the afflicted, — who often had to run in order to save their lives from the mobs sent to destroy them. But they were at all times watched over and protected by their spirit guides, and warned of approaching danger until their work was finished. And for three generations the early covenanters held fast to the communion of spirit, and were counselled and encouraged by their Master, who was often with them.

But, alas for suffering mortals! avarice and the mammon of unrighteousness increased and shut out the light of the Spirit, and the connection was broken; for, after the apostles and their co-laborers had passed over, there were none left to call them back, and the spiritual church of Jesus their Master was turned into an earthly commercial organization, where they had labored to increase their power to build up and strengthen their earthly kingdoms. She then spoke of their pleasure in being witnesses of the gathering up in spirit, where all could know and realize the importance of the grand consummation of their Master's triumphant labors. And, after expressing her gratitude for the pleasure of speaking, she withdrew.

One of the Hindoo women was next in council, where she told of the rapid progress her own people had made under the teachings of the great Star-Spirit, who was then engaged in teaching them the same as he taught those he was with when clothed in the flesh. And it was the opinion of her people that the Gentile nations, as they were now called, had made sad work about receiving him when He returned to them in spirit; and they had thought it was a pity they could not have had a better understanding about the importance of his return. But it was now very evident that if they had obeyed his precepts and been on the watch, as He had told them to do, they would have been much better prepared to receive him. She then expressed her grateful feelings for the many privileges her people had been permitted to enjoy, and they should ever feel grateful for the instructions they received from the great Star-Spirit, and would faithfully obey his precepts. After saying that the bow-and-arrow girl was waiting, she withdrew.

One of the Forest Maidens was then in council, where she spoke of the incomprehensible power of the Great Spirit, and of the magnitude of his vast dominions. She spoke of the millions of billions of the tribes of the red man's race that were in the upper hunting-grounds, and who had ever been near to the Great Spirit. She then spoke of the many tribes and nations of the pale-face race that had been buried up in the earth, with their cities and their temples and images, for turning away and disregarding the laws and the commands of the Great Spirit. She told them to look well after the scattered remnants of their tribes on the lower hunting-grounds, for the Great Spirit-Son had come for the last time, and all who disregarded his call would go the way many other rebellious tribes and nations had gone who had trifled with the covenants and the commandments of the Great Spirit when pilgrims on the lower hunting-grounds.

Whereupon India closed the session by invocation to the Great Spirit.

MARCH 29, 1874.—After India's invocation to the Great Spirit, again acknowledging their dependence, and asking for wisdom and strength sufficient for the accomplishment of their labors, he said that Josephus and Vespasian, Philo and Confucius, were present, and would each one report during the session; and, after a few encouraging remarks, he again withdrew.

Josephus was then in council, where he remarked that he felt a pleasure in again having the opportunity to speak, and said they had devoted much time to an investigation of the various manifestations of the spirit to the people of the present age, in contrast with the light that was given to the Jews at the time of their demand for a Messiah who could teach them of heavenly things. And it was well known that when the Saviour of man was among them in the flesh, his wonderful labors were but little known or noticed by the law-making and ruling class. It was true they talked of it at times in their councils, but they were not willing to believe in his divine mission, or that such marked results could ever flow from it. They well knew that many intelligent Jews, who had witnessed the power of the Spirit which was manifested through Jesus, did believe he was the true Messiah; but there was so much opposition and persecution, that they made no public avowal of their faith; and it was allowed to go on until their national troubles accumulated on every hand as had been foretold by Jesus, and also by his disciples; but even then, he said, they were not prepared to acknowledge the trouble, but tried to explain that their misfortunes were the result of other causes. Their national destruction and suffering were now a matter of history, and should be a warning to other nations not to trifle with the evidence given of the ever-living Spirit, when sent to teach them of their temporal as well as of their eternal welfare. He then addressed a few encouraging words to his people who had been gathered up around the platform of Eternal Justice, where, he said, they were all glad to bow and to acknowledge that Jesus, the humble and forgiving Nazarene, was in truth their true Messiah; and after giving expression to his pleasure that he could be a witness of the grand consummation, he retired.

Vespasian was next in council, where he spoke of the things that he himself had witnessed connected with the terrible judgments inflicted upon the Jews as well as others who inhabited their country. He told of the fearful suffering and of the blood and carnage among the people at Jerusalem at the time of the destruction of the city and temple by the Romans under the command of his son Titus, and he affirmed that a wing of the army was removed after they had commenced the siege, in order that all that would might flee to the mountains, as Jesus had told them; for they had no desire to secure their destruction; and he had often asked himself in spirit why he was made the instrument to inflict such a dreadful chastisement on a rebellious and stiff-necked people; but the answer would come back to him from the compassionate and forgiving Jesus, asking why He had to be buffeted and spat upon, and suffer the agonies of the cross. But it was true they were blind in their zeal; they had the offer of his kingdom, and had voluntarily shut themselves out, and had endured the afflictions of the second death, and let it stand for a warning to the nations of the present age, as well as for others, that may still come forth as by the fiat of a mighty power from the unfolding mysteries of time. After speaking of the magnitude of their present gathering, he expressed his pleasure in being called to stand as a witness among the people with whom he was identified during his earthly pilgrimage, and then retired.

Philo, the Jewish historian, was the next in council, where he spoke of the vast and incomprehensible power of the great Creator, and of the various manifestations of the spirit as seen in the closing cycles of time. He then spoke of his own people as a nation, and of their struggle in their fleshly forms with the surrounding elements with which they had to contend; and he thought they had done all they could in order to leave their footprints on the passing panorama. It was true they had suffered by their own experience from the errors they committed in their struggle for an earthly kingdom, and they had all bowed in humble submission to the mighty power of spirit that controls the destinies of the nations; and he also knew that many errors had been incorporated into the history of their own earthly pilgrimage that had darkened the understanding of the people of the present age; and he would cheerfully unite with others in the work of restoring the covenants and commandments, that all may have the light of the Spirit to pilot them over their earthly Jordans and up to the great platform of Eternal Justice built up by Jesus, whom they rejected and crucified, who was the true Messiah, and who only could give the password into the kingdom of his Father. He then spoke a few cheerful words of encouragement, and told of his own pleasure for an opportunity of expressing his opinion, and said that enough had been already recorded, and then withdrew.

The familiar voice of Confucius was the next in council, where he spoke in words of approbation, and told them their work of cleaning themselves up would soon be completed. He talked to the assembled nations and tribes as the children of one great family, and said they had done well, and the Great Father was satisfied, and would now receive them in his kingdom; told them it was only their leaders, who had deceived them, that would have to return in order to finish up their work and purify the records they had left behind them, which were still deceiving others. He then spoke of Sapphira, and said they were all frightened when she acknowledged the fault of herself and of her husband, and told of what had been the result. He was glad they had told the truth, for the truth had set them free, and all would be satisfied, for the doors of the Great Father's eternal kingdom would be opened, where they would see his people, and see the Father and the Son with all his happy children together. He did rejoice now in their behalf, for it had grieved him when he had to tell them of their many transgressions, for he knew it filled them with sorrow; but then he was upon the platform of Eternal Justice, where he had to speak the truth; and he was glad they had told the truth, for they had freed themselves and would be happy, and they could cross over where all were ready to receive them. He then spoke of the vastness of the dominions of the Great Father, whose wisdom was beyond comprehension; and after again encouraging those who were set apart to be witnesses of their labors, asking for strength to be given them sufficient to sustain them to the end, he once more withdrew.

One of the Hindoos was the next in council, where he spoke of the gratification his people had received in listening to the remarks of those who had been speaking; said two of them — Josephus and one of the others — were well known to them, for they used to come to their country to fight with them at a time when his nation was increasing in temporal power, and the others were afraid of losing their own temporal existence. They had heard of the one who was known by the name of Confucius, and were pleased to see and hear him speak, for they had heard of a speaking god that he used to tell about by the name of Allah; and the people of his country knew about it at the same time, for one of the idols they used to worship was then called by that name. He said Confucius was a bright spirit, and knew about all their earthly gods.

After which, India again closed the session by invocation to the Great Spirit.

APRIL 1, 1874. — After India's invocation to the Great Spirit, he made the following statement in connection with the twenty-sixth anniversary of the spirit-rap which had awakened mortals to a knowledge of the immortality of their friends in spirit. He stated that the band had visited every country on the planet the previous evening, in order to note what progress had been made in spirit development during the past year as manifested by the various associations who had met together in commemoration of the wonderful event; and whatever expression had been given in evidence of the knowledge which had been imparted was gathered up and placed in endurable form by the angels who kept the record of the things of time. He then remarked they had made provision for the annual return of the event, and that Webster, who was president of the America they had built up in spirit, would preside and give directions connected with the evening's entertainment. After which, he again retired.

Webster was the next in council, where he reviewed with apparent satisfaction a portion of their labors in spirit. He spoke with evident pride of the platform of Eternal Justice, around which the nations had been gathered. He spoke of the child that was born in our own country twenty-six years ago, and of the great interest by which it had been watched through the delicate stages of its childhood by the spirit-world as it passed from childhood to youth, and from its youth to a full-grown maiden, who was now preparing her garments in order to stand in her place and perform her part in the affairs of life. He then spoke of the sorrowful condition of national affairs at Washington, in contrast with what had been accomplished in spirit, where their New America was represented by the leaders who had proved faithful from the earliest set-

tlement down to the present time. He spoke of Scott and his
soldiers, and of their labors in the new organization. He
spoke of Everett and the school which had been successfully
established in spirit, and of the chair of justice that was sent
to Washington, with many important results which had already
been accomplished; but as these things had been spoken of
and recorded before, it was unnecessary, he said, for him to
prolong his remarks further than to say it was arranged, in order to commemorate the great event for which they were then
assembled, that Miss Landon and others, with their schools
from the celestial sphere, would form a union on the great
platform with the teachers and children of the new school,
after which the parents of their earthly witnesses would have
an opportunity to speak. He then remarked that he felt grateful for the position which had been assigned to him, for its
magnitude was far beyond the comprehension of mortals;
and, after encouraging all to be faithful to their trust, he withdrew.

Miss Landon was the next in council, where she with others
had come with their schools, as she said, from the paradise of
their Great Father's love, in order to mingle and commingle
with others, for all were his children and the recipients of his
untold blessings; and she told the children, as they went forth
to scatter their flowers, to see that none were forgotten, for
many of those present were the chosen leaders of other circles
in spirit, who were invited guests that had come to see and to
be witnesses of the evening's entertainment. She then spoke
of a tall stranger who was standing in amazement by the side
of one of their leaders, who had been active in the organization of the school with which they had come to mingle and
encourage, for they were the unfortunate children who had
been neglected during their sorrowful earthly existence, but
who were now fast gaining a knowledge of the wisdom and
love of their Creator. She spoke of the transitory and perishable nature of all earthly things. She told the stranger,
who was still standing in wonder, ignorant of everything in
connection with the spirit, that his earthly fame was also perishable, and that the trappings which he had striven so hard
to gather about him would soon be scattered, and his name
dropped from the roll and forgotten, while others who were
striving for earthly fame would take his place in the memory
of the few that were called his friends. She then spoke of
their accumulated and lasting pleasure in spirit in connection

with the work which had been already accomplished, and of the building up of the great platform of Eternal Justice, around which all could gather; and, in evidence of their progress, she mentioned the names of those of the school-children designated to take a part in the public entertainment of the evening; whereupon, after a few words of. gratitude to the Great Father of all for the present manifestation of his wisdom and of his mercy, she retired.

The children whom she had called by name were the next in council, where each one spoke of their happy condition, and of the friendship and care of their teachers who had devoted their time in teaching them the practical parts in connection with their own existence, and of their duties to each other. They told of their great pleasure in being permitted to mingle with those who had as yet seemed to have been less favored, and scatter the beautiful flowers which they were all taught to cultivate with their own labor, as they now mingled together in order to cheer them on their way. After the children's remarks, which were equally creditable to themselves and to their teachers, they withdrew.

The father and the mother of the two earthly witnesses were the next in council, where each one gave an interesting account of the nations and tribes who had answered to the call of the Angel of Time, and gathered around the great platform of Eternal Justice which had been built up in spirit, and where all that were prepared could cross over and enter into rest. They spoke of the surprise which had been experienced as the ancient tribes had gathered together apparently in the same condition they had occupied during their earthly pilgrimage in order that each one might know their place. And, after each one had spoken of the magnitude of the work of changing the condition of the spirits of the dark sphere, and of the importance of the results among mortals, they again withdrew.

One of the Hindoos was the next in council, where he spoke of the things they had been permitted to enjoy during the evening's investigation. He called it a grand exhibition, and said that his people with their Box were assigned a position in the centre of the platform, where the children had nearly covered the Box up with an endless variety of flowers. And the old general who had the command of the soldiers was also about covered up, and was having a joyful time with the school-children, for there seemed to be no end of their beautiful flowers, and they were apparently all delighted in trying to make each other happy. And his people were at all times contented and happy when they could see the great Star-Spirit look pleased, as he always did when the children were at work distributing their flowers. He then said the bow-and-arrow girl had come, and he retired.

One of the Forest Maidens was next in council, where she referred to the scenes around them as another evidence of the power and love of the Great Spirit for his pale-face children. And she entreated earnestly that every obstacle that was in the way might be removed, that all should cross over and be together. She then told them that the river that seemed to separate them was only imaginary, but they must press forward, and the mists would depart. After a few encouraging words for the white squaw and her brave, who had sat quietly year after year in their wigwam in order to keep the council-fire bright and assist in forwarding the work of the Great Spirit's Central Son, she gave directions for the archers, who were the mighty warriors of the red man's race that were on the trail of the balance of the pale-faces.

Whereupon India closed the session by invocation to the Great Spirit, again returning thanks for what had been already accomplished, and asking for wisdom and for strength sufficient in order to complete their labors.

APRIL 5, 1874. — After India's invocation to the Great Spirit, he said John the revelator was present, and would close up the investigation of the New Testament records, and would then designate who was to follow. He then spoke encouragingly of their labors, and compared the condition of the friendless wanderers in spirit to a member of an earthly family who had been enticed away from his home and from those who had cherished and loved him, and gone out into the world and partaken of its evils, until, broken down in health and deserted by those with whom he had revelled, and who had no interest in his welfare, he resolves as soon as possible to return to the loved ones of his childhood; and, as he winds his way back in sorrow and in rags, trembling with fear as he approaches the cottage of his happier days among the loved ones, where now he stands by the roadside in anxiety and inquires of a passing stranger who lives in yonder cottage, he is told, and out of common sympathy for his condition he is invited in to rest. But, alas! how all things have changed:

there is none there now that know him, for some have gone out one way and some another; and those that remain see nothing in the stranger that awakens the family affection; and disconsolate he turns to the lonely corner, and kneels down in order to relieve his spirit of the accumulated burdens; when, lo and behold! the sound of a word that was once familiar reveals the secret, and he is again recognized and restored to his place in the family circle, where joy and returned affection softens the memory of past afflictions. And, again, after a few encouraging words, he retired.

John the revelator was next in council, and remarked that he was thankful for another opportunity to add his testimony with others in evidence of the work that had already been accomplished in spirit by the aid and direction of their Master; and as he now could stand upon the everlasting platform of Eternal Justice around which the nations and tribes of the earth had been called in judgment, in charity, and love, he did bow in adoration and praise to the Great Father and the Son for the continued manifestations of their wisdom seen through the labors of those in the higher spheres who had sustained and upheld them in the work in order to clear away the darkness that held the spirits of the earth in bondage and fear, imprisoned around their tombs and under their altars, that all might be gathered up and brought into the everlasting covenants, and be partakers of their glory. It was true that his own spirit had expanded with love and forgiveness when he had beheld the lost and scattered tribes coming in from continent to continent, from island to island, and from the mountain-side and plain, all satisfied as they anxiously bowed in acknowledgment of the truth and of the glorious triumph of their Master's mission, for it was the reality of what was long before shown to him in a vision. And they were ready now to go forth among the inhabitants of the earth, and finish the work, where the vials would be poured out until they were willing to receive the covenant of the communion of spirit and obey the commandments. He then pointed to the living temple that was but a little beyond them, and spoke of the many mansions and of the stars that were eternal emblems of the Great Father's love. He then spoke of the labors and trials of Jesus their Master, who had re-established the covenant of the communion of spirit with mortals, and prepared the way that all might enter into his Father's heavenly kingdom, where they would partake of his glory. After a few cheerful remarks, he said that his brother Pierpont would be the next one to speak, and assured all that the time had surely come for the fulfilment of the prophecies; and after telling us to be faithful to our trust, again retired.

Pierpont was then in council, and said he was thankful for another opportunity of speaking through the vocal organs of an earthly sister in evidence of the magnitude of the work already accomplished through the mission of the blessed Saviour, for although he had had a foretaste of what he was to expect in spirit, it was impossible for human language to portray the reality of what they had witnessed in the gathering together of the ancient tribes. He then spoke of the disturbed condition of the inhabitants of the present age, and especially those of our own country, who were fast breaking away from the bondage of education, and looking into broader fields in search of mental food, hoping to satisfy the demands of the spirit without knowing why they were disturbed. But the time for a closing cycle foretold by prophet and seer had arrived, and countless millions of spirits had gone forth to accomplish the work, and would not be withdrawn until all was finished. He then spoke of our patience and endurance in connection with the spirits in building up the platform of Eternal Justice upon an everlasting foundation that the coming storms could not disturb; and they loved to come and say a few words as they had opportunity, for it strengthened them in their work with mortals; and they all rejoiced for what had been so quietly and so successfully accomplished. He then said that his brother Lincoln was present, and desired the pleasure of another interview, and he would retire.

Lincoln, the martyr, was the next in council, where he remarked that he had been called upon to make some sacrifice in the good work, and he felt to rejoice in what had been accomplished. He then spoke of the disturbed condition of the politicians who seemed by every move they made only to get further into trouble, and thought many of them were anxious to inaugurate another war in order to cover up their errors; but said it was not their intention to let them get out in any such way. It was true that changes were fast approaching in a way that was unexpected by mortals. He spoke of the chair of justice that had been sent to Washington, and of the change which had already transpired among them;

said it was a marvel to see how their selfish plots had been uncovered, and exposed to the toiling and overburdened people. He spoke cheeringly of the work which had been successfully accomplished in spirit, and said the everlasting kingdom based upon the broad platform of Eternal Justice was constantly increasing in strength, while mortals were losing power over their earthly principalities, and their trouble would multiply until the covenants were acknowledged and the law of justice re-established; and none had a right to complain. Whereupon, after a few pleasant remarks in connection with personal affairs, he retired.

A person of Irish nationality was the next in council, where he spoke of the condition of the people of his own country, and expressed his gratitude for the many privileges which had been extended to them before the council, for it had enabled them to organize in spirit, and strengthened their labors for the advancement of the people of their own nationality; and they did feel to adore the blessed Saviour who had done so much in order to redeem them from their fallen condition which had kept them in ignorance and in bondage. But now they rejoiced to know that a platform had been erected where Justice had found a seat, and where Charity and Judgment would be administered until the love of the Father, manifested by and through Jesus their Saviour, was again felt and acknowledged by sin-sick earthly mortals. After again expressing his own gratitude, he spoke in behalf of his countrymen, and said they would ever feel grateful for their blessings which would lead them from their earthly bondage into the light and love of the Great Father's eternal kingdom, and then withdrew.

One of the Hindoos was next in council, where he spoke of the pleasure and gratitude of his people as he told of their love for the great Star-Spirit, who was preparing them to go and see the Father; he then spoke of the great celebration, and of the notice that was taken of them, and of the Box the Star-Spirit had given to them to keep. He spoke of the pleasure of their women and children, who had the same kind of dress at the exhibition as those of the invited guests who had sat with them and with the Star-Spirit who had given them their place in the centre of his great platform. After saying that the bow-and-arrow girl would not speak, and the Star-Spirit had told them they must take good care of their little goddess while the others were away with instructions for their spirit warriors all over the lower hunting-grounds of their race, he retired.

Whereupon India closed the session by invocation to the Great Spirit.

APRIL 11, 1874. — After India's invocation to the Great Spirit, he said, owing to the health of their media, they would have a short session, and that Joan D'Arc, and one of the Hindoo women, and the red squaw, would be the only ones to speak at the present session. He then spoke of the perseverance of one who had formerly been a neighbor of the family when their media was a child with her parents in a neighboring State, and who had been for some time laboring in order to make herself manifest; and such efforts often absorbed the individuality of the media, and left them in a disturbed condition, without any explanation of the cause. He then said that hereafter no such interference would be allowed; that Deepwater and the "Healer" would only be allowed to control during the vacancy between the regular sessions, and that other spirits who were so anxious to make themselves known must make their application through them. Whereupon, after the usual encouragement, he again withdrew.

Joan D'Arc was the next in council, where she told them she had come forth at the call of the angel of time at the head of a mighty army in spirit, who were marshalled by the valiant warriors of old in order to do battle in the great cause of Justice and Truth,—she that was once the poor little maid at the inn, where she did see and talk with the spirits who had been clothed in mortal forms, and who showed her the armies in the heavens that were then ready to go forth and defend the rights of her countrymen and lead them on to victory. And she was controlled by a spirit warrior who upheld her frail body, and led the army of her country forth triumphant. One dynasty was dethroned, and another established, when she should have obeyed the counsel of her spirit guides, and retired from the earthly conflicts; but ambition and avarice came between and shut out her heavenly visions, and she was left to pay the penalty of her disobedience until she was relieved, and finally escaped from the strife and cruelty of the kings and rulers of earthly principalities. She had joined the armies in spirit who were again sent forth in countless millions to battle for the oppressed.

"O, rulers of the crumbling kingdoms of earth, what now is the condition of your toiling people? O, why have you allowed both body and spirit to be chained in bondage until their wail of sorrow has disturbed the heavenly spheres whose mighty and victorious hosts are again marshalled forth, led by the valiant warriors of old, in order to re-establish justice and execute judgment among mortals? And one by one will your kingdoms disappear, as one by one you are called to render up an account before the recording angel of time, who has kept the records of your selfish abominations." After speaking of her severe trials during her earthly pilgrimage, she encouraged us to be faithful to our trust, and then retired.

One of the Hindoo women was the next in council, where she had come to speak of the gratitude of her people for the many and great blessings they were enjoying, and for the opportunity given to them to learn from the people of other nations. The great Star-Spirit had been teaching them to return to their natural condition, and not be unnecessarily anxious about anything, for it could do no good, and many times retarded the development of the things in which they were the most interested. He had told them to examine cautiously, and see if the people of their own nationality who were still in the flesh, were prepared to receive the teachings of the Spirit; and, if they were, they would find other media like the one they call their goddess, with whose vocal organs they had learned to speak; and in the same way they could learn others to teach them. She then spoke of the great exhibition to commemorate the Star-Spirit's triumph over the darkened scenes of earth, and said it was an event never to be forgotten by her people; for they were clothed in a new dress, and placed by the great Star-Spirit in the middle of the platform, where they were shown wonderful things; yes, such things as they as a people had never expected to see. But they did hope to be worthy of the attention they had received by their obedience to the star-spirit's precepts. They had taken the new dresses from their children, and laid them aside for another suitable occasion, for they did not think it proper for children to appear in such fine dresses for every-day apparel; they had observed, where such things were allowed, they were soon taught to be ungrateful. She did not know whether she had much more to say. She felt grateful for our attention, and, if it was proper, she desired us to speak to the Great Father and to the great Star-Spirit for her people. After saying the bow-and-arrow girl had come, she retired.

One of the Forest Maidens was the next in council, and told them she had come from the upper hunting-grounds of the red man's race to the council-fire of the white squaw and her brave, to listen to the talk of the Great Spirit's pale-face children; for He had sent out his archers from the upper hunting-grounds to know why the cry of sorrow and of injustice was coming up from his white children, who had been intrusted with the lower hunting-grounds of the red man. She then told of the time when the red children of the Great Spirit covered his lower hunting-grounds, and were contented and happy; for he taught them, as he taught the birds, to know their place in his earthly kingdom, and be satisfied; they knew, when they were done with the lower, they would answer the call of the Great Spirit, and go to his upper hunting-grounds, and be nearer to him. And they found he was satisfied with his red children, for they had not departed from the laws the Great Spirit had given to his white children through prophet and seer, and by covenant and commandment; and still the cry of suffering and of injustice was heard. The Great Spirit sent to his white race his central Son, that was near to his heart of hearts, who you have said was born in sin and cradled in poverty that He might bear with you in your affliction, and endure the scoffing and buffetings in order to tell you of his Father's mansions, and lead the way to his everlasting kingdom of joy and peace. "But how have you paid the Great Spirit and his great Central Son for all of this love, you pale-face races? No wonder that you stand shaking in all of your places, for the Great Spirit knows you all, and the time has come when you must answer his call and stand upon the platform of Eternal Justice, where the Book of Life is opened."

Whereupon India closed the session by invocation to the Great Spirit.

APRIL 12, 1874. — After India's invocation to the Great Spirit, he said there were so many anxious for an opportunity to speak, it was difficult to decide which ones could have the privilege. He then remarked that Calhoun and Franklin would be the first, and during their remarks it would be decided who would have the coveted privilege of following; and, after a few encouraging remarks, he again withdrew.

Calhoun was then in the council, and remarked that he felt grateful for the privilege assigned to him in order to have a few words with his northern and eastern, as well as his western friends; and now, since they were allowed to meet together on the broad platform of God's Eternal Justice, it was his privilege to inform them there were many things connected with their own advancement that required their immediate attention, — personal affairs concerning their country's good, which they had too long neglected. And then told them he had been up and down through the northern States, and everywhere found contention about unjust taxation, with strife and discontent among the people, with pauperism and crime rapidly increasing, and no prospect for any relief. And he would say to his western friends, that they had monopolized the beautiful lakes and rivers, and cut down the forests, and driven the native red man from his home into the distant and barren mountains, where their wives and children were starving, and where they had been and were still watched over by the government hirelings with the lash, which had shown to the world that there were other lashes and other kinds of bondage a thousand times more cruel than the one held over the black man's race by his southern taskmaster. He then requested them to withdraw their forces from the slaveholding States, where they had already demoralized the black man, and taught him to lie and steal, and where many were starving; for their snow and ice had followed their armies in their devastation of the once beautiful and prosperous southern States, where contentment and happiness were wont to surround their homes, but where now the lovely flowers had refused to bloom. And he asked that in justice they should look after and try to ameliorate the fallen condition of their own people, who were fast becoming a scoff and a by-word to other nations of the earth, and leave the black man of the southern States to those whose duty it was to elevate and improve their condition. He then spoke of the fearful results flowing from craft and avarice that were hastening the downfall of nations, and again retired.

Franklin was then in the council, where he said he had come to give his boys a few words of instruction in connection with their present work with the press; told them they must put on a little more pressure, for there were still many things that must be shown up to the people. They must tell that many good, old, gray-headed Americans were starving for bread, and could get no employment, for all work was now performed by the laboring people of other countries; and tell them how the nations across the water are laughing at them in their troubled condition to find prisons and asylums for the criminals and the paupers that have cunningly and wrongfully been shipped into their marts of trade. He assured them that such things must be told, for it was the demand of justice. It was not right for the people of our country to be made to bear all the burdens that flowed from the errors of the people of other nations; and he wanted his boys to publish the truth as it was to the world. He told them they must gather around the compositors and impress them; and if that would not do, call off their attention and slip in a paragraph or two of their own. And there are the church-boys: you all know she has been a babbler of many things. But the time has now arrived when they must all be shown up in their true condition. "Well, well; and here are the women too, and they are anxious about their cause. So, my boys, be faithful, and attend to them all." He knew they had done well the past year, but they must try and do a little better — yes, a little better the present year. He then remarked that he was pleased with the opportunity of again giving his boys their instruction, and said we must be patient and take good care of our health, for many things would be told through the public press, and talked about among the people before the end of the present year. After saying that it was decided that Forrest should say a few words, he told us to be cheerful, and then retired.

· Forrest was the next in council, and said he had been favored by the privilege of using the platform of Eternal Justice for the present purpose of addressing a few words to his friends who had gathered around him in the green room of the spirit world; and as the great curtain was again rolled up, he was happy to see so many old and familiar faces awaiting and ready to receive him; and never before had he ever realized the truth that there was a part that each one had been called to perform; and as they could now take a view of the pit below them, after being called on to the great stage above to take their parts, they could all see, as the play progressed with tragedy and comedy, and farce after farce, that every one was an actor in the great drama of life. He had now learned that it was not himself who played the part of the noble Metamora, but it was the spirit of the true Metamora who at the time was reincarnated in his earthly body. And he would say to his friends one and all, who had got many parts to act, that it was better they should prepare and see that it was well done. He then described, in tragic style for the amusement of his friends, the initiation of a frightened spirit to its first immortal degree, and then spoke of the noble grandeur and beauty of the Forest Maiden who had been his guide in the spheres, and remarked if our people were as sincere in their devotion to that power they called God as the red man's race was in their constant devotion to the power they called the Great Spirit, we should be a much more happy and contented people. He felt truly grateful for the favor which had been extended to him, and that he was more than happy, for he had found such a vast and incomprehensible grandeur in the spheres through which he had travelled with his guide that had far transcended his most expanded imagination; and he was satisfied of the endless power and wisdom of the Great Grand Master. He then remarked that he was requested to say that a Forest Maiden was to follow, and would introduce to the platform one who had but recently been initiated into the mysteries of the spirit sphere, where the changing scenes had quickened their perceptions as the eye glanced with a new delight at the magnitude of Creation. He then retired.

One of the Forest Maidens with her charge was the next in council, where she introduced one as the judge, who had been interested in the work of the Great Spirit as well as in the work of the Great Spirit's Son. She then spoke of the important work which had been quietly going on; told him of the temple which had been erected in spirit, and of the platform of Eternal Justice which was built up piece by piece; and how the dark sphere, which the Great Spirit had shown to him, had been cleaned up; and she showed him the spirits which had so long been its unfortunate inhabitants. She then showed him the children and the schools which had been established for their improvement. "O, how surprised you look, good judge! But, then, this has been the work of the Great Spirit's Son, with the squaw and her pale-face brave, which he had found willing to assist him in his work. Now look this way, and behold the opening to yonder beautiful fields, where the spirits are all contented and happy. You see, good judge, they were the wandering and scattered tribes of Israel and of Judah, with Abraham, Isaac, and Jacob, and their numerous posterity, which the Great Spirit's Son has gathered into his kingdom. And if you look this way now, you see the children coming with their flowers from what they call the Paradise of God's Love. It is a beautiful sight to behold. And again, good judge, you can see in the distance the Garden of Eden, where a few commenced with the tree of life, whose branches have spread over the vast continents of the Great Spirit, and have borne the fruits you have now seen in his upper hunting-grounds. And now this way, good judge, and you shall see all those who have been enlightened by your teaching of the laws of the Great Spirit. You see that many smile as they approach you, for they have found what you taught them was true, and they are happy to greet you; and, as you gather around the one who has been faithful to the light given to him by the Great Spirit, and refused to soil the ermine of his office below, you are now to build him a platform a little higher than any of those who are gathering around him that is right. You will now place this beautiful chair upon the platform, and take the judge by his arms and assist him to his seat, and then place this crown which he has won upon his head. And now you can all see this partition between your platform and the great platform of Eternal Justice which is not yours, for none of you had thought to build it. What do I see? O, some of you are dissatisfied and are beginning to murmur. Well, open the trap-door, and let them go back until they are reconciled. For thus it must be, for the Great Spirit has said so." She then withdrew.

One of the Hindoos was next in council, and told of the gratification of his own people, and said they were much pleased with the one they called the actor. Spoke of the dress and of his fine appearance, and thought they would once liked to have had him for one of their earthly idols; but when he told about the painter with his brush that was making a panorama, some of his people were sorry when they heard of it. They had undertaken to build their pyramid in order to find out, if they could, where the Great Father was. They were afraid now it might be represented by the spirit-painter, and be an everlasting witness of their selfishness. They had spoken to the Star-Spirit about it, and were in hopes he would not have it put upon the great panorama. He then spoke of the bow-and-arrow girl, and of the surprise of the one she had called the "judge," when she showed him how much had been accomplished by the workers in spirit, and all without his knowledge. And he said the judge and his friends would soon find out now that the race of the red man was numerous, with a spirit-warrior on the trail of every pale-face.

And again India closed the session by invocation to the Great Spirit.

APRIL 15, 1874. — After India's invocation to the Great Spirit, he said the Quakeress, and Mrs. Otis, Mrs. Leavett, and Mrs. Pitcher, and one of the Hindoo women, were assigned to report the present session; and, after his usual encouragement, he again retired.

After which the earnest and friendly voice of Mrs. Townsend was again heard by the council. She spoke of what had been accomplished, and of the great pleasure they had enjoyed in witnessing the gathering together of the ancient tribes; said it was a grand sight to see them willingly bow before the humble and forgiving Nazarene, as they, tired and weary, gathered around his platform of Eternal Justice, and gladly acknowledged him to be their true Messiah, as they again united in their old songs of thanksgiving and praise to the God of Abraham, Isaac, and Jacob for their redemption. She then spoke of their gratitude for those who had patiently assisted them with their work, and affirmed that without such assistance it could not have been accomplished. But it was of no use to tell of its magnitude, for it would be impossible for mortals to fully comprehend it. "But then thou knowest, brother, that the work has now commenced with the inhabitants of our own country, and will not stop until they are made to see the light, and turn away from the darkness that has long enslaved them. So, be patient, and encourage our little sister who has at all times been faithful; and know that in due time you shall surely receive your reward." After saying she would soon have the pleasure of speaking again, and she would now give way for her sister Otis, she once more spoke a few encouraging words, and retired.

Mrs. Otis was the next in council, and said her anxiety in

behalf of her friend and brother, who had recently joined them in spirit, had procured for her the great pleasure to say a few words through the vocal organs of her earthly sister. She then stated that the condition which had been represented of her friend was a faithful reflex of his earthly surroundings; that it was for an object her friend had comprehended the situation, and was thankful. She then spoke of his noble qualities as a man, and stated that he had been a martyr during his political experience to his high sense of justice, and had given expression to it in his demand for freedom for the African race, with earnest words in their behalf that but few could comprehend. And she was sorry to say it, but it was true, that her own friends had not given him that protection and sympathy that his faithful labors had deserved. But their public display for its effects upon the rostrum over his mortal remains was well understood, and would have the desired influence over the successful occupant of the vacant chair. She then spoke of their present sphere, and of their increasing happiness which had been purchased for them by the labors of the blessed Saviour, who was also made to suffer, and who had endured for them all the agonies of Gethsemane and the torture of the cruel Cross. Said they were striving now by their efforts to ameliorate the afflictions of others, hoping sometime to merit his approbation; and she remarked that her dear friend, now that the cloud which had obscured the light had been removed, was anxious to be doing something, and would have the pleasure of being with them, and would speak for himself. She then expressed her gratitude for the privilege she had enjoyed, and said she was informed that she would soon have the pleasure of being with us to speak again, and would now retire and give place for another.

Mrs. Leavett was next in council, where she also spoke of the wonderful things they had been permitted to witness as the nations and tribes of the earth had answered to their call in spirit. She then spoke of her own sister, and said her case had been examined before the Great Judge, and they had become reconciled, and were satisfied, for many of the mysteries had disappeared when the great Book of Life was opened before them. After a few more encouraging words, she desired to be remembered to her friends that were pilgrims below, and also to the media through whom she was then speaking, and said she would be with them again when the roses were in bloom. She then retired.

Mrs. Pitcher was next in the council, and said it was true there had been a great gathering up in spirit, and they had got about through cleaning for the present. She then spoke of the affairs among mortals; said she had been to Washington and found the politicians as usual in a muddle, for they had become so deceptive they could not trust one another. But the time had now come when they would have to clean out the foul places all over the country. She thought the women that were then raiding on the rum-shops would find their own homes full of filth before they got through; said they would have to go to work themselves and clean up, for they were not going to do it for them: they had already had enough of it to look after in spirit. She said' they were going to show them now where their dirt had been hidden away, and see what effort they would make in order to have it removed, for by the old maxim all knew it was " a foul bird that would dirty its own nest." After saying their media had been faithful and would have her reward, and that she would soon be round again, but that others need not call for Molly Pitcher any more, as she had other things now to attend to, and should not answer their call, she retired.

One of the Hindoo women was the next in council, where she expressed her gratification with what she had heard; said the Star-Spirit had told her people that the two women who spoke first, and to whom they had listened with pleasure, had been educated in the schools with books, while the two that spoke last were instructed more by the Spirit. She then said that her people would ever feel grateful for the opportunities which had been extended to them in order that they might be present and listen to the views expressed by the people of the other nations. The Star-Spirit had taught them it was right to hear the opinions of others, and then use their own judgment in forming conclusions. It was the desire of her people to be good, for the great Star-Spirit had been good to them, and they wanted to gain or to merit his approbation. After again expressing her thanks for herself and people, she remarked that the bow-and-arrow girls would not speak until the next time, when it was said the men would occupy the time; she thought it looked as though they wanted a larger mark at which to shoot their arrows, after their being so long among the archers of their own race. After which she retired.

Whereupon India closed the session by invocation to the

Great Spirit, once more expressing gratitude for all they had accomplished.

APRIL 19, 1874. — After India's invocation to the Great Spirit, he remarked that Lee and Sumner, one of the Hindoos, and one of the Indian women, would speak the present session; and, after speaking again of the anxiety that was now manifested by all, he once more retired.

Lee was next in the council, where, after giving expression to his pleasure for all they had been permitted to enjoy, he spoke of their northern friend who had so recently been initiated into their New America which had been organized and built up in spirit, and where for the first time it could be truly said they had no north no south, no east no west, — where they had all laid aside their weapons of warfare, and entered into a perfect union upon the great platform of Eternal Justice, — and where he could in truth say that it was a pleasure to meet so many of his former friends and associates on a higher plane, where the prejudice of former opinions was forever laid aside, and where they could now see themselves as they had been seen by others. It was true their northern and their eastern brothers, in their zeal to free the colored man and subjugate and humble the southern States, were instigated more by their love of power than by the principles of justice. It was true the southern planter had two votes for each five of his colored workmen; and it was also true that those who opposed them had all the votes they desired to employ and had the means to control. But it was unnecessary, he said, for him to extend his remarks, for the present unhappy condition of their country conveyed its own lesson; and they had seen the contrast between that and what they were now permitted to see in spirit, with the humble Nazarene at the head, where, in the grand principle of fraternal Love and Eternal Justice, all had been accomplished. He then spoke of his gratitude for all he had been permitted to witness, and said he was too full of emotion to prolong his remarks, and would give way for one of his eastern brothers. He then retired.

Sumner was the next in council, where he first gave expression to his everlasting gratitude for the loved ones who had been permitted to come to his relief from the darkened conditions which had gathered around him during his earthly pilgrimage, and had covered him in spirit with a dark pall from which he had been resurrected, and was now submerged in the grandeur of the wonderful scenes before him; said he would willingly stand as a witness of the living truths that he in his blindness had not been able to comprehend, for he had devoted the full strength of his manhood in order to enforce the freedom of the black man's race from the bondage of his southern taskmaster, and in the strength of his will-force, urged on and encouraged by others, he had taken hold of the corner-stone of the temple of human slavery, and wrested it from its foundation, without making any provision for the terrible national results that were sure to follow; and for the past ten years, he said, his mental faculties had been overshadowed with a dark cloud, which it was impossible for him to penetrate, but which had kept him in a dissatisfied and unhappy condition. He was thankful and could rejoice now the cloud had been removed, and the light was penetrating his spirit vision; and thought the dreams of his youth would yet be realized in the things which had been shown to him around the great platform of Eternal Justice. After again expressing his gratitude, he said too much had been expected of the new-born, individualized spirit when it was permitted to speak to mortals through the vocal organs of an earthly form which it had never before inhabited; and told of his own amazement as mystery after mystery disappeared, as the mighty power and wisdom of the Great Creator continued to unfold before his relieved and elevated spirit vision. He then recognized a number of his old friends, who had again gathered around him to hear him speak, and after a few pleasant remarks in connection with their change, he retired.

One of the Forest Maidens was then in council, and told them she had come from the upper hunting-grounds of the red man near to the Great Spirit, to sit by the watch-fire at the wigwam of the white squaw, and listen to the talk of the pale-face braves. She then told the tall one of the pale-faces, who had spoken of his great zeal for the black man's race, that Africa was their rightful and proper place, and when he made his attack upon the corner-stone of the temple of slavery, which his white brothers had erected, he had forgotten to ask for justice for her race, who were the rightful owners of the hunting-grounds by the Great Spirit given; and they were not black in the face; and she would show him by permission the present condition of the remnant of her race. She then withdrew.

One of the Hindoos was next in council, where he spoke of the progress and gratification of his people from the opportunities they still enjoyed to hear the remarks that were made by others. It assisted them in forming their own opinions of what was right. He thought the bow-and-arrow girl would take the big man, who had but then made his appearance on their side, back to his counting-room, and he could pick up his pen and go to work again before the ink had time to dry; and he thought the man would have a better understanding from what had been said about justice than he had ever had before. He then spoke of the Star-Spirit, and said he was very busy; seemed to think something of importance would soon transpire, but did not know in what direction; and after asking us to speak to the Father for them, and they would do all they could in order to strengthen their little goddess, he retired.

Whereupon India closed the session by invocation to the Great Spirit, again acknowledging their dependence for strength and for wisdom sufficient for the accomplishment of their labors, which could come from no other source.

APRIL 26, 1874. — After India's invocation to the Great Spirit, he said one of the school-boys would first be heard, after which one who was then to be seen in the distance approaching the platform would have an opportunity to speak. Said the school-boy would be prepared to give the name after finishing his own remarks. After the stranger's report, Wadsworth, the pirate, was the next in order, and he would designate the one who was to follow. He then retired.

One of the school-boys was the next in council, where he said he was one of the newsboys that Everett their teacher had found with many others in their misfortune, who was at the time around their former haunts of vice and suffering in New York. And, after speaking of their changed condition, and of their improvement in the schools which had been organized in spirit, he related the following in connection with his former experience before he was relieved of his body which so often had to go hungry. Said he was out on the promenade looking around, and hard up as usual, when he saw the old man Astor coming along, and he watched his opportunity and whipped a handkerchief from the old man's pocket, and then ran along and gave it to him, saying he had found it, and thinking, if he was honest and gave it back to him, he would get a dime, and with it could buy a loaf of bread. "But," said he, "what do you think he said? Well, he said, 'You little thief, you stole that handkerchief out of my pocket; and if you don't get out of my sight in a moment, I will call a watchman and send you over to the Island.' Yes, sir, that is true; and that is the way a rich man paid me for trying to be honest;" for he called for a watchman to take him to the station, and he had to run, hungry as he was, in order to keep out of prison. Well, he said, at the time it was a trifling affair, but he had not forgotten it; and in order to get even, he had invited Astor to come to their new home. He then asked as a special favor, that he might have an opportunity to speak, for he was poor enough now himself, and could appreciate the blessing. And then, after renewing his thanks for himself and his fellow school-companions, he gave way for his new friend.

Astor was himself the next in council, where he remarked that he was glad to find one place where the beggar and the millionnaire could meet upon the same platform. He then told of his troubles and of his sorrows, and of their accumulations in spirit, as he had tried to watch over his earthly possessions. Said he had often and earnestly prayed that he might be withdrawn and given something to look after that was more substantial. He felt now that he would rejoice when the time arrived when he could exchange his bank-stock for anything that would cover his present nakedness. After expressing his gratitude for the attention which he had received, and hoping it might lead to a change in his condition, he retired.

Wadsworth, the pirate, was the next in council, where he told of his experience in the dark sphere in spirit, and how they had earnestly begged and prayed for deliverance. He said it seemed as though they had been fighting over their old battles, where the agonizing groans and the shrieks for help were heard on every side for an endless age, before the light from a higher sphere could penetrate their dark condition. After speaking of their change and of the gratitude of himself and his companions for their release, he remarked that one who had assisted with others in their labors for their elevation was present, and he would retire that she might have the privilege of making a few remarks. And he withdrew.

The voice of a woman was next heard in council, where she said that England was the country of her nativity, and she had been over sixty years in the spheres after a long and also eventful earthly pilgrimage. She then spoke in beautiful language of the wonderful changes that had taken place, and of her own anxiety for the welfare and elevation of the friends that her change had left struggling in the elements below. She spoke of the trials and sufferings of the Saviour who triumphed over the powers of darkness, and had returned in spirit to finish his work and release the imprisoned spirits. She encouraged us to persevere with them in their labors, that the darkness that was fast increasing over the minds of mortals might be forever removed. She then expressed her thanks for the use of the vocal organs of her earthly sister, and retired.

One of the Hindoos was then in council, where he told with evident pride of the great change which had also come to his people, and of their love for the great Star-Spirit who had told them of the Father which they were now all anxious to see; said he was not going to stay, for the bow-and-arrow girls were waiting to speak; but he had come only for a few moments to let us know they were doing well, and were also thankful for all they had received.

One of the Forest Maidens was next heard in the council, where she told them of the magnitude and of the grandeur of the upper hunting-grounds of the Great Spirit; told them to persevere in their labors, and they would learn more of his great power, and of his wisdom and love for his pale-face children who had been intrusted with the lower hunting-grounds of the red man, and who had shut out the light of the Great Spirit by their own evils and by their avarice for each other's wampum. She told them they must clear away their own darkness, and learn to respect the law of Eternal Justice, and the smile of the Great Spirit would return when they removed the stumbling-blocks they left in the way of the balance of their tribes on the lower hunting-grounds.

Whereupon India again closed the session by invocation to the Great Spirit.

MAY 3, 1874. — After India's invocation to the Great Spirit, he said that Elijah and Matthew would each have an opportunity to speak, and that many others were very anxious to be heard; but that only two or three who would be designated could have the desired privilege. He then spoke a few encouraging words in connection with their labors; said all were pleased with what had already been accomplished, and withdrew.

Elijah, the prophet, was then in council, where he spoke of the closing cycle, and of the covenant of the communion of spirit; and said it was true the Ancient of Days had come, and he had seen their promised Shiloh, around whom they had long been told the wandering and scattered tribes and nations of the earth should gather. And they did rejoice, and had renewed their songs of thanksgiving and praise for their redemption, although he had not the capacity then or even now to comprehend the wonderful mystery of the power and of the wisdom and love of the God of Israel, who had watched over and protected them all during their long and weary pilgrimage. After saying it was true that he had been an instrument through which the Spirit had warned the people of his age of the darkness and sorrow that would enshroud them when they shut out the light of the High and Holy One by their disregard of his covenants and commandments, so he had been permitted to return to the people of the present age, and through the vocal organs of another mortal form he had and would again renew the warning for all to beware how they trifled with God's high and holy laws. He then repeated a few words of encouragement, and again withdrew.

Matthew was the next in council, where he said he had come as another witness of the trials and sufferings of their Master during his labors in behalf of a fallen race. He told of the covenant with Spirit, and said that all who held to it after their Master's resurrection were instructed and enlightened by their heavenly counsel. He told of their doubts and fears, and of the scoffs and jeers of their opposers, and of the wonderful change the closing cycle had produced as they sat in council upon the platform of Eternal Justice, and had seen their Master surrounded by loved ones seated upon his throne of glory; while those who had scoffed and jeered, and crucified him in the flesh, had gladly bowed before him, and in their presence had acknowledged his right to be the King of kings. After speaking of their pleasure when witnessing the gathering together of the lost and scattered tribes as the crowning glory of their Master's earthly mission, he said it was true the mystery was fulfilled, and they had already been doubly rewarded for all their earthly sorrows. He then spoke of the self-will and blindness of the people of the present age, and of the darkness and the sufferings that must result from their disregard of the call of the Spirit, and then retired.

King was again in council, where he spoke of their work, and of what had been accomplished, and the pleasure himself and co-laborers had received in compensation for their service among the unfortunates in the dark sphere; but as the grand results had before been reported, he would not prolong his present interview, and gave way. After introducing a spirit known in California by the name of Miss Carter, he withdrew.

Miss Carter next expressed her gratitude for the privilege of speaking through the vocal organs of her earthly sister, and related many things of interest to those in the council that had transpired during her own earthly pilgrimage; said she had been for about twenty years an inhabitant of the spirit-sphere, and was anxious to do something, if possible, in order to improve the condition of her friends that were still groping their way among mortals; after which she retired.

Kemble was the next one before the council, where he complained of still being in trouble, and said he had not done as well as he should, with the light and knowledge that were intrusted to him when he had an opportunity to have been useful among mortals. He was evidently anxious to get away from the Indian guides who had been appointed to show him his work; said as yet he could see no end to the sorrows he had voluntarily brought upon himself and others, and bitterly lamented his sad condition. After asking for assistance, he retired.

One of the Forest Maidens was the next one before the council, where she, in beautiful and appropriate words, reviewed the statements the others had made; and then spoke of the mighty power and wisdom of the Great Spirit, and of the magnitude of the work already accomplished by the Great Spirit's Son in building up his great platform of Eternal Justice. She then retired.

One of the Hindoos was next before the council, where he spoke of the progress his people were making in spirit, and of the great interest they all had taken in the teachings of the great Star-Spirit, whose precepts and examples they had all found to be a great pleasure to them to obey.

Whereupon India again closed the session by invocation to the Great Spirit, in thankfulness for his continued blessings.

May 10, 1874.— After India's invocation to the Great Spirit, once more asking for wisdom and strength sufficient for their labors and for continued protection for their earthly witnesses, he said it would not be necessary for him to designate the ones that were present in order for them to speak; each one would give the name of the one who was to follow in the order as they were called before the council. He then withdrew.

A sailor-boy was the next before the council, where he spoke of his pleasure in again having an opportunity to speak; said he was still assigned the duty of looking after the mariners of the ocean; and, after having made his report, he retired.

Dickens was the next one in council, where he gave an interesting account of his experience in spirit, and acknowledged his authorship of the "Drood Mystery" through the amanuensis which he had found, and then stated that he had been assigned the duty to look after one of our popular clergymen not far from the famous city of Brooklyn. After expressing his thanks, he introduced an English woman by the name of Ellingworth, and retired.

His friend was the next one in the council, and gave an interesting statement of her own experience in connection with her country. She then spoke of the wonderful work which had been accomplished in spirit, and of the great pleasure the gathering up of the wandering and long scattered tribes had afforded herself and her associates in spirit; and after giving expression of her thanks to the great Creator for his continued mercy, she withdrew.

One of the Hindoos was the next before the council, and again spoke of the progress of his people in spirit, and said they had been sending ambassadors to their countrymen that were teaching them to turn away from their earthly idols, and to be looking up for the great Star-Spirit. After giving some instructions concerning their speaking goddess, he withdrew.

One of the Forest Maidens was the next before the council, where she reviewed the statements which had been made, and told them how much had been lost by their turning away from the counsel of the Great Spirit, and following after their own selfish and earthly devices. She then spoke encouraging and approving words to her confiding Hindoo brothers, and told them to persevere in their upward search, and they would find the Great Spirit. She then spoke of the sorrowful condition of the pale-faces on the lower hunting-grounds, who had turned away from the light and the love of the Great

Spirit, and were wandering in fear of each other in the darkness their own evils had created.

Whereupon India again closed the session by invocation to the Great Spirit.

MAY 19, 1874. — After India's invocation to the Great Spirit, again thanking him for another privilege of assembling together in spirit in connection with their earthly witnesses, and asking for renewed strength and wisdom sufficient for their work, he said the present session would be assigned to the friends of the family in connection with the birthday of their media; after which, making a few appropriate remarks concerning the magnitude of their labors, he withdrew.

Miss Landon, with her school-children, was then before the council, where, after her own appropriate and beautiful remarks, a number of her scholars delivered the composition which they had prepared for the occasion; whereupon, after various remarks from other friends that were permitted to speak, they altogether made up a delightful evening entertainment.

After which, India closed the session by invocation to the Great Spirit, desiring that all present might unite in thanks for the wonderful manifestation of his continued blessings.

MAY 24, 1874. — After India's invocation to the Great Spirit, he said that Josephus was present for the purpose of saying a few words to those of his own day and age; after which others would occupy the balance of the session; he then withdrew.

Josephus, the historian of the Jews, was the next in council, where he again spoke of many things connected with the earthly labors of Jesus during their own physical pilgrimage, and of the seeming miraculous manifestations in evidence of the divinity of his heavenly mission, and of the suppression of the truth from the records of their national history. He then confirmed the statements in regard to the fearful judgments which were foretold by the One they disregarded, — that did follow in compensation for their wilful blindness, their unjust and cruel rejection and crucifixion of Jesus of Nazareth, whom they had now gladly acknowledged to be their true Messiah. He then addressed them with a few cheering words in connection with the present call of the angel of time, and of the gathering together of the scattered tribes in evidence of the fulfilment of the promises made to their forefathers, when they were wandering through the wilderness of doubts and fears, the lonely pilgrims of the earth. He also expressed his gratitude for the great privilege he had been permitted to enjoy of again speaking to his people through the vocal organs of another in the presence of earthly witnesses; after which he withdrew.

A woman of ancient days, who had once been a resident among the tribes of India, was then in the council, where she addressed those of her sex among the assembled tribes. She spoke of the grandeur of the scenes before them, and of their duties in connection with their present labors as sisters and mothers of the mighty host that had come up in answer to their call. She told them of their doubts and of their fears, and of their many sorrows, when they were faithful pilgrims of the earth; and she then pointed to the beautiful fields before them, which they would soon inherit in reward for their patient labors. And after a few more words of good cheer for them all, she expressed her thanks for the pleasure she had enjoyed from again speaking to her kindred through an earthly casket, and retired.

Parker was the next in council, and again addressed himself to those of his own country concerning their labors in connection with the present closing cycle. He pointed out to them with evident pride the work they had accomplished in spirit; spoke of their New America, and of the schools which had been established, and of the gathering up of the old people who were now contented and happy in their sphere; and, after giving further instructions to those who had not yet finished their work among mortals, he gave encouraging words to all, and again withdrew.

One of the Hindoo band, who had been intrusted with the old ark of the covenant once cherished by the wandering Israelites, was the next in council, where he told his people of how much the great Star-Spirit had done for them by teaching them the things he had taught to others when he was with them, and although they refused to receive him, his precepts could still be found in the Christians' Koran. After giving them instructions about the box the Star-Spirit had intrusted to their keeping, and telling all to obey his precepts, he withdrew.

One of the Forest Maidens was the next in council, where she had come with the many tribes of the red man's race in

answer to the call of the Great Spirit; and she told them of
the time when the race of the red man covered the lower
hunting-grounds, and was taught by prophet and sage who
had looked up to the Great Spirit for counsel. She told them
of the mighty warriors who with their many tribes had passed
up to the upper hunting-grounds, and were near to the Great
Spirit, and who had come as by his command with his great
Central Son to build up his platform among the pale-face race,
and re-establish the great law of Eternal Justice. She told
them of the many moons her sister squaws had stood by the
wigwam-door, as many from the hunting-grounds of the Great
Spirit had gathered around the council-fire of the pale-face
squaw and her brave, who had listened to the commands of
the Great Spirit who had sent out his archers whose bows
were strong, and whose arrows were bright, and they would
do His work. And the remnants of the scattered tribes of
the pale-faces would gladly turn back to the Great Spirit, and
obey the covenants and the commandments given to guide
them. After which, India closed the session by invocation
to the Great Spirit, once again expressing sincere thanks for
continued blessings.

MAY 31, 1874.— After India's invocation to the Great
Spirit, he said that Lafayette was present, and would be
the first one to report, and that he would designate the
one who was called to follow him; whereupon, after the
usual encouragement connected with their labors, he again
retired.

Lafayette was the next one in council, where he spoke of
many things in connection with the early struggle of the
Americans that finally resulted in their national independence.
He then spoke of his own country, and of his early love of
freedom which had identified him with the American Revolution that relieved them from the demands of the taskmasters
of other countries, and had opened the way for his present
appearance among those who had been firm in their demands
for national freedom. He then called out the names of a number of his compeers who had been foremost in the great
cause of human rights, and with whom he was again proud to
meet upon the great platform of Eternal Justice. He also
spoke of Arnold, and said he was then present, and would
have an opportunity to follow him with a few remarks; and
said it was evident that through his own weakness he had

proved in the end to have been the greatest traitor to himself when he voluntarily forfeited his own freedom. After speaking of the present sorrowful condition of the people of his own country, he expressed his approbation of the mighty work which had already been accomplished in spirit for the ultimate emancipation of a suffering race, and withdrew.

Arnold was next in council, where he again confirmed his previous report that his love for the enticing habit of gambling had been the sorrowful cause of his failure to fulfil his important trust. But he said his case had been examined before the council that was in session upon the great platform of Eternal Justice, and that he had been forgiven and assigned to duty with others who had forfeited their liberty in a similar way; and they had united in a covenant to work among mortals until the fearful curse of gambling was entirely eradicated from the human mind. After expressing his thanks for the favor shown to him, he said that Peter, who was known as "the great Russian ruler," was present in order to make a few remarks, and then retired.

Peter, the Russian ruler, was the next in council, where he confined his remarks to the people of his own country and age. He spoke of their labors for their national welfare, and also of the present glorious consummation as they had answered to the call of the angel of time, and found that their nationality had been protected, and that every tribe and kindred was now ready to stand in their place. He told them, as he had stood in his place, and witnessed with amazement the gathering up of the scattered tribes of the earth, he was overwhelmed with the evidence of the power and wisdom of the great positive Mind that had comprehended and controlled so grand a work. And then, after a few words of encouragement to his people, he gave thanks to the great Creator for their continued blessings, and withdrew.

One of the Hindoos was the next in council, where he spoke of the progress of his people, and then said, if the great man who had spoken before him had been a warrior and ruler over many people, the great Star-Spirit did not intrust them with the box which he had taken away from their forefathers, and had given it to his people, and was teaching them — as the others had been taught — the true meaning of the mystic symbols; and, after telling his people to be faithful to their trust, and to obey the instructions of the great Star-Spirit, who would take them all up to the Father, he retired.

One of the Forest Maidens was the next in council, and, after viewing the statements of the others, she told them of the " old sages" of her own race that were then in council near to the Great Spirit. She told of their happiness on the lower hunting-grounds before the pale-face race with their avarice had come to disturb the grand harmony of the Great Spirit's laws manifested throughout all nature. She told them of the tameness of the lower orders of the animal kingdom, surrounded with everything to supply their wants in their beautiful forest homes, and of the great variety of fish that sported playfully in their natural element which the Great Spirit in his bountiful wisdom had provided for food for his red children. She told them that the cry of suffering from the pale-face race had disturbed the harmony of the higher spheres; and although they pitied their fallen condition, it would have been better for them to have lived nearer to the Great Spirit, and to have obeyed his laws. And after a few words of instruction to the Great Spirit's archers of her own race, that were sent from their upper home to follow up the trail of the wandering and fighting pale-face race, she withdrew. Whereupon India once more closed the session by invocation to the Great Spirit.

JUNE 7, 1874. — After India's invocation to the Great Spirit, again asking for wisdom and for strength sufficient for their labors, he said they should appoint a committee in spirit of two who had proved the most worthy to represent the people of the towns in which they in spirit had labored. He then called the name of Sweet and of Brown to represent the town of Milford; after which he also called the name of Graham and of Griffin to stand for the town of Litchfield. When, after speaking of the many warnings which had been given to the inhabitants of the earth from the spirit spheres, and of the changes fast taking place, he again withdrew.

The parties named were the next in council, where each one spoke for himself, and acknowledged they had been residents of the towns as stated, where they had all been taught by the spirit, and each one gave a statement in regard to the present condition of the inhabitants of the towns, and then expressed their individual satisfaction in being called to stand as witnesses of the wilful blindness of mortals at the closing of the present cycle; after which they retired.

One of the Hindoo race was the next in council, where he

confirmed all his people had previously said about their progress, and then expressed it as his opinion that the time was near when the people of his own nationality would lay aside their dumb idols, and be looking after the great Star-Spirit which they had been told about in their Koran; and, after speaking of their own happy condition in spirit, he gave the usual instructions in behalf of their speaking goddess, and then withdrew.

One of the Forest Maidens was the next in council, where she said she had come where the council-fire was bright, with many of the mighty warriors of her own race, whom the Great Spirit had sent from his upper hunting-grounds, with his many archers to look after the fallen and sorrowful condition of the pale-face squaws and braves. She addressed words of good cheer to her confiding Hindoo friends, and told them to obey the precepts of the Great Spirit's Central Son, and they would have nothing to fear. After saying she would away to the Great Spirit and tell him all she had heard in the council where the scattered tribes had been gathered together around the great platform of Eternal Justice, and where the fair daughters of Israel and of Judah and the Gentile race had told of their sorrows, she retired.

Whereupon India closed the session by invocation to the Great Spirit, again acknowledging that he was the only true source of wisdom and power, and that it was the duty of all to ask, and for all to be thankful for their daily blessings.

JUNE 14, 1874. — After India's invocation to the Great Spirit, once more thanking him for another opportunity of meeting together with both spirits and mortals, and asking for wisdom and strength sufficient for their labors, he said that two were present as witnesses for St. Louis, and would be called in order to make their own statements; and then, after his usual encouragement, he again withdrew.

The next one in council gave the name of Mrs. Aversol; said she had been a resident of St. Louis, and had been a media, and was used by the Spirit in order to enlighten the people of that section of the country. She then further stated that she had found since her initiation into the spirit sphere that by her attending to the demands of others, she had neglected the things that pertained to her own vital interests, and by her so doing she had not attained a high position in the spheres. She desired that others should be instructed and warned in season, in order that they might be benefited by her own experience. And, after further stating such things as she desired before the council, she withdrew.

The next one in council gave the name of Ann Shaw, and she too had been a resident of St. Louis. She related before the council incidents connected with her earthly pilgrimage; said she had been unfortunate, and was cast off and neglected by all, and finally had thought to end her sorrows by leaving her body in the Mississippi River. But she had found in spirit those who had sorrowed with her in her affliction, and who had brought her before the council, where she was told that Justice had at last found a resting-place, and where she would be allowed to make her own statement; and, after finishing the story of her many wrongs, she withdrew.

Another of the Hindoos was the next in the council, where he asked that the Christian missionaries might all be recalled from the so-called "heathen" nation, for it was evident their labors were more needed among their own people. He said it had been the subject of much interest to them in spirit, and fears had been expressed that if such things were permitted to continue, the people of the heathen nations would soon become as much demoralized as the Christians themselves; and the great Star-Spirit had taught them to beware of evil communications, and never to follow the bad examples of others. And it was well known to them all that wherever the Christians had been, they had not practised the precepts inculcated by the Star-Spirit. After finishing his appeal, he withdrew.

One of the Forest Maidens was the next in council, where she told them she had come as by the command of the Great Spirit to listen to the talk of his pale-face squaws; and she told them their many sorrows were well known to the Great Spirit, for their white brothers had followed in the trail of the fighting kings and priests of Israel and of Judah, until darkness and strife had once more covered the lower hunting-grounds of the Great Spirit. She then told them of the great wisdom, and of the love, and of the beauty and harmony that reigned throughout the upper hunting-grounds of the Great Spirit. She told of how much his pale-face children had lost by turning away from the light given through prophet and sage, and through the covenants and the commandments of the Great Spirit. She told them it was enough. She had listened to their talk at the council-fire of the white squaw, and she would away and tell the Great Spirit of the many complaints of his pale-faces on the lower hunting-grounds of the red man, where the remnant of his once noble race had been driven to the mountains with their squaws and pappooses to starve.

After which, India again closed the session by invocation to the Great Spirit.

JUNE 21, 1874.— After India's invocation to the Great Spirit, he spoke of changes that were fast taking place among mortals, and of the darkened conditions that were sure to follow the withdrawal of the Spirit, which had everywhere been trifled with by those who should have been foremost in listening to its call. After speaking of the many obstacles under which they had labored in order to get a hearing, he withdrew.

Mrs. Hutchinson was the next in council, where she said she was called to represent the town of Lunenburg, of which for many years she had been a resident, and where she herself and others had been taught by the Spirit before she was called from her earthly pilgrimage. She related many things of interest as a witness of her changed condition, and said the inhabitants of the town were wedded to their earthly idols, and had turned a deaf ear to the call. After finishing her statement, she expressed her gratitude for the light which had been given to her, and then withdrew.

Paine was again in council, where he related many things in connection with his own experience of the blind, stubborn, and self-willed condition of the inhabitants of the earth. He told of how they had fought against the light which the higher powers had given through his own physical organization. He told of how they had scoffed at him, and had burned up the books which he had given to mortals — which would have led them out of their mental blindness, had they desired to follow the light. He then said he had found the One they had professed to worship, gathering up the starved and bleeding victims which they had cast out of their synagogues, and by their avarice and inhumanity had sent in ignorance, in poverty, and in rags, into the dark sphere in spirit, where even the "black coats" had been glad to fall in and follow until they stood in amazement before the great platform of Eternal Justice, where they had had to wait for further orders. After giving a few words of encouragement to all who worked for the unbinding and elevation of the race, he again retired.

One of the Hindoos was then in council, where he said it was a busy time with them all; but then his folks were all doing well and were satisfied, and they had told him to say they did not want the pennies the Christian children brought to their schools in order to assist in Christianizing the heathen. He said the matter had been well considered, and they had come to the conclusion that it was of more importance for the Christians to raise their pennies in order to help clothe and school their own poor children; said the great Star-Spirit was very busy now, and they did not see him as much as they had when he first came among them; but then he had promised to take them to the Father, and they were satisfied and obeyed his instructions. After giving directions about their goddess, he retired.

One of the Forest Maidens was then in council, where she told of the frightened and sorrowful condition of the Great Spirit's pale-face children, who started for the upper hunting-grounds without chart or compass or password, without a life-boat and guide to pilot them over an endless and a fathomless and a boundless ether ocean. She told them the Great Spirit had sent out his archers to clear away the many obstacles which had so long darkened the vision of the pale-faces on the lower hunting-grounds of the Great Spirit, and turn them away from the crumbling ruins of their earthly gods. And after giving instructions to her sister-squaws, who had guarded the wigwam-door of the pale-face squaw, where the council-fire was ever bright, and where many a pale-face had told the story of their many wrongs, she withdrew.

After which India once more closed the session by invocation to the Great Spirit.

JUNE 28, 1874.—After India's invocation to the Great Spirit, thanking him for another gathering of both spirits and mortals, and asking for wisdom and strength sufficient for their labors in order that all might be approved, he stated that one by name of Mill would speak for his countrymen, and then Chocorua the mountain-chief would speak for himself; and, after giving some cheerful words, he withdrew.

Mill was next in council, where he spoke of his countrymen and their condition; told of his own condition; said that the erysipelas in his throat had released him from his earthly pilgrimage. He then spoke of his earthly labors in behalf of his fellow-man, and said he had advocated the emancipation of woman from her thraldom, and had favored her political enfranchisement before his changed condition; but since he had received more light, he had now altered his former opinion on that subject, although he was still in favor of her having equal rights in her home and by the side of her husband; but it should be her duty to attend to her household affairs, and devote her spare time to the more important duty of teaching the children intrusted to her care the covenants and the commandments of God, and by so doing she would soon find that greater good had been accomplished for herself and her offspring, and for humanity, than it would have been possible to do by wasting her valuable time in trying to regulate the commercial and political affairs of the nation. He then spoke of his honest doubts, before his change, of man's individualization continuing beyond the tomb, and of his amazement when he awoke to a consciousness of his error, and to the busy scenes of life beyond the vale of mortals. After saying all that he desired, he gave expression to his thanks for the privilege given to him to solve a great mystery, and then retired.

Chocorua was the next in council, where he said he had come before the great platform of Eternal Justice to acknowledge that when he destroyed the wives and children of his white brothers, he was not just, for his white brothers had done him no wrong. He was satisfied that his own young brave — whom he had accused his white brothers of slaying — had been removed from the hunting-grounds of his tribe by an accident, and he had now come to say to his white brothers that he had been sorry for the wrong he had done to them, and to ask them to forgive him. He then told of the many moons during which he had clung around the mountain-top where his earthly remains had been left, disregarding the entreaties of his tribe to go up nearer to the Great Spirit; but now he had seen that justice had been once more established, and felt satisfied; after which he retired.

The next in council was the deaf and dumb patient that was before the council some two years previous, at the time the schools were established among the children in spirit. He said he had recovered his speech, and had been instructed in the schools, and had come to thank all for the interest that had been taken in his welfare. He then told of how the dumb had been taught to speak, and the deaf to hear, the blind to see, and the lame to leap for joy; said they had been commissioned to go in a happy band together, and assist in removing such misfortunes and sorrows from the suffering inhabitants of the earth; and, after thanking all who had been interested in their welfare, he retired.

One of the Hindoos was the next in council, where he said that his people were also thankful for all that had been done for them. He spoke of the Star-Spirit, and how he had given them the Box, and had taught them the language of the symbols which it contained, and its design to elevate the spirit and draw it away from its earthly idols; and he had taught them the same things in another form that was found in the Christians' Koran. He said the great Star-Spirit was good, and had been kind to his people, and they were satisfied he would take them to the Father; said his people often talked of it, and had come to the conclusion that the Christian people would feel their own condemnation when they awoke to a consciousness of the way they had used the Star-Spirit. After saying they had all sent their love to their goddess, he withdrew.

One of the Forest Maidens was the next in council, where she had come with more of the red man's race from the upper hunting-grounds to do the bidding of the Great Spirit; and they had followed in the trail of the Great Spirit's great Central Son, who had opened the way through the dark sphere of spirit, and had awakened all, and sent his messengers to summon them to appear before the great platform of Eternal Justice, where Israel and Judah with their many tribes, and where the Gentile race who had followed in the bloody trail of their forefathers, had all stood trembling over the memory of their evil doings, and in fear of the mighty power of the Great Spirit. She then told of the mighty warriors of her race, who had left the upper hunting-grounds, and were out on the war-path after the remnant of the pale-face race still left on the lower hunting-grounds, who had turned away from the covenants and from the commandments of the Great Spirit. After telling her sister squaws to see that the wigwam-door of the white squaw, where the council-fire was bright, was well guarded until their work was finished, and the remnants of the scattered tribes on the lower hunting-grounds had been taught to obey the law of Eternal Justice, she retired.

India once more closed the session by invocation to the Great Spirit.

JULY 5, 1874. — After India's invocation to the Great Spirit, he said that Adams and Taylor, Van Buren, and, if there was time, others would have an opportunity to speak; and, after his usual encouragement, he withdrew.

Adams was then in the council, where he spoke of the great pleasure it afforded him to meet with so many of his countrymen who had gathered around the new platform. He then spoke of their own feeble labors in comparison with the magnitude of the work of their Saviour, who had crowned his labors for a blind and fallen race by establishing his great platform of Eternal Justice, and who had assigned to them a nationality in spirit of their own, where they could still unite in their labors for the amelioration and the elevation of their countrymen. And, after expressing his views in regard to the magnitude of the work connected with the present closing cycle, he gave thanks to the Great Creator for the privilege of knowing the Saviour and his co-laborers had found the instruments to assist in their glorious work among the inhabitants of their own beloved America, and retired.

Taylor was the next in council, where he expressed his pleasure for another opportunity of meeting with so many of his countrymen who had rallied around the new platform and pledged themselves to stand shoulder to shoulder in the approaching battle; said it was a matter of gratification to his own feelings that he was permitted to see so many of his countrymen in the front ranks who had been martyrs in the great cause of human emancipation during their earthly pilgrimage; and, although it was evident that there were yet plenty seemingly surrounded and intrenched and barricaded with their earthly principalities who would continue to oppress and oppose them, yet they could console themselves with the knowledge now that they had tried and faithful leaders at their head, who knew how to organize and when and where to move in order to accomplish the victory. And, after giving expression of his feelings of satisfaction to know that he had been found worthy to stand as one among them, he withdrew.

Van Buren was the next in council, where he related things in connection with their preparation in spirit for the work set apart for them to accomplish. He told them of the patient labors of their Saviour, who by perseverance had finally triumphed in spirit over every opposing force, and whose power was already shaking the principalities and powers of earth to the bottom of their sandy foundations. He said he was rejoiced to meet with so many of his former friends and associates who had gathered around the great platform of Eternal Justice, where the prejudices and the mistakes which they had fostered during their earthly pilgrimage could now be laid aside, and they could commence and rebuild upon the true foundation; said he felt grateful for the pleasure he had experienced by speaking through the vocal organs of his earthly sister, and withdrew.

Scott was next in council, and again spoke of his boys that had enlisted under the new banner in spirit, and who were ever ready to engage in a conflict for the emancipation from the errors of their friends they had left behind. He said their weapons of warfare were perfect, and their balls were balls of electrical fire that never failed to accomplish their work. He spoke of the children and of the pleasant associations that returned as they were often permitted to gather around them and scatter their celestial flowers. Yes, he said, it was truly a heaven; and he should ever feel grateful for the new trust which had fallen to his lot. And, after issuing his commands to his soldiers, he again withdrew.

One of the Hindoos was next in council, where he said he had not got much to say; but he had stepped in for a moment to let us know his people were all doing well, and that it was a busy time with them all in spirit. He thought something would soon transpire. He then told the bow-and-arrow girl she must not stay long, for it was evident those other fellows had used up the strength of their little goddess; and, after saying that his folks were very thankful for what they had seen and heard, he withdrew.

One of the Forest Maidens was the next in council, where she had come to the camp-fire at the wigwam of the white squaw, and she had listened to the talk of the pale-face braves, and would away and tell the Great Spirit, for the Great Spirit was ever pleased when his white braves talked together, and obeyed the law of Eternal Justice in their dealings with each other; and, after a few words with the archers that were sent upon the war-path to do the bidding of the Great Spirit among the pale-face race, she withdrew.

After which India again closed the session by invocation to the Great Spirit.

JULY 12, 1874. — After India's invocation to the Great Spirit, once more thanking Him for protection and strength for the accomplishment of their labors, he spoke of their efforts in order to teach and quicken the spirits of mortals, and elevate their thoughts from the transitory and perishable things of time to the more enduring and imperishable things of eternity. Said it was the return of the Great Media who had done so much for a selfish and fallen race, and said it would have been far better for those who have turned away and scoffed at their labors if they had never heard that the "second coming" of Jesus of Nazareth was to be in spirit. After a few encouraging words, he said a French woman was present, and would have an opportunity to speak, and withdrew.

One who said she was known among mortals by the name of Madame de Stael was the next in council, where she spoke of things connected with her earthly pilgrimage; said she was a native of France, where she had labored for the emancipation of her race from their earthly thraldom, and where she had once been banished from her home and country for speaking too freely about the tyranny and oppression of man. She then said they had laid aside their robes, and had followed the lead of the blessed Saviour in his great work of inaugurating justice among the inhabitants of the dark sphere; and they did rejoice to know that mortals had felt their approach and were looking anxiously about in order to secure the foundations of their earthly principalities. She gave words of encouragement to her sister spirits; told them they could see through the dark vista of time when the great platform of Eternal Justice would have its place among the affairs of mortals; and, after expressing her gratitude, she retired.

A man by the name of Walker was then in council, where he said he was an American, and related many things connected with his earthly experience; spoke of his present surroundings; said no one could claim a thing that did not honestly belong to them; and, in order to have a claim that would be respected when they crossed the boundary line between time and eternity, their title must be good. Said he was permitted to make the above statement on account of the great interest he still felt for some of his friends that were not as yet relieved of their mortal forms; and, after expressing his gratitude, he urged them all to be vigilant, and withdrew.

One of the Hindoos was the next in council, and said it

was of no use for that last man taking the trouble of telling his friends about the conditions, for the same thing had been told by the Star-Spirit, and was in the Christians' Koran, and his friends had paid no attention to it. And now, if they wanted to cross the line with spots on them that every one could read, it was no one's fault but their own, and they would have to clean themselves up, for the great Star-Spirit had said so. He then said his people were doing well, and were preparing for a coming exhibition. He told the bow-and-arrow girl she must not stop long, and retired.

One of the Forest Maidens was next in council, and told them she had come from the upper hunting-grounds as by the Great Spirit sent to listen to the talk of his pale-face children. She told them of the vastness of his dominions, and of his mighty power. She told them the Great Spirit loved his white children when they obeyed his commandments and looked up to Him in thankfulness for their many blessings. She told of the old sages of her own race, who sat in council near to the Great Spirit, where they all knew of the many sorrows of the remnant of their race that was left among the pale-faces on the lower hunting-grounds of the red man; and she said she would return back to the upper hunting-grounds of the Great Spirit, and tell him all she had heard at the wigwam council of the white squaw and brave who had the records of the scattered tribes called up in judgment.

And India again closed the session by an invocation to the Great Spirit.

JULY 19, 1874. — After India's invocation to the Great Spirit, he said a man known by the name of Martin, and his friend, would have an opportunity to make their reports, after which an Irish girl would have the privilege of speaking. He then made a few encouraging remarks in connection with the importance and the necessity of their work that would culminate in a reunion of mortals with their friends who had passed beyond the veil. He then withdrew.

The next one in council said he was known by the name of Sandy Martin, and had devoted much of his time during his earthly pilgrimage to the important business of "driver of a public stage," in which capacity he gave many a poor and weary traveller, who was short of means, a free ride in order to help him along on his way; and as yet, he said, he had no occasion to regret it. Said he had sought for his present interview in order to prepare the way for one of his fellow-townsmen who was once called a "major," but who in fact had not proved to be much of a major after all; for he was evidently still in trouble, and was anxious to make the trip again through the mortal in order to unload a part of his burdens, trusting it might in the end result in some relief. And after relating a few of the reminiscences that formerly occurred along his own familiar route, he expressed his thanks for his new experience, and left.

His friend, the "major," was the next in council, and voluntarily relieved himself of the things which had troubled his mind. He told them that through the instrumentality of interested friends he finally secured a position that he was not at the time competent to fill; and he had defrauded the public treasury, and had also wantonly maltreated others intrusted to his charge, who had been deprived of their liberty for the violation of law, and whom it was his duty to see that they were treated with humanity, trusting that it might have resulted in their ultimate improvement. He then related how the memory of the past was ever present, and that wherever he went his burdens followed in order to torment him. He had begged and he had prayed, but found no relief; and if there was anything in his power to accomplish by way of compensation, he was ready and willing to perform it, if it would relieve him from his present condition. He then said, if he had been kept at the plough, where he might have obtained an honest and an independent living, it would have been much better for himself, as well as for all others with whom he had come in contact. He then expressed thanks for the privilege of speaking, and to all that could sympathize with him in his afflictions, and withdrew.

The Irish girl was the next in council, where she related the following: Said she was one of the poor, friendless, and homeless little girls that were gathered together by the good spirits who had clothed and schooled them; and she had been told by one of the lady teachers she would be likely to find her father by having an opportunity to speak before such a vast multitude of other spirits. She then said that her father had preceded her to the spirit sphere, and she had not been able as yet to find him; but they were told by their teachers that now all the poor children who had been cared for and schooled in spirit, would have the privilege given to them soon of going to their parents and friends, and assist in leading them out of the purgatories that ignorance and the prejudice of conditions had forced them into during their earthly lives, up into the new tabernacle which the Saviour had now prepared for them in spirit.

She was evidently delighted with her opportunity of speaking, and seemed to be anxious for the time to arrive when she could be with her parents. And, after thanking all who had been instrumental in improving the sorrowful condition of the unfortunate spirits, she retired.

The next one in council was an American boy whose only friends he had known, he said, he found among the hovels of the poor in New York; but he had found good friends, who had compassion on his forsaken and friendless condition in spirit, and he had been clothed and schooled. He thanked those who had been interested in the establishment of their schools, and spoke of the kindness of their teachers, and said they were promised that at the next session of the council there would be an opportunity for some of the poor boys to give evidence of their improved condition by an exhibition of their scholarship; and, after again expressing his thanks, he retired.

One of the Hindoos was next in council. Said he could not stay long, for his folks were all busy preparing for the exhibition, and that some of their children would also have an opportunity to make an exhibition of their improved condition in contrast with the Christian children. He said his folks were thankful to all who had been instrumental in the great work of progression; but more especially were they thankful to the great Star-Spirit, who had opened the way and was preparing them to go with him to the Father. After saying his folks all sent their love to their little goddess, he retired.

One of the Forest Maidens was next in council, where she told them she had come from the upper hunting-grounds of the Great Spirit who had sent her to the wigwam of the white squaw, where the council-fire was bright, to listen to the talk of his pale-face children, who had come from the lower hunting-grounds of the red man's race. She told them the Great Spirit was pleased with the improved condition of all the sorrowing ones who had been gathered out of the purgatories and the hells of the dark sphere created by the avarice and the ignorance, by the selfishness and the blindness of his white children, who have turned away from the light of the

Great Spirit given by prophets and sages of old. She told of the love of the Great Spirit manifested by sending his great Central Son to light up the way and call them above their perishable kingdoms which they had built through blood and strife on the lower hunting-grounds of the red man. After giving instructions to her sister squaws to guard well the wigwam of the white squaw, she said she would away back and tell the Great Spirit all. She then withdrew.

After which, India again closed the session by invocation to the Great Spirit, once more acknowledging that his mighty power and wisdom were everywhere made manifest, and that without him nothing could exist; and that all should ask and give thanks for the blessings they were receiving.

JULY 26, 1874. — After India's invocation to the Great Spirit, he said the session would be devoted to an examination of the school which had been established for the improvement of the neglected and the unfortunate ones which had been gathered up in spirit; and that Washington, Franklin, and Webster, with Channing and Everett, besides many others who had been connected with the schools among mortals, were present and interested in the intended exhibition; and that Everett would take the lead, and make the necessary arrangements among the children. He then withdrew.

Everett was next in council, where he said they had arranged for the evening's entertainment an exhibition to all who were interested in the laws of eternal progress, of the wonderful improvements the children had made in their schools since they had been gathered together and organized in spirit. He then told them they commenced by teaching all the English language; they then established order in the different classes, and taught them to spell and to read, with a correct understanding of what they were given to learn; and after they had learned to read well, they had taught them the different branches of arithmetic, then geography, and then botany and astronomy. He then remarked that it was with much pleasure to himself and his present associates to be able to introduce one of their pupils from each branch in order to prove the success of their system. After expressing his gratitude to the Great Creator for their increased happiness, he withdrew.

The children were next before the council, where one from each class was examined in the different branches which had been taught them in their "spirit schools," with much credit to themselves and their teachers, judging from the evidence manifested by the great surprise which all expressed who had the pleasure of witnessing their advanced and happy condition. And as the last of the Christian children, after their examination, had told of their changed condition, and given forth expressions of gratitude for the loved ones who had come into the dark and friendless sphere, where they found them in their rags, and had relieved them, they all retired.

The next surprise was given by the introduction of one of the Hindoo little girls, who was before the council, where she was examined, and gave proof of a still higher advancement. She told of a school which the great Star-Spirit had established among her people, where the children were taught the language of flowers, which they were instructed were the alphabet of all creation, and unfolded to them the history of the planet which they inhabited. She invited the Christian children to come up to their school, and see if they could interpret the language of the beautiful flowers. She then recited an inspired lesson as a specimen of what they were taught by a few of the great variety of flowers; and, after saying they could never cease to be thankful for all the great Star-Spirit had done for them, she withdrew.

White Fawn, the Indian girl, was the next in council, where she told of the progress her tribes had made in spirit from what she had been taught among the Great Spirit's good paleface children. She told them the children of her tribes and race had got a school in which they were taught to love the Great Spirit for his wisdom manifested through the bountiful provision made for all things created; and the love of the Great Spirit taught them to be kind and charitable to each other. The Great Spirit's good pale-face children had taught her tribes to spell and to read; they had taught them how to cultivate the fruits and the flowers, and they had beautified the gardens around their homes in their upper hunting-grounds through the knowledge received from the Great Spirit's good pale-face children. And she wanted all to look up to the Great Spirit in confidence and in love, and thank him for their daily blessings; for she could see day after day how much had been done for her and for her tribes, and she loved the Great Spirit who was so wise; she was always fearful of doing wrong to incur his displeasure. And, after expressing her gratitude for the improved condition of herself and her tribes, she thanked the good pale-faces for their instruction, and then withdrew.

Whereupon India once more closed the session by invocation to the Great Spirit.

AUGUST 2, 1874. — After India's invocation to the Great Spirit, he mentioned the names of Edmonds, King, Agassiz, and Paine, and said that Mrs. Townsend and Fanny Fern, and, if there was time, others were anxious to speak, and that after the present session they would have a vacation of one month; and, after they organized again, they should commence a revision of the account of their labors. After a few encouraging remarks in connection with what had already been accomplished, he retired.

The parties named above were next in council, where each one made a statement in connection with their own experience, and of the magnitude of the work necessarily connected with the present closing cycle; and, after making their arrangements for the appointed vacation, the last one of them retired.

One of the Hindoos was next in council, where he spoke of the exhibition of the school-children, and of the great pleasure his folks experienced from their opportunity of being present and from a knowledge that their own children were not considered inferior to the Christians' children. Said they had expected there would be some change, for the bulletin-boards were all turned, and the messages on them were read from the other way; but it would make no change with them, and they would take good care of the goddess during the vacation, for they did not want to go away until the great Star-Spirit was ready to take them to his Father. After telling the bow-and-arrow girl that she could take his place and say a few words, but should not stop long, he withdrew.

One of the Forest Maidens was next in the council, where she told of the number of her race who once inhabited the lower hunting-grounds of the red man, and who now had their wigwams in the upper hunting-grounds near to the Great Spirit; and of the mighty warriors who had gone forth with the archers to mark the wigwam-doors of the pale-faces, who had followed the trail of the fighting kings and priests of Israel and of Judah, who had turned away from the covenants and the commandments of the Great Spirit. She told of the Great Spirit's great Central Son, who had come to the lower hunting-grounds of the red man with a mighty host to establish His own platform of Eternal Justice among the remnant of the pale-face race. After telling her sister squaws to guard well the wigwam-door of the white squaw until the council-fire was again kindled, while she would away and tell the Great Spirit of the doings of the pale-faces all over the hunting-grounds, she retired.

Whereupon, after instructions, India once more closed the session by invocation to the Great Spirit, again thanking Him for his ever-present power and wisdom to guide and protect their labors; and, after a few cheerful words in connection with the appointed vacation, he withdrew.

SEPTEMBER 6, 1874. — After a pleasant vacation through the month of August, the necessary arrangements were made to witness the renewed labors of the council.

India was present, and opened the session by invocation to the Great Spirit, who alone had power to stay and control the elements, who had watched over and guarded them in their outgoings, and who had again brought them together with spirits and mortals with increased strength and wisdom to pursue their labors. He spoke of the school-children and of their enjoyment during their vacation; said they had assembled and were again organized and ready to pursue their studies. He also spoke of the fearful condition among mortals, who had turned away and scoffed at the manifestation of the ever-living Spirit, and were trying to console themselves by treasuring up the perishable things of time. After saying that King would make a few remarks, and could designate the one that was called to follow, and that when they had completed their organization the work of arranging the record of their labors would be commenced, he retired.

King was next in council, where, after expressing his own gratification, he said it was a great pleasure to them all to know the doors were again to be thrown open in order to forward a glorious work that would ameliorate the suffering condition and eventually would elevate a fallen race. He said it was true they had sat together during the vacation, and had wept· in sorrow over the blindness of their earthly friends, until Jesus their Saviour came among them and dried up their tears by showing them how their labors would finally be triumphant. He spoke cheerfully of the work already accomplished; told of the pleasure it afforded them to witness the gathering together of the children in order once more to commence their investigations in the pursuit of knowledge ; said one of the boys by the name of Jeff was present, and would make his own statement in evidence of their improved condition; after which one of the old mothers would also make a few remarks. And then, after again thanking the high controlling Power that upheld and sustained them in their labors, he retired.

Jeff was next in council, where he confirmed the previous statements in regard to their suffering condition in the dark sphere in spirit; said he had gnawed his crust, and displayed what few rags he was allowed, during his miserable life on earth among the sorrowing poor of New York, and they had found nothing to better their condition in spirit until their new friends had found them out and had compassion on their ignorance and poverty, and had gathered them up and clothed them, and were teaching them in their schools that the Higher Powers had some object that would eventually be accomplished through their creation. He spoke in praise of the kindness of their teachers, and gave evidence by his remarks of his own progression ; said they had no necessity now to steal in order to appease their hunger, or to skulk around and try to hide on account of their nakedness. It was true they did appreciate their improved condition, and his school companions united with him in love to all who had been their saviors ; and, after leaving his thanks for the one through whose vocal organs he had spoken, he retired.

The next in council gave the name of Perkins. Said she was one of the early mothers of America, and that her and her old man's home was in the State of Vermont. She related reminiscences of the early history of the country, and told of their great interest in the present gathering in spirit. She then turned and told Parson Peabody not to be so anxious, for she could do nothing for him : he was no better than she was, or her old man either. If he had been, he would not be there now, after all his pious pretensions. She then spoke of the present condition of their country, which they had labored so hard to sustain during its infancy, and said they had often felt in their spirit homes as if they wanted to wallop the young hussies with their canes for causing so much sorrow by their idleness and by their foolish extravagance. She then spoke of the increased happiness of the old folks in their present social gatherings, and thought some change was in preparation, and that they would soon be permitted to appear in a new sphere. And, after saying the old folks had all united in sending their love to the ones who had assisted in gathering them together, she said she would go, for they were curious to have her tell them her new experience.

The next one in council claimed to be a king by the name of O'Dyer; said he had come to claim a place for the African race in the kingdom of King Jesus. He then told of Enoch, Seth, and Noah, of Shem, Ham, and Japheth. He told of the cycle of time during the age of the patriarchs; spoke of Abraham, Isaac, and Jacob, and of Joseph and Benjamin, and seemed familiar with the history of the different tribes of Israel and of Judah; told of Moses and Aaron, of Joshua and Daniel. He told of the fighting kings and priests that controlled the wandering tribes until the coming of their promised Shiloh, around whom the tribes and nations of the earth must gather. He said King Jesus had been held in bondage to the earth by all who had professed to be his followers, and told Him to go and tell the Father they were ready to acknowledge his right to reign; and said that all who had oppressed the African race must answer before the great platform of Eternal Justice which King Jesus had established. He then said it was a work that had to be accomplished in order that his kingdom might commence; and they were ready now to engage in the conflict that could only end in the removal of the powers and the principalities and kingdoms of the earth, which through avarice and injustice had increased their sighs and groans, and held the race in bondage. He then withdrew.

One of the Hindoos was next in council, where he said his folks were much pleased to know the time had arrived for them to assemble where they could again listen to the statements made by the representatives of the scattered tribes as they were called up before the council; said they had had a lovely time during the vacation, and they did not know but they were all going to be annihilated by the one who had last spoken, for he seemed like one who had great power; but when he spoke to the great Star-Spirit, and said he was ready to acknowledge his rights, all their fears departed. He then remarked that the bow-and-arrow girl assigned the privilege to speak was engaged, and would not appear until the next session, when she would bear witness of the things in connection with the history of her own race. And, after saying his folks desired to be remembered to their speaking goddess, and would do what they could to give her strength, he withdrew.

And once again India closed the session by invocation to the Great Spirit, acknowledging their own dependence and their gratitude for wisdom and for strength combined sufficient for all that had been accomplished.

AT a sitting on the 12th of September, 1874, the "healer" was present, and made a few sensible remarks about the popular scandal that was then in every one's mouth. He asked which were suspended the highest in the heavens — the Protestants or the Catholics; and said the Catholics, bad as they were, kept such scurrilous conduct out of sight of the people.

A woman, who seemed to be giving instruction to a band of spirits, was the next to control. She also referred to the subject which the "healer" had been speaking about; and told of the effect such things produced among those who had been deprived of their earthly forms. She was pleased with the opportunity of speaking, and said there was another one whom they desired might have an opportunity to say a few words, and then retired.

The next speaker was a slave from a Georgia plantation; said his master had come here with a large company of black boys, and was going to teach them to make stump speeches. He then addressed himself to his companions, told them their master had been good to them; said master and mistress, and young master and young missis, were all good to them. They had their plantation, and gave them work, clothed them, and gave them plenty to eat; said they were of a superior mind, and had a right to control; and when the black folks behaved themselves, they were contented and happy. He then said his master bought his shoes for the plantation of the people in the eastern States; but said, when black man wear shoes two weeks, they go to pieces,— good for nothing,— often nothing but paper put in the place where there should be good leather used in their manufacture. Said black man got whipped by the overseers when his shoes were gone, though he was not to blame, as the shoes were good for nothing; and they were going to have white folks know that such things were not right.

AT the next session, on the evening of the 13th, India opened by invocation, and then spoke at some length of their work in spirit, and said, on account of the health of the media, they should not prolong the session. He then said John, one of the Twelve, would make a few remarks. ·

John was the next present, and spoke of the pleasure it afforded him to have the opportunity of speaking. He addressed himself to his co-workers in spirit, and spoke of their triumphant connection with mortals, and of the work that was about being completed; and, after the usual encouragement, he retired.

One of our Hindoo friends made a few remarks; after which, India closed by invocation.

SUNDAY, SEPTEMBER 20, 1874. — After India's invocation, he said the time had now arrived for all who adhered to the communion of spirit to stand firm in their work, and not be weakened or discouraged by those who had turned away and were pursuing the perishable things that were earthly; said they needed all the material force that was in connection with them in order to complete their work. He then said that Wesley desired to make a few remarks, and then would designate who was to follow.

Wesley was then present, and said he was again thankful he had been found worthy to be intrusted with a part in the finishing-up work, and spoke with firmness to his own followers in spirit; said he still believed in the freedom of the will, and could foresee the time when all would freely bow the knee in thankfulness to the blessed Saviour, and gladly enter his kingdom. He then said Edmonds was present, and desired to make a few remarks; and, after giving the usual encouragement, he retired.

Edmonds was next present, and said he had many things he was anxious to say. He then spoke of those he had left in their physical forms who had professed a faith in the communion of spirit, and said it grieved him to know so many were turning away from the high and holy marriage covenant, which had originated and been sanctioned for the happiness of mortals high up in the spheres, and was alone instrumental in preventing the connecting link between spirit and mortal from being severed. He then told his followers he regretted the mantel that represented their faith had not fallen upon the shoulders of a more worthy leader, and told them they must gather around him, and they would ask for more strength from those above, in order to prevent their friends of the same faith, whom they had left behind, from turning back and being lost in the conflicting elements of the earth. He was thankful for the opportunity of being present; said he would persevere in his labors until he attained a position on the platform of Eternal Justice. He then announced the presence of Shakspeare and Booth, but he could not say who would have the pleasure of speaking; whereupon he retired.

The familiar voice of Booth was the next one heard. Said the teacher had given way for the scholar, and he was again permitted to take his part on the great stage of eternal progress as the green curtain rolled up in order to display another scene in the affairs of life. He then pointed backward through the marble archways of time, and spoke of the representatives of a race who to them was unknown, but coming forth in answer to the archangel's call, prepared to take their place on the great platform of Eternal Justice. He described their anxious and cautious step as they came forward and raised the corner of their dark and ancient visors in order to see and listen to the once familiar voices of their little ones, who had come down from the higher spheres in order to greet them on their way. He then feelingly portrayed the grandeur of the work as worthy of the High and Holy One, and of his Son, their Saviour, who had voluntarily endured the cross that He might elevate a fallen race. He then spoke of his own boy, who had been found worthy to take his part, and said he was still anxious to be remembered; and, if there were others who had a similar part to perform, they must stand firm in the day of trial. After the usual encouragement, he retired.

One of the Forest Maidens was next present, and spoke to the representatives that had been called forth, whom she called "salamanders with woolly heads," whose chains had been broken by command of the Great Spirit, who had ordered them forth to partake in the work of emancipating their race.

After which, the familiar voice of one of our Hindoo friends was again heard, and said all his folks were greatly pleased with what they had seen, and were wondering what would come next in answer to the instructions of the Star-Spirit. And after India's invocation, the session closed.

SEPTEMBER 27, 1874. — After India's invocation, he said that arrangements would be made for commencing the work of compiling the records of their labors, and the friends that stood nearest would have the privilege of calling the more distant relatives of both families, that all that were ready and willing might have an opportunity to enter into the covenant. Then, after giving an appropriate charge in connection with their various duties, he said that Parker and White and Cook would each have the opportunity of making a few remarks; after which, he retired.

Parker was present, and said, although much of his time was necessarily employed in another direction, he was happy to be known as one of our band, and thankful the work was progressing. He spoke of the faithful and untiring labors of those foremost in the work, and said he had felt their influence before he was called from his earthly labors. He then spoke encouraging words to those who had gathered around him in spirit, and said they would press on until their labors, united with others, had achieved a glorious victory, and then retired.

White, of the "Banner," was next present, and made a statement in connection with his own experience. He was thankful for the opportunity of speaking again, and gave encouragement to all who had the privilege of entering into the covenant. He felt grateful to know so much had been accomplished, and spoke of his own labors, and embarrassments he had encountered for the truth while battling in his earthly form; and of others who were still faithful, although so poorly requited for their labors by their earthly friends. Said he hoped to have an opportunity of again speaking soon; and, after the usual assurance of success, he retired.

Cook, one of a noted pirate band, was next present, and was pleased to have an opportunity to speak, for he was ready for action; and then said our country was covered with land pirates from shore to shore. He spoke of the terrible condition they were in during their first experience in spirit life, until the blessed Saviour penetrated their dark and dismal sphere, and called them forth, and told them they were his brothers, and that he had a mission for them to perform among the inhabitants of the earth, where he and others were working in order to establish a law of Eternal Justice. He said, most gladly they had responded to the call as they came forth as it were to a newness of life, and were commissioned and sent to the earth to battle for the right; for it was well they knew "by the twinkle of the miser's eye in what direction his stolen treasure lay." He felt grateful that he was found worthy to stand as a representative of those of his profession, and he would guarantee none of them would flinch until their work was finished. He said Jesus was the bright star who had lighted up the dark sphere in spirit with his love and sympathy, and all had come forth to obey his commands. After giving forth a beautiful prayer to the Father of all for his remembrance of those who had participated in their redemption, he retired.

One of our Hindoo friends was next present, and wanted to know whom that fellow meant by the "bright star." He guessed it must be their Star-Spirit, who was preparing them and getting every one in readiness to show them to the Father. He had only come for a minute to say that they were all well, and the Star-Spirit had told them to give all the strength they could to their little goddess; said the bow-and-arrow girl was waiting to speak, and he would retire, and let her shoot her arrows at the pale-faces.

One of the Forest Maidens was then present, and said, "Brave, wherever you see life, you see the Great Spirit; you hear Him in the winds, as they move the beautiful forests, or stir the waters of the mighty ocean; and, wherever there is motion, it is the Great Spirit speaking to his children. So, brave, as you have been chosen to sit in council with the spirits of the Great Spirit, see that every mark in the record is made in the order of justice, that it may receive the approval of the Great Spirit;" for, as she came down to the lower hunting-grounds, she found some of the Great Spirit's spirits dressed in black cowls, suspended a little above the beautiful earth, with a great key hanging to their girdles. And she told the Great Spirit, and the Great Spirit said, What key? He gave them no key to hide the knowledge that was sent by his Central Son, who opened the way for all into the upper hunting-grounds. After addressing those who had gathered in council around the platform of Justice, she withdrew, and India again closed by invocation to the Great Spirit..

OCTOBER 4, 1874. — After India's invocation to the Great Spirit, he said that Peter, one of the Twelve, would be present, and after his remarks he would designate who should follow. Peter was then present, and spoke of the changes which had transpired since his own experience during his physical life, and of the trials and hardships the little band their Master gathered around him had to endure in order to acquire a knowledge of their spirit home ; and then said the key that was intrusted to him was the key of knowledge, that opened the way from the darkened scenes of earth up to the higher mansions which the Father had prepared for his earthly children. The key that was intrusted to him he had come to bestow upon another, trusting that all might receive the light, and become partakers of the blessings. He then spoke of the great triumph of their Master's work, and of the rejoicing of the lost and scattered tribes that were gathered together in spirit around the platform of Eternal Justice; and said the little band that was with their Master during his lonely wanderings, when despised and rejected, were now permitted to sit together in council and be partakers of his glory. He then introduced his friend and brother Metamora as the representative of a mighty race, and withdrew.

Metamora next said he stood with his red warriors face to face with his white brothers on the platform of Justice. Metamora and his warriors loved justice, but his white brothers had not always dealt in justice with his race. Metamora was glad the time had come when they could meet their white brothers without their weapons of war, and talk about justice for the remnant of the red man's race that were still residents of the lower hunting-grounds of the Great Spirit. The Great Spirit gave his red children the lower hunting-grounds east and west, north and south, and they had never bowed their knee in slavery to their white brothers. They were an ancient and a numerous race, and near to the Great Spirit. His white brothers should find out who they were. Metamora and his red brothers would meet their white brothers, when they would talk of justice. He then told us to be faithful in the work the Great Spirit had given us to do, for we had nothing to fear; the Great Spirit had sent out his red children from his upper hunting-grounds, and they were now at every man's wigwam engaged in the great work of justice; but he would go and let his white brother Forrest speak.

Forrest was the next in council, and said he felt proud to stand on the same stage by the side of his brave red brother who had been talking of justice; and as the green curtain was rolling up, he was pleased to see so many of his former friends who had gathered around the platform in order to cheer him as he was again called to take his stand upon the stage in a higher sphere, where the scenery was more ancient and on a grander scale. He then recited from the panorama before him for the evening's entertainment the appearance of the inhabitants of the planet for ages before the Chinese established an empire. He traced them from China on to the eastern continent where the Garden of Eden was inhabited, and in the rambling of the tribes through the different countries they established until the time of Abraham; then on to the time the gray-haired sage received the covenants and the commandments on Mount Sinai, and taught them to the people. He told them that every move was represented on the panorama before them, true to the condition of the inhabitants of the planet at each closing cycle of time. He then turned from Israel to Judah, and pointed out the Saviour in the streets of Jerusalem, with his little band of outcast and despised followers, who could not comprehend the grandeur of his mission, but in spirit had realized the truth of the resurrection, and were still waiting to participate in the fullness of their Master's glory, before whom all nations in spirit as well as he himself had bowed. After speaking of the beauty of the scenery and the magnitude of the stage on which he had been called in order to take his part, where avarice and envy were left behind, he felt the necessity of returning to his childhood in order to become perfect in his part of the play; and then gave expression to feelings of gratitude for the pleasure he was permitted to enjoy, and retired.

One of the Hindoos was the next in the council, and said he was much pleased with all he had seen; but he saw that in one place, to which some fellows had gone to smash up a temple, they threw their box, or one just like it, out of the window. His folks were all looking on, and thought it was queer such smashing work should be made among the things that belonged to the gods which ought to have been sacred; but then no one could disturb it now without getting smashed up themselves, for the Star-Spirit had given it to them to keep. Said he only came for a moment, and as the bow-and-arrow girl was waiting, he would go and let her speak.

One of the Forest Maidens was next in the council; said she had come to the watch-fire where the Great Spirit's pale-face children had met together to talk with his red children from his upper hunting-grounds. She spoke of the many tribes that once inhabited the lower hunting-grounds of the Great Spirit, and of the labors of the Great Spirit's

Central Son, who had gathered them around his platform; and she would away back to the Great Spirit, and tell of all she had seen and heard at the council where the scattered tribes and nations had been gathered together and gladly acknowledged his wisdom and power through the love made manifest to the pale-face race by the patient labors of his great Central Son.

After which, India again closed the session by invocation to the Great Spirit, with an acknowledgment of his right to govern, and with renewed thanks for all that had been accomplished that received his approval.

OCTOBER 11, 1874. — After India's invocation to the Great Spirit, which was a beautiful appeal for help and strength for the earth's inhabitants to be prepared for the approaching conditions so fast overshadowing them, and saying that White, of the "Banner," had introduced one of his Boston friends at the platform, and he would be allowed to make a few remarks, he again retired.

A man by the name of Head was next in council; said he was formerly a resident of Boston, and had been connected with the "Banner," and said he still had some demands on that institution which he was anxious to have settled up during the coming season; said he was familiar with the crooks and turns about the city. He then asked for help from the platform of Justice to aid him in his work, for he well knew where the pure liquors were kept, and how few there were who ever got a taste before all were in the possession of the many who had made their fortunes by their poisonous adulterations, and then joined in the cry of prohibition. He said Choate was present; and he was glad he had taken the responsibility of seeing that justice commenced its work with all that had been wronged in that direction, and then retired.

Choate was again in council, where he said that his friend Bennett and himself had discussed the question of prohibition before the council, and it had been decided that if pure wines and liquors were good for the rich man and his friends, they were also equally good for the poor man, whose strength was often reduced from the effects of his daily toil; but whose demand could only be supplied from the poisonous adulterations and false imitations that unprincipled men everywhere forced into the markets in order to supply the demand for a stimulant that by every principle of law and justice should be pure. It was well known to them that most of the evils of which their earthly friends complained were in some way the result of their own wrongs. He knew his Boston friends often spoke of him with pride; but was he any better than his poor brother? Both came into the world as little fledgelings, and all were dependent on the conditions and circumstances by which they were surrounded. If he had become stronger than his brother in his earthly development, it was his duty to see that just laws were made and enforced for his brother's protection; and he held that all who were intrusted with power, and neglected that duty, should be held accountable for the wrongs of which they complained; and he appealed to the platform of Eternal Justice, and to the holy angels that were high in the heavenly spheres above them, that it should be the law. He then said his appeal had been sanctioned and ordered to be so recorded. After speaking of the action of the prohibitionists, and of the effect it was producing on commercial affairs, he said they would have a busy time through the approaching season, and they should make a strong effort for the adoption of a law based upon justice, and ultimately put away all poisonous adulterations from the marts of trade, which at present were producing fearful results among the people. He then announced the presence of his friend and colleague, who was anxious to speak, and retired.

His friend Bennett was the next in council, and there said, although he had done so little when in his earthly form, he was thankful for the opportunity of being called to stand a representative in a cause of such vital importance. He then spoke of his labors during the past winter among the representatives of his own State for the adoption of a law that would protect the people; said they found it difficult to find men, after they were impressed with the necessity of such laws, who would stand firm until such laws were enforced; for the wealth accumulating fast by a traffic in the filthy and poisonous imitations which had filled the markets, was freely used in order to delay the demands of justice; but said they would strengthen their force, and look well to their cause until they were triumphant. He then made a strong appeal for the one who had stood high in the estimation of the people, that he might realize the effects of his terrible fall, and not think to turn it off with a laugh, and come before the platform of Eternal Justice with his crime upon him. "May he truly acknowledge his fault, and warn and caution the people to beware and shun the downward paths which are multiplying on every hand, in which so many find nothing but degradation and woe." He then said there was a woman present, who, he had no doubt, was anxious to say something in behalf of her sex, and he would retire.

The next one before the council said her name was Menkin, and she was anxious to say a word in regard to her sex in connection with the subject that was then before the platform of Justice. She would say there were other kinds of intemperance that they too freely indulged in, which were quite as pernicious in their general effects as that of drinking poisoned rum; and she would say to her earthly sisters everywhere, who were the leaders of the fashions and follies of life, if they would lay aside their foolish and extravagant dress and their wanton parade, and clothe themselves with a less expensive and more becoming apparel, and go out into the by-ways of life and gather up, and hold up, and strengthen their weaker sisters, they would shut up the flood-gates of destruction, and inaugurate a temperance reform that would receive the approbation of the high and holy angels, and soon have less of the surrounding evils to complain. Said she was thankful for all she had suffered, for it strengthened her spirit for the approaching conflict. After addressing a few words of encouragement, she spoke of the daughters of Israel and of Judah, who had travelled through the red sea of affliction, but at last had willingly bowed with gratitude and praise to their Messiah who had led them up to their promised land. She then withdrew.

One of the Hindoos was present a few moments. He said his folks understood all about this prohibition business, for they had been out with the great Star-Spirit, and they had seen the officers who were sent out to enforce the laws make a big fuss looking around after the little black bottles; but when they came to the places where the big casks were kept, and where the pipes and such things with which it was made were stored, they always found some flaw in their papers, and went away satisfied, saying they had no right to interfere. And when it was sent from foreign countries, and had to be pure, it was taken out in demijohns and sent round among the big folks — who were in power — as a present; whereupon they filled up the casks with a much cheaper article, and said it was good enough for the folks who had to pay for it. His people were all well posted about such things, for their gods had formerly consumed large amounts of it; and they thought it was not wonderful when they had to stand out in the cold. Said they were all glad their little goddess through whom they spoke was getting along well; that the bow-and-arrow girl was waiting, — she would stop but a moment, — and then withdrew.

One of the Forest Maidens was present. She had come from the upper hunting-grounds of the Great Spirit to listen to the talk of his pale-face children. She would go and tell the Great Spirit that the cry of suffering, of want, and of injustice was everywhere heard among the remnants of the scattered tribes that still inhabited the lower hunting-grounds, where they had turned away from the light of the Spirit, and had disregarded the covenants and the commandments of the Great Spirit, — and where, by creed and by craft, and by the power of their own selfish inventions, their darkness and sorrows had increased, and shut out the light and the love of the Great Spirit. "O Great Spirit, hear the cry of despair from the remnant of the red man's race, who have been driven from the beautiful forest homes of their forefathers, by the covetousness and the injustice of their pale-face brothers, away into the cold, barren mountains to starve! O Great Spirit, hear their wail of sorrow as they look to thy great power and ask for help and for protection! Great Spirit, raise up thy great arm of power, and soon will the remnant of the pale-face race stand shaking with affright! Send thy mighty winds, and open the doors of their storehouses, where they through avarice have hidden away the products of the hunting-grounds, and let their brothers and their squaws and their pappooses cry for bread! O Great Spirit, show thy displeasure, and they will return to Thee and to thy Central Son, and gladly beg for protection."

After which, India closed by invocation to the Great Spirit.

OCTOBER 18, 1874. — After India's invocation, he spoke at some length of the condition of mortals during their earthly pilgrimage; said it was a frequent contest between the demands of the flesh and the demands of the spirit, as they journeyed along together; but it was too often decided in favor of the earthly, and the spirit was shut out from a knowledge of its immortal home, and made to suffer. Said it would improve both by working in harmony together, that the spirit might be prepared for the change when the time arrived for the separation. He then said that Peabody, and his friend by the name of Dow, and Aristotle, would speak first during the evening; after which he retired.

Peabody was next in council, and said he felt proud of the position he had been called to fill on the platform of Eternal Justice, as he had been permitted to examine every plank that was squared up and fitted to its place, and he knew that every condition of humanity had been sought out by their Master, and duly represented; said he had been permitted to introduce his old friend Dow, who was a fellow-townsman many years past at Exeter, in New Hampshire, and who still felt interested about the schools at that place. He then withdrew.

Dow was the next in council, and said he had long contemplated on having the pleasure he was then permitted to enjoy; for he had been anxious to realize the change of the new birth through the earthly casket; and his acquaintance and friendship with a guardian of the one through whom he was then speaking, with the influence of his friend Peabody, had placed him in a position to have his desire gratified; while there was another matter he was interested about and desired to represent before the platform of Justice. He wanted the students and the teachers at the college in their old town, in which his friends and himself had taken great interest, should be made to acknowledge the claims of the Spirit, and be witnesses for the people that it was from the spirits they got their inspiration; for he had been a witness of the progress which hundreds of spirits had made who were allowed to come and experience the great change produced by entering and speaking through an earthly organization; and it was time for mortals to realize the importance of such connection. He then spoke of the labors and sufferings of the One who volunteered to unite the broken link between the sphere of earth and the higher spheres of spirit, and of the gratitude manifested by all as they gathered around in acknowledgment of his glorious victory; and retired.

Aristotle was the next in council, and spoke of the importance of the inhabitants of earth having a better understanding of the law of propagation, of pregnancy and birth; that the mother should know how to watch over and guard the little offspring intrusted to her care, and protect it from the magnetic touch of all that was not in harmony with the elemental condition necessary for its perfect unfoldment. Said it was necessary that the two who formed the union in compliance with the marriage covenant should understand and live in obedience to the law in order to insure a more perfect development of the little angels they were instrumental in bringing into life. He said he had closed up his laboratory for scientific investigation in spirit, and should again commence his labors with mortals, for it was the understanding in spirit that the covenants and commandments of God must be re-established among the inhabitants of earth, and he knew how essential it was that the magnetic touch of spirit-fingers should mingle with the affairs of man in order to bring them into harmony with the immutable and eternal laws that come from above. He then withdrew.

One of the Hindoos was then present a few moments; said he had not much to say, but they wanted to keep their place open, for they should want to say something by-and-by. They were doing all they could for their goddess; and the bow-and-arrow girl was waiting to speak; but she must not stay long, for there was no necessity for it. And why, if her Great Spirit was so much bigger than their Star-Spirit, did not she bring him along with her, that his people might have a chance to see him? Whereupon he withdrew.

One of the Forest Maidens was present, and spoke of the mighty work of the Great Spirit's Son, who had gathered together in spirit all the nations of the Great Spirit's lower hunting-grounds to sit in council; and she too had come by command of the Great Spirit from his upper hunting-grounds, with twelve of the wise and ancient sages of her race, who by command of the Great Spirit would join the council. She then spoke of Israel and of Judah with their twelve tribes, and said each tribe was represented by twelve in council. She then turned to the representatives of "the woolly-headed race," as she called them, and told them to go with her. She showed them where the Great Spirit's pale-face children had warred with each other in many bloody conflicts,—father against son, and son against father,—to break the chains that held their race in bondage. She told them to look up in thankfulness to the Great Spirit, and not stand shaking as with affright, for all were brothers. She then told of the great council that had been called together by command of the Great Spirit, and his great Central Son, in order to prepare for a higher birth, and to see to it that every sign and mark was right, if they would learn more of the vast dominions and of the mighty power of the Great Spirit.

After which, India addressed his invocation to the Great Spirit, asking for light and strength for all that their work might be acceptable when finished among mortals, who had again turned away from the light of the Spirit, and were wandering in a wilderness of darkness, and of doubts, and of fears, resulting from the violated commandments and from their own disregard of the great law of Eternal Justice. They had wantonly cast aside the present manifestation of the ever-living Spirit, and clung to the musty records of a past cycle of time of which nothing but the shadow had been left.

OCTOBER 25, 1874. — After India's invocation, he made a few remarks, and then said that Ashmalaw, the Indian spirit who formerly controlled the girl by the name of Graham, who would still be remembered, was then present with her guide, and both would have an opportunity to speak; said the girl would give the name of the one that was assigned to follow; after which he retired.

Ashmalaw was next in council, and said he had come to the watch-fires where justice had been provided with a platform, for Ashmalaw loved justice; and he had brought the one the Great Spirit had sent him to speak through to his pale-faces on the red man's hunting-grounds, to tell them to learn and deal in justice with all; and was glad that many that heard his voice had been called to stand before the platform of Justice to answer for the scoffs and jeers in which they paid the pale-face squaw, who was used to tell them by the command of the Great Spirit of their injustice. And he had come with the squaw to the council to bear testimony of the way their labors had been received. Said he had been with his tribe since the squaw's call to the upper hunting-grounds until the Great Spirit say, "Ashmalaw, take the squaw, and go to the council and tell the pale-faces of their wrongs."

The Graham girl was next present, and gave an interesting account of her reception in spirit; said she was not conscious at first of her separation from her body, but supposed it had been taken as formerly by another spirit in order to speak to the people. Said the one who had controlled her was with her, and took her by the hand and led her away seemingly a long distance until she began to feel the loss of her body and refused to go further; but she had since learned the object was to prevent her seeing her perishable body deposited in the ground. When she was conscious of her condition, she was very lonely and discontented; said that Ashmalaw did what he could in order to pacify her. She then asked to see her mother, but was not permitted to do so. She said, finally, that at one time she felt so lonely and bad that she began to cry, and a little group of spirits were gathered around her, — whereupon a spirit (whom she had heard speak through another media, and knew the voice to be India's) came to them, and told who she was, telling them she was a poor, friendless girl who had no opportunity for instruction; and said she must be taken to a school in spirit, where she would be educated. She then said they were very kind to her, and she was taken away higher up and put into a school where she had been until the present time, and where the beautiful angels had come to them daily and imparted lessons of instruction. Said she had been contented and happy in her new home, where all anxiety about her earthly condition had been removed, until now they had told her she was prepared to go and be a teacher to her own townspeople who had entered the spirit sphere, and where she would soon be able to satisfy them that she was not an impostor and had no desire to deceive them. She spoke with much feeling of her previous condition before entering spirit life; said she had often felt like trying to destroy herself, which feeling had been caused by the mistrust and unbelief of those around her; said she had been permitted to know of the work that was going on in spirit, — that Ashmalaw had come with her and had told her she would now have the opportunity of visiting her friends in spirit that she had been anxious to see. After desiring that she might be remembered to her friends that were still known among mortals, she said she would retire, for Dickens was present to take her place.

Dickens was next in council. Said he was glad of another opportunity to speak, for there was much that he was still anxious to say to mortals; said the streams of inspiration were let loose and were flowing into many channels; and he wanted all that received the light to have manhood enough to acknowledge to the people that it was not they themselves that were the great and the mighty power, but that it was the power that came down from above. He, Dickens, had written many things during his pilgrimage with mortals, and when received after they came from the press, he thought they were not suitable for the present age; but they had gone forth, and Dickens could not get them back; and he knew now that it was not Dickens, but it was a power behind Dickens giving forth truths in order to awaken and prepare the public mind for the "death of Old Theology;" for, he said, there were many who were still occupying high places before the people who were overflowing in their pride of intellect that was given through inspiration, and who, if they did not soon begin to speak the truth, would have to step "down" and "out." After addressing himself to his friends who had gathered around in spirit, he expressed thanks for the pleasure he had experienced, and retired.

One of the Hindoos was then in council a few moments, and said his people as a nation were fast turning away from the doctrines which the Christians had been trying for centuries to propagate among them; but they had no confidence in a people who did not practise the precepts they inculcated as a guide for others. He said the bow-and-arrow girl had come; he would go with his own people, who were being taught by the great Star-Spirit.

One of the Forest Maidens was next in council; said she had come from the upper hunting-grounds of the red man near to the Great Spirit, down to the platform of Justice where many braves were holding council. She spoke of the eleven who were called around the platform of Eternal Justice by command of the Great Spirit's Central Son, and of the race who first covered the lower hunting-grounds of the red man, and said she would away back to the Great Spirit and tell of the many tribes and nations that had heard the call of the angel of time, and had gathered around the great platform, where many of the pale-face braves had now learned that justice and judgment must be restored among the remnants of their own race.

After which, India again closed the session by invocation to the Great Spirit, once more acknowledging their dependence, and encouraging them in their labor.

NOVEMBER 1, 1874.— After India's invocation to the Great Spirit in thankfulness for his numerous blessings, and asking for instructions if in any way their labors had not been acceptable, he said, that on account of a birthday arrival of one of their number, the evening exercises would be specially arranged in order to commemorate its memory; said Confucius and Mahomet would be the first to speak, after which Miss Landon and the children would have an opportunity for their exhibition.

Confucius was again in council, and spoke of the birthday of the one they had met to commemorate and give encouragement concerning the amount of good their labors had already accomplished, and of the many obstacles which had been thrown in their way in order, if possible, to prevent its fulfilment; and then recited the amount of labor and time devoted to the gathering in of the lost and scattered tribes of Israel, and of their changed condition; said that the patience and perseverance of the two they had chosen to be their earthly witnesses had crowned their labors with success. After speaking of the darkness fast enshrouding the scoffers, who had turned away from the light sent by the Great Creator, and were clinging to their perishable earthly principalities that had no power to save in the day of anguish, he said the other paths would be guarded until all was finished, and then their joy would be complete. He then addressed his co-laborers in spirit who were inspired by the examples of their Master, who left his high estate, and, clothed in the flesh and in the form of the meek and lowly Nazarene, had worked his way through in order to give light to all and lead them up to the Great Father's eternal kingdom. After renewing his encouragement and giving assurance of a reward for the faithful, he retired.

Mahomet was next in council. Said he was thankful that a birthday had arrived which gave him an opportunity of speaking to his own people through an earthly casket; for it revived the memory of the time when his own earthly organism was used by spirits to encourage and enlighten the darkened condition of a covetous and cruel race. He spoke of the Koran, and of the many times he had stood up to speak to his people, sustained and upheld by an invisible spirit band, who were working for the amelioration of suffering mortals. He told of his own elevated condition through spirit power, and of his fall back to the principalities of earth, and of how terrible had been his sufferings. He next spoke of Moses, who held up the spirit banner to the wandering Israelites who clung to their earthly Jordans; then of Emmanuel, who left his seat at his

Father's throne, and labored and suffered at Jerusalem, where he triumphed over the monster who had held the race in bondage, — and of his labors in the dark sphere in spirit, until all were resurrected and had bowed down in acknowledgment of his glorious triumph around the great platform of Eternal Justice. He then gave an account of his own experience, and of how his people had clung to him in spirit, and said he was glad the time had arrived when he could cross over the big waters and commence his work anew. He then withdrew.

Miss Landon was next present with her school of celestial spirits from their Paradise of God's Love, with their flowers. Two of them were allowed to speak in connection with the birthday remembrance.

Then one of the Hindoos cheerfully made a few remarks in favor of Mahomet; said he was one of their speaking gods who had told them about the great Star-Spirit, and they were pleased with his present opportunity of speaking.

One of the Forest Maidens then spoke of her own race, and said they made up the number twelve of the long-lost tribes who had gathered together around the Great Spirit's Central Son on the broad platform of Eternal Justice. She told them of the vastness of the dominions of the Great Spirit, and of his great and incomprehensible power; and wished them to remember that, whatever might be their color, they were all the children of the Great Spirit, and had been the recipients of his endless blessings all over the lower hunting-grounds.

After which, India spoke of the magnitude of the wonderful work which had already transpired, which they knew was far beyond the comprehension of mortals; but which would ultimately result in their elevation, for peace and contentment in spirit would eventually harmonize the earthly sphere. He then closed the session by a beautiful invocation to the Great Spirit, again acknowledging their dependence, and asking for wisdom and for sufficient help for the successful re-establishing of the sacred covenants and commandments. Whereupon, after speaking of the object of the present birthday commemoration as an event connected with the closing of the gospel dispensation in spirit, and establishing a new epoch of time that would soon be of great importance in the approaching cycle among mortals, he gave the usual encouragement for all to remain faithful in their work, and withdrew.

NOVEMBER 8, 1874. — After India's invocation, he said that Jackson and "Stonewall" Jackson would have the opportunity to speak first, and they would give the names of those who would follow. He then withdrew.

Jackson was next present. He expressed his pleasure for an opportunity of again speaking on the platform of Justice, and referred to the people's triumph at the ballot-box the past week as an evidence of the good results of their labors. He then addressed his fellow-statesmen who had gathered in council, spoke to Washington and Jefferson and Madison, congratulated Adams over the people's triumph in his State, and then said, as they all, presidents and statesmen, members of congress and judges, had been intrusted with power from the people, and permitted to tread the halls where justice should have been administered, — O, what was the reason, when they were called before the platform of Eternal Justice, where the great Judge was sitting in his purity, that each one of them had to hang down his head in shame over the corrupt and fallen condition of their countrymen? He said it was true he was a poor waif that was floated to them, and asked them if they could point out any act where he had failed to do his duty when he was intrusted with power. He then called on Washington — who was still at their head, and who had been intrusted with the chair of justice in spirit — to look well to it and see that every man did his duty who had enrolled his name in support of the new constitution for their country, for, by that Eternal Power that surrounded and sustained them, justice should be meted out to all. Not one of them should relax his efforts until the wail of suffering caused by injustice ceased to be heard. He told them, now that the change had commenced, they must see that the people, who were asking for their rights, were supplied with leaders that would not deceive them. And let the clergy, who were ever ready to be with them, and who had prayed over them, also be up and out to undo their work, as each and every one of them knew now how great had been their failures; for the cry of distress from pauperism and prostitution, with crimes of every nature, was heard on every hand. After a few words of encouragement, he withdrew.

Another by the name of Jackson was next in council, and said he felt grateful for another opportunity to speak on the great platform. He told of his trials and sufferings, and of the trials and sufferings of the southern people resulting from their parricidal war. Although their suffering was a judgment following their treatment of their colored servants, it had been terrible to endure; and, although he was called on to defend his State from the encroachments of those who would interfere, his heart was not in the work, for he felt guilty and ashamed to be called up in judgment with his hands dripping with his brothers' blood. How could he expect anything but banishment from all that was pure and good? He also would say to his brothers of the eastern, and of the northern and western States, who had been called to stand up and answer before the platform of Eternal Justice, that they were not justified in the part they had taken, for there was a black pall still hanging over their own States, gathering up from the sighs and groans of the neglected ones of whom they had once been the trusted guardians, while the thief and the midnight assassin they had created were standing ready, waiting for plunder at every keyhole; and the Pacific States would soon be submerged, in order to cleanse the land of the blood which was shed in their struggle for the Mammon of unrighteousness. He then said it was announced that Franklin desired to speak; and, after encouraging all in their work, he gave way.

Franklin was again heard in the council. He said he only wanted to say a few words, for the reports of the past week had been very satisfactory from all the States. Said his boys had done bravely, and he had no complaints to make, for all of them had done well; but he wanted it understood now he must have another band. Congress would soon be sitting, and the State councils would be gathering together, and there was much to do, and his boys were all busy. He must have another band, if it took all those who were on the platform. "What, do you all say yes? Well, boys, all say yes! Now, boys, I want you to scatter yourselves to every important point, and keep a good watch. You found a good many of short weight last week, and they had to step down. You will find others that will have to come down. See that everything is on the bulletin-boards, and once in a while put in a paragraph for our two friends here, for they are watching and know where it comes from. Now I have got through for this time; so all of you away, and look sharp to your calling." He then gave a few cheering words of encouragement, and said, if it was agreeable, Mrs. Franklin would like to speak a few moments; said he should be with us again during the season, and retired.

Mrs. Franklin was next in council, and said she was with the band in their labors, but had not sought for an opportunity before in order to speak for herself. She told of the magnitude of the labors of the band, and of how much the patient endurance of their little earthly sister had encouraged and assisted them in their work. She then spoke of the school-boy for a comparison, referred to his first efforts in order to learn how the light of knowledge was impressed on his brain from the lessons prepared by other minds, and after arriving to manhood he still gathered the light from the books that others had left behind, in order to pilot him on his way; and such, she said, had been their condition in spirit. All were groping their way in the dark until Jesus, their Saviour, left his Father's throne, and came down to light up the dark sphere in spirit, and cheer them on to higher knowledge. She then said that it had been our privilege to know something of the grandeur of his triumph, and how his glorious light had been reflected on them all, until the dark sphere was lighted up, and a platform of Eternal Justice firmly established, — also schools inaugurated, where the poor and the ignorant, and the forsaken and neglected ones of earth were gathered in and cultivated, where all received that care and attention that were their due by right during their earthly pilgrimage. She said their labors were now among the inhabitants of the earth, and they asked for mantles of charity from the higher spheres in spirit to enable them to finish their work, and carry the light reflected from the blessed Saviour to every nation, until all should see the glory of his mission, lay down their weapons, and prepare to enter his kingdom, where there were joy and peace in the Holy Spirit. She then spoke of the wonderful changes that were putting the inhabitants of the earth in commotion; and she thought, after the darkness they had brought upon themselves, they would rejoice again to see the light. She then said she had a favor to ask. It was that "Pompey" should have an opportunity to speak. She saw him near to the platform, and knew he was anxious; said she, with a delegation of spirits, had been sent ambassadors to his dominions, where he had shown them every possible attention, and had been their escort from Rome to Arabia and Egypt, and all through the beautiful country where he had been a humane ruler, and where his own people still loved and clung to him in spirit. She then said her kind husband was still her companion, and it was delightful for those who had been united in the physical to remain united in spirit, although at times their work might be in opposite directions. Some time she hoped to have the pleasure of speaking with us again; but as one of the confiding Hindoos was waiting, she would retire.

The Hindoo was next in council, and said he had only stepped in a moment to say a few words. He was glad the woman who had been speaking told about their Star-Spirit, for there did not appear to be a great many that knew how real good the great Star-Spirit had been, while all of his people felt as though they wanted to go away somewhere and pound their heads on the ground for their ingratitude. Their women had asked the Star-Spirit for those mantles of charity, that they might go and teach such things to their own people; but as the bow-and-arrow girl, who was looking after the red man's race, was then waiting to speak, he would retire.

One of the Forest Maidens was next in council, and said she had come by the command of the Great Spirit from his upper hunting-grounds. She had followed their trail to the wigwam of the pale-face squaw, where many braves sat in council, and she told them, as by the command of the Great Spirit, to lay aside their mantles of charity, and clothe themselves in coats of mail, and go among the remnant of their races, and faithfully work until the cry of suffering and injustice was no more heard upon the lower hunting-grounds of the Great Spirit. Then they could put on their mantles of charity as they gathered around the platform of Eternal Justice, erected by the toil and suffering of the Great Spirit's Central Son, who had endured their scoffs and jeers that he might lead them away from the purgatories and the Hades of their own creating into the light and the love of the Great Spirit's eternal kingdom. She told them to mind their chart, and look well to the signs and passwords, or they would soon again be submerged in their own darkness. After a few words of instruction for the mighty warriors of her own race, she retired.

India again closed the session by invocation to the Great Spirit, once more thanking him for their blessings, and for the privilege of again meeting with spirits and mortals in council, and after a few encouraging words for the final accomplishment of their arduous labors, he once more withdrew.

NOVEMBER 15, 1874. — After India's invocation, he said Washington and Clay and Adams would first speak, after which, if there was time, one or two others would have an opportunity before the Hindoo and Forest Maiden spoke. He then referred to the great anxiety of many, and withdrew.

Washington was again in council, and said he appreciated the privilege of speaking again of things in which his countrymen should be interested ; and after recognizing among those around him Jefferson, Madison, Monroe, Jackson, and the Adamses, with many of the older statesmen, he spoke of the responsible trust they had taken upon themselves during their earthly pilgrimages, and how far they had all come short, during their administrations, in wisely protecting the interests of the people intrusted to their charge. He then spoke of the platform of Eternal Justice, around which they had been called to answer for the condition of their country, and of the laws promulgated by a righteous judge, who himself had partaken of the earthly, in order to enlighten and lead them all up to his Father's kingdom. He then spoke of their America in spirit, and of the new constitution which they had all voluntarily signed, where every right of the people was protected by the law of justice ; and told them they must now return to the old halls, surrounded by the scenes of their earthly lives, and renew their labors until the new constitution, which proclaims freedom for every race, was firmly established ; then, and not till then, would justice be again recognized among the affairs of men. He spoke with much feeling of the increase of population, and of the changed condition of the laboring class, whose interests had been sadly neglected by their trusted guardians. He spoke of fearful things that were overshadowing their countrymen, and counselled vigilance by each and every one, until their country, where liberty first had its birth, should again proclaim freedom for the spirit, from the rock-bound Atlantic away to, and beyond, the mild Pacific shores. After giving directions for their work through the approaching season, he said their time was limited, and gave way.

Clay was the next in council, and was thankful he had not attained the position of president of his country, for he was relieved of a terrible responsibility which others who had were held to by the law of justice ; said it was not a pleasant thing to be arraigned in spirit and questioned by those in authority about the condition of a people that were intrusted to them, and for whose condition they were held accountable. He then spoke of the time when he and his colleagues whom he now could see gathering about the great platform of Justice, once stood side by side in the halls of congress, clothed with authority from the people, whose inherited rights, sealed by the sacred blood of their fathers, it was their duty to have protected by the inauguration of laws that would have secured the public lands to the laboring man and his posterity. Now they could listen to the cry of poverty among their countrymen, and see pauperism and crime everywhere on the increase, while the lands which should have been their heritage were given away by townships to favorite monopolies, and bought up with capital from the foreign aristocracies, who would, if they could, have strangled freedom when it was first rocked in the cradle of liberty. He knew how it was, and how it had been; the poor man's condition was never thought of in the halls of legislation. He could vote for the lucky man that secured the nomination, and take off his hat, if he had one, and hurrah for the winning party. After that he could stand to one side, and starve for all his party cared; for they had no further thought of the poor man and his family until they wanted his vote at another election. He, too, was glad they had all been called to stand around the platform of Eternal Justice, where the Just Judge proclaimed freedom for all; and they would take their old places in the halls of congress, where their voices were once familiar, and work as best they could until justice for all, with freedom for body and spirit, was proclaimed from shore to shore. After a few words of encouragement, he gave way for his friend, J. Q. Adams.

Adams next made a few remarks; said he still felt proud of his old State, for it was evident from their last vote that the people were anxious, and wanted to do what was right as near as they could understand it. He then spoke of the financial embarrassments, and of the depression of business and its causes; of the increase of population, caused by the desire of the poor laboring people of other nations to breathe the air of a free country; and they had gathered their little bundles together, and braved the dangers of the ocean by thousands and hundreds of thousands, all for the love of freedom. He then spoke of the accumulation of wealth from the industry of the people, where the sound of the hammer on the anvil and the hum of the wheel in the mill had been heard throughout the land, — and of craft and idleness and extravagance, with their fearful consequences, which were crippling the energies of the people; said the time had come for a change, for the Saviour of man had returned, and would establish his kingdom, — all things earthly would have to give place for the law of Eternal Justice. He then spoke of their New America in spirit, where the rights of all had been secured, and where they had renewed their pledge to be vigilant in their work in the approaching contest. He then gave a few words of encouragement, and said the same power which had sustained himself and others in their struggle for the right would continue to surround, sustain, and uphold them; whereupon he withdrew.

One of the mariners was next present; said he had just arrived in port with his sailing craft and colors flying, in order to report that all was well on the ocean; said he had got his papers renewed; asked to be remembered to his former companions, and then requested that Paul Jones might have an opportunity to report, and was off on another cruise.

One of the Hindoos was next in council for a few moments. He stepped in to say his people were doing well, and that some of them had been to that place our folks called a "congress," where the wise men met to make the laws for the government of the people. They had said there were a good many unsettled accounts that would make a stir the coming season, for one of the speaking gods had kept a short-hand statement of all their sly affairs, and was going to make them settle up. Said his folks wanted a place in the record by themselves, for they were going to commence and make a congressional report; but the bow-and-arrow girl was waiting and anxious to speak, and he would go.

One of the Forest Maidens then said that she too had come to the wigwam where the squaw and brave sat in council. She had listened to the much talk from the prominent leaders, who were once looked up to as big chiefs among the palefaces on the lower hunting-grounds of the Great Spirit. She told of a white tent embroidered with beautiful flowers outside of the wigwam, where the old sages of her race were sitting in council with the many chiefs that belonged to the pale-face races. She spoke of the white chief who was again intrusted with the chair of justice — how he was asking the old sages of the red man's race about the condition of the Great Spirit's lower hunting-grounds. Many, many moons ago, when the beautiful forest covered the hunting-grounds, and the wild animals, and the fish in the talking waters, were protected, and supplied the red man's race with food, they looked up to the Great Spirit in gratitude for all their daily blessings, and they were happy and contented as they gambolled in their native parks with the deer and the antelope, with no one to disturb or make them fearful of the mighty power of the Great Spirit. But the pale-face race, with their covetousness, spied out the beautiful forest home of the red man, and with their many inventions for destruction they had covered the once happy hunting-grounds with the blood of their brothers; they had turned away from the covenants of the Great Spirit given by sages and seers; they had disregarded the precepts inculcated by the Great Spirit's Central Son, and darkness and doubt, want and starvation, with the wail of sorrow from their own injustice, had disturbed the harmony of the upper hunting-grounds of the Great Spirit, and the frown of the Great Spirit was making the pale-face race stand shaking with affright all over the lower hunting-grounds.

After which, India again gave instructions connected with their present labors, and spoke with evidence of much feeling about the darkness fast accumulating over mortals; after which he closed the session by another invocation to the Great Spirit, asking for wisdom and for strength sufficient for their labors, and then withdrew.

NOVEMBER 18, 1874.— At this special seance, set apart for a hearing from Pompey, the Roman general, and Paul Jones, the naval hero, our Irish friend, the "healer," was present, and said he was assigned the privilege, in the absence of the leader of the circle, to preside for the evening; and pleased he said he was to know he was found worthy of so high an honor. He then spoke of the commotion among the inhabitants of the earth in their struggle for temporal power; said his people, the Catholics, well knew the time had arrived for the birth of the spirit, and they were strengthening their organizations for the purpose of controlling the same for their own benefit; but, he said, we had nothing to fear as individuals; keep quietly at our work, and all would be well; for the blessed Saviour would see that no sect made a monopoly of the spirit for their own special aggrandizement. He said, as we had been kind enough to sit for others, he would not occupy the time, and retired.

Pompey was next present, who said it was true he had found a casket, but what was it without the gem, — the ever-living Spirit, which put it in motion? Death, cold death, was everywhere found in the earthly. Where were the seers and sages of the past, or of the present, who could tell how the spirit inhabited its earthly casket, or tell how it took its departure? They could see the shaking frame, and hear the rattling of the teeth, and see the dry bones as they returned to the dust; but they told nothing of the spirit, or of its home beyond. He was delighted with the privilege of speaking, told of their condition in the dark sphere in spirit, when it was announced that a bright spirit had descended from above that gave them light, and was calling the nations to judgment. He had come for his commission, that himself and his people might engage in the approaching conflict, for they wanted Jesus to be triumphant, and see him crowned in a kingdom that was worthy of his labors. In answer to a question concerning the ancient oracles, he said they did consult with spirits, but they were the spirits of their friends and followers in the dark sphere, who knew nothing of the bright spheres above them, for no one had told them of a risen Saviour who had triumphed over death and penetrated through the dark sphere. In answer concerning their speaking the English language, he said they had teachers and interpreters, and spirits progressed as well as mortals; said the records of the past, as they had been kept by earthly historians, were very imperfect. He then spoke of the Saviour's triumph in their dark sphere, and of the platform of Justice around which they were resurrected, and of their mission now among the nations of the earth, where they should work until all bowed in acknowledgment of the Saviour's rights. After again expressing his gratitude, he retired.

Jones, the mariner, was the next in council. He said that he too had answered the call, and come into port to have his papers right for the coming battle; for of what avail were the trials and sufferings of Jesus, if the principalities of earth through creed and craft denied his call, and refused to accept his reign? He was glad the time had come when he also could join the heavenly hosts who had come down from the higher spheres, and had engaged in the great battle of truth and justice, led on by the Friend and Saviour of man. No wonder the inhabitants of earth were beginning to fear and tremble, for the elements were in commotion in answer to the call, for the bride was not prepared to receive the Bridegroom. He was pleased with his commission and ready for his work; said he would hand in his papers when he arrived again in port; told us to keep to the lee shore, and mind our main-stays, and all would be right; whereupon he retired.

His sister was next present; said she had come without the knowledge of her brother, and by permission should go with him on his voyage. She spoke of the time when they were children, and were fondled on the knees of their loving parents, and told that the time would come when a bright star should make its appearance, and light up the darkened minds of the nations. She told of their sorrows when her brother had taken to the ocean during his earthly life, and they were told he was engaged in mortal combat. She told of their reunion in spirit through the light that was reflected from that bright star until fathers and mothers, sisters and brothers, and relatives were drawn together and were happy; and as her brother was again commissioned to go among the inhabitants of earth, where darkness and temptation led them to mortal combat, she could now go with him and help sustain him in his work. She then retired.

The "healer" was next present; and, after a few appropriate remarks, commended all to the care of the blessed Saviour, and the session closed.

NOVEMBER 22, 1874. — After India's invocation, he said Chase, and Ames, and the scientist Agassiz, would have an opportunity to speak. He then made mention of things that were transpiring, and gave directions concerning the same, and retired.

Chase was next in council, where he made no claim to the title of judge in spirit. He was pleased, although the least worthy, to be remembered among those of his friends and countrymen who were called before the platform of Justice, where all were united in a work that would enlighten and elevate the inhabitants of earth. Said he was truly thankful for all he had received. He thanked his enemies as well as his friends; said our enemies often proved our best friends by telling of our failings, and making us more watchful over our weakness when transacting the business affairs of life. He could see around him the presidents and statesmen, judges, and all who had stood high in council, both east and west, and north and south, — true men, who had left behind their differences of opinion and united under the lead of the Saviour of man, who was still working for the progress and elevation of the human race. Yes, he was glad, although least of all, to be counted as one among them, and he would gladly return to the scenes of his earthly life, and labor with his brother-man until the higher laws were obeyed, and until justice, with which no one had a right to contend, had finished its work. He then spoke of the unsettled condition of our national affairs, and of the restless condition of the people; and said there would be many a conflict before the right could prevail. After again expressing thanks for all of his trials, he gave place for his friend.

Ames was the next in council, and said he was thankful he had been a little sharp in his business affairs, for it had taught him where to look for others who were more tricky than himself. He too was glad to stand with others who had been called from the scenes of their earthly labors, and he was thankful that he could be permitted to go back and do his work over, for there were still those in congress who had tried to make a cat's-paw of him in order to hide their own rascality. He said many of them, who had time to review the past and get a higher conception of the law of justice, were in a better condition to go to congress, and they would go back and stay until congressmen learned that they were the guardians of the people, and that they must make just laws and see they were enforced for the people's protection. He said he had been shovelling around, and there was still a great deal of rubbish that would have to be moved before Justice could find a permanent resting-place among the affairs of men. He spoke of the changes that were taking place, and thought others would improve from the many lessons an all-wise Power was manifesting to the inhabitants of earth. After the usual thanks for the attention he had received, he retired.

The scientist Agassiz was next in council, and expressed his thanks for another privilege of being present for the purpose of speaking through an earthly casket. He told of the order and harmony he had found in all of his researches, from matter in its crude form up to the individualized spirit; said he had followed it from the little granite pebble to the worm, and from the worm through all its slimy changes up to man. How grand and perfect was the workmanship of the Master Mind! Man and woman — living temples organized through matter by the infusion of a little germ that was quickened by the living Spirit — they were growing up to be inhabitants for the world above; but why had he failed to comprehend it? He had analyzed and reconstructed among the fossils, and, as far as he could go, he found the evidence of a Master Workman, but he failed to find the living Spirit that quickened all things into motion. Now he was a living spirit thrown out of his earthly tenement with a body to sustain him, and he bowed in reverence and humble submission to that Power which he could not see or comprehend. He said he leaped over valleys and mountains in his freedom in spirit, and everywhere found the same manifestation of order and perfection throughout the extent of his vision. He had the children for his companions, and they had supplied him with what he had been deficient in the physical. They had taken him to the tops of the crystal mountains, where they had looked down among the inhabitants of earth who were struggling away in their material forms, cutting down mountains, making new channels, exporting and importing from other continents, little knowing how much such things disturb the elements, for the order in nature was so perfect that each part must return back to its own. He then said the language of earth was not sufficient for an expression of his gratitude for all he found in the home of the spirit, where every desire was satisfied, and he would jump at the call of his brother scientists of earth whenever they sent out a thought in his direction. Said he was more than thankful for the hour's entertainment, which should not depart from his memory, and then retired.

One of the Hindoos was the next in council, and said he was glad when the man told that each part would have to return back to where it belonged, for he thought his folks would get back some things that belong to them. He was glad for the little bow-and-arrow girl, for her people would also have all that belonged to them; but he should not stop long. He wanted to say his folks had sent ambassadors to Washington for the season, and they should know themselves what was transpiring at the capital of the nation; they asked the Star-Spirit, who told them they might do so. Now he would retire, and let one of the bow-and-arrow girls come; but she could not stay long, for it was evident their goddess must be a little tired.

One of the Forest Maidens was next in the council, where she told them that she too had come from the upper hunting-grounds as by the command of the Great Spirit, where the tribes from the lower hunting-grounds had gathered together around the great platform of Eternal Justice, built up, piece by piece, by the Great Spirit's Central Son. She told them it was not strange so many of them stood trembling with affright in their new places, as they now heard of the condition of the balance of their suffering races, who had been following in their trail over the beautiful hunting-grounds, where by their craft and their creeds they had brought many to need, who had turned away from the light and from the love of the Great Spirit, and were unprepared for the white mantle that would soon cover the hunting-grounds where many of the pale-faces had no wigwams; and she would away back and tell of the many big storehouses that were full of the products of the hunting-grounds, when the white squaws and their pappooses were looking up to the Great Spirit crying for bread.

After which, India again closed the session by invocation to the Great Spirit, once more asking for wisdom sufficient that the results of their labors might be approved.

NOVEMBER 27, 1874. — After India's invocation, he said Lee, and Burns, and Hutchinson, would have the privilege of speaking; after which two old people by the name of Ripley would come in and join with the band of old folks in spirit; also one by the name of Thomas would have a call before the session closed. After speaking of the effect it would produce on those in the physical by the elevation of those in spirit, he retired.

Lee was again in council, and spoke of the pleasure they enjoyed after coming into union on the platform of Eternal Justice, where they had all been taught a higher conception of national life and its many duties; said the coming year would be one of action between the contending forces, and that matter with its mouldy and perishable forms would fall before the ever-living Spirit. After a few words of instruction to those in spirit who were gathered in council, saying they would stand by the covenant until the work was finished, he retired.

The poet Burns was next in council, and gave all a friendly greeting; said he had studied well in spirit in order to master the English language, and had been told he had done well, and he was preparing to return to the lads and lasses of his own country, where the spirit of craft and bigotry was giving way to the spirit of truth; for they had learned that the ghost they had seen was not the old devil the priest prayed up the chimney and out into the air. O, no! it was their fathers and friends come back to tell them of their beautiful home above so fair. After reciting a poem connected with his present experience, and then expressing thanks to the eternal powers, he withdrew.

One of the Hutchinsons was next present, and spoke of his own imperfections which had clung to him in spirit, and said by careful investigation he had been taught it was a part of his inherited condition that had to be endured until overcome by natural growth. He was pleased with the privilege of speaking, and left cheering words for his friends who were still battling with their earthly condition in order to triumph over their own imperfections.

One of the old grandfathers of the Revolution, by the name of Ripley, was then present. Said he had been told to come this way, and he would feel more satisfied about some things that had disturbed him and his old companion in spirit. Said he was very old when he was taken from his affectionate old wife, and he was lonely and discontented in spirit, waiting for her to come to him. Said he went back to the house, and stayed out round in the cold, waiting for her to come, and after she did come they were both a little more contented. They had seen a great many people going up and down in spirit, but no one had taken much notice of them. He had brought his war papers along, and had thrown them up on to the platform. They were told that was the place where they would examine them, and see that they all received what was their due, for they had contended with foreign despots that their children might enjoy the blessings of a free country. Said the men who came on their side, who contended in the last war, could not tell what they had been fighting for. He was glad they were having a settlement, and he would go and let his companion come and speak, for he wanted her to keep up with him, and wherever they went they would go together.

The old grandmother then made a few remarks; spoke of her age and infirmities, and of her pleasure when, relieved of her frail body, she found herself in company again with her old man. Said they had jogged along together without making much disturbance, for the old ladies were ashamed of the extravagant hussies who had come into their places, and by their folly had ruined their country. She hadn't much to say, and she would go along with her old companion. She then remarked that the one who stood next to her in spirit looked as though he had never done a good act in his life ; and after expressing thanks for herself and companion, she retired.

One by the name of Thomas was next in council, where he affirmed the old lady was right in her remark, for he felt as though he had never done anything right. It was true he had occupied prominent positions, and had distributed other men's money for charitable objects; but he had done nothing on his own account, and he truly felt his naked condition ; said he had been terribly broken up as he found himself in spirit, and as yet he could hardly realize his condition. He could see others coming and going on every side, but no one said anything to him, or seemed to want to have anything to do with him. How it would continue, or what would be his condition, he did not know. Said the people kept crowding in apparently every second, and did not seem to get any further; and one man had remarked he was afraid the place would break down. He was glad he had been remembered, and said he felt some relief from the pleasure he received in again speaking with mortals ; and, if they could do anything that would better his condition after he left, he would be forever thankful, for, he said, he had taken no comfort after moving into his new mansion before his recent change, and even that was gone from him now. He thought he would have to return to the market-place and wait, but the thought, he said, was not encouraging. After expressing his thanks, he withdrew.

One of the Hindoos was next in council, where he told of the gratitude of his own people for the privileges they had received and of the progress they made from their opportunity of listening to the statements made by others. They felt bad for the man, although he had had his good things during his earthly pilgrimage, and had not troubled himself about others who had nothing ; and he could stand in the market-place now, and wait until he was wanted. He guessed he would not be lonesome — there were plenty in the same fix to keep him company ; but he thought the man was glad that we had called for him, for he shrugged his shoulders when he went away. He then said they would ask the Star-Spirit if they could go to him and take him something that would make him feel better ; if the Star-Spirit said it would be right for them to go, they would do so, and try and do something for his relief; but, as one of the bow-and-arrow girls was waiting to speak, he would retire.

The Forest Maiden next told of the terrible wail of suffering from those in want of bread, which had fearfully disturbed the Great Spirit in his upper hunting-grounds; and the Great Spirit said, " Red squaw, go down and mark well the doors of all who have hoarded up the fruits of the harvest in their big storehouses; then count the many they have cast out with nothing to eat; and go to the wigwam council of the white squaw and brave, and see to it that the records are true." And she would return and tell the Great Spirit that the white brave who sat in council knew what to do. She then withdrew.

Whereupon India closed the session by invocation to the Great Spirit.

DECEMBER 6, 1874. — After India's invocation to the Great Spirit, by whose power and wisdom all things were sustained, he said the time was growing short, and there was great anxiety in spirit manifested by those who had stood off and been indifferent to the work. They were now crowding up and asking for " a hearing." He said the people of the earth would soon be anxious to learn that the phenomena of spirit were realities; that a man named Graves, and a woman by name of Chase, and one Mrs. Ham, would have an opportunity to speak, and, if there was time for others, their names would be given. He then retired.

Graves was next in council, and acknowledged that, when a pilgrim with mortals, he had done many things that a man of his age at the time should have been ashamed of. And he had long desired an opportunity to confess his faults, which had sadly debarred his progress in spirit. He said the school of his profession had fallen from that high standing they once occupied, and had tampered with the laws of the Great Creator in their greed for mammon, until there were but few women in the country whose functions for reproduction had not been injured. He was glad the time had arrived for a settlement, when a higher standard of morals would again be enforced, which he hoped might be a benefit to him as well as others. After a few general remarks concerning the corruption of the age, he said his wife and daughter were in a sphere high above him; but he was anxious the spots might be washed out with which he had stained himself during his physical life, that he might be allowed to take his place with his family in spirit. He then retired.

Mrs. Chase was next in council, and said she had been a neighbor to the media during her own earthly pilgrimage, and was very anxious to learn more of her family affairs. She wanted to be located where she could have them all, or a place for them, when they came to see her. She complained of her husband's want of order; said he was no better calculated to manage a home now than when on their old farm in Stratham; said he showed the same disregard to her counsel now that he did then. She had noticed appearance of some change going on around them, and she was anxious now for another move, where they could all have their homes, and go to work, and fix up, and be contented. She then withdrew.

Mrs. Ham was next present, and said she was an aunt of the media, and she had waited and watched and wondered why her time did not come to speak. She had seen hundreds of others of every color and condition pass through and go away rejoicing. She had seen the gathering up of the ancient nations who had been clothed in new garments, and the sphere above opened to receive them as she had sat in wonder and amazement at the grandeur of the work. Lo and behold! a new garment had been prepared for herself. She spoke of her earthly trials, and told of how rheumatic pains had distorted her body, and how thankful she was when relieved. She spoke of Jesus as the blessed Saviour who himself had suffered and knew how to sympathize with others in their affliction. She told of his labors in the dark sphere in spirit, where all had been gathered up and clothed, and a platform of Justice established. And after saying the work had now commenced with mortals, she expressed her thanks to the Great Creator, and desired she might be remembered, and then withdrew.

One of the Hindoos was the next one heard for a few moments. After saying what he desired, he gave way for one of the Forest Maidens.

She spoke of the love of the Great Spirit for his numerous tribes, and of his great Central Son who had suffered and was still working for the elevation of all the Great Spirit's earthly children; and now she, and her sisters before, had laid aside their robes in their upper hunting-grounds, and clothed themselves in garments suitable to their work, as they were sent by the Great Spirit to see and to know why there was so much complaint of want and suffering from every tribe and nation among the pale-faces on the hunting-grounds. She had come to the wigwam of the white squaw to listen, and she would come again, when the white blanket covered the beautiful hunting-grounds, and see that the braves, with their big storehouses, went out and relieved the cold and starving ones who were crying to the Great Spirit, day and night, and night and day, for only a small ration from the vast productions of his bountiful lower hunting-grounds. After a few words of instruction for the numerous archers of the red man's race, she withdrew.

India again closed the session by invocation to the Great Spirit, commending all to his great fatherly care, and asking for sufficient wisdom to guide to insure the approval of all which had been in accord with Justice.

DECEMBER 20, 1874. — After India's invocation to the Great Spirit, he said they were making preparation to celebrate the birthday of the Great Media in spirit, and would hold the session on the eve of the twenty-fifth. He then said the present session was assigned to the women who desired to make a few remarks, and that Mrs. Washington, Mrs. Webster, also Mrs. Franklin and Mrs. Adams, each one would speak for herself, and withdrew.

Mrs. Washington was then in council, and said she had come to invite their sisters of other nationalities to join them in their celebration of the birthday of the Saviour of man on the platform of Eternal Justice that was built up in their New America in spirit. She spoke of the pleasure it afforded them to meet together in anticipation of the approaching birthday of him who had borne the agonies of Gethsemane and the cross in their behalf. She said, although they did mourn over the fallen condition of their country, it was from the old that their New America was now born in spirit, and they were proud to find one daughter and son of America through whom they could still work. She spoke of George, and of the contentment and the happiness they received in connection with their present work. She then gave way.

Mrs. Franklin was next present, and said she was thankful for another privilege to say a few words; told of the pleasure her friend Pompey enjoyed at the time of his interview. She said they were all very busily employed in working out conditions for the ushering in of justice among the inhabitants of earth, and that Benny was watching every point where type and wire could be used in order to enlighten the people and draw their minds away from their perishable earthly principalities. After addressing her co-worker, she withdrew.

Mrs. Webster then spoke of the pleasure that herself and Daniel enjoyed in the parts they had been called to represent, and how pleased she was that her husband's hands had not been stained with his brothers' blood ; how they had sorrowed over the terrible condition of their country, and how they rejoice in the work of establishing a platform of Eternal Justice, where all could meet without dissimulation, and work as brothers should work in the cause of humanity with him who had sacrificed so much and still sorrowed over their fallen condition. Said they should all be together again on the eve of the birthday of their blessed Saviour, and that all their countrymen felt a just pride in meeting together in spirit to honor and acknowledge the wonderful work accomplished through the labors and sufferings of Jesus the Nazarene. She then gave way for Mrs. Adams, who expressed her pleasure that herself and sisters could stand among the representatives of their country, although they had sorrowed in spirit over its fallen condition, for many had turned away from the precepts and examples of their fathers, who had toiled and sacrificed that their children might inherit a free country. And said there could be no excuse devised in their behalf, for they had turned away from the law and the prophets, and disregarded the teachings of all histories, and were rushing headlong to national destruction. She then said, although they still had their family representatives in the old State they had loved so much, she wanted to have justice established, no matter who or how much they had to suffer, for they had all been unmindful of their duties when protecting the rights of the people, and let them all go back to the plain floors and scanty fare of their forefathers, and they might learn to appreciate the blessings of liberty that were purchased with blood, and she retired.

Another of the Forest Maidens was next present, and said she had come from the upper hunting-grounds of the red man, where the Great Spirit said, " Squaw, go make room." She sent out the warriors of her race, and said to the Great Spirit there was room. And the Great Spirit then said, " Go, squaw, and see that the women are ready to celebrate the birthday in spirit of my Central Son." And she said, " Great Spirit, it is eighteen hundred and seventy-four years, and the birthday of your great Central Son has never been celebrated."

He said, "Go, squaw, and see that all is ready." She said, should she go to the fair daughters of India, or to the tribes of Ephraim, who hung their harps on the willows, or should she go to the daughters of Israel — or where should she go? And the Great Spirit said, "Go, squaw, to the despised and neglected ones that were sent from my hunting-grounds all tattered and torn, all friendless and alone." And she had come to the wigwam of the white squaw, where she found them gathered around the great platform of Eternal Justice, all dressed and waiting for the Great Spirit's Central Son. Then the Great Spirit said, "Squaw, where are the fathers and mothers and brothers? Go and see if all have been gathered together." She looked again, and she found them crying and asking, "O, where are my daughters? and where is my son?" Then she pointed and told; but they could not believe, for their daughters were wantons, and their sons were deceivers. No, it could not be so. But the mighty archers had brought them together, and they were awaiting the birthday of the Great Spirit's Central Son, who also had been crucified.

Then one of the Hindoos said that his folks were getting ready to celebrate the birthday of their Star-Spirit, and three of their gods would be in the procession in front of the box and symbols. He then told of how the ancient priests deceived the people by having one of their number secreted in disguise to answer questions; whereupon India closed by invocation to the Great Spirit.

DECEMBER 25, 1874. — After India's invocation to the Great Spirit, asking for the approval of their labors, he spoke of the trials and hardships of the Great Media whose birth through the physical they had now assembled to commemorate. He spoke of the condition of mortals at the time of the birth, and also of the manner of his reception at Jerusalem, — how he suffered from the terrible opposition of the Jews, who were so strongly wedded to their earthly principalities, and of their final overthrow and scattering among the different nationalities. He then spoke of the triumph of the Great Media over death and the darkness of the tomb that held the tribes in bondage, and of those looking for light who gladly received him and followed after him as he passed through the dark sphere in spirit; and then told of his present advent in spirit, and of his reception, — how his great heart of hearts sorrowed over the condition of humanity; how he had to turn the second time from those who had professed to be his followers, and go to the haunts of vice among the suffering and sorrowing ones that were rejected and cast out; and then told of his labors in spirit as their leader in the work of cleaning up the dark sphere, and having all prepared to present to the Great Spirit, his Father and the Father of all, on this the anniversary of his birthday in spirit. He then spoke of the pleasure the fathers and mothers and their children were enjoying for this their privilege of being present, saying they thanked those who had prepared them for the greatest of known celebrations ever connected with this planet and beyond the capacity of mortals to comprehend. When, after saying John was then prepared to follow him, he withdrew.

The apostle John was next present, and spoke of the great joy they experienced as witnesses of their Master's triumphant reception in spirit; saying they were standing as it were on a sea of glass, where all the tribes of Israel and of Judah were gathered together, with all the Gentile race gathered from the dark sphere in spirit, and prepared for an offering to the Great Father as part of the fruits of their Master's labors. He then spoke of the Ark of the Covenant, and the ancient sages with whom it was intrusted, who stood by it surrounded by those found worthy to bring it on to the platform. He then pointed up through an opening in the spheres, where their Master was approaching at the head of an innumerable train of little children who had never known corruption. "See, he has in his arms a little form! As they advance, he lays it on the box, and is teaching them the mystery of the spirit entering the physical temple under the 'second covenant.' And here we see is a Jew with a miniature temple on his back, pressing his way forward. He is a representative of his race who are urging him forward. You can see how he agonizes in his efforts to ascend the platform where he can ask my Master to forgive him and his race. And upon that answer will depend the national prosperity of his people. And now he is putting the wedding-ring on the fingers of those who were separated in their earthly lives through misfortunes; how their parents are now rejoicing to again meet their long-lost children whom they never expected to see, who went down in the whirlpools of dissipation and vice which man still permits to infest the earth!" Their final triumph over such condition in spirit was the crowning glory of their Master's great work, where all gladly bowed the knee to acknowledge him the King of kings, as he delivers up the kingdom to his Father with all he had gathered in, and where for a season he will remain with them until those left behind finish up their work with mortals. Then, and not till then, will all be prepared for a happy union, when they meet again in spirit. After a few encouraging words for those who had to remain, he gave way.

One of the Forest Maidens was next present, and said she had come with her race to the celebration of the birthday of the Great Spirit's Central Son, who had been gathering the many sent from the lower hunting-grounds of the red man all tattered and torn, and where all were still suffering from the bad seed they had sown, and where they must stay until they stopped the cry of the Great Spirit's children that were still in the purgatory they had made, and were asking for bread.

One of the Hindoos next told of the pleasure they had received in connection with the birthday of their great Star-Spirit. He spoke of the little form of a child that he had placed on the box, and said the Star-Spirit was teaching his people about the covenants; after which they should put box and all with their other earthly gods, and then the Star-Spirit would show them to his Father. He also told about the children that had come with the Star-Spirit, carrying their beautiful flowers; said they often had had a grand time when they desired to honor their earthly gods; but no one, nor all they ever had, could compare with the vastness of the Star-Spirit's present celebration. When India again closed the session by invocation to the Great Spirit.

DECEMBER 27, 1874. — After India's invocation to the Great Spirit, thanking him for wisdom and strength sufficient to accomplish their labors with the spirits in bondage, he said he should not speak with them again until the end of the ensuing three months, at which time he would be present and open the session as usual. After instructions for keeping up the connection with the council by an evening session once a week, when they would assemble and give evidence of their presence, and answer necessary inquiries by writing through the hand of the media, he said that a spirit was present who was anxious to be heard, and would have an opportunity to speak after he had withdrawn; and, if there was time, another one would be authorized to follow. When, after a few encouraging words in reference to their labors, he retired.

The next in council said he had sought for an opportunity to offer a few remarks in his own behalf. He said he had formerly been known among the Freewill Baptists of New Hampshire and Massachusetts, and had officiated in the capacity of a clergyman with those of that faith, and that he was honest and anxious at the time to enlighten and improve the condition of mortals. And in evidence that his labors were not unfruitful, he introduced to the council one of the sisters of his order, who made a few appropriate remarks, and then sang a beautiful hymn commencing with the words, "Jesus, lover of my soul;" and then she retired.

The next one in council said he felt grateful for the present opportunity to say a few words, for he had lived during his earthly pilgrimage with his family at Exeter, and was well acquainted with the one who had spoken. He had been a resident of the town of Stratham, and, although he had never been a clergyman, he had loved justice and disliked and opposed the deception and the hypocrisy among the leaders of the pretended followers of Jesus. He was gratified with the work which had been accomplished in the dark sphere of spirit, where Jesus, their leader, had found true followers in his labors of compassion among the fishermen and the beggars who had been cast out by the temple-builders regardless of their natural rights; but they had found their Saviour in Jesus of Nazareth, who had gathered them up and again taught them of a common humanity by the establishing of his great platform of Eternal Justice which had already disturbed the mammon-hunters among mortals. After expressing his own gratification, he remarked that one of the old American mothers was waiting in order to say a few words, and he would retire.

One of the mothers of the American Revolution was the next in council, where she spoke of the trials and deprivations they had to endure in their struggle for national freedom. She told of their present happiness after witnessing the gathering up of the tribes of Israel and of Judah, as well as the lost and forsaken ones neglected and cast out from the Gentile nations. She spoke of their wonderful change as they had been awakened from their dark condition by their knowledge of the love of the blessed Saviour, who was leading them all into the Great Father's kingdom; and, after giving expression to her own feelings of gratitude to know they had not been forgotten, she withdrew.

One of the Hindoos was next in council, where he had come to say that his folks were also thankful and that they still clung fast to the great Star-Spirit, who had given them the box and taught them the true meaning of its symbols; and said they had not much of anything else to take with them up to the Great Father's kingdom, unless they went back and gathered up their dumb idols of brass and of stone; that those things were not wanted when they had the love and the light of the Star-Spirit to guide them all on their way. After giving evidence of the gratitude of his people, he withdrew.

One of the Forest Maidens was next in council, where she told of the mighty power and of the endless love of the Great Spirit that never failed. Said it would be good for all to follow in his trail. She then told of how he had opened the doors of his eternal kingdom, and sent down his spirits to enlighten the pale-faces on the lower hunting-grounds; and how they had trifled with them, and laughed, and scoffed, and treated all with scorn. "O Great Spirit, judge them as they have judged thy spirits; make them tremble and shake with affright for their disregard of thy high and holy commandments, until they return and willingly acknowledge Thee through the various manifestations of thy spirits! O Great Spirit, make them to know that thy great arm is stretched out in evidence of thy mighty power, and that thy valiant and trusty spirit-warriors have gone forth at thy command to re-establish thy Law of Eternal Justice with the remnant of the pale-face race!"

After a few encouraging words, India said he would be present during the vacation, and, when necessary, he would write through the hand of the media. He then closed the session by invocation to the Great Spirit, again asking for wisdom and strength to guide them, that mortals might awake from their moral death, and, if possible, yet be saved from the approaching mental darkness and national destruction.

The following quotations, which have been selected from the sayings of Jesus, and others that are recorded in Matthew's Gospel, confirm the events that have been reported by the spirits at the present closing cycle of time.

"And there followed him great multitudes of people from Galilee, and from Decapolis, and from Jerusalem, and from Judea, and from beyond Jordan.

"And he opened his mouth and taught them, saying:

"Blessed are the meek, for they shall inherit the earth.

"Blessed are they who hunger and thirst after righteousness, for they shall be filled.

"Blessed are the merciful, for they shall obtain mercy.

"Blessed are the pure in heart, for they shall see God."

"When the Son of Man shall come in his glory, and all the holy angels with him, then shall he sit upon the throne of his glory; and before him shall be gathered all nations, and he shall separate them one from the other, as a shepherd divideth his sheep from the goats.

"For the Son of Man shall come in the glory of his Father, with his angels.

"And then he shall reward every man according to his works."

"And they said, Whence hath this man this wisdom, and these mighty works?

"Is not this the carpenter's son? Is not his mother called Mary?

"For he taught them as one having authority, and not as the scribes."

"Fear them not, therefore, for there is nothing covered that shall not be revealed, and nothing hid that shall not be made known."

THEREFORE, in closing this record, which has been patiently given by the heavenly messengers in order to enlighten and quicken the lonely spirits of the countless millions that will inhabit the beautiful earth during the incoming cycle, we would affirm that many things have been told and shown which mortals at the present time will not comprehend; but enough has been given that should satisfy the rational mind that all who would have a part in the first resurrection, and avoid the pains of the second death, must obey the covenants and the commandments, and follow the lead of Jesus the Saviour, who through his love and compassion for a covetous and fallen race has won the grand title of the Son of God, who has cleared away the darkness and opened a passage for the individualized spirit to a higher sphere, where scoffers and crucifiers, where thieves and robbers, where murderers, adulterers, and liars cannot enter, but must suffer the anguish of a living death in spirit, until they have paid the penalty in compensation to the demands of the broken Law; while those who have handed down the various statements which this book contains for your instruction will meet you, at the close of another cycle of time, upon the Great Platform of Eternal Justice, ever-living witnesses that it was a true and a faithful record.

www.ingramcontent.com/pod-product-compliance
Lightning Source LLC
Chambersburg PA
CBHW031415230426
43668CB00007B/316